STOCHASTIC OPTIMIZATION IN CONTINUOUS TIME

This is a rigorous but user-friendly book on the application of stochastic control theory to economics. A distinctive feature of the book is that mathematical concepts are introduced in a language and terminology familiar to graduate students of economics. Although the topics are standard in many mathematics, economics, and finance books, they are illustrated with many real examples documented in the economic literature. Moreover, the book emphasizes the dos and don'ts of stochastic calculus, and cautions the reader that certain results and intuitions cherished by many economists do not extend to stochastic models. A special chapter (Chapter 5) is devoted to exploring various methods of finding a closed-form representation of the value function of a stochastic control problem, which is essential for ascertaining the optimal policy functions. The book also includes many practice exercises for the reader. Notes and suggested readings are provided at the end of each chapter for more references and possible extensions.

Fwu-Ranq Chang is an associate professor of economics at Indiana University, Bloomington. He received a Ph.D. in economics from the University of Chicago and a Ph.D. in mathematics from the State University of New York at Stony Brook. Professor Chang has published papers in leading journals of economics and mathematics, including *Econometrica*, the *Review of Economic Studies*, the *Journal of Economic Theory*, the *Proceedings of the American Mathematical Society*, and the *Journal of Optimization Theory and Applications*. He has been a Visiting Scholar at Chicago and the Center for Economic Studies (CES) at the University of Munich, and is a Research Fellow of the CESifo Research Network.

Stochastic Optimization in Continuous Time

FWU-RANQ CHANG
Indiana University

CAMBRIDGE
UNIVERSITY PRESS

PUBLISHED BY THE PRESS SYNDICATE OF THE UNIVERSITY OF CAMBRIDGE
The Pitt Building, Trumpington Street, Cambridge, United Kingdom

CAMBRIDGE UNIVERSITY PRESS
The Edinburgh Building, Cambridge CB2 2RU, UK
40 West 20th Street, New York, NY 10011-4211, USA
477 Williamstown Road, Port Melbourne, VIC 3207, Australia
Ruiz de Alarcón 13, 28014 Madrid, Spain
Dock House, The Waterfront, Cape Town 8001, South Africa

http://www.cambridge.org

© Fwu-Ranq Chang 2004

First published 2004

Printed in the United States of America

Typeface Times New Roman PS 10.5/13 pt.   *System* LATEX 2ε [TB]

A catalog record for this book is available from the British Library.

Library of Congress Cataloging-in-Publication Data

Chang, Fwu-Ranq, 1947–
Stochastic optimization in continuous time / Fwu-Ranq Chang.
p. cm.
Includes bibliographical references and index.
ISBN 0-521-83406-6
1. Economics–Mathematical models.   2. Stochastic control theory.   I. Title.
HB135.C444   2004
330′.01′51923–dc22   2003061745

ISBN 0 521 83406 6 hardback

To my mother and in memory of my father

Contents

List of Figures

Preface

This is an introduction to stochastic control theory with applications to economics. There are many texts on this mathematical subject; however, most of them are written for students in mathematics or in finance. For those who are interested in the relevance and applications of this powerful mathematical machinery to economics, there must be a thorough and concise resource for learning. This book is designed for that purpose. The mathematical methods are discussed intuitively whenever possible and illustrated with many economic examples. More importantly, the mathematical concepts are introduced in language and terminology familiar to first-year graduate students in economics.

The book is, therefore, at a second-year graduate level. The first part covers the basic elements of stochastic calculus. Chapter 1 is a brief review of probability theory focusing on the mathematical structure of the information set at time t, and the concept of conditional expectations. Many theorems related to conditional expectations are explained intuitively without formal proofs.

Chapter 2 is devoted to the Wiener process with emphasis on its irregularities. The Wiener process is an essential component of modeling shocks in continuous time. We introduce this important concept via three different approaches: as a limit of random walks, as a Markov process with a specific transition probability, and as a formal mathematical definition which enables us to derive and verify variants of the Wiener process. The best way to understand the irregularities of the Wiener process is to examine its sample paths closely. We devote substantial time to the zero sets of the Wiener process and the concept and examples of stopping times. It is the belief of the author that one cannot have a good grasp of the Wiener process without a decent understanding of the zero sets.

In Chapter 3 we define the stochastic integrals, discuss stochastic differential equation, and examine the celebrated Ito lemma. The Ito integral is defined as the limit of Riemann sums evaluated only at the left endpoint of each subinterval and hence is not a Riemann integral. However, this formulation fits economic reasoning very well, because under uncertainty future events are indeed nonanticipating. It is similar to the discrete-time formulation in which an economic agent makes a decision at the beginning of a time period and then subjects herself to the consequences after the state of nature is revealed. These mathematical tools enable us to study the Black–Scholes option pricing formula and issues related to irreversible investment. To make the presentation self-contained, we include a brief discussion of the heat equation and Euler's homogeneous equation. More importantly, we caution the reader throughout the chapter that some of results and intuitions cherished by economists may no longer be true in stochastic calculus.

The second part of the book is on the stochastic optimization methods and applications. In Chapter 4 we study the Bellman equation of stochastic control problems; a set of sufficient conditions, among them the transversality condition, for verifying the optimal control; and the conditions for the existence and differentiability of the value function. We guide the reader through a step-by-step argument that leads to the Bellman equation. We apply this solution method to many well-known examples, such as Merton's consumption and portfolio rules, demand for index bonds, exhaustible resources, the adjustment-cost theory of investment, and the demand for life insurance. We also derive the Bellman equation for a certain class of recursive utility functions to broaden the scope of applications to models with variable discount rates. Most of all, we wish to show that setting up the Bellman equation for a stochastic optimization problem in continuous time is as easy as setting up the Lagrange function in a static, constrained optimization problem. We hope applied economists will find this powerful tool readily accessible.

In Chapter 5 we discuss various methods of finding a closed-form representation for the value function of a stochastic control problem. In many economic problems, the functional form of the value function is absolutely essential to ascertain the optimal policy functions. We present the commonly employed methods systematically, from brute force to educated guess. Some of the problems are solved using more than one method so that the reader can compare the method's strengths and weaknesses. We also introduce the *inverse optimum* methodology that enables us to ascertain the underlying economic structure from the observed policy functions. The chapter title, "How to Solve It," which is borrowed from Pólya's book, summarizes the spirit of the presentation. We hope researchers will find this chapter useful.

In Chapter 6 we investigate two classes of economic problems related to the boundaries of a controlled diffusion process. The first class of problems relates to the nonnegativity constraint, which is not addressed in the mathematical literature. Specifically, the mathematical solution to a controlled diffusion process assumes values on the whole real line, while the economic variables such as consumption and capital–labor ratios cannot be negative. We introduce several approaches to address this issue. As an example, we employ a reflection method to show that the capital–labor ratio in the stochastic Solow equation can never become negative. The second class of problems uses the optimal stopping time technique. We show the reader how to formulate and solve this type of problem through two well-known economic models: precautionary and transactions demand for money, and the tree-cutting problem. We also show that, even though the optimal policy function is implicitly defined, comparative dynamics can still be performed if we do the mathematics right.

The book includes many exercises, which follow immediately after each topic so that the reader can check and practice their understanding of the subject matter. Many of them are provided with useful hints; those, however, should be used only after an honest attempt has been made. Notes and suggested readings are provided at the end of each chapter for more relevant references and possible extensions. The "Miscellaneous Applications and Exercises" in the Appendix provide the reader with more applications to economics and can also be used as review exercises on stochastic optimization methods.

Acknowledgement

This book has grown out of a graduate course in mathematical economics I gave at Indiana University, Bloomington. A draft of this book was presented at the Center for Economic Studies of the University of Munich in 1999. Feedback from many experts at these two universities has greatly improved the presentation of the book. In particular, I would like to thank Jinwon Ahn, Manoj Atolia, Bob Becker, John Boyd, Hess Chung, Franz Gehrels, Slava Govoroi, Sumit Joshi, Peter Pedroni, and Pravin Trivedi.

Most of all, I would like to thank Buz Brock for introducing me to this interesting subject and for his intellectual inspiration, and Tassos Malliaris for his many suggestions, encouragement, and generosity, which played a very important role in getting this book off the ground. I would also like to thank Indiana University for financial support in the preparation of this book. Finally, I would like to thank my family for their support through thick and thin.

STOCHASTIC OPTIMIZATION IN CONTINUOUS TIME

1

Probability Theory

1.1 Introduction

In this chapter we introduce probability theory using a measure-theoretic approach. There are two main subjects that are closely related to economics. First, the concept of σ-algebra is closely related to the notion of information set used widely in economics. We shall formalize it. Second, the concepts of conditional probability and conditional expectation are defined in terms of the underlying σ-algebra. These are background materials for understanding Wiener processes and stochastic dynamic programming.

We keep proofs to the bare minimum. In their place, we emphasize the intuition so that the reader can gain some insights into the subject matter. In fact, we shall go over many commonly employed theorems on conditional expectation with intuitive explanations.

1.2 Stochastic Processes

1.2.1 Information Sets and σ-Algebras

Let Ω be a point set. In probability theory, it is the set of elementary events. The power set of Ω, denoted by 2^Ω, is the set of all subsets of Ω. For example, if the experiment is tossing a coin twice, then the set Ω is $\{HH, HT, TH, TT\}$. It is easy to write down all $2^4 = 16$ elements in the power set. Specifically,

$$2^\Omega = \{\varnothing, \{HH\}, \{HT\}, \{TH\}, \{TT\}, \{HH, HT\}, \{HH, TH\},$$
$$\{HH, TT\}, \{HT, TH\}, \{HT, TT\}, \{TH, TT\}, \{HH, HT, TH\},$$
$$\{HH, HT, TT\}, \{HH, TH, TT\}, \{HT, TH, TT\}, \Omega\}.$$

1

In general, the cardinality of the power set is $2^{|\Omega|}$, where $|\Omega|$ is the cardinality of the set Ω. Power sets are very large. To convince yourself, let the experiment be rolling a die twice, a rather simple experiment. In this simple experiment, $|\Omega| = 36$ and the cardinality of the power set is $2^{36} = 6.87 \times 10^{10}$. It would be impractical to write down all elements in this power set. What we are interested in is subsets of the power set with certain structure.

Definition 1.1 *A class $\mathcal{F}$ of subsets of Ω, i.e., $\mathcal{F} \subset 2^{\Omega}$, is an algebra (or a field) if:*

(i) $A \in \mathcal{F}$ implies $A^c \in \mathcal{F}$, where A^c is the complement of A in Ω.
(ii) $A, B \in \mathcal{F}$ imply that $A \cup B \in \mathcal{F}$.
(iii) $\Omega \in \mathcal{F}$ (equivalently, $\varnothing \in \mathcal{F}$).

Conditions (i) and (ii) imply $A \cap B \in \mathcal{F}$, because $A \cap B = (A^c \cup B^c)^c$.

Definition 1.2 *A class $\mathcal{F}$ of subsets of Ω is a σ-algebra if it is an algebra satisfying*

$$\text{(iv) if } A_i \in \mathcal{F}, \ i = 1, 2, \ldots, \text{ then } \bigcup_{i=1}^{\infty} A_i \in \mathcal{F}.$$

The Greek letter "σ" simply indicates that the number of sets forming the union is *countable* (including finite numbers).

Any $A \in \mathcal{F}$ is called a *measurable* set, or simply, an $\mathcal{F}$-set. We use $\mathcal{F}$ to represent the *information set*, because it captures our economic intuition. Conditions (i) through (iv) provide a mathematical structure for an information set.

Intuitively, we can treat a measurable set as an *observable set*. An object under study ($\omega \in \Omega$) is observable if we can detect that it has certain characteristics. For example, let Ω be the set of flying objects and let A be the set of flying objects that are green. Then A^c represents the set of all flying objects that are not green. Condition (i) simply says that if, in our information set, we can observe that a flying object is green (i.e., A is observable), then we should be able to observe that other flying objects are not green. That means A^c is also observable. Another example is this: if we were able to observe when the general price level is rising, then we should be able to observe when the general price level is not rising. Formally, if $A \in \mathcal{F}$, then $A^c \in \mathcal{F}$.

Condition (ii) says that, if we can observe the things or objects described by characteristics A and those described by characteristics B, then we should be able to observe the objects characterized by the properties of A or B. That is, $A, B \in \mathcal{F}$ imply $A \cup B \in \mathcal{F}$. For example, if we are able to observe when the price level is rising, and if we are able to observe the unemployment level is rising, then we should be able to observe the rising of price level *or* rising unemployment. The same argument applies to countably many observable sets, which is condition (iv). These mathematical structures make σ-algebras very suitable for representing information.

It is clear that the power set 2^Ω is itself a σ-algebra. But there are lots of σ-algebras that are smaller than the power set. For example, in the experiment of tossing a coin twice, $\mathcal{F}_1 = \{\Omega, \varnothing, \{HH\}, \{HT, TH, TT\}\}$ and $\mathcal{F}_2 = \{\Omega, \varnothing, \{HH, TT\}, \{HT, TH\}\}$ are both algebras. The information content of $\mathcal{F}_1$ is this: we can tell whether tossing a coin twice ends up with both heads or otherwise. The information content of $\mathcal{F}_2$ is this: we can tell whether both tosses have the same outcome or not. The reader should try to find other algebras in this setup. An obvious one is to "combine" $\mathcal{F}_1$ and $\mathcal{F}_2$. See the exercise below. We will return to these two examples in Example 1.12.

Exercise 1.2.1

(1) Verify that $\mathcal{F}_1$ and $\mathcal{F}_2$ are algebras.

(2) Show that $\mathcal{F}_1 \cup \mathcal{F}_2$, while containing $\mathcal{F}_1$ and $\mathcal{F}_2$, is not an algebra.

(3) Find the smallest algebra $\mathcal{G}$ that contains $\mathcal{F}_1$ and $\mathcal{F}_2$ in the sense that for any algebra $\mathcal{H}$ which contains $\mathcal{F}_1$ and $\mathcal{F}_2$, then $\mathcal{G} \subset \mathcal{H}$.

Definition 1.3 *A set function $P : \mathcal{F} \to \mathbb{R}$ is a probability measure if P satisfies*

(i) $0 \leq P(A) \leq 1$ for all $A \in \mathcal{F}$;

(ii) $P(\varnothing) = 0$ and $P(\Omega) = 1$;

(iii) if $A_i \in \mathcal{F}$ and the A_i's are mutually disjoint, then $P\left(\bigcup_{i=1}^\infty A_i\right) = \sum_{i=1}^\infty P(A_i)$.

Property (iii) is called *countable additivity*. The triplet $(\Omega, \mathcal{F}, P)$ is used to denote a probability space.

Example 1.4 *(Borel Sets and Lebesgue Measure) When $\Omega = \mathbb{R}$ (the whole real line) or $\Omega = [0, 1]$ (the unit interval), and the σ-algebra* *is the one generated by the open sets in $\mathbb{R}$ (or in $[0, 1]$), we call this σ-field the Borel field. It is usually denoted by $\mathcal{B}$. An element in the Borel field is a Borel set.*

Examples of Borel sets are open sets, closed sets, semi-open, semi-closed sets, F_σ sets (countable unions of closed sets), and G_δ sets (countable intersections of open sets). When $\Omega = [0, 1]$, $\mathcal{B}$ is the σ-algebra, and $P(A)$ is the "length" (measure) of $A \in \mathcal{F}$, we can verify that P is a probability measure on $\mathcal{B}$. Such a measure is called the Lebesgue measure on $[0, 1]$.

However, not all subsets of $\mathbb{R}$ are Borel sets, i.e., not all subsets of $\mathbb{R}$ are observable. For example, the Vitali set is not a Borel set. See, for example, Reed and Simon (1972, p. 33). For curious souls, the Vitali set V is constructed as follows. Call two numbers $x, y \in [0, 1)$ equivalent if $x - y$ is rational. Let V be the set consists of exactly one number from each equivalent class. Then V is not Lebesgue measurable.

A single point and, therefore, any set composed of countably many points are of Lebesgue measure zero. The question then is this: Are sets with uncountably many points necessarily of positive Lebesgue measure? The answer is negative, and the best-known example is the Cantor set.

1.2.2 The Cantor Set

Since the Cantor set contains many important properties that are essential to understanding the nature of a Wiener process, we shall elaborate on this celebrated set. The construction of the Cantor set proceeds as follows. Evenly divide the unit interval $[0, 1]$ into three subintervals. Remove the middle *open* interval, $(1/3, 2/3)$, from $[0, 1]$. The remaining two closed intervals are $[0, 1/3]$ and $[2/3, 1]$. Then remove the two middle open intervals, $(1/9, 2/9)$ and $(7/9, 8/9)$, from $[0, 1/3]$ and $[2/3, 1]$ respectively. Continue to remove the four middle open intervals from the remaining four closed intervals, $[0, 1/9]$, $[2/9, 1/3]$, $[2/3, 7/9]$, and $[8/9, 1]$, and so on indefinitely. The set of points that are not removed is called the *Cantor set*, $\mathfrak{C}$.

Any point in the Cantor set can be represented by

$$\sum_{n=1}^{\infty} \frac{i_n}{3^n}, \qquad \text{where } i_n = 0 \text{ or } 2.$$

For example,

$$\frac{7}{9} = \frac{2}{3} + \frac{0}{9} + \frac{2}{27} + \frac{2}{81} + \frac{2}{243} + \cdots,$$

i.e., $7/9 = (2, 0, 2, 2, 2, \dots)$. Similarly, $8/9 = (2, 2, 0, 0, \dots)$, $0 = (0, 0, 0, \dots)$, $8/27 = (0, 2, 2, 0, 0, 0, \dots)$, and $1 = (2, 2, 2, \dots)$. Therefore, the cardinality of the Cantor set is that of the continuum. Since the Lebesgue measure of the intervals removed through this process is

$$\frac{1}{3} + \frac{1}{9} \cdot 2 + \frac{1}{27} \cdot 4 + \cdots = \sum_{n=1}^{\infty} \frac{2^{n-1}}{3^n} = 1,$$

the Cantor set must be of Lebesgue measure zero.

The main properties that are of interest to us are three. First, here is a set with uncountably many elements that has a zero Lebesgue measure. Second, every point in the Cantor set can be approached by a sequence of subintervals that were removed. In other words, every point in the Cantor set is a limit point. Such a set is called a *perfect set*. Third, for any interval $I \subset [0, 1]$, it must contain some subinterval that was eventually removed, i.e., we can find a subinterval $J \subset I$ such that J and the Cantor set $\mathfrak{C}$ are disjoint: $J \cap \mathfrak{C} = \varnothing$. That is, $\mathfrak{C}$ is *nowhere dense* in $[0, 1]$. These three properties are the basic features of the zero set of a Wiener process, as we shall see later.

1.2.3 Borel–Cantelli Lemmas

Definition 1.5 *The limit superior and the limit inferior of a sequence of sets $\{A_n\}$ are*

$$\limsup_{n \to \infty} A_n = \bigcap_{n=1}^{\infty} \bigcup_{k=n}^{\infty} A_k,$$

$$\liminf_{n \to \infty} A_n = \bigcup_{n=1}^{\infty} \bigcap_{k=n}^{\infty} A_k.$$

Simply put, $x \in \limsup_{n \to \infty} A_n$ means x belongs to infinitely many A_k. In contrast, $x \in \liminf_{n \to \infty} A_n$ means x belongs to virtually all A_k, in the sense that there exists N such that $x \in A_k$ for $k \geq N$. Since $\mathcal{F}$ is a

σ-algebra, $\limsup_{n\to\infty} A_n \in \mathcal{F}$ and $\liminf_{n\to\infty} A_n \in \mathcal{F}$ if $A_n \in \mathcal{F}$. By definition, $\liminf_{n\to\infty} A_n \subset \limsup_{n\to\infty} A_n$.

Exercise 1.2.2 *Let*

$$A_n = \begin{cases} \left[0, 1 + \frac{1}{n}\right] & \text{if } n \text{ is even,} \\ \left[0, 2 + \frac{1}{n}\right] & \text{if } n \text{ is odd.} \end{cases}$$

Show that $\displaystyle\liminf_{n\to\infty} A_n = [0, 1]$ *and* $\displaystyle\limsup_{n\to\infty} A_n = [0, 2]$.

Exercise 1.2.3 *Let*

$$A_n = \begin{cases} \left[0, \frac{1}{n}\right] & \text{if } n \text{ is even,} \\ \left[-\frac{1}{n}, 0\right] & \text{if } n \text{ is odd.} \end{cases}$$

Show that $\displaystyle\liminf_{n\to\infty} A_n = \limsup_{n\to\infty} A_n = \{0\}$.

Exercise 1.2.4 *Let A and B be subsets of Ω. Define*

$$A_n = \begin{cases} A & \text{if } n \text{ is even,} \\ B & \text{if } n \text{ is odd.} \end{cases}$$

Show that $\displaystyle\liminf_{n\to\infty} A_n = A \cap B$, $\displaystyle\limsup_{n\to\infty} A_n = A \cup B$.

Theorem 1.6 *Let $A_n \in \mathcal{F}$. Then we have the following inequalities:*

$$P\left(\liminf_{n\to\infty} A_n\right) \leq \liminf_{n\to\infty} P(A_n) \leq \limsup_{n\to\infty} P(A_n) \leq P\left(\limsup_{n\to\infty} A_n\right).$$

Proof. See Billingsley (1995, Theorem 4.1). ∎

Corollary 1.7 *If* $\liminf_{n\to\infty} A_n = \limsup_{n\to\infty} A_n = A$, *then* $\lim_{n\to\infty} P(A_n) = P(A)$, *i.e., if $A_n \to A$, then $P(A_n) \to P(A)$.*

Theorem 1.8

(i) *(The First Borel–Cantelli Lemma):*

$$\sum_{n=1}^{\infty} P(A_n) < \infty \quad \Rightarrow \quad P\left(\limsup_{n\to\infty} A_n\right) = 0.$$

(ii) *(The Second Borel–Cantelli Lemma) Suppose A_n are independent events. Then*

$$\sum_{n=1}^{\infty} P(A_n) = \infty \quad \Rightarrow \quad P\left(\limsup_{n\to\infty} A_n\right) = 1.$$

Proof. See Billingsley (1995, Theorems 4.3 and 4.4). ■

Example 1.9 *(Value Loss Assumption and Asymptotic Stability of Optimal Growth) While the Borel–Cantelli lemmas may appear abstract, they have interesting economic applications. Recall that a standard model in first-year graduate macroeconomics is the discrete-time optimal growth problem: Let c_t, k_t, β, and $f(k)$ be, respectively, per capita consumption, capital–labor ratio, subjective discount factor, and production function. Then the problem is to find an optimal consumption program $\{c_t\}$ that solves*

$$\max_{\{c_t\}} \sum_{t=1}^{\infty} \beta^{t-1} u(c_t), \qquad s.t.\ k_t = f(k_{t-1}) - c_t,$$
$$t = 1, 2, \ldots, given\ k_0 > 0.$$

The value loss assumption is employed to ensure the asymptotic stability of optimal growth. By asymptotic stability we mean that the difference between two optimal growth programs under two different initial stocks will converge to zero. To prove such a strong result (independent of the initial stock), a value loss assumption is employed. Specifically, we assign a minimum value loss $\delta > 0$ to each time period in which the two optimal programs are parted by a distance at least $\varepsilon > 0$. The value loss assumption makes it impossible to have infinitely many such periods (otherwise, the program is not optimal), so that the asymptotic stability is possible.

To extend this theorem to stochastic cases, the first Borel–Cantelli lemma comes in handy. Given $\varepsilon > 0$, let A_n be the set of points in Ω such that, at time n, the difference between the realizations of these two *optimal programs is at least $\varepsilon > 0$. We shall assign for each $\omega \in A_n$ a minimal value loss $\delta > 0$. Then the* expected *value loss at time n is at least $\delta P(A_n)$, and the total expected value loss is at least $\delta \sum_{n=1}^{\infty} P(A_n)$. This being an optimal program, the expected value loss cannot be infinity. That is to say, the premise of the first Borel–Cantelli lemma is valid: $\sum_{n=1}^{\infty} P(A_n) < \infty$. It follows that $P(\limsup_{n \to \infty} A_n) = 0$. In words, the probability of those $\omega \in \Omega$ that belong to infinitely many A_n is zero. Thus, the time path of the difference between two optimal programs converges to zero with probability one. The interested reader is referred to Chang (1982) for more details.*

1.2.4 Distribution Functions and Stochastic Processes

Definition 1.10 *Let $(\Omega, \mathcal{F}, P)$ and $(\Omega', \mathcal{F}', P')$ be two probability spaces. Then $T : (\Omega, \mathcal{F}, P) \to (\Omega', \mathcal{F}', P')$ is measurable if $T^{-1}(B) \in \mathcal{F}$ for all $B \in \mathcal{F}'$. In particular, if $\Omega' = \mathbb{R}$, $\mathcal{F}' = \mathcal{B}$ (Borel field), and P' is Lebesgue measure, then T is a random variable.*

The term $T^{-1}(B)$ represents the *preimage* of B, or the *pullback* of set B. Recall that continuity of a mapping between two topological spaces is defined as follows: the pullback of any open set in the image space must be an open set in the domain. The concept of a measurable function is defined similarly, i.e., the pullback of a measurable set in the image space is a measurable set in the domain. A random variable is simply a special case of measurable functions.

Definition 1.11 *The distribution function of a random variable X, denoted by $F(X)$, is defined by*

$$F(x) = P(\{\omega \in \Omega : X(\omega) \leq x\}) = P[X \leq x]$$

(following Billingsley's (1995) notation) or, for any Borel set A,

$$F(A) = P(X^{-1}(A)) = P(\{\omega \in \Omega : X(\omega) \in A\}).$$

Clearly, $F(\cdot)$ is defined on Borel field with image in $\mathbb{R}$. Such a function is called a *Borel function*.

Given a random variable X, there are many σ-algebras that can make X measurable. For example, $\mathcal{F}$ is one. The σ-algebra generated by X, denoted by $\sigma(X)$, is the smallest σ-algebra with respect to which X is measurable; that is, $\sigma(X)$ is the intersection of all σ-algebras with respect to which X is measurable. For a finite or infinite sequence of random variables $\{X_1, X_2, \ldots\}$, $\sigma(X_1, X_2, \ldots)$ is the smallest σ-algebra with respect to which each X_i is measurable.

Example 1.12 *(Tossing a coin twice) Let*

$$X_1 = \begin{cases} 0 & \text{if heads in both tosses,} \\ 1 & \text{otherwise,} \end{cases}$$

$$X_2 = \begin{cases} 0 & \text{if same occurrence in both tosses,} \\ 1 & \text{otherwise,} \end{cases}.$$

Then $\sigma(X_1) = \mathcal{F}_1 = \{\Omega, \varnothing, \{HH\}, \{HT, TH, TT\}\}$ and $\sigma(X_2) = \mathcal{F}_2 = \{\Omega, \varnothing, \{HH, TT\}, \{HT, TH\}\}$. It is easy to show that $\sigma(X_1, X_2) = \mathcal{F}_1 \cup \mathcal{F}_2 \cup \{\{HH, HT, TH\}, \{TT\}\}$. For example, if $A = \{HH\} \in \mathcal{F}_1$ and $B = \{HH, TT\} \in \mathcal{F}_2$, then $A^c \cap B = \{TT\} \in \sigma(X_1, X_2)$. In words, if the result is "same occurrence in both tosses" but not "heads in both tosses," then it must be "tails in both tosses."

Exercise 1.2.5 *Let the experiment be rolling a die twice. Let X be the random variable of the sum of the two rolls.*

(1) Describe the probability space $(\Omega, \mathcal{F}, P)$, i.e., spell out Ω, find the smallest algebra $\mathcal{F}$ which makes X measurable, and let P be the usual probability.

(2) Write down the distribution function $F(x)$, and find $F(A)$ when $A = \{3, 4\}$.

(3) Let Y be the random variable that designates the larger of the two rolls. Repeat (1) and (2).

Hint. In (1), first find $X^{-1}(\{i\})$, $i = 2, 3, \ldots, 12$, and then choose $\mathcal{F} = \sigma(X) = $ the smallest algebra generated by X.

If the distribution function $F(x)$ has a derivative $f(x)$, which is called the density function of X, then $f(x)$ satisfies the equation

$$F(A) = \int_A f(x)\,dx.$$

Definition 1.13 *A stochastic process* $\{X(t) : t \in I\}$ *is a family of random variables, where I is the index set. If* $I = \mathbb{Z}$ *(integers), then* $\{X(t) : t \in I\}$ *is called a discrete (time) stochastic process, a time series, or simply a stochastic sequence. If* $I = [0, \infty)$ *or* $[0, 1]$*, then* $\{X(t) : t \in I\}$ *is called a continuous (time) stochastic process.*

A stochastic process can be thought of as a function defined on $I \times \Omega$, i.e., $X : I \times \Omega \to \mathbb{R}$ such that $X : (t, \omega) \mapsto X(t, \omega) = X_t(\omega)$. For a given $t \in I$, $X_t(\cdot) : \Omega \to \mathbb{R}$ is a random variable. For a given $\omega \in \Omega$, $X(\cdot, \omega) : I \to \mathbb{R}$ is a function mapping from the index set I to $\mathbb{R}$. Such a function is called a *sample function* (a *sample path*, a *realization*, or a *trajectory*). The range of the random variable X is called the *state space*, and the value $X(t, \omega)$ is called the *state* at time t for a given draw $\omega \in \Omega$. Thus, a sample function describes the states at different times for a given draw $\omega \in \Omega$. Sample functions play an important role in understanding the nature of a Wiener process.

Recall that the distribution function $F(x)$ of a random variable X is defined by $F(x) = P[X \leq x]$. Similarly, the finite-dimensional distribution function of a stochastic process $\{X(t) : t \in I\}$ is given by

$$F_{t_1, t_2, \ldots, t_n}(x_1, x_2, \ldots, x_n) = P\left[X_{t_1} \leq x_1, X_{t_2} \leq x_2, \ldots, X_{t_n} \leq x_n\right]$$

$$= P\left[\bigcap_{i=1}^{n} \{\omega \in \Omega : X_{t_i} \leq x_i\}\right].$$

In short, given a stochastic process, we can derive the entire family of finite-dimensional distribution functions and there are uncountably many of them. Is the converse true? That is, given a family of finite-dimensional distribution functions, $\{F_{t_1, t_2, \ldots, t_n}(x_1, x_2, \ldots, x_n) : t_i \in I, \ n \geq 1\}$, satisfying some regularity conditions (symmetry and compatibility), can we reconstruct a stochastic process and the underlying probability space such that the distribution functions generated by the reconstructed stochastic process are the ones originally given? The answer is affirmative and is formulated as Kolmogorov's existence theorem. See Billingsley (1995, section 36).

There is another issue here. Two stochastic processes $\{X(t) : t \in I\}$ and $\{Y(t) : t \in I\}$ are *stochastically equivalent* if, for all $t \in I$, $X(t) = Y(t)$ w.p.1, where "w.p.1" stands for "with probability one." The problem is: even with Kolmogorov's theorem, we may come up with two stochastically equivalent processes possessing the same finite-dimensional distribution functions such that one has continuous sample functions while the other has discontinuous sample functions. For example, let $I \times \Omega = [0, 1] \times [0, 1]$ and

$$X(t, w) \equiv 0, \, Y(t, w) = \begin{cases} 1 & \text{if } \omega = t, \\ 0 & \text{otherwise.} \end{cases}$$

In other words, it takes more than finite-dimensional distribution functions to determine the sample paths of a stochastic process. A concept of *separability* is in order. The reader is referred to Billingsley (1995) for details.

Mathematically, separability means countability. A stochastic process is separable if a countable set of points of time in I (which is a continuum) can determine the properties of the process. An important mathematical result is that any stochastic process has a stochastically equivalent, separable process. Thus, for any family of finite-dimensional distribution functions, there exists a separable process having the given family as its finite-dimensional distribution functions. *Unless otherwise specified, we are dealing only with separable stochastic processes.*

Last, but not least, we would like to know what ensures the continuity of sample functions of a separable process. A sufficient condition is given in the following

Theorem 1.14 *(Kolmogorov–Čentsov). A stochastic process $\{X(t) : t \in [0, T]\}$ has continuous sample functions w.p.1 if there exist positive numbers a, b, c such that*

$$E\left[|X_t - X_s|^a\right] \le c \, |t - s|^{1+b}$$

for all $0 \le s, t \le T$.

Proof. See Karatzas and Shreve (1991, p. 53). ∎

Arnold (1974, p. 24) called this theorem the *criterion of Kolmogorov*. It will become useful later when we try to show that a Wiener process has continuous sample paths w.p.1.

1.3 Conditional Expectation

Given a probability space $(\Omega, \mathcal{F}, P)$, the conditional probability of an event $A \in \mathcal{F}$ under a condition $B \in \mathcal{F}$ is $P(A \mid B) = P(A \cap B)/P(B)$. What we shall study in this section is $P[A \mid \mathcal{E}]$ and $E[X \mid \mathcal{E}]$ for a given σ-algebra $\mathcal{E} \subset \mathcal{F}$.

1.3.1 Conditional Probability

We begin with a heuristic discussion. What kind of mathematical object is a conditional expectation? First, we recognize that, in the end, we want to make sense of expressions like $E[E[X \mid \mathcal{E}_1] \mid \mathcal{E}_2]$, where $\mathcal{E}_1$ and $\mathcal{E}_2$ are two σ-algebras contained in $\mathcal{F}$, and X is a random variable. If we denote $Y = E[X \mid \mathcal{E}_1]$, then $E[E[X \mid \mathcal{E}_1] \mid \mathcal{E}_2] = E[Y \mid \mathcal{E}_2]$. Thus, if $E[E[X \mid \mathcal{E}_1] \mid \mathcal{E}_2]$ is defined, $Y = E[X \mid \mathcal{E}_1]$ has to be a random variable. That is, the conditional expectation *is* a random variable. Second, we recognize that expectations and probabilities are connected through the *indicator function*

$$I_A(\omega) = \begin{cases} 1 & \text{if } \omega \in A, \\ 0 & \text{if } \omega \notin A. \end{cases}$$

More precisely, $E[I_A] = P(A)$. We would expect $E[I_A \mid \mathcal{E}_1] = P[A \mid \mathcal{E}_1]$. If $E[I_A \mid \mathcal{E}_1]$ is a random variable, then so must be $P[A \mid \mathcal{E}_1]$.

Formally, the definition of conditional probability is defined as follows. Let A, B be two events, i.e., $A, B \in \mathcal{F}$. Suppose we can observe $\omega \in B$ or $\omega \in B^c$, but not ω itself. (This is referred to as having partial information.) Then we can ask the question: What is the probability of event A taking place, given the observation B? That is, what is $P(A \mid B)$? Similarly, what is $P(A \mid B^c)$?

We begin with the smallest σ-algebra $\mathcal{E} = \{\Omega, \varnothing, B, B^c\}$. We can define

$$P[A \mid \mathcal{E}](\omega) = \begin{cases} P(A \mid B) & \text{if } \omega \in B, \\ P(A \mid B^c) & \text{if } \omega \in B^c. \end{cases}$$

Even though we do not observe the realization of $\omega \in \Omega$ itself, we can calculate the random variable $P[A \mid \mathcal{E}]$. Conversely, given $P[A \mid \mathcal{E}]$, we know either $\omega \in B$ or $\omega \in B^c$ based on the value of $P[A \mid \mathcal{E}]$. The only exception is when $P(A \mid B) = P(A \mid B^c)$, but then, A and B are independent.

In the formulation above, events B and B^c represent a partition of Ω. The formulation can be extended to a family of events $\{B_1, B_2, \dots\}$ that partitions Ω. Let $\mathcal{E}$ be the σ-algebra generated by $\{B_1, B_2, \dots\}$. Then the conditional probability of $A \in \mathcal{F}$ given $\mathcal{E}$ is

$$P[A \mid \mathcal{E}](\omega) = P(A \mid B_i) \qquad \text{if } \omega \in B_i \text{ for some } i.$$

In this way, $P[A \mid \mathcal{E}] : \Omega \to [0, 1]$ is a random variable.

It is easy to verify that the conditional probability thus defined satisfies

$$0 \leq P[A \mid \mathcal{E}] \leq 1 \qquad \text{w.p.1}$$

and

$$P\left[\bigcup_{n=1}^{\infty} A_n \mid \mathcal{E}\right] = \sum_{n=1}^{\infty} P[A_n \mid \mathcal{E}] \qquad \text{if the } A_n\text{'s are mutually disjoint.}$$

Proposition 1.15 *$P[A \mid \mathcal{E}]$ is $\mathcal{E}$-measurable and integrable, satisfying*

$$\int_B P[A \mid \mathcal{E}] dP = P(A \cap B) \qquad \text{for all } B \in \mathcal{E}. \tag{1.1}$$

In particular,

$$\int_\Omega P[A \mid \mathcal{E}] dP = P(A).$$

Proof. For a formal proof, the reader is referred to Billingsley (1995). We shall sketch the proof here. The measurability of $P[A \mid \mathcal{E}]$ comes from the fact that the preimage of any interval $(a, b) \subset [0, 1]$ is the union of countably many (including finite number) B_j's. Since each $B_j \in \mathcal{E}$, that countable union of B_j's is also in $\mathcal{E}$. To understand (1.1), we begin with the simplest case, $B = B_i$ for some i. In that case, $\omega \in B_i$ implies $P[A \mid \mathcal{E}](\omega) = P(A \mid B_i)$. Next, we assume B is the disjoint union of B_1 and B_2. Then

$$\int_B P[A \mid \mathcal{E}] dP = P(A \mid B_1) P(B_1) + P(A \mid B_2) P(B_2) = P(A \cap B),$$

where the last equality is obtained by invoking Bayes's theorem. The argument can easily be extended to the case that B is a countable union of $\{B_i\}$. Finally, a special case of (1.1) can be seen from the fact that if $\mathcal{E} = \{\Omega, \varnothing\}$, the smallest σ-algebra, then $P[A \mid \mathcal{E}] = P(A)$, because Ω is the only nonempty measurable set. ∎

An event $A \in \mathcal{F}$ is *independent* of $\mathcal{E}$ if A is independent of B for all $B \in \mathcal{E}$. Similarly, two σ-fields $\mathcal{E}_1$ and $\mathcal{E}_2$ are independent if, for all $A \in \mathcal{E}_1$ and for all $B \in \mathcal{E}_2$, A and B are independent.

Proposition 1.16 *Event A is independent of $\mathcal{E}$ if and only if $P[A \mid \mathcal{E}] = P(A)$, a constant, w.p.1.*

Proof. Assume $P[A \mid \mathcal{E}] = P(A)$, a constant. Integrating both sides with respect to any $B \in \mathcal{E}$, and using (1.1), we have

$$P(A \cap B) = \int_B P[A \mid \mathcal{E}] dP = \int_B P(A) dP = P(A) \cdot P(B).$$

Conversely, assume A is independent of $\mathcal{E}$. Given any $B \in \mathcal{E}$, $P(A) \cdot P(B) = P(A \cap B)$. Using (1.1), we have

$$\int_B P[A \mid \mathcal{E}] dP = P(A \cap B) = P(A) \cdot P(B) = \int_B P(A) dP.$$

Since the choice of B is arbitrary, we must have $P[A \mid \mathcal{E}] = P(A)$ w.p.1. ∎

Definition 1.17 *A_1 and A_2 are conditionally independent with respect to $\mathcal{E}$ if*

$$P[A_1 \cap A_2 \mid \mathcal{E}] = P[A_1 \mid \mathcal{E}] \cdot P[A_2 \mid \mathcal{E}].$$

Notice that, in this case, the random variable $P[A_1 \cap A_2 \mid \mathcal{E}]$ is decomposed into a product of two random variables $P[A_1 \mid \mathcal{E}]$ and $P[A_2 \mid \mathcal{E}]$.
Recall that

$$\sigma(X_i : i \in I) = \text{the smallest } \sigma\text{-algebra generated by } \{X_i : i \in I\}.$$

We shall use the following notation:

$$P[A \mid X_i : i \in I] = P[A \mid \sigma(X_i : i \in I)].$$

1.3.2 Conditional Expectation

Now we are ready to define $E[X \mid \mathcal{E}]$. As with the concept of integration, the intuition comes from step functions. As we have seen earlier, $E[I_A \mid \mathcal{E}]$ is defined as $P[A \mid \mathcal{E}]$. Then, for $B \in \mathcal{E}$, we have

$$\int_B E[I_A \mid \mathcal{E}] dP = \int_B P[A \mid \mathcal{E}] dP = P(A \cap B) = \int_B I_A \, dP.$$

This equation relates the integral of the conditional expectation of the random variable I_A to the integral of the random variable itself.

A "step" random variable (a.k.a. a *simple* random variable, because it has a finite range) is

$$X = \sum_{i=1}^{n} c_i I_{A_i},$$

where $\{A_1, \ldots, A_n\}$ is a partition of Ω. Define the conditional expectation of a step random variable $X = \sum_{i=1}^{n} c_i I_{A_i}$ by

$$E[X \mid \mathcal{E}] = \sum_{i=1}^{n} c_i P[A_i \mid \mathcal{E}]. \tag{1.2}$$

Then, for any $B \in \mathcal{E}$,

$$\int_B E[X \mid \mathcal{E}] dP = \sum_{i=1}^{n} c_i \int_B P[A_i \mid \mathcal{E}] dP = \sum_{i=1}^{n} c_i P(A_i \cap B)$$

$$= \sum_{i=1}^{n} c_i \int_B I_{A_i} dP = \int_B \left(\sum_{i=1}^{n} c_i I_{A_i} \right) dP = \int_B X dP.$$

More generally, we have the following

Definition 1.18 *Suppose X is an integrable random variable on $(\Omega, \mathcal{F}, P)$ and $\mathcal{E}$ is a σ-algebra in $\mathcal{F}$. Then the conditional expectation of X given $\mathcal{E}$, denoted by $E[X \mid \mathcal{E}]$, is $\mathcal{E}$-measurable and integrable satisfying* *the functional equation*

$$\int_B E[X|\mathcal{E}]\,dP = \int_B X\,dP \qquad for\ all\ B \in \mathcal{E}. \qquad (1.3)$$

Proposition 1.19 *If X is $\mathcal{E}$-measurable, then*

$$E[X|\mathcal{E}] = X \qquad w.p.1. \qquad (1.4)$$

Proof. Clearly the difference of two $\mathcal{E}$-measurable functions,

$$Y = E[X|\mathcal{E}] - X,$$

is $\mathcal{E}$-measurable. Then from (1.3), $\int_B Y\,dP = 0$ for all $B \in \mathcal{E}$. Thus, $Y = 0$ w.p.1; otherwise, there would exist $B \in \mathcal{E}$ such that $P(B) > 0$ on which $Y \neq 0$, which implies $\int_B Y\,dP \neq 0$, a contradiction. ∎

As a random variable, $E[X|\mathcal{E}]$ is $\mathcal{E}$-measurable. This means that all of the information content in $\mathcal{E}$ is fully absorbed in $E[X|\mathcal{E}]$. Any attempt to squeeze out more information by taking the conditional expectation of $E[X|\mathcal{E}]$ with respect to $\mathcal{E}$ is futile, because $E[E[X|\mathcal{E}]|\mathcal{E}] = E[X|\mathcal{E}]$.

For easy reference, major properties of conditional expectations are summarized in the following

Proposition 1.20

(1) For any constants a and b and conditional expectations $E[X|\mathcal{E}]$ and $E[Y|\mathcal{E}]$,

$$E[aX + bY|\mathcal{E}] = aE[X|\mathcal{E}] + bE[Y|\mathcal{E}].$$

(2) If $X \geq 0$ w.p.1, then $E[X|\mathcal{E}] \geq 0$ w.p.1.
(3) If $X \leq Y$ w.p.1, then $E[X|\mathcal{E}] \leq E[Y|\mathcal{E}]$ w.p.1.
(4) If $X = b$, a constant, then $E[X|\mathcal{E}] = b$, for any $\mathcal{E}$.
(5) The triangle inequality holds:

$$|E[X|\mathcal{E}]| \leq E[|X||\mathcal{E}].$$

(6) Let $\{X_n\}$ be a sequence of random variables satisfying $\lim_{n\to\infty} X_n = X$ w.p.1 and $|X_n| \leq Y$, where X, Y are random variables

and Y is integrable. Then $\lim_{n\to\infty} E\left[|X_n| \mathcal{E}\right]$ *exists and satisfies*

$$\lim_{n\to\infty} E\left[X_n \mid \mathcal{E}\right] = E\left[X \mid \mathcal{E}\right] = E\left[\lim_{n\to\infty} X_n \mid \mathcal{E}\right].$$

(7) If $\mathcal{E} = \{\Omega, \varnothing\}$, *then* $E\left[X \mid \mathcal{E}\right] = E\left[X\right]$.

(8) If X is $\mathcal{E}$-*measurable, and Y and XY are integrable, then, w.p.1,*

$$E\left[XY \mid \mathcal{E}\right] = X E\left[Y \mid \mathcal{E}\right].$$

(9) Let $\mathcal{E}_1$ *and* $\mathcal{E}_2$ *be two* σ-*algebras in* $\mathcal{F}$ *such that* $\mathcal{E}_1 \subset \mathcal{E}_2$. *Then*

$$E\left[E\left[X \mid \mathcal{E}_2\right] \mid \mathcal{E}_1\right] = E\left[X \mid \mathcal{E}_1\right] = E\left[E\left[X \mid \mathcal{E}_1\right] \mid \mathcal{E}_2\right]. \qquad (1.5)$$

(10) Let X and $\mathcal{E}$ *be independent in the sense that* $\sigma(X)$ *and* $\mathcal{E}$ *are independent. Then* $E\left[X \mid \mathcal{E}\right] = E\left[X\right]$.

Proof. See, Billingsley (1995). For (1)–(6), see Theorem 34.2; for (8), Theorem 34.3; and for (9), Theorem 34.4. The rest are obvious. ∎

Property (1) is self-explanatory. Properties (2) and (3) are equivalent; both can be seen from setting $c_i \geq 0$ in simple random variables. Property (4) is a direct application of (1.4), because a constant function is always $\mathcal{E}$-measurable. Property (5) can be obtained by taking absolute values on both sides of (1.2). Specifically,

$$\left| E\left[X \mid \mathcal{E}\right] \right| = \left| \sum_{i=1}^{n} c_i P\left[A_i \mid \mathcal{E}\right] \right| \leq \sum_{i=1}^{n} |c_i| P\left[A_i \mid \mathcal{E}\right] = E\left[|X| \mid \mathcal{E}\right].$$

Property (6) is the so-called *conditional dominated convergence theorem*, which presents the conditions under which we can move the limit sign from outside the conditional expectation to inside, i.e., the limit of conditional expectations is the conditional expectation of the limit.

Property (7) is based on $P\left[A \mid \mathcal{E}\right] = P(A)$, so that $E\left[X \mid \mathcal{E}\right] = E\left[X\right]$ is true for simple random variables. An alternative explanation is more instructive. The concept of expectation has the effect of averaging things out. Similarly, the conditional expectation $E\left[X \mid \mathcal{E}\right]$ has the effect of averaging out everything in Ω except what is contained in the information set $\mathcal{E}$. If the σ-algebra is trivial, $\mathcal{E} = \{\Omega, \varnothing\}$, then everything in Ω is averaged out. Thus, we have (7).

The averaging concept applies to (8) as well. Let X be $\mathcal{E}$-measurable, i.e., X has fully absorbed what is contained in the information set $\mathcal{E}$. Then the attempt to average everything in Ω except what is in $\mathcal{E}$ would leave the X-component untouched. In other words, in the process of averaging with respect to $\mathcal{E}$, X can be treated like constants. Thus we can pull X out from under the expectation sign.

The intuition behind property (9) is still the averaging concept. Since $E[X \mid \mathcal{E}]$ averages out everything except what is in $\mathcal{E}$, repeated averaging leaves only the smaller σ-field untouched. This gives the first equality in (1.5). The second equality comes from the fact that $E[X \mid \mathcal{E}_1]$ is $\mathcal{E}_1$-measurable, and therefore, $\mathcal{E}_2$-measurable. Then (1.4) is directly applicable, i.e., $E[E[X \mid \mathcal{E}_1] \mid \mathcal{E}_2] = E[X \mid \mathcal{E}_1]$ w.p.1. Finally, property (10) can be seen from $X = \sum_{i=1}^{n} c_i I_{A_i}$, where A_i are $\sigma(X)$-measurable. Then independence implies that $P[A_i \mid \mathcal{E}] = P(A_i)$.

Exercise 1.3.1 *Let $\mathcal{E} \subset \mathcal{F}$ be a σ-algebra in the probability space $(\Omega, \mathcal{F}, P)$.*

   (i) Verify $E[E[X \mid \mathcal{E}]] = E[X]$.
   (ii) Verify $E[E[X \mid \mathcal{E}] Y \mid \mathcal{E}] = E[X \mid \mathcal{E}] E[Y \mid \mathcal{E}]$.
   (iii) What is $E[X \mid \mathcal{F}]$? Simplify it. Then compare it with property (4).

(Hint. X is $\mathcal{F}$-measurable.)

The following proposition says that if $\mathcal{E}_2$ is "more informative" than $\mathcal{E}_1$ in the sense that $\mathcal{E}_1 \subset \mathcal{E}_2$, then the dispersion of X about the conditional mean of $\mathcal{E}_2$ is smaller than that of $\mathcal{E}_1$. In other words, repeatedly updating information will reduce the conditional variance. The proof is a good exercise in the aforementioned properties.

Proposition 1.21 *If $\mathcal{E}_1 \subset \mathcal{E}_2$ and $E[X^2] < \infty$, then*

$$E\{(X - E[X \mid \mathcal{E}_2])^2\} \leq E\{(X - E[X \mid \mathcal{E}_1])^2\}, \tag{1.6}$$

and the equality holds if $E[X \mid \mathcal{E}_1] = E[X \mid \mathcal{E}_2]$.

Proof. Let $Y = X - E[X \mid \mathcal{E}_1]$, so that the right-hand side of (1.6) becomes $E[Y^2]$. Taking the conditional expectation of Y with respect to

$\mathcal{E}_2$, we obtain

$$E\left[Y\,|\,\mathcal{E}_2\right] = E\left[X\,|\,\mathcal{E}_2\right] - E\left[E\left[X\,|\,\mathcal{E}_1\right]\,|\,\mathcal{E}_2\right] = E\left[X\,|\,\mathcal{E}_2\right] - E\left[X\,|\,\mathcal{E}_1\right].$$

It follows that

$$\begin{aligned} X - E\left[X\,|\,\mathcal{E}_2\right] &= X - E\left[X\,|\,\mathcal{E}_1\right] - \{E\left[X\,|\,\mathcal{E}_2\right] - E\left[X\,|\,\mathcal{E}_1\right]\} \\ &= Y - E\left[Y\,|\,\mathcal{E}_2\right]. \end{aligned}$$

The left-hand side of (1.6) becomes $E\{(Y - E\left[Y\,|\,\mathcal{E}_2\right])^2\}$. Notice that

$$E\{(Y - E\left[Y\,|\,\mathcal{E}_2\right])^2\,|\,\mathcal{E}_2\} = E\left[Y^2\,|\,\mathcal{E}_2\right] - \{E\left[Y\,|\,\mathcal{E}_2\right]\}^2 \le E\left[Y^2\,|\,\mathcal{E}_2\right].$$

Taking the expected values on both sides, we are done. The inequality of (1.6) vanishes if $E\left[Y\,|\,\mathcal{E}_2\right] = 0$, which is exactly $E\left[X\,|\,\mathcal{E}_1\right] = E\left[X\,|\,\mathcal{E}_2\right]$. ∎

An immediate corollary of the above proposition is the so-called Rao–Blackwell theorem. In fact, if we choose $\mathcal{E}_1$ to be the smallest σ-algebra $\mathcal{E}_1 = \{\Omega, \varnothing\}$, and $\mathcal{E}_2 = \sigma\,(Y)$ for some random variable Y, then we have

$$E\{(X - E\left[X\,|\,Y\right])^2\} \le E[(X - \mu)^2],$$

where $\mu = E\left[X\right]$. Denote by σ_X^2 the variance of X, the Rao–Blackwell theorem is simplified as

$$\sigma_{E[X\,|\,Y]}^2 \le \sigma_X^2.$$

Exercise 1.3.2 *Verify the following equality: if $\mu = E\left[X\right]$, then*

$$E[(X - \mu)^2] = E\{(X - E\left[X\,|\,Y\right])^2\} + E\{(E\left[X\,|\,Y\right] - \mu)^2\}.$$

Hint. It suffices to show that

$$E\{(X - E\left[X\,|\,Y\right])(E\left[X\,|\,Y\right] - \mu)\} = 0.$$

For this, you need to show

$$E\{XE\left[X\,|\,Y\right]\} = E\{(E\left[X\,|\,Y\right])^2\}.$$

To complete the proof, you should recognize that

$$E \{XE [X | Y]\} = E \{E [XE [X | Y] | Y]\}$$

and that $E [X | Y]$ is $\sigma (Y)$-measurable, implying

$$E [XE [X | Y] | Y] = E [X | Y] \cdot E [X | Y].$$

1.3.3 Change of Variables

Next, we turn our attention to the case of change of variables. By definition, the expected value of a random variable X is $E (X) = \int_\Omega X dP$ when we follow the measure-theoretic approach. But, in statistics, economists typically write it as $E (X) = \int_\mathbb{R} x \, dF(x)$. What is the justification?

Given two probability spaces $(\Omega, \mathcal{F}, P)$ and $(\Omega', \mathcal{F}', P')$, let $T : \Omega \to \Omega'$ be a measurable transformation from $\mathcal{F}$ to $\mathcal{F}'$. We can define a measure PT^{-1} on $\mathcal{F}'$ by way of P as follows:

$$(PT^{-1})(A') = P(T^{-1} A') \qquad \text{for all } A' \in \mathcal{F}.$$

Theorem 1.22 *(Change of Variables) Suppose f is a $\mathcal{F}'$-measurable, real-valued function on Ω' such that fT is $\mathcal{F}$-measurable on Ω. Then f is integrable with respect to PT^{-1} if and only if fT is integrable with respect to P, and*

$$\int_{T^{-1}A'} f(T\omega)P(d\omega) = \int_{A'} f(\omega')(PT^{-1})(d\omega'), \qquad A' \in \mathcal{F}.$$

In particular, if $A' = \Omega'$, we have

$$\int_\Omega f(T\omega) P(d\omega) = \int_{\Omega'} f(\omega')(PT^{-1})(d\omega').$$

Proof. See Billingsley (1995, Theorem 16.13). ∎

In the event that $T = X$ (a random variable), $\Omega' = \mathbb{R}$, $\mathcal{F}' = \mathcal{B}$, and $f : \mathbb{R} \to \mathbb{R}$ is the identity function ($f(x) = x$), then

$$E [X] = \int_\Omega X(\omega) P(d\omega) = \int_\mathbb{R} x(PX^{-1})(dx)$$

Recall that the distribution function is $F(x) = P[X \le x]$. Then

$$dF(x) = F(x + dx) - F(x) = P[X \le x + dx] - P[X \le x]$$
$$= P[x \le X \le x + dx] = (PX^{-1})(dx).$$

Thus, we have

$$E[X] = \int_{\Omega} X(\omega) P(d\omega) = \int_{\mathbb{R}} x \, dF(x).$$

This is the theoretical justification. Proceed in the same way and define

$$P[x \le X \le x + dx \mid \mathcal{E}] = dF(X \mid \mathcal{E}),$$

to arrive at

$$E[X \mid \mathcal{E}] = \int_{\mathbb{R}} x \, dF(X \mid \mathcal{E}).$$

Exercise 1.3.3 *Verify that, for a nonnegative random variable $X \ge 0$,*

$$E[X \mid \mathcal{E}] = \int_0^{\infty} P[X > x \mid \mathcal{E}] dx.$$

Hint. This conditional expectation is a natural extension of

$$E[X] = \int_0^{\infty} P[X > x] dx,$$

a useful expression to compute the first moment. Notice that

$$P[X > x] = 1 - F(x),$$

and $\int_0^{\infty} P[X > x] dx$ is the area above the distribution function $F(x)$.
    We shall verify the equality for the case that X has discrete and positive values, i.e., $X = \sum_{i=1}^{\infty} c_i I_{A_i}$, $c_i > 0$. Then

$$E[X] = \sum_{i=1}^{\infty} c_i E[I_{A_i}] = \sum_{i=1}^{\infty} c_i P(A_i) = \sum_{i=1}^{\infty} c_i P[x = c_i].$$

Geometrically, $c_i P[x = c_i]$ is a rectangle with base c_i and height $P[x = c_i]$. Ranking c_i's in ascending order, we see that $\sum_{i=1}^{\infty} c_i P[x = c_i]$, which

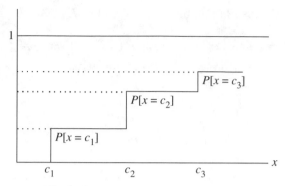

Figure 1.1: Expected value as an area.

is made up of rectangles, is the area above the distribution function. See Figure 1.1.

The extension to an arbitrary X, not necessarily nonnegative, is straightforward. In fact, we have

$$E[X] = \int_0^\infty P[X > x]\,dx - \int_{-\infty}^0 P[X \le x]\,dx.$$

The interested reader is referred to Cinlar (1975, pp. 24–26).

Example 1.23 *(Life Expectancy) It is usually assumed that the length of life, T, is a random variable and that there is a maximal date $\overline{T}$ beyond which no one will live. Assume the probability that one dies at age t is $\pi(t)$. Then the distribution function*

$$F(t) = \int_0^t \pi(s)\,ds$$

stands for the probability that one dies at or before time t. Clearly, $F(t)$ satisfies $F(\overline{T}) = 1$. By definition,

$$P[T \ge t] = 1 - F(t) = S(t)$$

is the survival function, i.e., the probability that one lives at least t years. Then the life expectancy is

$$E(T) = \int_0^{\overline{T}} t\pi(t)\,dt = -\,tS(t)\,|_0^{\overline{T}} + \int_0^{\overline{T}} S(t)\,dt = \int_0^{\overline{T}} S(t)\,dt.$$

In other words, the life expectancy can be represented by the area above the distribution function $F(t)$.

A finite $\overline{T}$ makes backward induction possible in many economic problems. However, a finite $\overline{T}$ can become logically inconsistent with the notion of uncertain lifetime when we do the comparative statics of increasing survival. Specifically, in a discrete-time model, if all conditional survival probabilities except in the last period are improved to unity, then there is nothing uncertain about the last period. With this consideration, allowing $\overline{T} \to \infty$ may be more desirable. In this case,

$$E(T) = \int_0^\infty S(t)\,dt = \int_0^\infty P\,[T \geq t]\,dt.$$

For more details, the reader is referred to Chang (1991).

1.4 Notes and Further Readings

Section 1.2 contains rather standard and rather selected subjects in probability theory. There are many good references, e.g., Arnold (1974), Billingsley (1995), Chung (1974), Cinlar (1975), Karatzas and Shreve (1991), Malliaris and Brock (1982). The last two also provide valuable historical development of the subjects in their notes. Besides Chang (1982), there are other stochastic versions of the value loss assumption, e.g., Brock and Majumdar (1978). For more applications of the Borel–Cantelli lemma to economics, the reader is referred to Joshi (1997a, 1997b, 2003).

Section 1.3 draws heavily from Billingsley (1995). What we emphasize here, however, is the intuition.

2

Wiener Processes

2.1 Introduction

In this chapter we introduce the concept and the major properties of a Wiener process. This stochastic process is essential in building the theory of stochastic optimization in continuous time. Unlike Chapter 1, we provide proofs for most of the theorems, because going through the proofs will enhance our understanding of the process under study.

We begin with a heuristic approach to the Wiener process. Specifically, the Wiener process can be generated as the *limiting process* of the random walk by letting the time interval go to zero. Then we introduce Markov processes, a subject familiar to economists. The purpose is to show that a Wiener process is a Markov process with a normally distributed transition probability. That gives us another perspective on Wiener processes. Finally, we formally define a Wiener process and show its major properties, using a measure-theoretic approach. Section 2.4.1 shows various ways to generate more Wiener processes from a given one. We stress that the understanding of the *zero set* is crucial to have a good grasp of this special stochastic process. We also stress that the sample path of a Wiener process is everywhere continuous and nowhere differentiable.

2.2 A Heuristic Approach

2.2.1 From Random Walks to Wiener Process

Recall that a random walk is a stochastic process such that, at each time interval $\triangle t$, it takes a step forward with probability p, and a step backward with probability $1 - p$, and such that all steps are mutually independent. Let S be the magnitude of each step. Then the random variable that represents each step Z can be characterized by

$$\Pr(Z = +S) = p \quad \text{and} \quad \Pr(Z = -S) = 1 - p = q.$$

Notice that Z is a Bernoulli trial with mean $E(Z) = (p - q) S$ and variance $V(Z) = 4pq S^2$.

Suppose the time elapsed is T. Evenly divide time interval $[0, T]$ into n subintervals, each having length $\Delta t = T/n$. That is, there are altogether $n = T/\Delta t$ steps taken, and the total displacement (the *partial sum*) is

$$X_n = \sum_{i=1}^{n} Z_i, \quad \text{where } Z_i \sim Z,$$

where the summation represents the independent sum of Z_i's. Thus, $X_n(T)$ is a Binomial process with

$$E(X_n(T)) = nE(Z) = \frac{T}{\Delta t}(p - q) S$$

and

$$V(X_n(T)) = nV(Z) = \frac{T}{\Delta t} 4pq S^2.$$

Suppose a limiting process can be generated from this Binomial process by letting $\Delta t \to 0$ (or $n \to \infty$) so that it has a mean μ and a variance σ^2 in unit time T, i.e., suppose

$$E(X_n(T)) \to \mu T \quad \text{and} \quad V(X_n(T)) \to \sigma^2 T.$$

That is, in the limit (with the understanding that Δt is arbitrarily small), we have the following equations

$$\frac{T}{\Delta t}(p - q) S = \mu T, \quad \frac{T}{\Delta t} 4pq S^2 = \sigma^2 T, \quad \text{and} \quad p + q = 1.$$

Solving these equations (squaring the first equation and adding it to the second equation), we obtain

$$S^2 = (\mu \, \Delta t)^2 + \sigma^2 \Delta t \approx \sigma^2 \Delta t,$$

since Δt is quite small. This leads us to choose, assuming $p > q$,

$$S = \sigma \sqrt{\Delta t}, \quad p = \frac{1}{2}\left(1 + \frac{\mu\sqrt{\Delta t}}{\sigma}\right), \quad \text{and} \quad q = \frac{1}{2}\left(1 - \frac{\mu\sqrt{\Delta t}}{\sigma}\right).$$

$$\text{(2.1)}$$

An important message falls out from this exercise. The size of each step S is of order $\sqrt{\Delta t}$. Recall the "big O" notation in elementary calculus. We write $S = O(\sqrt{\Delta t})$ if

$$\lim_{\Delta t \to 0} \frac{S}{\sqrt{\Delta t}} = k \qquad \text{for some constant } k.$$

This means that, as $\Delta t \to 0$, $S \to 0$, but it goes to zero only at the rate of $\sqrt{\Delta t}$. Then the *velocity* $S/\Delta t$ is of order $O(1/\sqrt{\Delta t})$, which goes to ∞ as $\Delta t \to 0$. This means that the instantaneous velocity

$$\lim_{\Delta t \to 0} \frac{S}{\Delta t}$$

does not exist. That is, in any finite interval, the realization of the limiting process has infinitely many spikes and therefore is *not differentiable*. As will be seen later, this limiting process is *nowhere differentiable* with probability one.

To verify that such a limiting process is normally distributed, let us compute the moment generating function (m.g.f.) of the limiting process. Since Z is Bernoulli, $X_n(T)$ is Binomial with

$$M_{X_n(T)}(\theta) = \left(pe^{\theta S} + qe^{-\theta S}\right)^n, \qquad n = \frac{T}{\Delta t}.$$

Using the equations in (2.1), we have

$$M_{X_n(T)}(\theta) = \left\{\frac{1}{2}\left(e^{\theta\sigma\sqrt{\Delta t}} + e^{-\theta\sigma\sqrt{\Delta t}}\right) + \frac{\mu\sqrt{\Delta t}}{2\sigma}\left(e^{\theta\sigma\sqrt{\Delta t}} - e^{-\theta\sigma\sqrt{\Delta t}}\right)\right\}^{\frac{T}{\Delta t}}.$$

Recall that

$$e^x = \sum_{n=0}^{\infty} \frac{x^n}{n!}.$$

Then

$$M_{X_n(T)}(\theta) = \left\{ 1 + \left(\mu\theta + \frac{1}{2}\theta^2\sigma^2 \right) \Delta t + o(\Delta t) \right\}^{\frac{T}{\Delta t}},$$

where $o(\Delta t)$ is the usual "little o", which represents terms converging to zero faster than Δt, i.e.,

$$\lim_{\Delta t \to 0} \frac{o(\Delta t)}{\Delta t} = 0.$$

Since $\Delta t = T/n$ and

$$\lim_{n \to \infty} \left(1 + \frac{b}{n} \right)^n = e^b,$$

as $\Delta t \to 0$ we have

$$M_{X_n(T)}(\theta) = \left\{ 1 + \left(\mu\theta + \frac{1}{2}\theta^2\sigma^2 \right) \frac{T}{n} + o(\Delta t) \right\}^n$$

$$\to \exp\left[\left(\mu\theta + \frac{1}{2}\theta^2\sigma^2 \right) T \right], \tag{2.2}$$

which is the m.g.f. of a normal distribution with mean μT and variance $\sigma^2 T$. The limiting process thus derived is called the Wiener process $W(T)$ (or the *Brownian motion*) with *drift* μ and *instantaneous variance* σ^2.

2.2.2 Some Basic Properties of the Wiener Process

If we change the time elapsed, then the Wiener process $W(T)$ is defined for all T. To follow the standard notation, we shall hereafter write it as $W(t)$, using a lowercase t. Notice that the above derivation depends only on the time elapsed, t, not on the initial time (which was set at 0). In other words, if we start at s instead of 0, then

$$W(s+t) - W(s) \sim N(\mu t, \sigma^2 t).$$

($W(s)$ stands for the initial position.) Equivalently,

$$W(t) - W(s) \sim N(\mu(t-s), \sigma^2(t-s)).$$

More importantly, from the properties of the random walk, the increment in displacements $W(t) - W(s)$ is not influenced by the increment $W(s) - W(0)$. In other words, $W(t) - W(s)$ and $W(s) - W(0)$ are independent. This is the so-called *independent increments property*. In particular, $\{\triangle W_t\} = \{W(t+1) - W(t)\}$, for integer t, are identically and independently distributed (i.i.d.).

We have just shown that the Wiener process is the limiting process of the random walk. However, that is not the only way to obtain it. As is well known, the Wiener process can also be approximated by a stochastic sequence other than the random walk. In the time series literature, economists are interested in discrete processes that are not i.i.d. but approximate the Wiener process.

Proposition 2.1 *A standard Wiener process ($\mu = 0$, $\sigma = 1$) has continuous sample functions w.p.1.*

Proof. From (2.2), the moment generating function is

$$M(\theta) = E\left(e^{\theta \triangle X}\right) = e^{\theta^2 \triangle t/2}.$$

A direct computation shows that

$$M'(\theta) = \theta M(\theta) \triangle t,$$
$$M''(\theta) = [1 + \theta^2 \triangle t] M(\theta) \triangle t,$$
$$M'''(\theta) = [3 + \theta^2 \triangle t] \theta M(\theta)(\triangle t)^2,$$
$$M^{(4)}(\theta) = [3 + 6\theta^2 \triangle t + \theta^4 (\triangle t)^2] M(\theta)(\triangle t)^2,$$

with $M^{(4)}(0) = 3(\triangle t)^2$. Hence,

$$E\left[|X_t - X_s|^4\right] = 3|t-s|^2. \tag{2.3}$$

By the Kolmogorov–Čentsov theorem, the proposition is proved if we choose $a = 4$, $b = 1$, and $c = 3$. ∎

Example 2.2 *Show that the covariance of a standard Wiener process* $X(t)$ *(with* $X(0) = 0$*) is*

$$E[X(s)X(t)] = \min\{s, t\}. \tag{2.4}$$

This is a direct application of the independent increments property. Assume without loss of generality that $0 \le s \le t$. *Then, by independence,*

$$E[X(s)X(t)] = E\{X(s)[X(t) - X(s)]\} + E[X(s)^2]$$
$$= E[X(s)]E[X(t) - X(s)] + E[X(s)^2] = 0 + s = s.$$

We can continue to study the further properties with this Wiener process $W(t)$ by investigating the associated forward and backward equations. However, we shall not pursue this avenue, because the major purpose of this section is to provide the reader with an overview of Brownian motion and to show how it is linked to the familiar random walk. Many of its important properties are natural outgrowths of an elementary probabilistic exercise, as we have just demonstrated.

2.3 Markov Processes

2.3.1 Introduction

Let $\{X_t : t \in I\}$ be a stochastic process with state space $\mathbb{R}$. Let $I = [t_0, T] \subset [0, \infty)$, the nonnegative real numbers, which are regarded as "time." Usually, $t_0 = 0$. Denote

$$\mathcal{F}_{[t_1, t_2]} = \sigma(X_t : t \in [t_1, t_2]),$$

where $[t_1, t_2] \subset [t_0, T]$. When $t_1 = t_0$, we simply write

$$\mathcal{F}_t = \sigma(X_s : s \in [t_0, t]), \qquad t \in I.$$

Clearly, $\{\mathcal{F}_t : t \in I\}$ is a family of increasing σ-algebras, i.e., $\mathcal{F}_s \subset \mathcal{F}_t \subset \mathcal{F}$ if $s < t$. Besides $\{\mathcal{F}_t\}$, there are other (and larger) families of increasing σ-algebras that contain the information embedded in $\{\sigma(X_s : s \in [t_0, t])\}$.

In his celebrated paper, Fama (1970) argues that capital markets are efficient, because prices "fully reflect" the available information. To characterize information sets, he calls the information set the *weak* form if it is generated by past prices alone; the *semi-strong* form if it is generated by past prices and all publicly available information; and the *strong* form if all private information is included.

Example 2.3 *(Weak Form Information) How do we estimate the expected stock price based on the information about past prices? Specifically, for $h > 0$, we try to find*

$$E\{X_{t+h}| X_0 = p_0, X_1 = p_1, X_2 = p_2, \ldots, X_t = p_t\},$$

where $X_0 = p_0, X_1 = p_1, \ldots, X_t = p_t$ are the observed past prices. We can characterize the σ-algebras $\{\mathcal{F}_t\}$ as follows. Let $A_0 = X_0^{-1}(p_0)$. Clearly, A_0 and $A_0^c = \Omega - A$ form a partition of Ω, i.e., $\mathcal{F}_0 = \{\Omega, \varnothing, A_0, A_0^c\}$. The cardinality of $\mathcal{F}_0$ is 2^2. Next, let $A_1 = X_1^{-1}(p_1)$ and $A_{01} = A_0 \cap A_1$. Then $A_0 - A_{01}, A_1 - A_{01}, A_{01}, and \Omega - (A_0 \cup A_1)$ form a partition of $\mathcal{F}_1$. The cardinality of $\mathcal{F}_1$ is 2^4 if $A_{01} \neq \varnothing$. By induction, we can in principle spell out all elements in $\mathcal{F}_t$, which has cardinality 2^n, where n is the number of mutually disjoint events that form a partition of Ω. Clearly, $\{\mathcal{F}_t : t = 1, 2, \ldots\}$ is an increasing sequence.

Definition 2.4 *A stochastic process $\{X_t : t \in I\}$ defined on a probability space $(\Omega, \mathcal{F}, P)$ is Markov if one of the following conditions is satisfied: for any s, t such that $t_0 \leq s \leq t \leq T$,*

(1) $P[X_t \in B \mid \mathcal{F}_s] = P[X_t \in B \mid X_s]$, where B is a Borel set;

(2) $P[A \mid \mathcal{F}_s] = P[A \mid X_s]$ for $A \in \mathcal{F}$;

(3) $E[Y \mid \mathcal{F}_s] = E[Y \mid X_s]$, where Y is $\mathcal{F}_t$-measurable and integrable;

(4) $P[A_1 \cap A_2 \mid X_t] = P[A_1 \mid X_t] \cdot P[A_2 \mid X_t]$, where $A_1 \in \mathcal{F}_{t_1}$, $A_2 \in \mathcal{F}_{[t_2,T]}$ and $t_1 < t < t_2 < T$; and

(5) for any Borel set B and any $\{t_i\}$ such that $t_0 \leq t_1 < t_2 < \cdots < t_n < t \leq T$, $P[X_t \in B \mid X_{t_1}, X_{t_2}, \ldots, X_{t_n}] = P[X_t \in B \mid X_{t_n}]$.

All five conditions hold w.p.1.

For a formal proof of equivalence, the reader is referred to Chung (1982, p. 3) or Doob (1953, pp. 80–85). Conditions (1) and (2) are equivalent if we identify A as the preimage $X_t^{-1}(B)$. Both say that only the information at time s is useful. Information before time s is "forgotten." This is the "lack of memory" property. Condition (3) says the same thing except that it is expressed in the conditional expectation form. Condition (4), on the other hand, clearly spells out an important property: that, given the information set of the present, events occurring in the past and those occurring in the future are independent. Condition (5) is a weaker form of (1) in that there are only a finite number of X_{t_i} in the information set. To prove (1) from (5), however, we need Kolmogorov's existence theorem.

2.3.2 Transition Probability

Recall that the distribution function of a random variable is defined as the probability of the preimage of a Borel set, i.e., $F(B) = P(X^{-1}(B))$, and $F(B)$ is a Borel function. The *conditional distribution function* can be defined similarly. Specifically, for any random variable X and Borel set B,

$$F(B \mid \mathcal{E}) = P[X \in B \mid \mathcal{E}] \qquad \text{for a given } \sigma\text{-algebra } \mathcal{E} \subset \mathcal{F}.$$

The conditional distribution function thus defined is a random variable with domain Ω. If $X = X_t$ and $\mathcal{E} = \sigma(X_s)$, then the conditional distribution function of B given X_s becomes

$$F(B \mid X_s) = P[X_t \in B \mid X_s].$$

This enables us to define the *transition probability* $P(s, X_s, t, B)$ as a conditional distribution function.

Definition 2.5 *The transition probability of a Markov process* $\{X_t : t \in I\}$ *is*

$$P(s, X_s, t, B) = P[X_t \in B \mid X_s] \qquad \text{w.p.1.}$$

When a particular value of X_s is observed, i.e., when the event $[X_s = x]$ is given, we can define the transition probability as a function of four arguments s, x, t, B (with $s \leq t$) such that

$$P(s, x, t, B) = P[X_t \in B \mid X_s = x].$$

This transition probability can be viewed from two different angles. First, by construction, $P(s, x, t, \cdot)$ is a probability measure on a Borel field. Second, $P(s, \cdot, t, B)$ is a Borel function, because the information set on which we are conditioning is $X_s^{-1}(A)$, for any Borel set A.

Proposition 2.6 *(Chapman–Kolmogorov Equation) Given a Markov process $\{X_t : t \in I\}$, and $s \leq u \leq t$, the equation*

$$P(s, X_s, t, B) = \int_{\mathbb{R}} P(u, y, t, B) P(s, X_s, u, dy) \qquad (2.5)$$

holds w.p.1.

Proof. With probability one,

$$P(s, X_s, t, B) = P[X_t \in B \mid X_s] = P[X_t \in B \mid \mathcal{F}_s] = E\left[I_{X_t^{-1}(B)} \mid \mathcal{F}_s\right]$$

$$= E\left[E[I_{X_t^{-1}(B)} \mid \mathcal{F}_u] \mid \mathcal{F}_s\right] = E\left[P[X_t \in B \mid \mathcal{F}_u] \mid \mathcal{F}_s\right]$$

$$= E[P[X_t \in B \mid X_u] \mid \mathcal{F}_s] = E[P[X_t \in B \mid X_u] \mid X_s]$$

$$= E[P(u, X_u, t, B) \mid X_s].$$

Using the notation $X_u = y$ (X_u assuming value y), we have, w.p.1,

$$P(s, X_s, t, B) = \int_{\mathbb{R}} P(u, y, t, B) P[dy \mid X_s]$$

$$= \int_{\mathbb{R}} P(u, y, t, B) P(s, X_s, u, dy),$$

and the proposition is proved. ∎

A Markov process $\{X_t : t \in I\}$ is *stationary* if $P(s+u, x, t+u, B) = P(s, x, t, B)$. In particular, if $u = -s$, then $P(s, x, t, B) = P(0, x, t - s, B)$, which depends only on three arguments: $t - s$, x, and B. We simply denote it by $P(t - s, x, B)$. What we are interested is a special case of stationary Markov processes.

To set up the next definition, we denote by $N(x, t)$ the normal distribution with mean x and variance t, and by $\delta_x(\cdot)$ the delta function,

$$\delta_x(y) = \begin{cases} 1 & \text{if } y = x, \\ 0 & \text{if } y \neq x. \end{cases}$$

Definition 2.7 *The Wiener process* $\{W_t : t \in I\}$ *is a stationary Markov process defined on* $I = [0, \infty)$ *with stationary transition probability* $P(t, x, \cdot) \sim N(x, t)$ *for* $t > 0$, *and* $P(t, x, \cdot) = \delta_x(\cdot)$ *for* $t = 0$. *More precisely, for* $t > 0$,

$$P(t, x, B) = \int_B \frac{1}{\sqrt{2\pi t}} \exp\left\{-\frac{|y - x|^2}{2t}\right\} dy, \qquad (2.6)$$

and for $t = 0$,

$$P(t, x, B) = \begin{cases} 1 & \text{if } x \in B, \\ 0 & \text{if } x \notin B. \end{cases}$$

Proposition 2.8 *The Wiener process defined above satisfies the following three properties. For any* $\varepsilon > 0$, *we have*

$$\lim_{t \to 0} \left(\frac{1}{t}\right) \int_{|y-x|>\varepsilon} P(t, x, dy) = 0, \qquad (2.7)$$

$$\lim_{t \to 0} \left(\frac{1}{t}\right) \int_{|y-x|\le\varepsilon} (y - x) P(t, x, dy) = 0. \qquad (2.8)$$

and

$$\lim_{t \to 0} \left(\frac{1}{t}\right) \int_{|y-x|\le\varepsilon} (y - x)^2 P(t, x, dy) = 1. \qquad (2.9)$$

Proof. For any $\varepsilon > 0$, and for any y satisfying $|y - x| > \varepsilon$,

$$\exp\left\{-\frac{|y - x|^2}{2t}\right\} \le \exp\left\{-\frac{\varepsilon^2}{2t}\right\}.$$

Then

$$\left(\frac{1}{t}\right) \int_{|y-x|>\varepsilon} P(t, x, dy) = \left(\frac{1}{t}\right) \int_{|y-x|>\varepsilon} \frac{1}{\sqrt{2\pi t}} \exp\left\{-\frac{|y - x|^2}{2t}\right\} dy$$

$$\le \int_{|y-x|>\varepsilon} \frac{1}{\sqrt{2\pi}} t^{-3/2} \exp\left\{-\frac{\varepsilon^2}{2t}\right\} dy.$$

Hence,

$$\left(\frac{1}{t}\right) \int_{|y-x|>\varepsilon} P(t, x, dy) \to 0 \qquad \text{as } t \to 0.$$

This proves (2.7). Next, for any $\varepsilon > 0$,

$$\left(\frac{1}{t}\right) \int_{|y-x|\leq\varepsilon} (y-x)P(t, x, dy) = \int_{x-\varepsilon}^{x+\varepsilon} \frac{(y-x)}{t\sqrt{2\pi t}} \exp\left\{-\frac{|y-x|^2}{2t}\right\} dy$$

$$= -\frac{1}{\sqrt{2\pi t}} \exp\left\{-\frac{|y-x|^2}{2t}\right\} \Big|_{y=x-\varepsilon}^{y=x+\varepsilon}$$

$$= 0.$$

This proves (2.8). Finally, for any $\varepsilon > 0$, using integration by parts, we have

$$\left(\frac{1}{t}\right) \int_{x-\varepsilon}^{x+\varepsilon} \frac{1}{\sqrt{2\pi t}} (y-x)^2 \exp\left\{-\frac{|y-x|^2}{2t}\right\} dy$$

$$= -\frac{(y-x)}{\sqrt{2\pi t}} \exp\left\{-\frac{|y-x|^2}{2t}\right\} \Big|_{y=x-\varepsilon}^{y=x+\varepsilon}$$

$$+ \int_{x-\varepsilon}^{x+\varepsilon} \frac{1}{\sqrt{2\pi t}} \exp\left\{-\frac{|y-x|^2}{2t}\right\} dy$$

$$= -\frac{2\varepsilon}{\sqrt{2\pi}} t^{-1/2} \exp\left\{-\frac{\varepsilon^2}{2t}\right\} + \int_{x-\varepsilon}^{x+\varepsilon} \frac{1}{\sqrt{2\pi t}} \exp\left\{-\frac{|y-x|^2}{2t}\right\} dy.$$

Notice that

$$\int_{x-\varepsilon}^{x+\varepsilon} \frac{1}{\sqrt{2\pi t}} \exp\left\{-\frac{|y-x|^2}{2t}\right\} dy \to 1 \qquad \text{as } t \to 0$$

because the variance, $\sigma^2 t$, is going to zero, so that the support of the density function lies entirely inside the interval $(x - \varepsilon, x + \varepsilon)$. It follows that

$$\left(\frac{1}{t}\right) \int_{\leq\varepsilon} (y-x)^2 P(t, x, dy) \to 0 + 1 \qquad \text{as } t \to 0.$$

This proves (2.9). ∎

The three properties in the proposition are the building blocks for a diffusion process.

2.3.3 Diffusion Processes

Definition 2.9 *A Markov process $\{X_t : t \in I\}$ with state space $\mathbb{R}$ and continuous sample functions, w.p.1, is called a diffusion process if its transition probability $P(s, x, t, B)$ satisfies*

$$\lim_{t \to s} \frac{1}{t - s} \int_{|y-x|>\varepsilon} P(s, x, t, dy) = 0; \tag{2.10}$$

there exists a real-valued function $\mu(s, x)$ such that

$$\lim_{t \to s} \frac{1}{t - s} \int_{|y-x|\le\varepsilon} (y - x) P(s, x, t, dy) = \mu(s, x); \tag{2.11}$$

and there exists a real-valued function $\sigma^2(s, x)$ such that

$$\lim_{t \to s} \frac{1}{t - s} \int_{|y-x|\le\varepsilon} (y - x)^2 P(s, x, t, dy) = \sigma^2(s, x). \tag{2.12}$$

Clearly, the Wiener process defined above is a diffusion process with $\mu = 0$ and $\sigma^2 = 1$. The functions $\mu(s, x)$ and $\sigma^2(s, x)$ are called the *(local) drift* and the *(local or instantaneous) variance* respectively. In higher-dimensional cases, $\mu(s, x)$ is a vector, while $\sigma^2(s, x)$ becomes the covariance matrix Σ. In that case, the factor $(\mathbf{y} - \mathbf{x})^2$ stands for the matrix product $(\mathbf{y} - \mathbf{x})^T(\mathbf{y} - \mathbf{x})$, where $(\mathbf{y} - \mathbf{x})^T$ is the transpose of the row vector $\mathbf{y} - \mathbf{x}$.

Notice that equation (2.11) is a *truncated* instantaneous first moment, because it is defined only on $|y - x| \le \varepsilon$, not on $\mathbb{R}$. Similarly, (2.12) is a truncated instantaneous second moment. In general, even if these truncated moments exist, the true instantaneous moments may fail to exist. The next proposition says that if an instantaneous moment of order greater than 2 exists and equals zero, then (2.11) and (2.12) become true moments.

Proposition 2.10 *If there exists* $\delta > 0$ *such that*

$$\lim_{t \to s} \frac{1}{t-s} E\left[|X_t - X_s|^{2+\delta} \mid X_s = x\right]$$

$$= \lim_{t \to s} \frac{1}{t-s} \int_{\mathbb{R}} |y-x|^{2+\delta} P(s,x,t,dy) = 0, \quad (2.13)$$

then

$$\lim_{t \to s} \frac{1}{t-s} E\left[X_t - X_s \mid X_s = x\right] = \mu(s,x), \quad (2.14)$$

$$\lim_{t \to s} \frac{1}{t-s} E[(X_t - X_s)^2 \mid X_s = x] = \sigma^2(s,x), \quad (2.15)$$

and (2.10) *holds as well.*

Proof. To prove this, we observe that

$$\int_{\mathbb{R}} |y-x|^k P(s,x,t,dy)$$

$$= \int_{|y-x| \le \varepsilon} |y-x|^k P(s,x,t,dy) + \int_{|y-x| > \varepsilon} |y-x|^k P(s,x,t,dy),$$

and that, for $k = 0, 1, 2$,

$$\int_{|y-x| > \varepsilon} |y-x|^k P(s,x,t,dy)$$

$$= \int_{|y-x| > \varepsilon} |y-x|^{k-2-\delta} |y-x|^{2+\delta} P(s,x,t,dy)$$

$$\le \varepsilon^{k-2-\delta} \int_{\mathbb{R}} |y-x|^{2+\delta} P(s,x,t,dy).$$

The latter, after dividing by $t - s$, converges to zero as $t \to s$. This shows that, for $k = 1, 2$, the truncated moments are the true moments. In the event $k = 0$, the above inequality implies (2.10) immediately. ∎

Example 2.11 *For a Wiener process, we shall show that the third moment is zero (i.e., we choose $\delta = 1$) to ensure the existence of the first two true* *moments. This is because, using (2.6) and integration by parts,*

$$\lim_{t \to s} \frac{1}{t - s} E\left[|X_t - X_s|^3 |X_s = x\right]$$

$$= \lim_{t \to s} \frac{1}{t - s} \int_{-\infty}^{\infty} \frac{|y - x|^3}{\sqrt{2\pi (t - s)}} \exp\left\{-\frac{(y - x)^2}{2(t - s)}\right\} dy$$

$$= -\frac{(y - x)^2}{\sqrt{2\pi(t - s)}} \exp\left\{-\frac{(y - x)^2}{2(t - s)}\right\}\Bigg|_{y=-\infty}^{y=\infty}$$

$$+ \int_{-\infty}^{\infty} \frac{2(y - x)}{\sqrt{2\pi (t - s)}} \exp\left\{-\frac{(y - x)^2}{2(t - s)}\right\} dy$$

$$= 0 - \frac{2}{\sqrt{2\pi}} (t - s)^{1/2} \exp\left\{-\frac{(y - x)^2}{2(t - s)}\right\}\Bigg|_{y=-\infty}^{y=\infty} = 0.$$

The instantaneous moments (2.14) and (2.15) have very intuitive interpretations. Equation (2.14) represents the *mean velocity* of $\{X_t : t \in I\}$, i.e.,

$$\lim_{t \to s} \frac{1}{t - s} E\left[X_t - X_s \mid X_s = x\right] = \lim_{t \to s} E\left[\frac{X_t - X_s}{t - s} \bigg| X_s = x\right] = \mu(s, x).$$

Similarly, (2.15) represents the instantaneous rate of variance. In fact, they can be expressed as

$$E\left[X_t - X_s \mid X_s = x\right] = \mu(s, x)(t - s) + o(t - s),$$
$$E\left[(X_t - X_s)^2 \mid X_s = x\right] = \sigma^2(s, x)(t - s) + o(t - s),$$

and (2.10) can be written as

$$P\left[|X_t - X_s| > \varepsilon \mid X_s = x\right] = o(t - s),$$

which has the interpretation that large changes in X_t over a short period of time elapsed are improbable, and are dominated by the time elapsed.

Since the increments $W_t - W_s$ of a Wiener process are distributed as $N(0, t - s)$, we can write

$$X_t - X_s = \mu(s, x)(t - s) + \sigma(s, x)(W_t - W_s) + o(t - s).$$

Letting $t \to s$, we arrive at the following stochastic differential equation:

$$dX_s = \mu(s, x)\, ds + \sigma(s, x)\, dW_s. \qquad (2.16)$$

That is, we have heuristically demonstrated that a diffusion process $\{X_t\}$ satisfies (2.16). It can be shown that every solution to (2.16) is also a diffusion process, if $\mu(s, x)$ and $\sigma(s, x)$ are continuous in (s, x). See Friedman (1975, p. 115).

Finally, we look at the density function of W_t,

$$f(t, x, y) = \frac{1}{\sqrt{2\pi t}} \exp\left\{-\frac{(y - x)^2}{2t}\right\}. \qquad (2.17)$$

It is clear that

$$f(t, x + z, y + z) = f(t, x, y) \qquad \forall z.$$

Thus, a standard Wiener process is stationary both in time and in space. The transition probability of a Wiener process is, by definition, $p(s, x, t, y) = f(t - s, x, y)$. Then, a direct computation shows that $p(s, x, t, y)$ satisfies the following *backward equation*:

$$\frac{\partial p(s, x, t, y)}{\partial s} + \frac{1}{2}\frac{\partial^2 p(s, x, t, y)}{\partial x^2} = 0 \qquad \text{for fixed } t \text{ and } y. \quad (2.18)$$

Mathematically, we can learn all about the Wiener process through this backward equation.

Exercise 2.3.1 *Using the density function $f(t - s, x, y)$ of $W_t - W_s$ and using integrations by parts repeatedly, show that (2.3) is valid.*

2.4 Wiener Processes

We have shown that a Wiener process is a stationary Markov process with transition probability (2.6) for $t > 0$ and $\delta_x(\cdot)$ for $t = 0$. It has a density function in the form of (2.17). We have also shown that, as a diffusion process, the standard Wiener process ($\mu = 0$, $\sigma = 1$) satisfies $W_t - W_s \sim N(0, t - s)$. That is, the density function of $W_t - W_s$ is $f(t - s, x, y)$ as defined in (2.17). Such a process has several important properties:

(i) It is a process with continuous sample functions w.p.1.

(ii) It satisfies the independent increment property. Specifically, if $(s, t) \cap (u, v) = \varnothing$, then $W_t - W_s$ and $W_v - W_u$ are independent.

(iii) $W_t - W_s \sim N(0, t - s)$, with density $f(t - s, x, y)$.

(iv) The initial value $W_0 = 0$ w.p.1.

As it turns out, all these properties are the defining conditions for a (standard) Wiener process.

Definition 2.12 *A standard Wiener process is a stochastic process satisfying (i)–(iv).*

2.4.1 How to Generate More Wiener Processes

There are lots of Wiener processes. Given one Wiener process, there are ways to generate more. The following proposition summarizes them all.

Proposition 2.13 *If $\{W_t : t \in I\}$ is a Wiener process, then so are*

(a) $\{cW_{t/c^2} : t \in I\}$, $c \neq 0$,

(b) $\{W_{t+s} - W_s : t \in I\}$, s *fixed,*

(c) $\{tW_{1/t} : t > 0\}$, *with the definition $tW_{1/t} \equiv 0$ at $t = 0$.*

Proof. For a formal proof, the reader is referred to McKean (1969, p. 9) or Billingsley (1995, p. 504). ∎

The transformation in (a) is known as *Brownian scaling*. It says that if we want to double the value of the process then we should reduce the time interval to one-fourth its value. This is because the variance of a Wiener process is linear in time and because doubling the value of the process will quadruple the variance. Formally, let $X_t = cW_{t/c^2}$. Notice that the transformation, t/c^2, simply rescales the time interval from $[s, t]$ to $[s/c^2, t/c^2]$. Since $E(W_t - W_s) = 0$, we must have $E(W_{t/c^2} - W_{s/c^2}) = 0$. Thus,

$$E(X_t - X_s) = cE(W_{t/c^2} - W_{s/c^2}) = 0.$$

Similarly,

$$V(X_t - X_s) = V\left[(cW_{t/c^2} - cW_{s/c^2})\right] = c^2 V(W_{t/c^2} - W_{s/c^2})$$

$$= c^2 \left(\frac{t}{c^2} - \frac{s}{c^2}\right) = t - s.$$

The rest of the conditions, such as the continuity of sample functions and $X_0 = 0$ w.p.1, are obvious.

The transformation in (b) is known as the *differential property* of the Brownian motion. It is a *translation* of the process $\{W_t : t \in I\}$ in the $(t, W_t(\omega))$ coordinates, i.e., it simply shifts the starting point of the sample function from $(0, W_0(\omega))$ to $(s, W_s(\omega))$. There is no rescaling or changing the value of the process.

The last case, (c), is quite interesting and important. The following geometric description of case (c) will be useful. In terms of sample functions, $Z_t = W_{1/t}$ is nothing but an *inversion* of W_t with respect to $t = 1$. That is, the value of Z_t at time $t \in (0, 1]$ is identified with the value of $W_{1/t}$, where $1/t \in [1, \infty)$. Similarly, the value of Z_t with $t \in [1, \infty)$ is identified with the value of $W_{1/t}$, where $1/t \in [0, 1]$. This makes $(1, W_1(\omega))$ a fixed point of the inversion. However, this is not the only thing happening in case (c). The inverted values are multiplied by time t. Still, the point $(1, W_1(\omega))$ remains the fixed point under inversion and multiplication, $tW_{1/t}$.

To simplify the notation, let $Y_t = tW_{1/t}$, $t > 0$, and define $Y_0 = W_0$ w.p.1. Again, inversion and multiplication will offset each other in computing the variance of $Y_t - Y_s$, because the variance of the Wiener process W_t is linear in time. Formally, it is useful to write, for $s < t$,

$$Y_t - Y_s = tW_{1/t} - sW_{1/s} = (t - s)W_{1/t} - s(W_{1/s} - W_{1/t}).$$

Since $0 < 1/t < 1/s$, the differences $W_{1/s} - W_{1/t}$ and $W_{1/t}\ (= W_{1/t} - W_0)$ are independent. It follows that $E[Y_t - Y_s] = 0$. Similarly,

$$V[Y_t - Y_s] = V[tW_{1/t} - sW_{1/s}] = V\left[(t - s)W_{1/t} - s(W_{1/s} - W_{1/t})\right]$$

$$= (t - s)^2\, V[W_{1/t}] + s^2 V[W_{1/s} - W_{1/t}]$$

$$= (t - s)^2 \left(\frac{1}{t}\right) + s^2 \left(\frac{1}{s} - \frac{1}{t}\right) = t - s.$$

It is also quite obvious that Y_t has continuous sample functions for all $t > 0$.

It remains to show the continuity of Y_t at $t = 0$. In fact, this property drives many of the important properties of the Wiener process. As $t \to 0$, the variance of $W_{1/t}$ is $1/t$, which approaches ∞. Therefore, $W_{1/t}$ is unbounded. However, the standard deviation of $W_{1/t}$ is only $O(1/\sqrt{t})$ as $t \to 0$. Thus, as $t \to 0$, $W_{1/t}(\omega)$ is dominated by t for "most" of $\omega \in \Omega$ in the sense that

$$t W_{1/t} \to 0 \quad \text{in probability} \qquad \text{as } t \to 0.$$

This observation is equivalent to

$$(1/t) W_t \to 0 \quad \text{in probability} \qquad \text{as } t \to \infty.$$

This result can be formulated as the well-known weak law of large numbers, because

$$W_t = \sum_{i=1}^{t} (W_i - W_{i-1})$$

if t is an integer.

Proposition 2.14 *(Weak Law of Large Numbers) For the Wiener process W_t, we have*

$$\lim_{t \to \infty} P\left[\left| \frac{1}{t} W_t \right| \geq \varepsilon \right] = 0.$$

To complete the verification that case (c) is also a Wiener process, we need to prove $P[\lim_{t \to 0} t W_{1/t} = 0] = 1$, not just $t W_{1/t} \to 0$ in probability as $t \to 0$. This requires, among other things, the first Borel–Cantelli lemma. The interested reader should consult Billingsley (1995, p. 504) for further details.

The next proposition follows from the fact that case (c) is indeed a Wiener process.

Proposition 2.15 *(Strong Law of Large Numbers) For the Wiener process* W_t, *we have*

$$P\left[\lim_{t\to\infty}\frac{1}{t}W_t = 0\right] = 1.$$

Proof. It follows immediately from the fact that $Y_t = tW_{1/t}, t > 0$, and $Y_0 = W_0$ w.p.1 is also a Wiener process. Then, by the continuity of sample functions,

$$P\left[\lim_{t\to 0}Y_t = 0\right] = P\left[\lim_{t\to 0}tW_{1/t} = 0\right] = 1,$$

which is equivalent to $P\left[\lim_{s\to\infty}\frac{1}{s}W_s = 0\right]$, using the change of variables $s = 1/t$. ∎

Exercise 2.4.1 *Show that* (2.4) *is satisfied for all three cases in Proposition* 2.13. *In fact, McKean (1969) uses* (2.4) *as part of a definition for the standard Wiener process.*

2.4.2 Differentiability of Sample Functions

By inversion and multiplication, we have a new Wiener process $Y_t = tW_{1/t}$. Rewrite it as $(1/t)Y_t = W_{1/t}$. The quantity $(1/t)Y_t = (1/t)(Y_t - Y_0)$ is the slope of Y_t relative to $Y_0 = 0$. As $t \to 0$, it becomes the *derivative* of Y_t at $t = 0$, if the limit exists. To study the nature of this derivative, it suffices to look at the behavior of $W_{1/t}$ as $t \to 0$ or the behavior of W_t as $t \to \infty$.

Is W_t bounded w.p.1 as $t \to \infty$? If so, then the set

$$B = \left\{\omega : \sup_t |W_t(\omega)| < \infty\right\}$$

must be of probability one, if it is measurable. However, B may not be measurable, because it is the supremum over a continuum of t. We can, however, replace it with a measurable one by starting with a separable version of $\{W_t : t \in I\}$. Specifically, let $D = \{t_i : i = 1, 2, \ldots\}$ be the countable *dense* set of points of time in $[0, \infty)$, and let

$$A = \left\{\omega : \sup_{t_i \in D} |W_{t_i}(\omega)| < \infty\right\}.$$

The set A is measurable, because it can be written as countable union and/or intersection of measurable sets, viz.,

$$A = \bigcup_{a=1}^{\infty} \bigcap_{i=1}^{\infty} \left\{ \omega : |W_{t_i}(\omega)| \leq a \right\}.$$

Then the difference between A and B is contained in a set of probability zero. In this way, the question becomes: Is $P(A) = 1$?

The next proposition says that $P(A) = 0$. Since D is dense in $[0, \infty)$, we may assume $t_i \to \infty$ as $i \to \infty$. With this notation, we shall prove the following:

Proposition 2.16 *With probability one,*

$$\inf_{t_i} W_{t_i} = -\infty \quad and \quad \sup_{t_i} W_{t_i} = +\infty. \tag{2.19}$$

Proof. Assume, without loss of generality, that $1 \in D$. Using Brownian scaling, for each time t, we choose the scale c to be $1/\sqrt{t}$ in $X_t = cW_{t/c^2}$ and study the random variable X_1. That is,

$$X_1 = \left(\frac{1}{\sqrt{t}} \right) W_{1/(1/t)} = \left(\frac{1}{\sqrt{t}} \right) W_t$$

This establishes a relationship between X_1 and W_t, namely, $W_t = \sqrt{t} X_1$. An immediate implication of this relationship is that whether W_t is bounded or not is determined by $\sqrt{t}$ and a fixed random variable X_1. Then

$$A_i^a = \{ \omega : |W_{t_i}(\omega)| \leq a \} = \left\{ \omega : |X_1(\omega)| \leq \frac{a}{\sqrt{t_i}} \right\}.$$

Since $t_i \to \infty$ as $i \to \infty$, we have $P(A_i^a) \to 0$ as $i \to \infty$. Obviously, $P(\bigcap_{i=1}^{\infty} A_i^a) \leq P(A_i^a)$ for all i. It follows that $P(\bigcap_{i=1}^{\infty} A_i^a) = 0$ for all a. By the subadditivity of the probability measure $P(\cdot)$, we have

$$P(A) = P\left(\bigcup_{a=1}^{\infty} \bigcap_{i=1}^{\infty} A_i^a \right) \leq \sum_{a=1}^{\infty} P\left(\bigcap_{i=1}^{\infty} A_i^a \right) = 0.$$

In other words, we have shown

$$\sup_{t_i} |W_{t_i}| = +\infty \qquad \text{w.p.1.}$$

Now look at the following two sets:

$$F_1 = \left\{ \omega : \sup_{t_i} W_{t_i} = +\infty \right\}$$

and

$$F_2 = \left\{ \omega : \inf_{t_i} W_{t_i} = -\infty. \right\} = \left\{ \omega : \sup_{t_i} (-W_{t_i}) = +\infty \right\}.$$

Since $\{-W_t : t \in I\}$ is a version of $\{W_t : t \in I\}$, F_1 and F_2 differ by a set of probability zero. From the fact that

$$F_i \subset \Omega - A \subset F_1 \cup F_2, \qquad i = 1, 2,$$

and the fact that $P(\Omega - A) = 1$, we have

$$P(F_i) \le P(\Omega - A) = 1 \le P(F_1 \cup F_2) = P(F_i).$$

Hence, $P(F_1) = P(F_2) = 1$. ∎

Exercise 2.4.2 *Why can we assume, without loss of generality, $1 \in D$?*
Hint. Otherwise let $b \in D$. Choose $c = \sqrt{b/t}$ in Brownian scaling. Show that $W_t = \sqrt{t/b} X_b$.

Now we can address the differentiability issue. Using (2.19), we can conclude that the slope of $Y_t = t W_{1/t}$ is $(1/t) Y_t = W_{1/t}$, which diverges as $t \to 0$. That is to say, the Wiener process $\{Y_t : t \in I\}$ is *not* differentiable at $t = 0$ w.p.1. (The divergence can be obtained by picking a subsequence $\{t_i\}$). Similarly, for any given $s > 0$, $\{W_{t+s} : t \in I\}$ is not differentiable at s w.p.1 (by using the differential property of the Wiener process $W_{t+s} - W_t$). In other words, we have just shown that, for any $t \ge 0$, there exists a set B_t with $P(B_t) = 0$ such that for all $\omega \notin B_t$, $W_t(\omega)$ is not differentiable at t.

This is a pointwise (in time) statement. To extend it to "W_t is *nowhere differentiable* w.p.1," we need to find a set B with $P(B) = 0$ such that, for all $\omega \notin B$, W_t is not differentiable at all t.

Proposition 2.17 *The sample paths of a Wiener process are, w.p.1, everywhere continuous and nowhere differentiable.*

Proof. See Billingsley (1995, Theorem 37.3). ■

Exercise 2.4.3 *"Nowhere differentiability w.p.1 can easily be proved if we choose $B = \bigcup_t B_t$." True or false?*

2.4.3 Stopping Times

Definition 2.18 *Let $\{\mathcal{F}_t\}$ be an increasing family of σ-algebras with respect to the Wiener process $\{W_t : t \in I\}$. The stopping time τ (with respect to $\{\mathcal{F}_t\}$) is a random variable $\tau : \Omega \to I$ such that the sets $[\tau < t] \in \mathcal{F}_t$ for all t.*

For each $\omega \in \Omega$, the random variable τ effects a choice of time for the process W_t to "stop". The following quotation from Chung (1974, p. 259) should be helpful: the stopping time "is usually rather a momentary pause after which the process proceeds again: time marches on!"

Proposition 2.19 *The random time τ is a stopping time if and only if $[\tau \leq t] \in \mathcal{F}_t$ for all t.*

Proof. For necessity, we note that

$$[\tau \leq t] = \bigcap_{n=1}^{\infty} \left[\tau < t + \frac{1}{n} \right] \in \bigcap_{n=1}^{\infty} \mathcal{F}_{t+1/n} = \mathcal{F}_t.$$

Conversely, if the stopping time is defined by $[\tau \leq t] \in \mathcal{F}_t$, then

$$[\tau < t] = \bigcup_{n=1}^{\infty} \left[\tau \leq t - \frac{1}{n} \right] \in \mathcal{F}_t.$$

This proves the equivalence. ■

In the proof we assume the increasing family of σ-algebras is *right continuous* in the sense that $\mathcal{F}_t = \bigcap_{s \geq t} \mathcal{F}_s$. For related topics, the reader is referred to Karatzas and Shreve (1991).

Example 2.20 *(Constant Time) Let* $\tau \equiv t_0$ *for some* t_0. *This is a stopping time, because*

$$[\tau < t] = \begin{cases} \Omega & \textit{if } t > t_0, \\ \varnothing, & \textit{if } t \leq t_0. \end{cases}$$

A constant time is a stopping time.

Example 2.21 *(First Passage Time) Given b, let*

$$\tau_b = \min \{t \geq 0 : W_t = b\}.$$

That is, τ_b *is the first time the process* W_t *hits state b. Since* $W_0 = 0$ *w.p.1, the continuity of sample functions ensures that* W_t *is always less than b until time* τ_b. *Afterwards, it can go either way.*

To verify that the first passage time is indeed a stopping time, we need to show that $[\tau_b \leq t] \in \mathcal{F}_t$ *for all t. By definition, for any* $\omega \in [\tau_b \leq t]$, *there exists a unique s (the smallest s),* $s \leq t$, *such that* $W_s(\omega) = b$. *That is, we have*

$$[\tau_b \leq t] = \bigcup_{\substack{s \leq t \\ s:smallest}} \{\omega : W_s(\omega) = b\}.$$

Each $\{\omega : W_s(\omega) = b\}$ *is in* $\mathcal{F}_s$ *and hence is in* $\mathcal{F}_t$. *However,* $[\tau_b \leq t]$ *may not be* $\mathcal{F}_t$-measurable, because it is written as the uncountable union of measurable sets. To overcome this problem, we partition the time interval* $[0, t]$ *by points* $t_k^{(n)} = tk/2^n$, *where* $k = 0, 1, \ldots, 2^n$, *and define*

$$A = \bigcap_{m=1}^{\infty} \bigcup_{k,n} \left\{\omega : W_{k/2^n}(\omega) \geq b - \frac{1}{m}\right\}.$$

As a countable intersection–union of $\mathcal{F}_t$-measurable sets, $A \in \mathcal{F}_t$.

Our claim is $[\tau_b \leq t] = A$. *First, we show that* $A \subset [\tau_b \leq t]$. *By the definition of A,* $\omega \in A$ *means for any integer m, there exist k and n such that the state* $W_{k/2^n}(\omega)$ *is at least* $b - 1/m$. *This means that there is a point in time, denoted by* $k/2^n \leq t$, *at which the corresponding state* $W_{k/2^n}(\omega)$ *is greater than* $W_t = b - 1/m$. *With* $m \to \infty$, $W_{k/2^n}(\omega)$ *must reach b before time t.*

Next, we show that $[\tau_b \leq t] \subset A$. *Let* $\omega \in [\tau_b \leq t]$, *and let s be the first passage time associated with* ω. *Then there are k and n such that s is* *in the interval $[(k-1)/2^n, k/2^n]$. In fact, by the continuity of the sample function, we shall pick k and n to make the interval $[(k-1)/2^n, k/2^n]$ quite small in the sense that, for a given $m > 0$,*

$$|W_{k/2^n}(\omega) - W_s(\omega)| < 1/m.$$

Then

$$W_{k/2^n}(\omega) > W_s(\omega) - 1/m = b - 1/m.$$

This proves $[\tau_b \le t] = A$ and τ_b is a stopping time.

There are many economic applications of the first passage time. We shall mention two in the following examples.

Example 2.22 *(Transactions Demand for Money) The classical Baumol–Tobin model shows that the time path of money is of sawtooth type and the economic agent replenishes her money stock whenever she uses up cash. The optimal transactions demand for money minimizes the sum of the transactions costs and the cost of foregone interest earnings.*

In the stochastic case, if we assume the stock of money follows a Wiener process with a negative drift, then the time path of money is no longer of sawtooth type. The first time her real cash balance reaches $M_t = 0$ is the time for her to go back to the bank. Such a model is of great interest in studying the elasticities of money demand due to precautionary and transactions motives. See Frenkel and Jovanovic (1980), Chang (1999), and Chapter 6.

Example 2.23 *(Wicksellian Tree-Cutting Problem) The classical Wicksellian tree-cutting problem can be summarized as follows. A tree (asset value) has a given growth pattern. The question is when to cut the tree (or retire the asset) so that the net present value is maximized. Given the growth pattern, the timing is related to the size of the tree. Thus, the question is the optimal cutting size of a tree. The problem becomes a Faustmann problem when there are rotations, i.e., when there are cutting and replanting. In the stochastic case, we shall assume the growth of a tree follows a Wiener process with positive drift. The first time the tree reaches the optimal cutting size is the time to cut (and replant if it is a rotation problem). Details are in Chapter 6.*

Example 2.24 *(The Explosion Time) Let $\tau_n = \min\{t : W_t = n\}$ be an increasing sequence of stopping times. Define the explosion time as the limit of stopping times, i.e., $\tau_\infty = \lim_{n\to\infty} \tau_n$. This is a stopping time, because, if the first time the process reaching value $n + 1$ occurs before time t, then its first time reaching value n must occur before time t, i.e., $[\tau_{n+1} < t] \subset [\tau_n < t]$. Then*

$$[\tau_\infty < t] = \bigcap_{n=1}^{\infty} [\tau_n < t]$$

is clearly $\mathcal{F}_t$-measurable.

An application of the explosion time to economics is the following example.

Example 2.25 *(Steady State Distribution of Stochastic Optimal Growth) The stochastic version of the Solow growth equation, which will be studied extensively in the next few chapters, is a stochastic differential equation of the form (2.16). The solution of the equation is known to exist up to the explosion time. With uncertainty, it is possible that the growth process derived from the stochastic Solow equation may explode in finite time with a positive probability. Chang and Malliaris (1987) showed that, under certain reasonable conditions, the explosion time is ∞ w.p.1, and that the optimal growth process neither explodes nor degenerates to zero in finite time, so that a nontrivial steady state is ensured. Details are in Chapter 6.*

Exercise 2.4.4 *Is the* last leaving time *– the opposite of the first passage time,* $\max\{t : W_t = b\}$ *– a stopping time? Why? The answer should become transparent after we cover the zero set of the Wiener process. The term "last leaving time" comes from McKean (1969, p. 10).*

Let $\mathcal{F}_\tau$ (the *stopping time σ-algebra*) be the σ-algebra consists of all measurable sets A such that $A \cap [\tau \leq t] \in \mathcal{F}_t$ for all t. Roughly speaking, $\mathcal{F}_\tau$ is the σ-algebra generated by $\{W_t : t \leq \tau\}$, i.e., it is the information set of W_t up to time τ. For a formal proof of this intuition, the reader is referred to Protter (1990, p. 6, Theorem 6).

Lemma 2.26 *The stopping time σ-algebra $\mathcal{F}_\tau$ is indeed a σ-algebra.*

Proof. Suppose $A \in \mathcal{F}_\tau$, i.e., $A \cap [\tau \le t] \in \mathcal{F}_t$ for all t. We shall first show that $A^c \in \mathcal{F}_\tau$. Using the fact that $[\tau \le t]^c = [\tau > t]$, we have

$$
\begin{aligned}
A^c \cap [\tau \le t] &= \{A^c \cap [\tau \le t]\} \cup \varnothing \\
&= \{A^c \cap [\tau \le t]\} \cup \{[\tau > t] \cap [\tau \le t]\} \\
&= \{A^c \cup [\tau > t]\} \cap [\tau \le t] = \{A \cap [\tau \le t]\}^c \cap [\tau \le t].
\end{aligned}
$$

Since $A \cap [\tau \le t] \in \mathcal{F}_t$, for all t, we must have $\{A \cap [\tau \le t]\}^c \in \mathcal{F}_t$ for all t. By the definition of stopping time, $[\tau \le t] \in \mathcal{F}_t$. Hence, $A^c \cap [\tau \le t] \in \mathcal{F}_t$ for all t. Similarly, if $A, B \in \mathcal{F}_\tau$, then

$$
(A \cup B) \cap [\tau \le t] = \{A \cap [\tau \le t]\} \cup \{B \cap [\tau \le t]\} \in \mathcal{F}_t
$$

for all t. The argument extends to countable unions of sets. Finally, $\Omega \cap [\tau \le t] = [\tau \le t] \in \mathcal{F}_t$ for all t. $\blacksquare$

Example 2.27 *(The Stopping Time σ-Algebra of a Constant Time) Suppose τ is a constant time, $\tau \equiv t_0$, for some t_0. Then*

$$
[\tau \le t] = \begin{cases} \Omega & \text{if } t \ge t_0, \\ \varnothing & \text{if } t < t_0. \end{cases}
$$

Then $A \in \mathcal{F}_\tau \Leftrightarrow A \cap [\tau \le t] \in \mathcal{F}_t$ for all $t \Leftrightarrow$

$$
\begin{aligned}
A \cap \Omega &= A \in \mathcal{F}_t && \text{if } t \ge t_0, \\
A \cap \varnothing &= \varnothing \in \mathcal{F}_t && \text{if } t < t_0.
\end{aligned}
$$

In other words, we have $A \in \mathcal{F}_t$ for all $t \ge t_0$. Therefore,

$$
\mathcal{F}_\tau = \bigcap_{t \ge t_0} \mathcal{F}_t.
$$

Since $\{\mathcal{F}_t\}$ is an increasing family, $\mathcal{F}_\tau = \mathcal{F}_{t_0}$.

This example shows that $\mathcal{F}_\tau$ is a stochastic version of $\mathcal{F}_{t_0}$, which makes the intuition that $\mathcal{F}_\tau$ is the information set up to time τ plausible.

Exercise 2.4.5 *Suppose τ and τ' are stopping times. Show that, if $\tau \le \tau'$ w.p.1, then $\mathcal{F}_\tau \subset \mathcal{F}_{\tau'}$.*

Hint. First note that

$$[\tau' \leq t] \subset [\tau \leq t] \qquad if \ \tau \leq \tau' \ w.p.1.$$

Then show that, if $A \in \mathcal{F}_\tau$, then

$$A \cap [\tau' \leq t] = A \cap [\tau \leq t] \cap [\tau' \leq t] \in \mathcal{F}_t \qquad for \ all \ t.$$

The following theorem on stopping times is of fundamental importance in theory and in applications.

Theorem 2.28 *(Dynkin–Hunt) If τ is a stopping time, then conditional on $\tau < \infty$, the process defined by $\{W_t^*\} = \{W_{t+\tau} - W_\tau\}$ for $t \geq 0$ is a Wiener process independent of $\mathcal{F}_\tau$, i.e., $\sigma(\{W_t^* : t \geq 0\})$ is independent of $\mathcal{F}_\tau$.*

Proof. See McKean (1969, p. 10) or Billingsley (1995, Theorem 37.5). ∎

The Dynkin–Hunt theorem says that Wiener process begins afresh at any stopping time. It reduces to the differential property of Proposition 2.13(b) when we have a constant stopping time. This theorem is also known as the strong Markov property. We shall return to stopping times in Chapter 6.

2.4.4 The Zero Set

Now we are ready to study the Wiener process at close range through the so-called *zero set*. Let $Z(\omega) = \{t : W_t(\omega) = 0\}$ be the set of zeros for a given $\omega \in \Omega$. In words, $Z(\omega)$ is the set of times at which the sample path of the Wiener process W_t crosses the time axis. The set $Z(\omega)$ is nonempty, because, by definition, $W_0 = 0$ w.p.1, i.e., $0 \in Z(\omega)$ w.p.1. For the purpose of exposition, we shall break the argument into seven parts.

(1) There are infinitely many zeros. These zeros are unbounded.

From (2.19), there is a set B with probability zero such that, for all $\omega \notin B$, $\inf_i W_i = -\infty$ and $\sup_i W_i = +\infty$. We can find a sequence of i's such that $W_i \to +\infty$. Similarly, we can find another sequence of

j's such that $W_j \to -\infty$. In fact, the j's can be so chosen that each is nested between two i's. In particular, $W_j < 0$ and $W_i > 0$. Thus, as $i \to \infty$ and $j \to \infty$ the sample function of the Wiener process changes sign infinitely many times. By the continuity of the sample function, it must have crossed the time axis infinitely many times. Hence, there are infinitely many zeros. By construction, these zeros are unbounded.

(2) $t = 0$ is the limit point of other zeros, i.e., there are infinitely many zeros "near" $t = 0$.

To show this, we examine a sequence $Y_i = i W_{1/i}$, $i = 1, 2, \ldots$. As shown earlier, Y_i is a Wiener process and therefore satisfies (2.19). That is, there is a set B with probability zero such that, for all $\omega \notin B$, $\inf_i Y_i = -\infty$ and $\sup_i Y_i = +\infty$. Again, we can find a sequence of i's such that $Y_i \to +\infty$, and another sequence of j's, each of which is nested between two i's, such that $Y_j \to -\infty$. It follows that $W_{1/j} < 0$ and $W_{1/i} > 0$. Thus, as $i \to \infty$ and $j \to \infty$ (i.e., as $1/i \to 0$ and $1/j \to 0$), the sample function of the Wiener process changes sign infinitely many times near $t = 0$. By the continuity of the sample function, it must have crossed the time axis infinitely many times. Thus, we have infinitely many zeros near $t = 0$. In other words, $t = 0$ is a limit point of other zeros.

(3) For any $r > 0$, let $\tau = \inf\{t : t \geq r, W_t = 0\}$. Then τ is the limit point of other "larger" zeros, i.e., there are infinitely many zeros to the right of τ.

By definition, τ is the first zero following r. Using the Dynkin–Hunt theorem, the process $\{W_t^*\} = \{W_{t+\tau} - W_\tau\}$ is also a Wiener process. As discussed in connection with the differential property of the Wiener process, what we have done is to move the origin of a particular realization from $(t, W_t(\omega)) = (0, 0)$ to $(\tau, 0)$ and translate the coordinates parallelly. The point $(\tau, 0)$ becomes the new origin, and the argument that "$t = 0$ is the limit point of other positive zeros" can be extended to "τ is the limit point of other larger zeros." Such a statement is valid for all $\omega \notin B_r$ with $P(B_r) = 0$, where B_r exists for each r. Again, this is a pointwise statement on the limit point property of zeros.

(4) All zeros are limit points of other zeros.

Formally, what we would like to have is that, w.p.1, all zeros are limit points. That is, there is a set B with $P(B) = 0$ such that, for all $\omega \notin B$

and for any $t > 0$, if $t \in Z(\omega)$, then t is a limit point of other points in $Z(\omega)$. For this purpose, we simply choose $B = \bigcup_{r:\text{rational}} B_r$. For then

$$P(B) \leq \sum_{r:\text{rational}} P(B_r) \leq 0.$$

The proof goes as follows. If t is the limit of smaller points of $Z(\omega)$, i.e., the points are coming from the left, then we are done. If not, we should be able to find some rational number r with $r < t$ such that t is the first zero following r. Since $\omega \notin B$ implies that $\omega \notin B_r$, this t is the limit point of larger points in $Z(\omega)$, as we have shown earlier.

(5) The zero set is nowhere dense, i.e., there is enough space to separate any two zeros.

Let a and b be any two zeros. Since the sample function of a Wiener process is nowhere differentiable, it is impossible that $W_t(\omega) = 0$ on $[a, b]$. (Otherwise, the sample function would be differentiable with derivative zero.) We may assume without loss of generality that there is some $t \in (a, b)$ with $W_t(\omega) > 0$. Then, by continuity, there is a subinterval $[c, d] \subset (a, b)$ such that $W_t(\omega) > 0$ on $[c, d]$. That is, we have found an interval $[c, d]$ with $Z(\omega) \cap [c, d] = \emptyset$. This shows that $Z(\omega)$ is nowhere dense in $[0, \infty]$.

(6) The cardinality of the zero set is that of the continuum.

The mathematical definition of a perfect set is most appropriate in describing the zero set. A set S is perfect if all points in S are limit points of S. Formally, S is perfect if (i) $S \neq \emptyset$, (ii) S is closed (so that the limit point stays in S), and (iii) if $x \in S$, then for any $\varepsilon > 0$, there exists some $y \in S$ such that $0 <| x - y |< \varepsilon$. Statement (4) says that $Z(\omega)$ is a perfect set. It is well known that a perfect set has the cardinality of the continuum. See Hausdorff (1962, p. 156).

(7) The zero set is of Lebesgue measure zero.

A nowhere dense set is *thin*. The following proof should be instructive. Let λ be the Lebesgue measure on I. To prove step (7), we first treat the Wiener process $W_t(\omega)$ as a mapping from the product space $I \times \Omega$ to $\mathbb{R}$, i.e., $W(t, \omega): I \times \Omega \to \mathbb{R}$. We also invoke a fact that this mapping is measurable with respect to the product measure $\lambda \times P$. Let

$$A = \{(t, \omega) : W(t, \omega) = 0\} .$$

Next we show that set A is very thin in the product space. By the Fubini theorem, we have

$$\iint_{I \times \Omega} I_A d(\lambda \times P) = \int_0^\infty P(\{\omega : W_t(\omega) = 0\}) dt = 0,$$

where the last equality is obtained because $W_t(\omega)$ has a normal distribution at any given t and therefore, $P(\{\omega : W_t(\omega) = 0\}) = 0$. In other words, we have $(\lambda \times P)(A) = 0$. But then the thinness of set A in the product space implies the thinness of the zero set. More precisely, the Fubini theorem implies that

$$\int_\Omega \lambda(Z(\omega)) P(d\omega) = \iint_{I \times \Omega} I_A d(\lambda \times P) = 0.$$

Hence, $\lambda(Z(\omega)) = 0$, w.p.1.

To summarize, we have

Theorem 2.29 *The set of zeros, $Z(\omega)$, is, w.p.1, perfect, unbounded, nowhere dense, and of Lebesgue measure zero.*

The above theorem says it all about the special characteristics of the Wiener process as seen from the zero set. We have already learned that the sample function has infinitely many spikes in any time interval, however small. Look at the points of time at which the sample function crosses the line $W_t(\omega) = 0$ (or any other horizontal line) in the $(t, W_t(\omega))$-plane. If we see one, we shall see a cluster of them (perfect set property). On the other hand, when they take off, we shall not see them for a while (nowhere dense property). Furthermore, there are lots of them, in fact, there is a continuum of them (perfect set property). Yet, the set is so thin that it contains no intervals (Lebesgue measure zero property). With all these properties put together, we have a Cantor set in action.

2.4.5 Bounded Variations and the Irregularity of the Wiener Process

In this subsection we shall revisit the irregularity (the sample function is everywhere continuous and nowhere differentiable) of the Wiener process through the concept of bounded variations. Recall that the variation with respect to a given partition $\{t_i\}$ of time interval $[s, t]$, where $s = t_0 < t_1 < t_2 < \cdots < t_{m-1} < t_m = t$, is

$$\sum_{i=1}^{m} \left| W_{t_i} - W_{t_{i-1}} \right|.$$

W_t is of bounded variations if all variations (with changing partitions) are bounded. A function of bounded variations is necessarily differentiable almost everywhere, i.e., at all points except a set of measure zero. Since W_t is nowhere differentiable, W_t cannot be of bounded variations. Then, there exists a sequence of partitions $\{t_k^{(n)}\}$ of the time interval $[s, t]$ in the form $t_k^{(n)} = s + (t - s) k / 2^n$, $k = 0, 1, \ldots, 2^n$, such that

$$\sum_{i=1}^{2^n} \left| W_{t_i} - W_{t_{i-1}} \right| \to \infty \quad \text{as } n \to \infty, \qquad \text{w.p.1.}$$

That is, a finer partition of the time interval will increase the values of variations without bounds.

This irregularity of the sample function could raise objections to a common practice in economics: we often derive the sample path by connecting the two adjacent observed points with a line segment. Such a practice is questionable if the underlying stochastic process is a diffusion process, because it would turn a nowhere differentiable sample function into a piecewise infinitely differentiable function.

2.5 Notes and Further Readings

Section 2.2 is largely taken from Cox and Miller (1965). Section 2.3 basically follows Arnold (1974). Section 2.4 is a mixture of McKean (1969) and Billingsley (1995). The terms "Brownian scaling" and "differential property of the Brownian motion," among others, are borrowed from McKean (1969). These books treat both one-dimensional and higher-dimensional Wiener process. However, we focus only on one-dimensional Wiener processes.

The definition of stopping time follows McKean (1969). A stopping time is also known as a Markov time or an optional time. See, for example, Billingsley (1995), Bhattacharya and Waymire (1990), and Chung (1982). Karatzas and Shreve (1991), however, make a distinction: the condition $[\tau \leq t] \in \mathcal{F}_t$ is associated with a stopping time, while the strict inequality $[\tau < t] \in \mathcal{F}_t$ is associated with an optional time. The two concepts coincide if the filtration is right-continuous. The interested reader should consult that book for details. On the implementation of Wiener processes and the econometric methods using discrete-time data, the reader is referred to Hansen and Scheinkman (1995) and Duffie and Glynn (1996).

Besides the aforementioned (Arnold (1974), Billingsley (1995), Cox and Miller (1965), and McKean (1969)), there are many good texts on Wiener processes. For example, any of the following books gives a comprehensive treatment on the subject: Bhattacharya and Waymire (1990), Chung (1982), Friedman (1975), Karatzas and Shreve (1991), and Knight (1981). For a good summary of the basic properties of Wiener processes, the reader is referred to Fleming and Rishel (1975) and Malliaris and Brock (1982).

3

Stochastic Calculus

3.1 Introduction

In many economic models, the dynamics of a given variable are typically characterized by a differential equation

$$\dot{x} = \mu(t, x). \tag{3.1}$$

This equation can also be expressed in differential form,

$$dx = \mu(t, x) dt.$$

It seems natural that we can extend this differential equation to a stochastic differential equation

$$dX_t = \mu(t, X_t) dt + \sigma(t, X_t) dW_t, \tag{3.2}$$

where W_t is a Wiener process. However, it should be noted that this stochastic differential equation is not the same as the result of adding a random shock to (3.1), because, if we divide (3.2) by dt on both sides, the right-hand side contains an expression, dW_t/dt, which is undefined. Thus, the stochastic differential equation does not represent the derivative of the state variable X_t with respect to time. What then is the meaning of (3.2)?

A differential equation can be interpreted as an integral equation. For example, equation (3.1) is equivalent to

$$x_t - x_0 = \int_0^t \mu(s, x) ds.$$

In the same vein, the stochastic differential equation (3.2) is associated with a stochastic integral equation

$$X_t - X_{t_0} = \int_{t_0}^{t} \mu(s, X_s) \, ds + \int_{t_0}^{t} \sigma(s, X_s) \, dW_s \qquad (3.3)$$

in the sense that a solution to (3.3) is taken as a solution to (3.2) and vice versa, provided that the second integral of (3.3) is defined.

In the next section, we shall provide a heuristic approach to the stochastic integral. We begin the study of stochastic integration with two examples that highlight the difference between the classic integral and the stochastic integral. Then we make an educated guess as to what mathematical conditions are important in stochastic integration. In section 3.3, we formally define an Ito integral and the class of functions on which the Ito integral is defined.

The celebrated Ito lemma is presented in two steps, with economic applications that follow directly from our formulation. First, we present the Ito lemma when the transformation is a time-independent (autonomous) function of an autonomous stochastic differential equation. The presentation begins with the one-dimensional Ito lemma, in which we emphasize the dos and the don'ts of stochastic calculus. It is followed by the two-dimensional Ito lemma when the two random shocks may be correlated. Then we present a multivariate Ito lemma with multiple sources of uncertainty for a time-dependent function, which has applications to Black–Scholes option pricing theory and to irreversible investment. The chapter concludes with a presentation of a vector-valued multivariate Ito lemma.

3.2 A Heuristic Approach

3.2.1 Is $\int_{t_0}^{t} \sigma(s, X_s) \, dW_s$ Riemann Integrable?

For the moment, let us assume that the second integral of (3.3) is defined as a Riemann integral. That is, the integral is the limit of Riemann sums. Recall that, for a given partition $t_0 < t_1 < \cdots < t_{n-1} < t_n = T$ of the time interval $[t_0, T]$ with $\delta_n = \max_i \{t_i - t_{i-1}\}$, the Riemann sum S_n with intermediate points τ_i $(t_{i-1} \leq \tau_i \leq t_i)$ is

$$S_n = \sum_{i=1}^{n} \sigma(\tau_i, X_{\tau_i}) (W_{t_i} - W_{t_{i-1}}).$$

Then $\sigma(s, X_s)$ is Riemann integrable if, as $n \to \infty$ and $\delta_n \to 0$, S_n converges w.p.1.

Example 3.1 *Let $\sigma(t, W_t) = 1$ w.p.1. Then $S_n = W_T - W_{t_0}$ for any partition. Clearly, S_n converges to $W_T - W_{t_0}$ as $n \to \infty$, and the integral becomes*

$$\int_{t_0}^{T} dW_t = W_T - W_{t_0}.$$

It behaves just like what elementary calculus would have suggested.

Before we present the next example, we need the following

Definition 3.2 *A sequence $\{C_n\}$ converges to C in mean square if*

$$E\left[|C_n - C|^2\right] \to 0 \qquad as\ n \to \infty.$$

Lemma 3.3 *Let $\{t_i\}$ be a partition of $[t_0, T]$, and let $\delta_n = \max_i \{t_i - t_{i-1}\}$. Then we have*

$$C_n = \sum_{i=1}^{n} \left(W_{t_i} - W_{t_{i-1}}\right)^2 \to T - t_0 \qquad in\ mean\ square \qquad (3.4)$$

as $n \to \infty$ and $\delta_n \to 0$.

Proof. By definition, (3.4) means that, as $n \to \infty$ and $\delta_n \to 0$,

$$E\left\{[C_n - (T - t_0)]^2\right\} \to 0.$$

Since

$$E[C_n] = \sum_{i=1}^{n} E\left[\left(W_{t_i} - W_{t_{i-1}}\right)^2\right] = \sum_{i=1}^{n} (t_i - t_{i-1}) = T - t_0,$$

equation (3.4) is equivalent to having the variance of C_n convergent to 0. It suffices to show that

$$E\left[C_n^2\right] = E\left\{\left[\sum_{i=1}^{n} \left(W_{t_i} - W_{t_{i-1}}\right)^2\right]^2\right\} \to (T - t_0)^2.$$

To this end, we expand C_n^2 as follows:

$$C_n^2 = \sum_{i=1}^{n} \left(W_{t_i} - W_{t_{i-1}} \right)^4 + \sum_{i \neq j}^{n} \left(W_{t_i} - W_{t_{i-1}} \right)^2 \left(W_{t_j} - W_{t_{j-1}} \right)^2.$$

As shown in Chapter 2, the fourth moment of the Wiener process is

$$E\left\{ \left(W_{t_i} - W_{t_{i-1}} \right)^4 \right\} = 3 \left(t_i - t_{i-1} \right)^2.$$

Since $\left(W_{t_i} - W_{t_{i-1}} \right)^2$ and $\left(W_{t_j} - W_{t_{j-1}} \right)^2$ are independent if $i \neq j$,

$$E\left[C_n^2 \right] = 3 \sum_{i=1}^{n} \left(t_i - t_{i-1} \right)^2 + \sum_{i \neq j}^{n} \left(t_i - t_{i-1} \right) \left(t_j - t_{j-1} \right)$$

$$= 2 \sum_{i=1}^{n} \left(t_i - t_{i-1} \right)^2 + \sum_{i=1}^{n} \sum_{j=1}^{n} \left(t_i - t_{i-1} \right) \left(t_j - t_{j-1} \right)$$

$$\leq 2\delta_n \sum_{i=1}^{n} \left(t_i - t_{i-1} \right) + \sum_{i=1}^{n} \left(t_i - t_{i-1} \right) \sum_{j=1}^{n} \left(t_j - t_{j-1} \right)$$

$$= 2\delta_n \left(T - t_0 \right) + \left(T - t_0 \right)^2 \rightarrow \left(T - t_0 \right)^2$$

as $\delta_n \rightarrow 0$. Notice that the inequality in the derivation follows from the fact that $\left(t_i - t_{i-1} \right)^2 \leq \delta_n \left(t_i - t_{i-1} \right)$. ∎

Example 3.4 *Let $\sigma \left(t, W_t \right) = W_t$. According to elementary calculus,*

$$\int_{t_0}^{T} x \, dx = \frac{1}{2} \left(x_T^2 - x_{t_0}^2 \right).$$

Is it true that

$$\int_{t_0}^{T} W_t \, dW_t = \frac{1}{2} \left(W_T^2 - W_{t_0}^2 \right)?$$

Notice that the Riemann sum with intermediate points τ_i is

$$S_n = \sum_{i=1}^{n} W_{\tau_i} \left(W_{t_i} - W_{t_{i-1}} \right).$$

If the Riemann integral exists, then S_n converges w.p.1. Since the integral is independent of the choice of τ_i, the difference between the Riemann sum evaluated at the right endpoint t_i of each interval $[t_{i-1}, t_i]$,

$$A_n = \sum_{i=1}^{n} W_{t_i} \left(W_{t_i} - W_{t_{i-1}} \right),$$

and the Riemann sum evaluated at the left endpoint t_{i-1} of each interval $[t_{i-1}, t_i]$,

$$B_n = \sum_{i=1}^{n} W_{t_{i-1}} \left(W_{t_i} - W_{t_{i-1}} \right),$$

should converge to the same limit w.p.1. In other words,

$$C_n = A_n - B_n = \sum_{i=1}^{n} \left(W_{t_i} - W_{t_{i-1}} \right)^2 \to 0 \qquad w.p.1.$$

But is it true? From (3.4), we know that $C_n \to T - t_0$ in mean square. By the Riesz–Fisher theorem, if a sequence $\{C_n\}$ converges to $T - t_0$ in mean square, then there is a subsequence of $\{C_n\}$ that converges to $T - t_0$ w.p.1. Therefore, $C_n \to 0$ w.p.1 is false.

This example clearly demonstrates that the integral $\int_{t_0}^{T} \sigma(t, X_t) dW_t$ cannot be a Riemann integral, because it is *not* independent of the choice of the intermediate points of a partition of $[t_0, T]$.

3.2.2 The Choice of τ_i Matters

Having shown that $\int_{t_0}^{T} W_t dW_t$ is not Riemann integrable, we shall demonstrate that the choice of τ_i dictates the value of S_n. To see this, we rewrite S_n as

$$S_n = \sum_{i=1}^{n} \left(W_{\tau_i} - W_{t_{i-1}} \right) \left(W_{t_i} - W_{t_{i-1}} \right) + \sum_{i=1}^{n} W_{t_{i-1}} \left(W_{t_i} - W_{t_{i-1}} \right),$$

$$(3.5)$$

using $W_{\tau_i} = \left(W_{\tau_i} - W_{t_{i-1}} \right) + W_{t_{i-1}}$. Using (3.4) and the fact that

$$W_{t_{i-1}} = \frac{1}{2} \left[\left(W_{t_i} + W_{t_{i-1}} \right) - \left(W_{t_i} - W_{t_{i-1}} \right) \right],$$

the second term of (3.5) becomes

$$\frac{1}{2} \sum_{i=1}^{n} \left(W_{t_i}^2 - W_{t_{i-1}}^2 \right) - \frac{1}{2} \sum_{i=1}^{n} \left(W_{t_i} - W_{t_{i-1}} \right)^2$$

$$\rightarrow \frac{1}{2} \left(W_T^2 - W_{t_0}^2 \right) - \frac{1}{2} \left(T - t_0 \right) \text{ in mean square,}$$

as $n \to \infty$ and $\delta_n \to 0$. It should be obvious to the reader that, unless the first term of (3.5) converges to $(T - t_0)/2$, this Riemann sum will have a result very different from the one implied by classical integration.

The first term of (3.5) involves τ_i, t_{i-1}, and t_i, which suggests that we should use a finer partition $\{\ldots, t_{i-1}, \tau_i, t_i, \tau_{i+1}, t_{i+1}, \ldots\}$, instead of the original partition $\{\ldots, t_{i-1}, t_i, t_{i+1}, \ldots\}$. That is, the term $W_{t_i} - W_{t_{i-1}}$ will be broken into $(W_{t_i} - W_{\tau_i}) + (W_{\tau_i} - W_{t_{i-1}})$. Define

$$D_n = \sum_{i=1}^{n} \left(W_{\tau_i} - W_{t_{i-1}} \right) \left(W_{t_i} - W_{\tau_i} \right)$$

Then

$$\sum_{i=1}^{n} \left(W_{\tau_i} - W_{t_{i-1}} \right) \left(W_{t_i} - W_{t_{i-1}} \right) = D_n + \sum_{i=1}^{n} \left(W_{\tau_i} - W_{t_{i-1}} \right)^2.$$

Repeating the proof of (3.4), *mutatis mutandis*, we have

$$\sum_{i=1}^{n} \left(W_{\tau_i} - W_{t_{i-1}} \right)^2 \rightarrow \sum_{i=1}^{n} \left(\tau_i - t_{i-1} \right) \qquad \text{in mean square.}$$

Similarly, by the independent increments property, we have $E(D_n) = 0$ and

$$E\left[D_n^2 \right] = \sum_{i=1}^{n} \left(\tau_i - t_{i-1} \right) \left(t_i - \tau_i \right) \leq \delta_n \sum_{i=1}^{n} \left(t_i - \tau_i \right) \leq \delta_n \left(T - t_0 \right),$$

which converges to 0 as $\delta_n \to 0$. In short, $D_n \to 0$ in mean square.

To summarize, we have, in mean square,

$$S_n \to \frac{1}{2} \left(W_T^2 - W_{t_0}^2 \right) - \frac{1}{2} (T - t_0) + \sum_{i=1}^{n} (\tau_i - t_{i-1}).$$

The value to which S_n converges is dictated by the choice of τ_i. Different choices of τ_i define different stochastic integrals. More precisely, since $t_{i-1} \leq \tau_i \leq t_i$, we can set $\tau_i = \lambda t_i + (1 - \lambda) t_{i-1}$, where $0 \leq \lambda \leq 1$. Then, in mean square,

$$S_n \to \frac{1}{2} \left(W_T^2 - W_{t_0}^2 \right) + \left(\lambda - \frac{1}{2} \right) (T - t_0).$$

The choice of the parameter λ clearly determines the limit of S_n.

Example 3.5 *(Ito Integral) Let $\lambda = 0$, i.e., we choose the left endpoint of the interval $[t_{i-1}, t_i]$. Then, in mean square,*

$$S_n \to \frac{1}{2} \left(W_T^2 - W_{t_0}^2 \right) - \frac{1}{2} (T - t_0).$$

In symbols,

$$\text{(Ito)} \int_{t_0}^{T} W_t \, dW_t = \frac{1}{2} \left(W_T^2 - W_{t_0}^2 \right) - \frac{1}{2} (T - t_0). \qquad (3.6)$$

Example 3.6 *(Stratonovich Integral) Let $\lambda = 1/2$, i.e., we choose the midpoint of the interval $[t_{i-1}, t_i]$. Then, in mean square,*

$$S_n \to \frac{1}{2} \left(W_T^2 - W_{t_0}^2 \right).$$

In symbols,

$$\text{(Strat)} \int_{t_0}^{T} W_t \, dW_t = \frac{1}{2} \left(W_T^2 - W_{t_0}^2 \right).$$

Notice that Stratonovich integral preserves the classical integration rule

$$\int_{a}^{b} x \, dx = \frac{1}{2} \left(b^2 - a^2 \right).$$

Example 3.7 *(Backward Integral) Let $\lambda = 1$, i.e., we choose the right endpoint of the interval $[t_{i-1}, t_i]$. Then, in mean square,*

$$S_n \to \frac{1}{2} \left(W_T^2 - W_{t_0}^2 \right) + \frac{1}{2} (T - t_0).$$

In symbols,

$$\int_{t_0}^{T} W_t \, dW_t = \frac{1}{2} \left(W_T^2 - W_{t_0}^2 \right) + \frac{1}{2} (T - t_0).$$

Notice the upper and lower limits of integration are written on the left. This notation follows McKean (1969).

Henceforth, we shall concentrate only on Ito integrals, unless otherwise specified.

3.2.3 In Search of the Class of Functions for $\sigma(s, \omega)$

The above examples illustrate some of the difficulties in the development of stochastic integrals. Having decided on the left endpoints of subintervals is only the first step. The next step is to decide the class of functions that can be used as integrands in $\int \sigma(t, X_t) dW_t$. Since $\sigma(t, X_t(\omega))$ is a function of (t, ω), we shall continue to denote it by $\sigma(t, \omega)$. In what follows we shall present a bird's-eye view of the theory of stochastic integration. The argument is heuristic.

We begin with a deterministic $\sigma(t, \omega)$, i.e., $\sigma : [t_0, T] \times \Omega \to \mathbb{R}$ is independent of ω. McKean (1969) calls it a *sure* function. Let $\sum_i \sigma(t_i, \omega) dW_{t_i}$ be the Riemann sum of $\int_{t_0}^{T} \sigma \, dW$ associated with a given partition. Then

$$E \left(\sum_i \sigma(t_i, \omega) dW_{t_i} \right)^2 = E \left[\sum_i (\sigma(t_i, \omega))^2 \left(dW_{t_i} \right)^2 \right]$$

$$+ E \left[\sum_{i \neq j} \sigma(t_i, \omega) \sigma(t_j, \omega) \left(dW_{t_i} \right) \left(dW_{t_j} \right) \right].$$

The assumption of a sure function enables us to pull $\sigma(t_i, \omega)$ and $\sigma(t_j, \omega)$ outside the expectation operator, i.e.,

$$E\left[\sum_i (\sigma(t_i, \omega))^2 \left(dW_{t_i}\right)^2\right] = \sum_i (\sigma(t_i, \omega))^2 E\left[\left(dW_{t_i}\right)^2\right]$$

$$= \sum_i (\sigma(t_i, \omega))^2 \, dt_i,$$

and

$$E\left[\sum_{i \neq j} \sigma(t_i, \omega) \sigma(t_j, \omega) \left(dW_{t_i}\right) \left(dW_{t_j}\right)\right]$$

$$= \sum_{i \neq j} \sigma(t_i, \omega) \sigma(t_j, \omega) E\left[\left(dW_{t_i}\right) \left(dW_{t_j}\right)\right] = 0,$$

using the independent increments property of $\{W_{t_i}\}$. Taking the limit, we arrive at the following isometry

$$E\left[\left(\int_{t_0}^T \sigma \, dW\right)^2\right] = E\left[\int_{t_0}^T \sigma^2(t, \omega) \, dt\right], \qquad (3.7)$$

if $\sigma(t, \omega)$ is deterministic and square integrable on $[t_0, T]$.

However, sure functions are not the only class of functions that enables us to pull $\sigma(t_i, \omega)$ and $\sigma(t_j, \omega)$ outside the expectation operator. All we need is that (1) $\{\mathcal{F}_t\}$ is an increasing family of σ-algebras, i.e., $\mathcal{F}_{t_i} \subset \mathcal{F}_{t_j}$ if $t_i < t_j$, and (2) the integrand $\sigma(t, \omega)$ is $\mathcal{F}_t$-measurable. Given these two conditions, we can conclude that both $\sigma(t_i, \omega)$ and $\sigma(t_j, \omega)$ are $\mathcal{F}_{t_j}$-measurable, since $t_i < t_j$. Then

$$E\left[\sum_i (\sigma(t_i, \omega))^2 \left(dW_{t_i}\right)^2\right] = E\left\{E\left[\sum_i (\sigma(t_i, \omega))^2 \left(dW_{t_i}\right)^2 \middle| \mathcal{F}_{t_i}\right]\right\}$$

$$= E\left\{\sum_i (\sigma(t_i, \omega))^2 E\left[\left(dW_{t_i}\right)^2 \middle| \mathcal{F}_{t_i}\right]\right\}$$

$$= \sum_i (\sigma(t_i, \omega))^2 \, dt_i$$

and

$$
E\left[\sum_{i\neq j}\sigma\left(t_i,\omega\right)\sigma\left(t_j,\omega\right)\left(dW_{t_i}\right)\left(dW_{t_j}\right)\right]
$$

$$
= 2E\left\{E\left[\sum_{i<j}\sigma\left(t_i,\omega\right)\sigma\left(t_j,\omega\right)\left(dW_{t_i}\right)\left(dW_{t_j}\right)\Big|\mathcal{F}_{t_j}\right]\right\}
$$

$$
= 2E\left\{\sum_{i<j}\sigma\left(t_i,\omega\right)\sigma\left(t_j,\omega\right)E\left[\left(dW_{t_i}\right)\left(dW_{t_j}\right)\Big|\mathcal{F}_{t_j}\right]\right\} = 0.
$$

Then (3.7) is reestablished.

Let us summarize what we have found. First, the underlying information structure $\{\mathcal{F}_t\}$ is an increasing family of σ-algebras. Second, the integrand $\sigma(t,\cdot)$ is $\mathcal{F}_t$-measurable, for all t. Third, the norm of the class of functions is the L^2 norm. In this way, we have established isometry (3.7) for $\sigma(t,\omega)\in\mathcal{M}^2([t_0,T]\times\Omega)$, a set to be defined below. These three conditions are the basic building blocks for stochastic integrals.

3.3 The Ito Integral

The probability space $(\Omega,\mathcal{F},P)$ is given.

Definition 3.8 *A family of σ-algebras $\{\mathcal{F}_t : t \in I\}$ is called a filtration, i.e., an increasing family, if $\mathcal{F}_s \subset \mathcal{F}_t \subset \mathcal{F}$ whenever $s \leq t$.*

Example 3.9 *(Standard Filtration) Let $\{W_t\}$ be the Wiener process. Then the σ-algebras generated by $\{W_t\}$ for all t,*

$$
\mathcal{F}_t = \sigma\left(W_s : s \leq t\right),
$$

form a filtration.

Usually, we take $\{\mathcal{F}_t : t \in I\}$ to be something "larger" than the standard filtration $\{\sigma(W_s : s \leq t\}$. Let $\mathcal{F}_\infty$ be the smallest σ-algebra on Ω containing all events in $\mathcal{F}_t$, i.e., if $A \in \mathcal{F}_t$ for some t, then $A \in \mathcal{F}_\infty$. Clearly, $\mathcal{F}_\infty \subset \mathcal{F}$.

Definition 3.10 *A filtered probability space is a probability space* $(\Omega, \mathcal{F}, P)$ *together with a filtration* $\{\mathcal{F}_t : t \in I\}$ *such that* $\mathcal{F}_\infty = \mathcal{F}$.

From now on, we assume that the probability space is a filtered probability space.

Definition 3.11 *A stochastic process* $\{X_t : t \in I\}$ *is nonanticipating with respect to a given filtration* $\{\mathcal{F}_t : t \in I\}$ *if* X_t *is* $\mathcal{F}_t$*-measurable.*

The term nonanticipating is self-explanatory in characterizing the relationship between the stochastic process $\{X_t : t \in I\}$ and the filtration $\{\mathcal{F}_t : t \in I\}$. A nonanticipating process is also known as an adapted process. Formally,

Definition 3.12 *A stochastic process* $\{X_t : t \in I\}$ *is adapted to the filtration* $\{\mathcal{F}_t : t \in I\}$ *if, for all* t, X_t *is* $\mathcal{F}_t$*-measurable.*

Definition 3.13 *A function* $\sigma(t, \omega) : I \times \Omega \to \mathbb{R}$ *is nonanticipating (or nonanticipative, according to Fleming and Rishel (1975)) if* $\sigma(t, \omega)$ *is* $\mathcal{F}_t$*-measurable for all* t.

We can view $\{\sigma(t, \cdot) : t \in I\}$ as a stochastic process. As a stochastic process, $\{\sigma(t, \cdot) : t \in I\}$ is adapted to $\{\mathcal{F}_t\}$. A sure function $\sigma(t)$ is always nonanticipating, because it is a constant function with respect to ω and constant functions are always measurable.

3.3.1 Definition

Now we shall formally define the class of functions on which the Ito integral is defined. Let $\mathcal{M}_0([t_0, T] \times \Omega)$ be the set of nonanticipating functions such that

$$\int_{t_0}^{T} |\sigma(t, \omega)|^2 \, dt < \infty \qquad \text{w.p.1.}$$

That is, $\sigma(t, \omega) \in \mathcal{M}_0([t_0, T] \times \Omega)$ means that (i) for a given t, $\sigma(t, \omega)$ is $\mathcal{F}_t$-measurable (nonanticipating) and (ii) for a given ω, the sample function $\sigma(t, \omega)$ is square integrable. Let $\mathcal{M}^2([t_0, T] \times \Omega)$ be the subset of $\mathcal{M}_0 ([t_0, T] \times \Omega)$ satisfying

$$E \left[\int_{t_0}^{T} |\sigma (t, \omega)|^2 \, dt \right] < \infty.$$

The extension from $\mathcal{M}^2 ([t_0, T] \times \Omega)$ to $\mathcal{M}^2 ([0, \infty) \times \Omega)$ is straight-forward. Notice that if $[a, b] \subset [c, d]$ then $\mathcal{M}^2 ([c, d] \times \Omega) \subset \mathcal{M}^2 ([a, b] \times \Omega)$. Therefore, we define

$$\mathcal{M}^2 ([0, \infty) \times \Omega) = \bigcap_{[a,b] \subset [0,\infty)} \mathcal{M}^2 ([a, b] \times \Omega),$$

i.e., $\mathcal{M}^2 ([0, \infty) \times \Omega)$ is the smallest set contained in all $\mathcal{M}^2 ([a, b] \times \Omega)$. In what follows we stay with $\mathcal{M}^2 ([t_0, T] \times \Omega)$ for our definition of an Ito integral.

Exercise 3.3.1 *Show that* $\mathcal{M}^2 ([t_0, T] \times \Omega) \subset \mathcal{M}_0 ([t_0, T] \times \Omega)$.
  Hint. Show that

$$E \left[\int_{t_0}^{T} |\sigma (t, \omega)|^2 \, dt \right] < \infty \quad \Rightarrow \quad \int_{t_0}^{T} |\sigma (t, \omega)|^2 \, dt < \infty \quad w.p.1.$$

Definition 3.14 *A function* $\sigma (t, \omega)$ *is called a step function (or a simple function, or a simple process) if there exists a partition of* $[t_0, T]$, $t_0 < t_1 < \cdots < t_n = T$, *such that* $\sigma (t, \omega) = \sigma (t_i, \omega)$ *for all* $t \in [t_i, t_{i+1})$, *where* $i = 0, 1, 2, \ldots, n - 1$.

It is important to recognize that, for each $\omega \in \Omega$, the sample function of a step function (as a function of t) behaves just like a step function in elementary calculus. Moreover, the sample function is right-continuous, possibly with jumps. It is also important to recognize that the partition $\{t_i\}$ is independent of ω. In fact, the step function can be written as $\sum_i \sigma (t_i, \omega) I_{[t_i, t_{i+1})}$. We may think of this step function as follows. We partition $I \times \Omega$ into many strips $\{[t_i, t_{i+1}) \times \Omega\}$. Inside each strip, the whole line segment (of fixed ω and varying t), $\{(t, \omega) : t \in [t_i, t_{i+1})\}$, is assigned the functional value $\sigma (t_i, \omega)$, the functional value of the left endpoint of the line segment. For different line segments (i.e., for different ω), the assigned functional values are generally different. That is, if $\omega \neq \omega'$, then $\sigma (t_i, \omega) \neq \sigma (t_i, \omega')$ in general.

Denote by

$$S^2 = \{\sigma \in \mathcal{M}^2 ([t_0, T] \times \Omega) : \sigma \text{ is a step function}\}$$

the set of step functions.

Definition 3.15 *The Ito integral of a nonanticipating step function $\sigma(t, \omega)$ is defined as the Riemann sum evaluated at the left end-points,*

$$I(\sigma)(\omega) = \int_{t_0}^{T} \sigma(t, \omega) \, dW(t) = \sum_{i=0}^{n-1} \sigma(t_i, \omega) [W(t_{i+1}) - W(t_i)].$$

Notice that the Ito integral thus defined is itself a random variable, i.e., $I(\sigma) : \Omega \to \mathbb{R}$.

Proposition 3.16 *Major properties of Ito integrals are:*

(1) If $\sigma(t, \omega) \in S^2$, $g(t, \omega) \in S^2$, and a and b are constants, then

$$\int_{t_0}^{T} [a\sigma(t, \omega) + bg(t, \omega)] \, dW(t)$$

$$= a \int_{t_0}^{T} \sigma(t, \omega) \, dW(t) + b \int_{t_0}^{T} g(t, \omega) \, dW(t).$$

(2) For $a < b < c$, and $\sigma(t, \omega) \in S^2$,

$$\int_{a}^{c} \sigma(t, \omega) \, dW(t) = \int_{a}^{b} \sigma(t, \omega) \, dW(t) + \int_{b}^{c} \sigma(t, \omega) \, dW(t).$$

(3) If $\sigma(t, \omega) \in S^2$, then

$$E\left[I(\sigma) \mid \mathcal{F}_{t_0}\right] = E\left[\int_{t_0}^{T} \sigma(t, \omega) \, dW(t) \,\middle|\, \mathcal{F}_{t_0}\right] = 0 \qquad w.p.1. \quad (3.8)$$

(4) If $\sigma(t, \omega) \in S^2$, $g(t, \omega) \in S^2$, then

$$E\left[\left(\int_{t_0}^{T} \sigma(t, \omega)\, dW(t)\right)\left(\int_{t_0}^{T} g(t, \omega)\, dW(t)\right)\Big|\, \mathcal{F}_{t_0}\right]$$

$$= \int_{t_0}^{T} E\left[\sigma(t, \omega)\, g(t, \omega)\,|\, \mathcal{F}_{t_0}\right] dt. \tag{3.9}$$

In particular, when $\sigma = g$,

$$E\left[\left(\int_{t_0}^{T} \sigma(t, \omega)\, dW(t)\right)^2\Big|\, \mathcal{F}_{t_0}\right] = \int_{t_0}^{T} E\left[\sigma(t, \omega)^2\,|\, \mathcal{F}_{t_0}\right] dt. \tag{3.10}$$

Proof. Properties (1) and (2) are trivial. To prove (3), we note that if $\triangle W_{t_i} = W(t_{i+1}) - W(t_i)$, then

$$E\left[I(\sigma)\,|\, \mathcal{F}_{t_0}\right] = E\left[\sum_{i=0}^{n-1} \sigma(t_i, \omega)\, \triangle W_{t_i}\,\Big|\, \mathcal{F}_{t_0}\right]$$

$$= \sum_{i=0}^{n-1} E\left[\sigma(t_i, \omega)\, \triangle W_{t_i}\,|\, \mathcal{F}_{t_0}\right]$$

$$= \sum_{i=0}^{n-1} E\left\{E\left[\sigma(t_i, \omega)\, \triangle W_{t_i}\,|\, \mathcal{F}_{t_i}\right]\,|\, \mathcal{F}_{t_0}\right\}.$$

Since $\sigma(t_i, \omega)$ is $\mathcal{F}_{t_i}$-measurable,

$$E\left\{E\left[\sigma(t_i, \omega)\, \triangle W_{t_i}\,|\, \mathcal{F}_{t_i}\right]\,|\, \mathcal{F}_{t_0}\right\}$$
$$= E\left\{\sigma(t_i, \omega)\, E\left[\triangle W_{t_i}\,|\, \mathcal{F}_{t_i}\right]\,|\, \mathcal{F}_{t_0}\right\} = 0,$$

using the fact that $E\left[\triangle W_{t_i}\,|\, \mathcal{F}_{t_i}\right] = 0$ w.p.1. Thus,

$$E\left[I(\sigma)\,|\, \mathcal{F}_{t_0}\right] = 0.$$

To prove (4), we note that

$$\left(\sum_{i=0}^{n-1} \sigma\left(t_i, \omega\right) \triangle W_{t_i}\right)\left(\sum_{i=0}^{n-1} g\left(t_i, \omega\right) \triangle W_{t_i}\right)$$

$$= \sum_{i=0}^{n-1} \sigma\left(t_i, \omega\right) g\left(t_i, \omega\right)\left(\triangle W_{t_i}\right)^2 + \sum_{i<j} \sigma\left(t_i, \omega\right) g\left(t_j, \omega\right) \triangle W_{t_i} \triangle W_{t_j}$$

$$+ \sum_{i<j} \sigma\left(t_j, \omega\right) g\left(t_i, \omega\right) \triangle W_{t_i} \triangle W_{t_j}.$$

Then the left-hand side of (3.9) is

$$E\left[\left(\sum_{i=0}^{n-1} \sigma\left(t_i, \omega\right) \triangle W_{t_i}\right)\left(\sum_{i=0}^{n-1} g\left(t_i, \omega\right) \triangle W_{t_i}\right) \middle| \mathcal{F}_{t_0}\right]$$

$$= \sum_{i=0}^{n-1} E\left\{E\left[\sigma\left(t_i, \omega\right) g\left(t_i, \omega\right)\left(\triangle W_{t_i}\right)^2 \middle| \mathcal{F}_{t_i}\right] \middle| \mathcal{F}_{t_0}\right\}$$

$$+ \sum_{i<j} E\left\{E\left[\sigma\left(t_i, \omega\right) g\left(t_j, \omega\right) \triangle W_{t_i} \triangle W_{t_j} \middle| \mathcal{F}_{t_j}\right] \middle| \mathcal{F}_{t_0}\right\}$$

$$+ \sum_{i<j} E\left\{E\left[\sigma\left(t_j, \omega\right) g\left(t_i, \omega\right) \triangle W_{t_i} \triangle W_{t_j} \middle| \mathcal{F}_{t_j}\right] \middle| \mathcal{F}_{t_0}\right\}$$

Since $\sigma\left(t_i, \omega\right) g\left(t_j, \omega\right) \triangle W_{t_i}$ is $\mathcal{F}_{t_j}$-measurable, we have

$$\sum_{i<j} E\left\{E\left[\sigma\left(t_i, \omega\right) g\left(t_j, \omega\right) \triangle W_{t_i} \triangle W_{t_j} \middle| \mathcal{F}_{t_j}\right] \middle| \mathcal{F}_{t_0}\right\}$$

$$= \sum_{i<j} E\left\{\sigma\left(t_i, \omega\right) g\left(t_j, \omega\right) \triangle W_{t_i} E\left[\triangle W_{t_j} \middle| \mathcal{F}_{t_j}\right] \middle| \mathcal{F}_{t_0}\right\} = 0.$$

Similarly,

$$\sum_{i<j} E\left\{\sigma\left(t_j, \omega\right) g\left(t_i, \omega\right) \triangle W_{t_i} E\left[\triangle W_{t_j} \middle| \mathcal{F}_{t_j}\right] \middle| \mathcal{F}_{t_0}\right\} = 0.$$

Thus,

$$E\left[\left(\int_{t_0}^{T} \sigma(t,\omega)\,dW(t)\right)\left(\int_{t_0}^{T} g(t,\omega)\,dW(t)\right)\Big|\,\mathcal{F}_{t_0}\right]$$

$$= \sum_{i=0}^{n-1} E\left\{\sigma(t_i,\omega)\,g(t_i,\omega)\,E\left[\left(\Delta W_{t_i}\right)^2\Big|\,\mathcal{F}_{t_i}\right]\Big|\,\mathcal{F}_{t_0}\right\}$$

$$= \sum_{i=0}^{n-1} E\left\{\sigma(t_i,\omega)\,g(t_i,\omega)\,\Delta t_i\,\big|\,\mathcal{F}_{t_0}\right\}$$

$$= \int_{t_0}^{T} E\left[\sigma(t,\omega)\,g(t,\omega)\,|\,\mathcal{F}_{t_0}\right]dt.$$

When $\sigma = g$, (3.9) becomes (3.10). ∎

Property (3) is the so-called *martingale property* or *zero-expectation property*. The term martingale will be defined later. The special case of (4) given by equation (3.10) is the isometry mentioned earlier.

Next, we extend the definition of Ito integrals from S^2 to all $\sigma(t,\omega) \in \mathcal{M}^2([t_0, T] \times \Omega)$. Recall from elementary calculus that the integral of a function f is defined as the limit of integrals of the step functions that approximate f. In the same vein, if we know that S^2 is dense in $\mathcal{M}^2([t_0, T] \times \Omega)$, then the Ito integral of $\sigma(t,\omega)$ can be defined as the limit of integrals of step functions that approximate $\sigma(t,\omega)$. To this end, we need the following lemma.

Lemma 3.17 *For any $\sigma(t,\omega) \in \mathcal{M}^2([t_0, T] \times \Omega)$, there exists a sequence of step functions $\{\sigma_n(t,\omega)\}$ in S^2 such that*

$$\lim_{n \to \infty} E\left[\int_{t_0}^{T} |\sigma_n(t,\omega) - \sigma(t,\omega)|^2\,dt\right] = 0$$

and as $n \to \infty$

$$\int_{t_0}^{T} \sigma_n(t,\omega)\,dW_t \to \int_{t_0}^{T} \sigma(t,\omega)\,dW_t \qquad \text{in mean square.}$$

Proof. See Arnold (1974, Lemma 4.4.12). ∎

Definition 3.18 *Assume a family of step functions $\{\sigma_n(t, \omega)\}$ converge in mean square to $\sigma(t, \omega) \in \mathcal{M}^2([t_0, T] \times \Omega)$. Then there exists a random variable, the Ito integral, denoted by $I(\sigma) = \int_0^T \sigma(t, \omega) dW(t)$, such that, as $n \to \infty$,*

$$E\left[\left|\int_{t_0}^T \sigma_n(t, \omega) dt - \int_{t_0}^T \sigma(t, \omega) dt\right|^2\right] \to 0.$$

Remark 3.1

(1) It goes without saying that the Ito integral thus defined satisfies the properties listed in Proposition 3.16 with S^2 replaced by $\mathcal{M}^2([t_0, T] \times \Omega)$. For a formal proof, the reader is referred to Friedman (1975, Theorem 2.8).

(2) The stochastic integral can also be defined on $\mathcal{M}_0([t_0, T] \times \Omega)$, a larger class of functions. Assume a family of step functions $\{\sigma_n(t, \omega)\}$ satisfies

$$\int_{t_0}^T |\sigma_n(t, \omega) - \sigma(t, \omega)|^2 dt \to 0 \qquad \text{in probability}$$

and $\text{plim}_{n \to \infty} \int_{t_0}^T \sigma_n(t, \omega) dW(t)$ *exists and is unique; then we define*

$$I(\sigma) = \underset{n \to \infty}{\text{plim}} \int_{t_0}^T \sigma_n(t, \omega) dW(t).$$

In this case, however, the statement for isometry requires an additional condition:

$$E\left[\int_{t_0}^T |\sigma(t, \omega)|^2 dt\right] < \infty.$$

As mentioned earlier, a stochastic differential equation such as (3.2) is defined in terms of a stochastic integral equation (3.3). Now we can provide a formal definition.

Definition 3.19 *Let $\{X_t : t \in I\}$ be adapted to $\{\mathcal{F}_t : t \in I\}$. Suppose there exist $\sigma(t, \omega)$ and $\mu(t, \omega)$, where $\sigma(t, \omega) \in \mathcal{M}^2([t_0, T] \times \Omega)$,*

$\{\mu(t, \omega) : t \in I\}$ *is adapted to* $\{\mathcal{F}_t : t \in I\}$, *and* $\mu(t, \omega)$ *is integrable w.p.1, i.e.,*

$$\int_{t_0}^{T} |\mu(t, \omega)| \, ds < \infty \qquad \text{w.p.1,}$$

so that

$$X_t = X_{t_0} + \int_{t_0}^{t} \mu(s, \omega) \, ds + \int_{t_0}^{t} \sigma(s, \omega) \, dW_s.$$

Then we say that

$$\mu(t, \omega) \, dt + \sigma(t, \omega) \, dW$$

is the stochastic differential of the process $\{X_t : t \in I\}$, *and we denote it by* dX_t. *Such a process is also called an Ito process.*

3.3.2 Martingales

Given an Ito integral $\int_{t_0}^{T} \sigma(u, \omega) \, dW(u)$, where $\sigma(u, \omega) \in \mathcal{M}^2([t_0, T] \times \Omega)$, define a new stochastic process

$$X_t = \int_{t_0}^{t} \sigma(u, \omega) \, dW(u) = \int_{t_0}^{T} I_{[t_0, t]} \sigma(u, \omega) \, dW(u). \qquad (3.11)$$

Notice that $I_{[t_0, t]} \sigma(u, \omega) \in \mathcal{M}^2([t_0, T] \times \Omega)$. Similar to (3.8), we have

$$E\left[X_t \mid \mathcal{F}_{t_0}\right] = E\left[\int_{t_0}^{T} I_{[t_0, t]} \sigma(u, \omega) \, dW(u) \,\middle|\, \mathcal{F}_{t_0}\right] = 0 \qquad \text{w.p.1.}$$

Furthermore, for $t_0 \le s \le t \le T$,

$$X_t - X_s = \int_{s}^{t} \sigma(u, \omega) \, dW(u) = \int_{t_0}^{T} I_{[s, t]} \sigma(u, \omega) \, dW(u).$$

Then, the zero-expectation property

$$E[X_t - X_s \mid \mathcal{F}_s] = 0 \qquad \text{w.p.1}$$

implies that

$$E[X_t \mid \mathcal{F}_s] = E[X_s \mid \mathcal{F}_s] = X_s \qquad \text{w.p.1.} \qquad (3.12)$$

A stochastic process satisfies (3.12) is known as a martingale. The whole derivation tells us that the stochastic process $\{X_t\}$ generated by the Ito integral is a martingale. Notice that if $\sigma(u, \omega) \equiv 1$, then $X_t = W_t$. This shows that the Wiener process is a martingale.

Martingales play an important role in the theory of stochastic processes and in economics. A formal discussion will be useful.

Definition 3.20 *Given a filtration* $\{\mathcal{F}_t : t \in I\}$, *a stochastic process* $\{X_t\}$ *is a martingale if* $\{X_t\}$ *is adapted to* $\{\mathcal{F}_t\}$, *is integrable (i.e.,* $E(|X_t|) < \infty$), *and is such that*

$$X_s = E[X_t \mid F_s] \qquad \text{for } t_0 \leq s \leq t \leq T.$$

It is a submartingale if the equality is replaced by

$$X_s \leq E[X_t \mid F_s] \qquad \text{for } t_0 \leq s \leq t \leq T;$$

it is a supermartingale if the equality is replaced by

$$X_s \geq E[X_t \mid F_s] \qquad \text{for } t_0 \leq s \leq t \leq T.$$

The notion of a martingale is closely related to gambles. According to Elliot (1982, p. 16), a martingale is a part of a horse's harness which prevents the horse from raising its head too high. Through horse racing the word became a gambling term. A martingale means a fair game in the sense that the expected return from gambling, $E[X_t \mid F_s]$, will be the same as keeping what you currently have, X_s. In submartingale, the expected return is greater than what you have now. A supermartingale is the opposite of a submartingale: the expected return is lower than what you have now. If you are risk-neutral, you should continue to bet if the game is a submartingale; if it is a supermartingale, however, you should quit while you can. This intuitive explanation makes it easier to memorize the direction of the inequality – it is "super" to quit gambling.

Proposition 3.21 *(Major Properties of Martingales)*

(1) Let $\{X_t\}$ and $\{Y_t\}$ be two martingales. Then so is $\{aX_t + bY_t\}$, where a and b are constants. In particular, $\{X_t - Y_t\}$ and $\{-X_t\}$ are martingales too.

(2) $\{X_t\}$ is a submartingale if and only if $\{-X_t\}$ is a supermartingale.

(3) If $\{X_t\}$ is a martingale and $X_t \in L^p$, $p \geq 1$, then $\{|X_t|^p\}$ is a submartingale, while $\{-|X_t|^p\}$ is a supermartingale.

(4) If $\{X_t\}$ is a martingale, then $\{X_t^+\}$ and $\{X_t^-\}$ are submartingales, where

$$X_t^+ = \max(X_t, 0), \qquad X_t^- = -\min(X_t, 0) = \max(-X_t, 0).$$

Proof. Properties (1) and (2) are evident. To prove (3), we first note that $\phi(x) = |x|^p$, $p \geq 1$, is a convex function. Then by (the conditional) Jensen's inequality for convex functions,

$$E[\phi(X) \mid \mathcal{E}] \geq \phi(E[X \mid \mathcal{E}]),$$

we have

$$E\left[|X_t|^p \mid F_s\right] \geq |E[X_t \mid F_s]|^p = |X_s|^p.$$

Thus, $\{|X_t|^p\}$ is a submartingale. Using (2), $\{-|X_t|^p\}$ is a supermartingale. To prove $\{X_t^+\}$ is a submartingale, we note that the function $\phi(x) = \max(x, 0)$ is a convex function because, for $0 \leq \lambda \leq 1$,

$$\max\{\lambda x + (1 - \lambda)y, 0\} \leq \lambda \max\{x, 0\} + (1 - \lambda)\max\{y, 0\}.$$

Then apply Jensen's inequality as before. To show $\{X_t^-\}$ is a submartingale we simply notice that $\{-X_t\}$ is also a martingale. ∎

Exercise 3.3.2 *Suppose X_t is defined by (3.11). Show that:*

(1) One has

$$E\left[X_s X_t \mid \mathcal{F}_{t_0}\right] = \int_{t_0}^{\min(s,t)} E\left[\sigma(u)^2 \mid \mathcal{F}_{t_0}\right] du;$$

in particular,

$$E\left[|X_t|^2 \mid \mathcal{F}_{t_0}\right] = \int_{t_0}^{t} E\left[\sigma(u)^2 \mid \mathcal{F}_{t_0}\right] du.$$

(2) If $t_0 \leq s \leq t \leq v \leq u \leq T$, then

$$E\left[(X_t - X_s)(X_u - X_v) \mid \mathcal{F}_{t_0}\right] = 0.$$

Hint. For (1), let $s \leq t$. Then $X_s X_t = X_s(X_t - X_s) + X_s^2$. For (2), show that $I_{[s,t]} \cdot I_{[v,u]} = 0$ w.p.1.

Example 3.22 *(Consumption Is a Submartingale) In his celebrated paper, Hall (1978) argued that the time path of consumption is a random walk. The result is attractive because current consumption helps predict future consumption. His reasoning can be summarized as follows. Let ρ, r, and c_t be, respectively, the subjective discount rate, the market interest rate, and consumption at time t. The standard discrete-time utility maximization condition is the Euler equation:*

$$E_t[u'(c_{t+1})] = \left(\frac{1+\rho}{1+r}\right) u'(c_t).$$

Under certain conditions, the Euler equation can be transformed into

$$E[c_{t+1}] = \lambda c_t,$$

where λ is determined by taste parameters and the market interest rate.

We shall show that consumption is a submartingale ($\lambda \geq 1$) if $\rho = r$. In this case the Euler equation implies that $E_t[u'(c_{t+1})] = u'(c_t)$, i.e., the time path of marginal utility of consumption is a martingale. Now assume $u''' > 0$, so that u' is convex. As we shall see in Chapter 5, $u''' > 0$ is a necessary condition for a utility function to exhibit decreasing absolute risk aversion. In the $(c, u'(c))$ plane, the graph of $u'(c)$ is downward sloping and convex to the origin. Since the inverse function is the mirror image of the original function with the $45°$ line as the mirror, the graph of $(u')^{-1}$ is also strictly decreasing and convex to the origin. Thus, $(u')^{-1}$ is a convex function. By Jensen's inequality, we obtain

$$c_t = (u')^{-1}[u'(c_t)] = (u')^{-1}\{E_t[u'(c_{t+1})]\}$$
$$\leq E_t\{(u')^{-1}[u'(c_{t+1})]\} = E_t c_{t+1}.$$

Notice that the equality holds (i.e., consumption is a martingale) if u' is linear, or if u is quadratic.

3.4 Ito's Lemma: Autonomous Case

When the drift and the instantaneous variance of (3.2) are independent of time t, the corresponding stochastic differential equation is called autonomous and is written as

$$dX_t = \mu(X_t)dt + \sigma(X_t)dW_t. \tag{3.13}$$

To understand the rules of stochastic differentiation, we begin with autonomous case.

3.4.1 Ito's Lemma

The easiest way to remember Ito's lemma is as the stochastic version of the *chain rule* for differentiation. Recall that in the deterministic case, if x satisfies a differential equation $\dot{x} = f(x)$, then any transformation of x, say $y = h(x)$, where h is a differentiable function, satisfies another differential equation,

$$\frac{dy}{dt} = \frac{d}{dt}[h(x)] = h'(x)\dot{x} = h'(x)f(x).$$

The key to this result is that the first-order approximation applies, i.e., $dx = f'(x)dt$, and hence $d[h(x)] = h'(x)f(x)dt$. In terms of "little o" we have

$$\Delta[h(x)] = h'(x)f(x)\Delta t + o(\Delta t).$$

The question which Ito's lemma addresses is this: If X_t satisfies (3.13), what is dY_t, where $Y_t = h(X_t)$?

Since dX_t/dt does not exist in the stochastic case, the first-order approximation of ΔY_t is certainly inappropriate. The question is to how high an order of the Taylor series expansion we should go. To investigate, we expand ΔY_t to get

$$\Delta Y_t = h'(X_t)\Delta X_t + \frac{1}{2}h''(X_t)(\Delta X_t)^2 + \frac{1}{6}h'''(X_t)(\Delta X_t)^3 + \cdots.$$

Then

$$E\left[\Delta Y_t\right] = h'\left(X_t\right) E\left[\Delta X_t\right] + \frac{1}{2} h''\left(X_t\right) E\left[\left(\Delta X_t\right)^2\right]$$

$$+ \frac{1}{6} h'''\left(X_t\right) E\left[\left(\Delta X_t\right)^3\right] + \cdots .$$

Since

$$\left(\Delta X_t\right)^2 = \left(\mu \Delta t + \sigma \Delta W_t\right)^2 = \mu^2 \left(\Delta t\right)^2 + 2\mu\sigma \Delta t \Delta W_t + \sigma^2 \left(\Delta W_t\right)^2 ,$$

$$\left(\Delta X_t\right)^3 = \mu^3 \left(\Delta t\right)^3 + 3\mu^2\sigma \left(\Delta t\right)^2 \Delta W_t + 3\mu\sigma^2 \left(\Delta t\right)\left(\Delta W_t\right)^2$$

$$+ \sigma^3 \left(\Delta W_t\right)^3 ,$$

and recalling that Wiener process W_t satisfies $E\left[\Delta W_t\right] = 0$, $E\left[\left(\Delta W_t\right)^2\right] = \Delta t$, and $E\left[\left(\Delta W_t\right)^k\right] = o\left(\Delta t\right)$ for $k \geq 3$, we have

$$E\left[\Delta Y_t\right] = h'\left(X_t\right) \mu\left(X_t\right) \Delta t + \frac{1}{2} h''\left(X_t\right) \sigma^2 \left(X_t\right) \Delta t + o\left(\Delta t\right).$$

In the limit, all higher-order terms of Δt vanish, i.e., $o\left(\Delta t\right) \to 0$ as $\Delta t \to 0$. Thus,

$$E\left[dY_t\right] = h'\left(X_t\right) \mu\left(X_t\right) dt + \frac{1}{2} h''\left(X_t\right) \sigma^2 \left(X_t\right) dt$$

$$= \left[h'\left(X_t\right) \mu\left(X_t\right) + \frac{1}{2} h''\left(X_t\right) \sigma^2 \left(X_t\right)\right] dt.$$

The second term on the right-hand side of the above equation, $\frac{1}{2} h''\left(X_t\right) \sigma^2 dt$, highlights the difference between the deterministic differentiation rule and the stochastic differentiation rule. The drift of dY_t is not $h'\left(X_t\right) \mu\left(X_t\right)$, but $h'\left(X_t\right) \mu\left(X_t\right) + \frac{1}{2} h''\left(X_t\right) \sigma^2 \left(X_t\right)$. This leads us to the following

Theorem 3.23 *(Ito's Lemma) If $h\left(\cdot\right)$ is twice continuously differentiable, then $Y_t = h\left(X_t\right)$ satisfies the following stochastic differential equation:*

$$dY_t = \left[h'\left(X_t\right) \mu\left(X_t\right) + \frac{1}{2} h''\left(X_t\right) \sigma^2 \left(X_t\right)\right] dt + h'\left(X_t\right) \sigma\left(X_t\right) dW_t.$$

$$(3.14)$$

Proof. See, for example, McKean (1969, pp. 32–35), Gikman and Sko-rohod (1969, pp. 387–389), Arnold (1974, pp. 96–99), and Friedman (1975, pp. 81–84). ∎

It is easier to remember Ito's lemma through a direct computation up to the second order,

$$
\begin{aligned}
dY_t &= h'(X_t)\, dX_t + \tfrac{1}{2} h''(X_t)(dX_t)^2 \\
&= h'(X_t)[\mu(X_t)\, dt + \sigma(X_t)\, dW_t] \\
&\quad + \tfrac{1}{2} h''(X_t)[\mu(X_t)\, dt + \sigma(X_t)\, dW_t]^2,
\end{aligned}
$$

and then using the following "multiplication table":

$$
\begin{array}{c|cc}
\times & dW & dt \\
\hline
dW & dt & 0 \\
dt & 0 & 0
\end{array}
\tag{3.15}
$$

Example 3.24 *(Polynomials) In elementary calculus,* $d(x^n) = nx^{n-1}dx$, $n \geq 2$. *In stochastic calculus, if* X_t *satisfies (3.13), then*

$$
\begin{aligned}
d\left(X_t^n\right) &= nX_t^{n-1}dX_t + \tfrac{1}{2} n(n-1) X_t^{n-2}(dX_t)^2 \\
&= \left[n\mu X_t^{n-1} + \frac{\sigma^2}{2} n(n-1) X_t^{n-2} \right] dt + nX_t^{n-1}dW_t.
\end{aligned}
$$

It is different from the elementary calculus unless, of course, $\sigma = 0$.

Example 3.25 *(Fundamental Theorem of Calculus) In elementary calculus, the fundamental theorem of calculus is*

$$
h(b) - h(a) = \int_a^b h'(x)\, dx.
$$

In stochastic calculus, it becomes

$$
h(W_t) - h\left(W_{t_0}\right) = \int_{t_0}^t h'(W_s)\, dW_s + \frac{1}{2} \int_{t_0}^t h''(W_s)\, ds.
$$

When $h(x) = x^2/2$, we have

$$\frac{1}{2}\left(W_t^2 - W_{t_0}^2\right) = \int_{t_0}^{t} W_s \, dW_s + \frac{1}{2}\int_{t_0}^{t} ds,$$

which is (3.6).

Example 3.26 *(Rate of Change) Traditionally, we use $d\log x$ to represent the rate of change in x, because*

$$d\log x = \frac{dx}{x},$$

by using elementary calculus. This is no longer valid in the stochastic case. Indeed,

$$d\log x = \frac{dx}{x} - \frac{1}{2}\left(\frac{dx}{x}\right)^2.$$

Certainly, we should not use $d\log y / d\log x$ to represent an elasticity in the stochastic case.

Example 3.27 *(Exponential Function) It is straightforward to verify that, if X_t satisfies (3.13), then*

$$de^{X_t} = e^{X_t}dX_t + \frac{1}{2}e^{X_t}(dX_t)^2 = e^{X_t}\left[dX_t + \frac{1}{2}(dX_t)^2\right]$$
$$= e^{X_t}\left[(\mu + \sigma^2/2)\,dt + \sigma\,dW\right] \neq e^{X_t}dX_t.$$

Again, $de^{X_t} = e^{X_t}dX_t$ if $\sigma = 0$.

3.4.2 Geometric Brownian Motion

Definition 3.28 *An autonomous stochastic differential equation with $\mu(X_t) = aX_t$ and $\sigma(X_t) = bX_t$, where a and b are constants, i.e., an equation of the form*

$$dX_t = aX_t \, dt + bX_t \, dW_t, \tag{3.16}$$

is called a geometric Brownian motion.

Proposition 3.29 *There is a closed-form solution to (3.16), which is of the form*

$$X(t) = X(0)\exp\left\{(a - b^2/2)t + bW(t)\right\}$$
$$= X(0)\exp\left\{(a - b^2/2)t\right\}\exp\left\{bW(t)\right\}, \qquad (3.17)$$

and the sign of the solution X (t) is, w.p.1, dictated by the initial condition X (0).

Proof. Let $y(t) = \log X(t)$. By Ito's lemma,

$$d\left[\log X(t)\right] = \frac{dX(t)}{X(t)} - \frac{1}{2}\frac{[dX(t)]^2}{X(t)^2} = (a\,dt + b\,dW) - \frac{1}{2}b^2\,dt$$
$$= (a - b^2/2)\,dt + b\,dW.$$

Integrating both sides, we have

$$\log X(t) - \log X(0) = \int_0^t (a - b^2/2)\,ds + \int_0^t b\,dW$$
$$= (a - b^2/2)t + bW(t).$$

Taking exponential on both sides and using the fact that $\log [X(t)/X(0)] = \log X(t) - \log X(0)$, we arrive at (3.17). Since exponential functions are always positive, $X(t)$ has the same sign as $X(0)$. ∎

Remark 3.2

(1) Notice that the initial condition X (0) is in general a random variable, although in most economic problems it is treated as a constant.

(2) Even though the diffusion process W (t) is unbounded, X (t) can become bounded on one side. For example, if X (0) > 0 w.p.1, then X (t) > 0 w.p.1. In this case, the process is bounded from below. This will be useful when a nonnegativity constraint on the variable is required. It should be noted that X (t) > 0 even if a and b are negative. A similar argument applies if X (0) < 0 w.p.1.

(3) It is instructive to compare (3.16) with the discrete-time counterpart

$$X_{t+1} = (1 + a)X_t + bX_t\varepsilon_{t+1}.$$

If ε_{t+1} is normally distributed, there is no way we can prove $X_t > 0$ w.p.1. Even if X_0 is large, there is still a positive probability, albeit very small, that $X_1 < 0$, because ε_1 is not bounded from below. If the nonnegativity constraint of the variable becomes an issue, then the normal distribution may not be an appropriate assumption to make.

Proposition 3.30 *If $X(t)$ is a geometric Brownian motion, then so is $X^i(t)$ for $i \geq 2$.*

Proof. If $X(t)$ is a geometric Brownian motion satisfying (3.16), then, by Ito's lemma,

$$d\left(X^i\right) = iX^{i-1}dX + \frac{1}{2}i\,(i-1)\,X^{i-2}\,(dX)^2$$

$$= \left[ia + \frac{1}{2}i\,(i-1)\,b^2\right]X^i\,dt + ibX^i\,dW$$

for all $i \geq 2$. This shows that $X^i(t)$ is also a geometric Brownian motion. ∎

Proposition 3.31 *The mean and variance of a geometric Brownian motion are, respectively,*

$$E[X(t)] = X(0)\,e^{at}$$

and

$$V[X(t)] = X^2(0)\,e^{2at}\left(e^{b^2 t} - 1\right).$$

Proof. From (3.17),

$$E[X(t)] = X(0)\exp\left\{(a - b^2/2)\,t\right\}E\left[\exp\left\{bW(t)\right\}\right],$$

since $\exp\left\{(a - b^2/2)\,t\right\}$ is a real number independent of ω. Next, we recognize that $\exp\{bW(t)\}$ has a lognormal distribution, whose moments are well known. In particular, if X is a normal distribution, then

$$E[e^X] = \exp\left\{E[X] + V[X]/2\right\}. \tag{3.18}$$

It follows that

$$E[X(t)] = X(0) \exp\{(a - b^2/2)t\} \exp\{(b^2/2)t\} = X(0) e^{at}.$$

To find the variance, let $Y(t) = X^2(t)$. As shown before, $Y(t) = X^2(t)$ is another geometric Brownian motion satisfying

$$dY(t) = (2a + b^2)Y(t) dt + 2bY(t) dW(t).$$

Therefore,

$$V[X(t)] = E[X^2(t)] - \{E[X(t)]\}^2 = X^2(0) e^{(2a+b^2)t} - [X(0) e^{at}]^2$$
$$= X^2(0) e^{2at} (e^{b^2 t} - 1). \qquad \blacksquare$$

Example 3.32 *(Higher Moments of a Geometric Brownian Motion)
Given a geometric Brownian motion* (3.16), *we can compute all moments of $X(t)$ as follows. Since $X^i(t)$ is also a geometric Brownian motion, we have, for $i \geq 2$,*

$$d\left(X^i\right) = \left[ia + \frac{1}{2}i(i-1)b^2\right] X^i dt + ibX^i dW.$$

Integrating both sides,

$$X^i(t) - X^i(0)$$
$$= \left[ia + \frac{1}{2}i(i-1)b^2\right] \int_0^t X^i(s) ds + ib \int_0^t X^i(s) dW(s).$$

If we assume $X^i(s) \in \mathcal{M}^2(I \times \Omega)$ for all s, i.e., if $\int_0^t E[X^{2i}(s)] ds < \infty$, so that $E\left[\int_0^t X^i(s) dW(s)\right] = 0$, then

$$E[X^i(t)] = E[X^i(0)] + \left[ia + \frac{1}{2}i(i-1)b^2\right] \int_0^t E[X^i(s)] ds.$$

Let $y(s) = E[X^i(s)]$. Then the above equation reduces to

$$y(t) = y(0) + \left[ia + \frac{1}{2}i(i-1)b^2\right] \int_0^t y(s) ds,$$

or the first-order differential equation

$$dy = \left[ia + \frac{1}{2}i\,(i-1)\,b^2 \right] y\,dt.$$

The solution is well known (by separation of variables):

$$E\left[X^i\,(t)\right] = y\,(t) = y\,(0) \exp\left\{ \left[ia + \frac{1}{2}i\,(i-1)\,b^2 \right] t \right\}$$

$$= E\left[X^i\,(0)\right] \exp\left\{ \left[ia + \frac{1}{2}i\,(i-1)\,b^2 \right] t \right\}.$$

Notice that all moments ($i \geq 2$) shown above approach ∞ as $t \to \infty$ as long as the expected growth rate a is nonnegative. On the other hand, if $ia + \frac{1}{2}i\,(i-1)\,b^2 < 0$, then $E\left[X^i\,(t)\right] \to 0$ as $t \to \infty$. For example, when $i = 2$, the condition for stochastic stability is $a + \frac{1}{2}b^2 < 0$.

Example 3.33 *(Forward-looking vs. Backward-looking) We know that the Ito integral is different from other stochastic integrals because it is forward-looking (right-continuous). In the deterministic case, the rate of change of $X(t)$ can be computed as $[X(t + \Delta t) - X(t)]\,/\,X(t)$ or as $[X(t) - X(t - \Delta t)]\,/\,X(t)$ with $\Delta t > 0$. That is not so in the stochastic case. We shall use geometric Brownian motion to make the point. From (3.17), the forward-looking rate of change of process X is*

$$\frac{X(t+\Delta t) - X(t)}{X(t)} = \frac{X(t+\Delta t)}{X(t)} - 1$$

$$= \exp\left\{ (a - b^2/2)\,\Delta t + b\,\Delta W_t \right\} - 1$$

Then, by (3.18),

$$E\left[\left| \frac{X(t+\Delta t) - X(t)}{X(t)} \right| \mathcal{F}_t \right]$$

$$= \exp\left\{ (a - b^2/2)\,\Delta t \right\} \exp\left\{ (b^2/2)\,\Delta t \right\} - 1$$

$$= \exp\left\{ a\,\Delta t \right\} - 1.$$

Hence,

$$\lim_{\Delta t \to 0} \frac{1}{\Delta t} E\left[\frac{X(t + \Delta t) - X(t)}{X(t)} \middle| \mathcal{F}_t\right] = a,$$

as expected. In contrast, the backward-looking rate of change is

$$\frac{X(t + \Delta t) - X(t)}{X(t + \Delta t)}$$

$$= 1 - \frac{X(t)}{X(t + \Delta t)} = 1 - \exp\left\{-(a - b^2/2)\Delta t - b\Delta W_t\right\}.$$

Then,

$$E\left[\left|\frac{X(t + \Delta t) - X(t)}{X(t + \Delta t)}\right| \mathcal{F}_t\right]$$

$$= 1 - \exp\left\{-(a - b^2/2)\Delta t\right\} \exp\left\{(b^2/2)\Delta t\right\}$$

$$= 1 - \exp\left\{-(a - b^2)\Delta t\right\}.$$

Hence,

$$\lim_{\Delta t \to 0} \frac{1}{\Delta t} E_t\left\{\frac{X(t + \Delta t) - X(t)}{X(t + \Delta t)} \middle| \mathcal{F}_t\right\} = a - b^2.$$

3.4.3 Population Dynamics

Let $X_i(t)$ be the number of offspring, net of deaths, from person i at time t. Let h be the length of time elapsed, and n be the expected growth rate of the population, the same for all i. At time $t + h$, person i will be subject to two types of shocks: system-wide shocks and idiosyncratic shocks, both of which have zero mean and satisfy the independent increment property. Moreover, system-wide shocks and idiosyncratic shocks are independent. Formally,

$$X_i(t + h) = nh + \sigma\eta(t, h) + v_i\varepsilon_i(t, h)$$

satisfying

$$E_t(\eta) = E_t(\varepsilon_i) = 0, \qquad E_t(\eta^2) = E_t(\varepsilon_i^2) = h,$$

$$E_t(\eta \varepsilon_i) = E_t(\varepsilon_i \varepsilon_j) = 0, \qquad E_t(\eta(t,h)\eta(t+kh,h)) = 0,$$

$$k = \pm 1, \pm 2, \ldots$$

where n, σ and v_i are constants. Denote the total population at time t by $L(t)$. Given $L(t) = L$, the change in population is

$$L(t+h) - L(t) = \sum_{i=0}^{L} X_i(t+h)$$

$$= nhL + \sigma \eta(t,h)L + \sum_{i=0}^{L} v_i \varepsilon_i(t,h).$$

It is easy to show that

$$\frac{1}{h} E[L(t+h) - L(t) \mid L(t) = L] = nL,$$

and that

$$\frac{1}{h} V[L(t+h) - L(t) \mid L(t) = L]$$

$$= \frac{1}{h} E\left[\left(\sigma \eta(t,h)L + \sum_{i=0}^{L} v_i(t,h)\varepsilon_i\right)^2 \bigg| L(t) = L\right]$$

$$= \sigma^2 L^2 + \sum_{i=0}^{L} v_i^2.$$

Under the assumption that all v_i's are bounded and approximately the same size,

$$\sum_{i=0}^{L} v_i^2 = \left(\frac{1}{L} \sum_{i=0}^{L} v_i^2\right) L \leq \left(\max_i \{v_i^2\}\right) L = O(L),$$

which is dominated by $\sigma^2 L^2$ for large L. Thus,

$$\frac{1}{h} V[L(t+h) - L(t) \mid L(t) = L] \to \sigma^2 L^2 \qquad \text{as } h \to 0.$$

This is the second moment of a diffusion process. The independent increment conditions

$$E_t \left(\eta \left(t, h \right) \eta \left(t + kh, h \right) \right) = 0, \qquad k = \pm 1, \pm 2, \ldots,$$

enable us to approximate the discrete-time dynamics as a diffusion process. In summary, we have

$$dL = nL \, dt + \sigma L \, dW. \tag{3.19}$$

Equation (3.19) shows that population growth follows a geometric Brownian motion whose population growth has expected rate n and instantaneous variance σ. If the initial condition $L(0) > 0$ is given, then

$$L(t) = L(0) \exp \left\{ \left(n - \sigma^2/2 \right) t \right\} \exp \left\{ \sigma W(t) \right\} > 0.$$

Notice that, even though the Wiener process $W(t)$ assumes unbounded negative values with positive probability, the size of the population is positive w.p.1 at all times, as it should be.

3.4.4 Additive Shocks or Multiplicative Shocks

Equation (3.19) shows that the *rate of growth* of population is a diffusion process with constant drift and variance:

$$\frac{dL}{L} = n \, dt + \sigma \, dW.$$

This is, the shock to population is a multiplicative shock. If, on the other hand, we assume the shocks are on the absolute magnitude of population, not the rate of growth, i.e., if we assume shocks are additive,

$$dL = nL \, dt + \sigma \, dW,$$

then

$$L(t) = L(0) + n \int_0^t L(s) \, ds + \sigma W(t).$$

Given the normality of a Wiener process, viz., $W(t) \sim N(0, t)$, population could become negative with positive probability, however small. The choice of additive or multiplicative shocks in economic modeling is crucial.

Example 3.34 *(Windfalls) In the deterministic case, the wealth dynamics of a consumer is*

$$\dot{A} = rA - c,$$

or

$$dA = (rA - c)\,dt,$$

where A, r, and c are, respectively, the wealth, the interest rate, and consumption. If the source of shocks is windfalls as Friedman (1963) defined them (i.e., unexpected gains or losses that have nothing to do with your wealth level), then it seems reasonable to set

$$dA = (rA - c)\,dt + \sigma\,dW.$$

But then the problem of negative wealth with positive probability arises.

On the other hand, if we model wealth uncertainty as a multiplicative shock, i.e., shocks are proportional to wealth,

$$dA = (rA - c)\,dt + \sigma A\,dW, \tag{3.20}$$

then wealthy people are subject to a larger windfall than the poor. Such an equation makes windfalls indistinguishable from fluctuations in the stock market, as we shall see later.

Example 3.35 *(The Ornstein–Uhlenbeck Processes) The historically oldest example of a stochastic differential equation is this:*

$$dX_t = -\alpha X_t\,dt + \sigma\,dW_t,$$

where α and σ are constants. The solution is easily obtained by a standard technique in differential equations. Specifically, convert the above equation into

$$e^{\alpha t}\left(dX_t + \alpha X_t\,dt\right) = e^{\alpha t}\sigma\,dW_t,$$

which becomes

$$d\left(e^{\alpha t}X_t\right) = e^{\alpha t}\sigma\,dW_t.$$

Integrating both sides from 0 to t, we have

$$X_t = e^{-\alpha t} X_0 + \int_0^t e^{-\alpha(t-s)} \sigma \, dW_s.$$

A version of the Ornstein–Uhlenbeck process has been used in economics for modeling the price of oil (and the prices of other raw commodities) in the mean-reversing form

$$dX_t = (X^* - X_t) dt + \sigma \, dW_t,$$

where X_t is the price at time t and X^* is the long run marginal cost of production. The solution to this mean-reversing process is

$$X_t = e^{-t} X_0 + \left(1 - e^{-t}\right) X^* + \int_0^t e^{-(t-s)} \sigma \, dW_s.$$

The argument for employing this process is that in the long run the price of oil should be drawn back to the marginal cost of production. (See, for example, Dixit and Pindyck (1994).) While this process may be more realistic, the price could be negative with a positive probability, at least theoretically.

A question naturally arises. Is geometric Brownian motion the only stochastic process that assumes positive value w.p.1? The following example should make the point.

Example 3.36 *Assume the diffusion process is of the form*

$$dX_t = \tfrac{1}{4} dt + \sqrt{X_t} \, dW_t.$$

Then $X_T \geq 0$ w.p.1 for any $T \geq 0$, if $X_0 \geq 0$. To prove it, consider

$$
\begin{aligned}
d\sqrt{X_t} &= \tfrac{1}{2} X_t^{-1/2} dX_t - \tfrac{1}{8} X_t^{-3/2} (dX_t)^2 \\
&= \tfrac{1}{2} X_t^{-1/2} \left(dX_t - \tfrac{1}{4} dt\right) = \tfrac{1}{2} X_t^{-1/2} \left(\sqrt{X_t} \, dW_t\right) \\
&= \tfrac{1}{2} dW_t.
\end{aligned}
$$

Integrating it from 0 to T, we have

$$\sqrt{X_T} = \sqrt{X_0} + \tfrac{1}{2} W_T.$$

Or, w.p.1,

$$X_T = \left(\sqrt{X_0} + \tfrac{1}{2} W_T \right)^2 \geq 0.$$

3.4.5 Multiple Sources of Uncertainty

Multiple sources of shocks are not uncommon in economics. For example, there are monetary shocks, and then there are real shocks due to technological changes or population growth. Some of them are independent, but many are not. The case in which shocks are not independent is commonly used in economic applications. In what follows we shall set up the notation and make it easy to apply.

Assume there are n *mutually independent* Wiener processes $\{W_t^i\}$, $i = 1, 2, \ldots, n$. By mutual independence we mean

$$(dW_t^i)(dW_t^j) = \begin{cases} dt & \text{if } i = j, \\ 0 & \text{if } i \neq j. \end{cases}$$

Assume there are k shocks in the model, each of which can be written as a linear combination of $\{W_t^i\}$

$$dz_t^i = \sum_{\ell=1}^{n} \lambda_\ell^i(t, \omega) \, dW_t^\ell, \qquad i = 1, 2, \ldots, k.$$

For easy computation, we assume each dz_t^i has unit norm, i.e., we assume $\left\{ \sum_{\ell=1}^{n} \left[\lambda_\ell^i(t, \omega) \right]^2 \right\}^{1/2} = 1$. Obviously, if the model does not have unit norm for some dz_t^i, we can always normalize them and redefine the terms. This normalization makes the notation much simpler. To see that, let

$$\lambda^{ij} = \sum_{\ell=1}^{n} \lambda_\ell^i(t, \omega) \lambda_\ell^j(t, \omega), \qquad i, j = 1, 2, \ldots, k,$$

be the correlation coefficient of dz_t^i and dz_t^j in the sense that

$$(dz_t^i)(dz_t^j) = \begin{cases} \lambda^{ij} dt & \text{if } i \neq j, \\ dt & \text{if } i = j. \end{cases} \tag{3.21}$$

Notice that the coefficient λ^{ij} satisfies $\left|\lambda^{ij}\right| \le 1$, because, by the Cauchy–Schwarz inequality,

$$\left|\sum_{\ell=1}^{n} \lambda_{\ell}^{i}\left(t, \omega\right) \lambda_{\ell}^{j}\left(t, \omega\right)\right| \le \sqrt{\sum_{\ell=1}^{n}\left[\lambda_{\ell}^{i}\left(t, \omega\right)\right]^{2}} \sqrt{\sum_{\ell=1}^{n}\left[\lambda_{\ell}^{j}\left(t, \omega\right)\right]^{2}} = 1.$$

In short, we have the following "multiplication table":

$\times$	dz^1	dz^2	$\cdot$	$\cdot$	$\cdot$	dz^k	dt
dz^1	dt	$\lambda^{12}\,dt$	$\cdot$	$\cdot$	$\cdot$	$\lambda^{1k}dt$	0
dz^2	$\lambda^{21}dt$	dt	$\cdot$	$\cdot$	$\cdot$	$\lambda^{2k}dt$	0
$\cdot$	$\cdot$	$\cdot$				$\cdot$	$\cdot$
$\cdot$	$\cdot$	$\cdot$				$\cdot$	$\cdot$
$\cdot$	$\cdot$	$\cdot$				$\cdot$	
dz^k	$\lambda^{k1}dt$	$\lambda^{k2}\,dt$	$\cdot$	$\cdot$	$\cdot$	dt	0
dt	0	0	$\cdot$	$\cdot$	$\cdot$	0	0

When $k = 2$, we often abbreviate λ^{12} as λ.

Next, we define the Ito integral of $\sigma\left(t, \omega\right)$ subject to independent shocks $\left\{W_{t}^{i}\right\}$, $i = 1, 2, \ldots, n$. Let

$$I\left(\sigma\right)\left(\omega\right) = \sum_{i=1}^{n} \int_{t_0}^{T} \sigma\left(t, \omega\right) dW_{t}^{i} = \int_{t_0}^{T} \sigma\left(t, \omega\right) \sum_{i=1}^{n} dW_{t}^{i}.$$

This definition can be extended to a vector-valued stochastic integral subject to $\{W^{i}\left(t\right)\}$, $i = 1, 2, \ldots, n$. Let

$$\mathbf{f} = \begin{pmatrix} f^1 \\ \vdots \\ f^m \end{pmatrix} : [t_0, T] \times \Omega \to \mathbb{R}^{m}$$

such that $f^{i} \in \mathcal{M}^{2}\left([t_0, T] \times \Omega\right)$. Then

$$I(\mathbf{f})\left(\omega\right) = \int_{t_0}^{T} \mathbf{f}(t, \omega) \sum_{i=1}^{n} dW^{i}\left(t\right) = \begin{pmatrix} \int_{t_0}^{T} f^1\left(t, \omega\right) \sum_{i=1}^{n} dW^{i}\left(t\right) \\ \vdots \\ \int_{t_0}^{T} f^m\left(t, \omega\right) \sum_{i=1}^{n} dW^{i}\left(t\right) \end{pmatrix}.$$

Again, Proposition 3.16 is satisfied. In particular, we have

Proposition 3.37 *Let* $|\mathbf{f}| = \sqrt{\sum_{i=1}^{m} |f^i|^2}$, *the Euclidean norm.*

(1) If $f^i \in \mathcal{M}^2\left([t_0, T] \times \Omega\right)$, *then*

$$E\left[\int_{t_0}^{T} \mathbf{f}(t, \omega)\, dW(t) \,\middle|\, \mathcal{F}_{t_0}\right] = \mathbf{0} \qquad w.p.1.$$

(2) If $\mathbf{f}(t, \omega)$ *and* $\mathbf{g}(t, \omega)$ *are nonanticipating (vector) processes, then*

$$E\left[\left(\int_{t_0}^{T} \mathbf{f}(t, \omega)\, dW(t)\right) \cdot \left(\int_{t_0}^{T} \mathbf{g}(t, \omega)\, dW(t)\right) \,\middle|\, \mathcal{F}_{t_0}\right]$$
$$= \int_{t_0}^{T} E\left[\mathbf{f}(t, \omega) \cdot \mathbf{g}(t, \omega) \,|\, \mathcal{F}_{t_0}\right] dt,$$

where " $\cdot$ *" stands for the dot product of two vectors. In particular,*

$$E\left[\left(\int_{t_0}^{T} \mathbf{f}(t, \omega)\, dW(t)\right)^2 \,\middle|\, \mathcal{F}_{t_0}\right] = \int_{t_0}^{T} E\left[(\mathbf{f}(t, \omega))^2 \,|\, \mathcal{F}_{t_0}\right] dt.$$

Exercise 3.4.1 *Assume*

$$dX = \mu X dt + \sigma_1 X dz_1 + \sigma_2 X dz_2,$$

where each z_i *is a standard Wiener process satisfying* $(dz_1)(dz_2) = \lambda\, dt$. *That is, the state variable* X *is subject to two possibly correlated shocks* dz_1 *and* dz_2. *Show that* $X(t) > 0$ *w.p.1 at all times if* $X(0) > 0$.
Hint. Show

$$X(t) = X(0) \exp\left\{\left(\mu - \frac{\sigma_1^2 + 2\lambda\sigma_1\sigma_2 + \sigma_2^2}{2}\right)t\right\}$$
$$\times \exp\left\{\sigma_1 z_1(t)\right\} \exp\left\{\sigma_2 z_2(t)\right\}.$$

Henceforth, we shall use z_t **to denote the standard Wiener process when there is only one source of uncertainty. When there are two or more shocks in the model, we shall use** z_t^i **in the context of (3.21) or the associated multiplication table. We keep the notation** $\{W^i(t)\}$ **only for a family of independent Wiener processes.**

3.4.6 Multivariate Ito's Lemma

Now let W'_t be another Wiener process satisfying $(dz_t)\,(dz'_t) = \lambda\,dt$, where λ is the correlation coefficient of dz_t and dz'_t.

Theorem 3.38 *(Ito's Lemma) Suppose X_t follows (3.13) and Y_t follows $dY_t = v\,(Y_t)\,dt + \theta\,(Y_t)\,dz'_t$. If $Z_t = h\,(X_t, Y_t)$, where h is twice continuously differentiable, then*

$$dZ_t = \left[\mu h_X + v h_Y + \left(\sigma^2/2\right) h_{XX} + \lambda\sigma\theta h_{XY} + \left(\theta^2/2\right) h_{YY}\right] dt$$
$$+ \sigma h_X\,dz_t + \theta h_Y\,dz'_t. \tag{3.22}$$

Proof. See, for example, McKean (1969, pp. 32–35), Arnold (1974, pp. 96–99), and Friedman (1975, pp. 81–84). ∎

The derivation is straightforward using the aforementioned method:

$$dZ_t = h_X\,dX_t + h_Y\,dY_t + \frac{1}{2}h_{XX}\,(dX_t)^2 + h_{XY}\,(dX_t)\,(dY_t)$$
$$+ \frac{1}{2}h_{YY}\,(dY_t)^2 .$$

What we have presented here is the case of two diffusion processes, which happens to be the most commonly used in economics. Ito's lemma for three or more diffusion processes can be done similarly. The formal presentation is at the end of this chapter.

Example 3.39 *(Integration by Parts) Suppose X_t follows*

$$dX_t = \mu_1\,(X_t)\,dt + \sigma_1\,(X_t)\,dz_t$$

and Y_t follows

$$dY_t = \mu_2\,(Y_t)\,dt + \sigma_2\,(Y_t)\,dz'_t,$$

with $(dz_t)\,(dz'_t) = \lambda\,dt$. Assume $Z = h\,(X, Y) = XY$. Then

$$d\,(XY) = Y\,dX + X\,dY + dX\,dY$$
$$= (\mu_1 Y + \mu_2 X + \lambda\sigma_1\sigma_2)\,dt + \sigma_1 Y\,dz_t + \sigma_2 X\,dz'_t.$$

Notice that this differs from the integration by parts (or the product rule) in elementary calculus,

$$d(XY) = Y\,dX + X\,dY,$$

by the term $dX\,dY = \lambda\sigma_1\sigma_2\,dt$. If, however, one of the stochastic differential equations is deterministic, i.e., if $\sigma_1(X_t) = 0$ or $\sigma_2(X_t) = 0$, or if they are independent, i.e., $\lambda = 0$, then the old rule of integration by parts applies.

Example 3.40 *(Real Cash Balance) Let M and P be the stock of money and the price level respectively. In the deterministic case, we have the following equation:*

$$\frac{d(M/P)}{(M/P)} = \frac{dM}{M} - \frac{dP}{P}.$$

That is, the rate of change in real cash balances is the difference between the money growth rate and the inflation rate. However, this formula is no longer valid in the stochastic case, because

$$d(M/P) = \frac{dM}{P} - \frac{M}{P^2}dP - \frac{(dM)(dP)}{P^2} + \frac{M}{P^3}(dP)^2$$

$$= \frac{M}{P}\left[\frac{dM}{M} - \frac{dP}{P} - \frac{dM}{M}\frac{dP}{P} + \left(\frac{dP}{P}\right)^2\right],$$

so that

$$\frac{d(M/P)}{M/P} = \frac{dM}{M} - \frac{dP}{P} - \frac{dM}{M}\frac{dP}{P} + \left(\frac{dP}{P}\right)^2.$$

To illustrate, let $dM_t = \mu_1 M_t\,dt + \sigma_1 M_t\,dz_t$ and $dP_t = \pi P_t\,dt + \sigma_2 P_t\,dz_t^2$. Then there is an extra term

$$\left(\frac{dP}{P}\right)^2 - \frac{dM}{M}\frac{dP}{P} = \left(\sigma_2^2 - \lambda\sigma_1\sigma_2\right)dt$$

in the drift. The old rule will remain true if the inflation rate is non-stochastic, i.e., $\sigma_2 = 0$, which, however, is the least interesting case. On the other hand, if $dP/P = dM/M$ (i.e., superneutrality), then the real *cash balance remains constant over time, just as in the deterministic case.*

Another implication is that the quotient rule in elementary calculus,

$$d\left(\frac{M}{P}\right) = \frac{P\,dM - M\,dP}{P^2},$$

does not hold in the stochastic case except in the case of superneutrality or $\sigma_2 = 0$.

Example 3.41 *(Rate of Change) In general,*

$$d\log\left(\frac{M}{P}\right) \le \frac{d\,(M/P)}{M/P}.$$

This is because

$$d\log\left(\frac{M}{P}\right) = d\,(\log M - \log P) = d\log M - d\log P$$

$$= \frac{dM}{M} - \frac{1}{2}\left(\frac{dM}{M}\right)^2 - \frac{dP}{P} + \frac{1}{2}\left(\frac{dP}{P}\right)^2$$

$$\ne \frac{dM}{M} - \frac{dP}{P} - \frac{dM}{M}\frac{dP}{P} + \left(\frac{dP}{P}\right)^2 = \frac{d\,(M/P)}{M/P}.$$

The difference between the two is

$$d\log\left(\frac{M}{P}\right) - \frac{d\,(M/P)}{M/P} = -\frac{1}{2}\left(\frac{dM}{M} - \frac{dP}{P}\right)^2 \le 0,$$

which, again, goes away under the assumption of superneutrality.

Example 3.42 *(Stochastic Solow Equation) The capital accumulation equation is*

$$dK = [F(K, L) - \delta K - C]\,dt,$$

where the production function, $F(K, L)$, is homogeneous of degree one in K and L, and δ is the depreciation rate. Assume the population dynamics follows (3.19). Treat the capital–labor ratio $k = K/L$ as a function of K and L, i.e., $k = h(K, L) = K/L$. Since $h_K = 1/L$, $h_{KK} = 0$,

$h_L = -K\,(1/L)^2,\ h_{LL} = 2K\,(1/L)^3$, *and* $h_{KL} = -(1/L)^2$, *we have*

$$dk = d\left(\frac{K}{L}\right) = \frac{dK}{L} - \frac{K}{L^2}dL - \frac{(dK)(dL)}{L^2} + \frac{K}{L^3}(dL)^2 .$$

Let $c = C/L$ *be the per capita consumption, and let* $f\,(k) = F\,(K/L, 1)$ *be the per capita output. Since* $(dK)(dL) = o\,(dt)$,

$$dk = \left[\frac{F\,(K,\,L) - \delta K - C}{L}\right]dt - \frac{K}{L}\frac{dL}{L} + \frac{K}{L}\left(\frac{dL}{L}\right)^2$$

$$= [f\,(k) - \delta k - c]\,dt - k\,(n\,dt + \sigma\,dW) + k\sigma^2\,dt$$

$$= \left[f\,(k) - \left(n + \delta - \sigma^2\right)k - c\right]dt - \sigma k\,dz.$$

Notice that when $\sigma = 0$, *we have the classical Solow equation*

$$\dot{k} = f\,(k) - (n + \delta)\,k - c.$$

From these examples, we can see that the differentiation rules in elementary calculus – such as the product rule, the quotient rule, and the chain rule – are no longer valid in stochastic calculus. The addition rule and the subtraction rule, however, remain true.

Example 3.43 *(Ito Integral Revisited) Suppose* $dX_t = \mu\,(X_t)\,dt + \sigma\,(X_t)\,dz_t$. *Then*

$$d\left(X^2\right) = 2X\,dX + (dX)^2 = 2X\,(\mu\,dt + \sigma\,dz) + \sigma^2\,dt$$

$$= \left(2\mu X + \sigma^2\right)dt + 2\sigma X\,dz.$$

In particular, if $\mu = 0$ *and* $\sigma = 1$, *then we have* $X_t = z_t$ *and*

$$d\left(z_t^2\right) = dt + 2z_t\,dz_t,$$

which is equation (3.6).

Exercise 3.4.2 *Is the solution to the geometric Brownian motion* (3.16) *unique for a given* $X\,(0)$?

Hint. Let $Y\,(t)$ *be another solution. Then, using* (3.22), *show that* $d\,(Y/X) = 0$ *w.p.1. The initial condition ensures that* $(Y/X)\,(0) = 1$ *and hence* $(Y/X)\,(t) = 1$ *w.p.1.*

3.5 Ito's Lemma for Time-Dependent Functions

Now assume X_t satisfies (3.2). Let $C^{1,2}([0, \infty) \times \mathbb{R})$ be the class of functions that are continuously differentiable in the first argument and are twice continuously differentiable in the second argument. Assume $Y_t = H(t, X_t)$, where $H(t, X_t) \in C^{1,2}([0, \infty) \times \mathbb{R})$. Using the method developed earlier,

$$dH(t, X_t) = H_t dt + H_X dX + \frac{1}{2} H_{XX}(dX)^2 + o(dt)$$

$$= \left(H_t + \mu H_X + \frac{1}{2}\sigma^2 H_{XX} \right) dt + \sigma H_X dz + o(dt).$$

Thus, we have

Theorem 3.44 *(Ito's Lemma) Let $H(t, X_t) \in C^{1,2}([0, \infty) \times \mathbb{R})$, where X_t satisfies (3.2). Then*

$$dH(t, X_t) = \left(H_t + \mu H_X + \frac{1}{2}\sigma^2 H_{XX} \right) dt + \sigma H_X \, dz_t. \qquad (3.23)$$

Proof. See, for example, McKean (1969, pp. 32–35), Gikman and Skorohod (1969, pp. 387–389), Arnold (1974, pp. 96–99), and Friedman (1975, pp. 81–84). ∎

That is, if the stochastic differential equation is not autonomous, then there is an extra term $H_t \, dt$ in Ito's lemma. A more general case is shown at the end of the chapter.

3.5.1 Euler's Homogeneous Differential Equation and the Heat Equation

Euler's Homogenous Differential Equation
The linear homogeneous differential equation

$$x^n y^{(n)} + b_1 x^{n-1} y^{(n-1)} + b_2 x^{n-2} y^{(n-2)} + \cdots + b_n y = 0$$

is called Euler's homogeneous differential equation. A particular solution can be found by substituting $y = x^\lambda$ to obtain $I(\lambda) x^\lambda = 0$, where

$$I(\lambda) = \sum_{i=0}^{n} b_{n-i} \lambda (\lambda - 1) \cdots (\lambda - i + 1) = \sum_{i=0}^{n} b_{n-i} \binom{\lambda}{i} i!$$

(with $b_0 = 1$) is the *indicial equation*. Thus, x^λ is a solution to Euler's differential equation if λ satisfies $I(\lambda) = 0$. Note that $I(\lambda)$ is a polynomial of degree n in λ. If λ is a double root of $I(\lambda) = 0$, then both x^λ and $x^\lambda \log x$ are solutions. When $n = 2$, the indicial equation is

$$\lambda (\lambda - 1) + b_1 \lambda + b_2 = 0,$$

and the solutions are

$$\lambda_1 = \frac{1 - b_1 + \sqrt{(1 - b_1)^2 - 4b_2}}{2},$$

$$\lambda_2 = \frac{1 - b_1 - \sqrt{(1 - b_1)^2 - 4b_2}}{2}.$$

Therefore, the general solution to this case of Euler's equation is of the form $A_1 x^{\lambda_1} + A_2 x^{\lambda_2}$.

On the Heat Equation
The heat equation, also known as the diffusion equation, is one of the most important equations in applied mathematics. It governs the diffusion of temperature in a (physical) body in time and space. Its canonical form is

$$\frac{\partial f}{\partial t} = k \left(\frac{\partial^2 f}{\partial x^2} + \frac{\partial^2 f}{\partial y^2} + \frac{\partial^2 f}{\partial z^2} \right),$$

where $f(t, x, y, z)$ measures the temperature at time t and place (x, y, z), and the coefficient k is called the *diffusivity*.

What we are interested is the one-dimensional equation

$$f_t = k f_{xx}, \qquad k > 0.$$

The closed-form solution to our equation is

$$f(t, x) = \int_{-\infty}^{g(t,x)} e^{-u^2} du,$$

where

$$g(t, x) = \frac{x}{2\sqrt{kt}}.$$

To verify this, we note that

$$g_t = -\frac{x}{4\sqrt{k}} t^{-3/2} = -2kg(g_x)^2.$$

Then from

$$f_t = e^{-g^2} g_t, \qquad f_x = e^{-g^2} g_x, \qquad \text{and} \qquad g_{xx} = 0,$$

we have

$$kf_{xx} = -2kge^{-g^2}(g_x)^2 = e^{-g^2} g_t = f_t.$$

There are variants of the heat equation that can be obtained through transformations. Two are of particular interest. If $h(t, x) = e^{rt} f(t, x)$, then $h_{xx} = e^{rt} f_{xx}$ and

$$h_t = re^{rt} f(t, x) + e^{rt} f_t = rh + kh_{xx}.$$

Notice that rh is added to the equation.

Next, if $y = b \log x$, then $\phi(t, x) = f(t, b \log x)$ satisfies

$$\phi_t = f_t, \qquad \phi_x = bf_y x^{-1}, \qquad \phi_{xx} = b^2 f_{yy} x^{-2} - bf_y x^{-2},$$

and hence the equation

$$b^{-2} k \left[x^2 \phi_{xx} + x\phi_x \right] = \phi_t.$$

Notice that the transformed heat equation now contains a component of Euler's homogeneous differential equation, $x^2 \phi_{xx} + x\phi_x$.

Combining these two transformations, we zero in on

$$\varphi(t, x) = e^{r(t-T)} f(a(t - T), b \log(x/c) + a(t - T)),$$

for some constants T and c. Then φ satisfies

$$\varphi_t = r\varphi + \frac{a}{b}\left(1 + \frac{k}{b}\right)x\varphi_x + \left(\frac{ak}{b^2}\right)x^2\varphi_{xx}. \qquad (3.24)$$

Notice that the right-hand side of (3.24) is a second-order Euler's differential equation.

3.5.2 Black–Scholes Formula

This subsection presents the celebrated formula for option pricing due to Black and Scholes (1973).

Consider the case of a European (call) option that gives one the right to buy one share of common stock at the time of maturity. The price that is paid for the stock when the option is exercised is called the exercise price. Assume that the short-term real interest rate is constant over time (i.e., there is a bond market) and the stock price X follows a geometric Brownian motion

$$dX = \mu X dt + \sigma X dz, \qquad (3.25)$$

with constant μ and σ. Assume further that there are no transactions costs in trading, no dividends or other distributions paid, no indivisibilities (i.e., we can buy or sell a fraction of an option), and no penalty for short selling.

Let $V(t, X)$ be the value of the option, as a function of time and the stock price. Consider the portfolio that, for every share of stock long, the investor has n units of option short. Then the value of the portfolio at any point of time is $X - nV$. The adjustment is done continuously in the sense that, throughout the time interval $[t, t + dt)$, we short $n(t, X_t)$ units of the option. Similarly, we short $n(t + dt, X_{t+dt})$ units of the option in the whole interval $[t + dt, t + 2 dt)$, and so on. All the while the stock price and the value of the portfolio vary with time. Then the change in the value of the portfolio from t to $t + dt$ is $dX - n \, dV$. By Ito's lemma,

$$dV = \left(V_t + \frac{1}{2}\sigma^2 X^2 V_{XX}\right)dt + V_X dX.$$

Thus, the change in the value of the portfolio becomes

$$dX - n \, dV = dX - nV_X dX - n\left(V_t + \frac{1}{2}\sigma^2 X^2 V_{XX}\right)dt.$$

Notice that $-n \left(V_t + \frac{1}{2}\sigma^2 X^2 V_{XX} \right) dt$ is risk-free, i.e., it contains no dz terms. Therefore, if we choose $n = 1/V_X$, i.e., $n(t, X_t) = 1/V_X(t, X_t)$, then the first two terms on the right-hand side of the above equation cancel each other and there is no dz term in $dX - (1/V_X) dV$. In other words, the portfolio of holding one unit of X and shorting $1/V_X$ units of V, when the adjustment is done continuously, is risk-free. A standard argument in finance (arbitrage) then implies that the return to this portfolio must be the same as its return from the bond market, or

$$-\frac{1}{V_X} \left(V_t + \frac{1}{2}\sigma^2 X^2 V_{XX} \right) dt = (r \, dt) \left(X - \frac{1}{V_X} V \right).$$

Rewrite this equation as

$$V_t = rV - rXV_X - \frac{1}{2}\sigma^2 X^2 V_{XX}. \tag{3.26}$$

This is the fundamental partial differential equation for option pricing, which is of the form (3.24). The value of the option can be obtained by solving the partial differential equation (3.26).

To complete the description of the problem, let c be the exercise price and T be the maturity date. Then the value of this call option is

$$V(T, X) = \max\{X - c, 0\} = \begin{cases} X - c & \text{if } X \geq c, \\ 0 & \text{if } X < c. \end{cases}$$

This equation serves as a boundary condition for (3.26).

Equation (3.26) is similar to (3.24) if we choose

$$-\frac{ak}{b^2} = \frac{\sigma^2}{2}, \qquad \frac{a}{b}\left(1 + \frac{k}{b}\right) = -r, \qquad \text{and} \quad k = 1.$$

Solving the equations, we obtain

$$b = \frac{2}{\sigma^2}\left(r - \frac{\sigma^2}{2}\right) \quad \Rightarrow \quad a = -\frac{2}{\sigma^2}\left(r - \frac{\sigma^2}{2}\right)^2.$$

This shows that the solution to the Black–Scholes equation (3.26) is of the form

$$V(t, x) = e^{r(t-T)} f\left(-\frac{2}{\sigma^2}\left(r - \frac{\sigma^2}{2}\right)^2 (t - T), \frac{2}{\sigma^2}\left(r - \frac{\sigma^2}{2}\right) \right.$$

$$\left. \times \left[\log\frac{x}{c} - \left(r - \frac{\sigma^2}{2}\right)(t - T) \right] \right).$$

This is equation (9) of Black and Scholes (1973).

Exercise 3.5.1 *Assume the stock price follows*

$$dX = \mu X\,dt + \sigma_1 X\,dz_1 + \sigma_2 X\,dz_2,$$

where each z_i is a standard Wiener process with $(dz_1)(dz_2) = \lambda\,dt$. That is, the stock price is subject to two possibly correlated shocks. Show that the heat equation for option pricing is

$$V_t = rV - rXV_X - \frac{1}{2}\left(\sigma_1^2 + 2\sigma_1\sigma_2 + \sigma_2^2\right) X^2 V_{XX}.$$

3.5.3 Irreversible Investment

The Value of Investment Opportunity
This line of research assumes that many, if not most, investment projects are irreversible in that there are sunk costs. To avoid bad investment, one will wait for the right time to invest, if one invests at all. In this sense, the opportunity to invest is just like an option that gives you the right to "exercise" (invest). This investment opportunity, therefore, commands a value, which is analogous to the value of a financial option. What then is the value of this investment opportunity?

Let X be the price of an investment project that follows a geometric Brownian motion (3.25), which is analogous to the stock price in the Black–Scholes model. Let $V(X)$ be the value of the investment opportunity, which is analogous to the value of the option in the Black–Scholes model. The risk-free portfolio can be obtained as follows. For each investment opportunity long, we short n units of the project (or any asset that is perfectly correlated with X) so that the net value of the portfolio is $V - nX$, and the adjustment is done continuously. The change in value of the portfolio in the time interval $[t, t + dt)$ is

$$dV - n\,dX = V'(X)\,dX + \frac{1}{2}\sigma^2 X^2 V''(X)\,dt - n\,dX.$$

Obviously, if we choose $n = V'(X)$, then

$$dV - V'(X)\,dX = \frac{1}{2}\sigma^2 X^2 V''(X)\,dt,$$

which contains no dz terms, i.e., it is risk-free. This risk-free portfolio must have a return $[V - V'(X)\,X]\,(r\,dt)$ for the duration of time dt, i.e.,

$$\frac{1}{2}\sigma^2 X^2 V''(X)\,dt = [V - V'(X)\,X]\,(r\,dt).$$

Thus, the value of investment is governed by the following equation:

$$\frac{1}{2}\sigma^2 X^2 V''(X) + rXV'(X) - rV = 0.$$

If the project carries dividends, then the change in value in the time interval $[t, t + dt)$ must allow for the loss in dividends in shorting n units of X. That is, if $\delta > 0$ stands for the dividend rate, then

$$dV - V'(X)\,dX = \frac{1}{2}\sigma^2 X^2 V''(X)\,dt - \delta V'(X)\,X\,dt.$$

In that case, the equation for the value of investment opportunity becomes

$$\frac{1}{2}\sigma^2 X^2 V''(X) + (r - \delta)\,XV'(X) - rV = 0,$$

which is an Euler's homogeneous differential equation of the second order.

The associated indicial equation is

$$\lambda^2 - \left[1 - \frac{2\,(r - \delta)}{\sigma^2}\right]\lambda - \frac{2r}{\sigma^2} = 0.$$

It is straightforward to verify that the discriminant of the quadratic equation is positive. This implies that there are two real roots. Since the product of the two roots is negative ($\lambda_1\lambda_2 = -2r/\sigma^2 < 0$), one of the roots is negative. However, this negative root can be ruled out by the boundary condition $V(0) = 0$ (the value of investment opportunity is zero if the underlying investment has no value). The positive root is

$$\lambda_1 = \frac{1}{2}\left\{\left[1 - \frac{2(r - \delta)}{\sigma^2}\right] + \sqrt{\left[1 - \frac{2(r - \delta)}{\sigma^2}\right]^2 + \frac{8r}{\sigma^2}}\right\} > 1.$$

Thus, the general solution is of the form $V(X) = A_1 X^{\lambda_1}$. For further discussion on this subject the reader is referred to Dixit and Pindyck (1994).

The Value of an Investment Project
Assume an investment project will produce a fixed flow of output. To simplify the argument, we assume that for each project there is exactly one unit of output produced per unit of time, i.e., we normalize it. The output price $\{X_t\}$ follows a geometric Brownian motion (3.25). Assume there is no operating cost. What is the value of the project?

Let the value of the investment project be $V(X)$. Form a portfolio as follows. The project holder will short n units of the output it produces, i.e., the portfolio is $V(X) - nX$. Again, the adjustment is done continuously. In the time interval $[t, t + dt)$ the project receives revenue Xdt and pays dividends $(\delta\, dt)(nX)$, so that the net revenue is $(1 - n\delta)Xdt$. In the same time interval, the capital gain is

$$dV - n\, dX = V'(X)dX + \frac{1}{2}\sigma^2 X^2 V''(X)dt - n\, dX.$$

The total change in the value of the portfolio is the sum of net revenue and the capital gains, $(1 - n\delta)Xdt + dV - n\, dX$. If we choose $n = V'(X)$, then the total change in value of the portfolio is

$$[1 - \delta V'(X)]Xdt + \frac{1}{2}\sigma^2 X^2 V''(X)dt,$$

which is risk-free. Therefore, it is equated to $(r\, dt)[V(X) - V'(X)X]$. Thus, we have the following equation:

$$\frac{1}{2}\sigma^2 X^2 V''(X) + (r - \delta)XV'(X) - rV(X) + X = 0.$$

A particular solution to this differential equation is $V_p(X) = X/\delta$, so that the general solution is of the form

$$V(X) = \frac{X}{\delta} + A_1 X^{\lambda_1} + A_2 X^{\lambda_2}.$$

The particular value of the firm, X/δ, is called the fundamental value. Again, for further discussion on this subject the reader is referred to Dixit and Pindyck (1994).

3.5.4 Budget Equation for an Investor

This example does not involve Ito's lemma. We present it here because we shall apply the same kind of argument employed in the previous two applications.

Suppose there are n assets, and the price of each asset follows a geometric Brownian motion

$$dP_i(t) = \mu_i P_i(t) dt + \sigma_i P_i(t) dz_i(t), \qquad i = 1, 2, \ldots, n.$$

Assume at time t the investor owns $N_i(t)$ units of asset i. Then the total wealth is

$$W(t) = \sum_{i=1}^{n} N_i(t) P_i(t).$$

Similarly to the previous two examples, the portfolio $\{N_i(t)\}$ remains unchanged over the time interval $[t, t + dt)$. Then the change in wealth over that time interval is

$$dW(t) = \sum_{i=1}^{n} N_i(t) dP_i(t),$$

if there is no consumption. Assuming the consumption pattern is constant in interval $[t, t + dt)$ in the same way as for portfolio selection, the budget equation becomes

$$dW(t) = \sum_{i=1}^{n} N_i(t) dP_i(t) - c(t) dt. \qquad (3.27)$$

An alternative way of deriving this budget equation is this: The wealth at the beginning of time t is the result of investment in the previous period:

$$W(t) = \sum_{i=1}^{n} N_i(t - dt) P_i(t).$$

From this wealth the consumer spends $c(t)\,dt$ on consumption and purchases $N_i(t)$ units of asset i, i.e.,

$$W(t) = \sum_{i=1}^{n} N_i(t) P_i(t) + c(t)\,dt. \tag{3.28}$$

Then the wealth at the beginning of time $t + dt$ is

$$W(t + dt) = \sum_{i=1}^{n} N_i(t) P_i(t + dt). \tag{3.29}$$

Subtracting (3.28) from (3.29), we have (3.27).

Let $s_i(t) = N_i(t) P_i(t) / W(t)$, the share of wealth in asset i, with

$$\sum_{i=1}^{n} s_i(t) = 1.$$

Then the budget equation (3.27) can be written as

$$dW(t) = \sum_{i=1}^{n} s_i(t) \mu_i W(t)\,dt - c(t)\,dt + \sum_{i=1}^{n} s_i(t) \sigma_i W(t)\,dz_i(t).$$

$$\tag{3.30}$$

When $n = 1$, the budget equation reduces to

$$dW = (\mu W - c)\,dt + \sigma W\,dz,$$

which is of the form (3.20).

Suppose the n-th asset is risk-free (i.e., $\sigma_n = 0$) with constant rate of return $\mu_n = r > 0$. Then the budget equation becomes

$$dW(t) = \sum_{i=1}^{n-1} s_i(t)(\mu_i - r)W(t)\,dt + [rW(t) - c(t)]\,dt$$

$$+ \sum_{i=1}^{n-1} s_i(t)\sigma_i W(t)\,dz_i(t).$$

This is a useful budget equation, as we shall see in the next two chapters.

Let $u(c(t), t)$ be the period utility function at time t (with discount), and $B(W_T, T)$ be the bequest function. Then the optimization problem for the investor is

$$\max_{\{c(t), s_i(t)\}} E\left\{\int_0^T u(c(t), t)\,dt + B(W(T), T)\right\} \qquad \text{s.t. (3.30)}.$$

The solution to this problem is the well-known consumption–portfolio rule. We shall deal with this problem in the next two chapters.

3.5.5 Ito's Lemma: General Form

In this subsection we examine Ito's differentiation rule when there are several underlying stochastic processes with multiple sources of uncertainty. The theorems may look complicated, but they are simply the second-order Taylor series expansion in elementary calculus, *from the viewpoint of application*. For real-valued functions, the gradient vector and the Hessian matrix are, respectively, the representations of the first and second derivatives. For vector-valued functions, the Jacobian matrix is the representation for the first derivative.

Real-Valued Functions
Now suppose $\mathbf{X}_t = (X_t^1, \ldots, X_t^n)^T \in \mathbb{R}^n$; $\mathbf{W}_t = (W_t^1, \ldots, W_t^m)^T$, the mutually independent Wiener processes; and $\boldsymbol{\mu} = (\mu^1, \ldots, \mu^n)^T$, where superscript T stands for the transpose of a matrix. That is, all vectors are column vectors. Let

$$dX_t^i = \mu^i(t, \mathbf{X}_t)\,dt + \sum_{j=1}^m \sigma_j^i(t, \mathbf{X}_t)\,dW_t^j, \qquad i = 1, 2, \ldots, n,$$

– in matrix form,

$$
\begin{pmatrix} dX_t^1 \\ \vdots \\ dX_t^n \end{pmatrix} = \begin{pmatrix} \mu^1 \\ \vdots \\ \mu^n \end{pmatrix} dt + \begin{pmatrix} \sigma_1^1 \cdots \sigma_m^1 \\ \vdots \qquad \vdots \\ \sigma_1^n \cdots \sigma_m^n \end{pmatrix}_{n \times m} \begin{pmatrix} dW_t^1 \\ \vdots \\ dW_t^m \end{pmatrix}_{m \times 1}.
$$

or, in a compact notation

$$
d\mathbf{X}_t = \boldsymbol{\mu}(t, \mathbf{X}_t)\, dt + \Sigma(t, \mathbf{X}_t)(d\mathbf{W}_t), \tag{3.31}
$$

where $\Sigma = \left(\sigma_k^i\right)$ is an $n \times m$ matrix.

Let $H(t, \mathbf{X}_t) \in C^{1,2}([0, \infty) \times \mathbb{R}^n)$. Denote by $H_i = \partial H / \partial X^i$. The quadratic expansion of $dH(t, \mathbf{X}_t)$ is

$$
dH(t, \mathbf{X}_t) = H_t dt + \nabla_{\mathbf{X}} H \cdot d\mathbf{X}_t + \frac{1}{2}(d\mathbf{X}_t)^T H_{\mathbf{XX}}(d\mathbf{X}_t),
$$

where $\nabla_{\mathbf{X}} H$ is the gradient vector of H, $H_{\mathbf{XX}}$ is the Hessian matrix of H, the dot in $\nabla_{\mathbf{X}} H \cdot d\mathbf{X}_t$ means the dot product, and the term $(d\mathbf{X}_t)^T H_{\mathbf{XX}}(d\mathbf{X}_t)$ represents the quadratic form of the second derivative. The first derivative is

$$
\begin{aligned}
\nabla_{\mathbf{X}} H \cdot d\mathbf{X}_t \\
= \sum_{i=1}^n H_i \left(\mu^i\, dt + \sum_{j=1}^m \sigma_j^i\, dW_t^j \right) \\
= \sum_{i=1}^n H_i \mu^i\, dt + \sum_{i=1}^n \sum_{j=1}^m H_i \sigma_j^i\, dW_t^j \\
= (\nabla_{\mathbf{X}} H \cdot \boldsymbol{\mu})\, dt + (\nabla_{\mathbf{X}} H)^T \Sigma(d\mathbf{W}_t).
\end{aligned}
$$

In spelling out the quadratic form, we note that

$$
(d\mathbf{X}_t)^T H_{\mathbf{XX}}(d\mathbf{X}_t) = \sum_{i=1}^n \sum_{j=1}^n H_{ij}\, dX_t^i\, dX_t^j.
$$

Since $\left(dW_t^i\right)\left(dW_t^j\right) = 0$ if $i \neq j$,

$$
\begin{aligned}
dX_t^i \, dX_t^j &= \left(\mu^i \, dt + \sum_{k=1}^{m} \sigma_k^i \, dW_t^k\right)\left(\mu^j \, dt + \sum_{k=1}^{m} \sigma_k^j \, dW_t^k\right) \\
&= \sum_{k=1}^{m} \sigma_k^i \sigma_k^j \, dt,
\end{aligned}
$$

by ignoring the $o\,(dt)$ term. Let

$$
\Sigma\Sigma^T = \left(\sigma^{ij}\right) = \left(\sum_{k=1}^{m} \sigma_k^i \sigma_k^j\right)_{n\times n},
$$

which is a $n \times n$ matrix. Then the second-order term becomes

$$
(d\mathbf{X}_t)^T \, H_{\mathbf{XX}} \, (d\mathbf{X}_t) = \sum_{i=1}^{n}\sum_{j=1}^{n} H_{ij}\sigma^{ij} \, dt = \mathrm{tr}\left(\Sigma\Sigma^T H_{\mathbf{XX}}\right) dt
$$

$$
= \mathrm{tr}\left(H_{\mathbf{XX}}\Sigma\Sigma^T\right) dt,
$$

where $\mathrm{tr}\,(A)$ stands for the trace of the matrix A, i.e., if $A = \left(a_{ij}\right)_{n\times n}$, then $\mathrm{tr}\,(A) = \sum_{i=1}^{n} a_{ii}$, the sum of the entries on the diagonal.

Theorem 3.45 *(Ito's Lemma) Let $H \in C^{1,2}\left([0, \infty) \times \mathbb{R}^n\right)$, and $\mathbf{X}_t$ satisfy* (3.31). *Then*

$$
dH\,(t, \mathbf{X}_t)
$$

$$
= \left(H_t + \sum_{i=1}^{n} H_i \mu^i + \frac{1}{2}\sum_{i=1}^{n}\sum_{j=1}^{n}\sum_{k=1}^{m} H_{ij}\sigma_k^i \sigma_k^j\right) dt
$$

$$
+ \sum_{i=1}^{n}\sum_{k=1}^{m} H_i \sigma_k^i \, dW_t^k
$$

$$
= \left(H_t + \sum_{i=1}^{n} H_i \mu^i + \frac{1}{2}\sum_{i=1}^{n}\sum_{j=1}^{n} H_{ij}\sigma^{ij}\right) dt + \sum_{i=1}^{n}\sum_{k=1}^{m} H_i \sigma_k^i \, dW_t^k.
$$

or

$$dH(t, \mathbf{X}_t) = \left[H_t + \nabla_{\mathbf{X}} H \cdot \boldsymbol{\mu} + \frac{1}{2} \mathrm{tr}\left(\Sigma \Sigma^T H_{\mathbf{X}\mathbf{X}} \right) \right] dt$$

$$+ (\nabla_{\mathbf{X}} H)^T \Sigma \, (d\mathbf{W}_t)$$

$$= [H_t + \mathcal{A}H] \, dt + (\nabla_{\mathbf{X}} H)^T \Sigma \, (d\mathbf{W}_t),$$

where

$$\mathcal{A} = \sum_{j=1}^{n} \mu^i \frac{\partial}{\partial X^i} + \frac{1}{2} \sum_{i=1}^{n} \sum_{j=1}^{n} \sigma^{ij} \frac{\partial^2}{\partial X^i \partial X^j}$$

is the backward operator.

Proof. See, for example, McKean (1969, pp. 32–35), Arnold (1974, pp. 96–99). ■

In stochastic analysis, the backward operator is a useful shorthand when we study the stochastic dynamic programming method.

Vector-Valued Functions
There is a straightforward extension from a real-valued function to a vector-valued function. Let

$$\mathbf{H} = \left(H^1, \ldots, H^\ell \right) : [0, \infty) \times \mathbb{R}^n \to \mathbb{R}^\ell.$$

Then Ito's lemma becomes

$$d\mathbf{H}(t, \mathbf{X}_t) = \mathbf{H}_t dt + (D_{\mathbf{X}}\mathbf{H})_{\ell \times n} \, d\mathbf{X}_t + \frac{1}{2} \left(\mathrm{tr}\left[\Sigma \Sigma^T H_{\mathbf{X}\mathbf{X}}^i \right] \right)_{\ell \times 1} dt,$$

where $(D_{\mathbf{X}}\mathbf{H})_{\ell \times n}$ stands for the Jacobian matrix of $\mathbf{H}(t, \mathbf{X}_t)$ with respect to $\mathbf{X}_t$, i.e.,

$$\begin{pmatrix} H_1^1 & \cdots & H_n^1 \\ \vdots & & \vdots \\ H_1^\ell & \cdots & H_n^\ell \end{pmatrix}.$$

Then, for $j = 1, 2, \ldots, \ell$, the j-th coordinate of $(D_{\mathbf{X}}\mathbf{H})_{\ell \times n} \, d\mathbf{X}_t$ is

$$\sum_{i=1}^{n} H_i^j \left(\mu^i \, dt + \sum_{k=1}^{m} \sigma_k^i \, dW_t^k \right) = \sum_{i=1}^{n} H_i^j \mu^i \, dt + \sum_{i=1}^{n} \sum_{k=1}^{m} H_i^j \sigma_k^i \, dW_t^k.$$

For the second-order term, we note that Σ is of dimension $n \times m$, Σ^T is of dimension $m \times n$, $H_{\mathbf{XX}}^i$ is of dimension $n \times n$, and hence $\Sigma \Sigma^T H_{\mathbf{XX}}^i$ is of dimension $n \times n$.

3.6 Notes and Further Readings

The example in section 3.2 comes from Arnold (1974). The setup in section 3.3 is influenced by McKean (1969), Gikhman and Skorokhod (1969), and Arnold (1974). We keep the term "nonanticipating" in the presentation, even though it is being replaced by the term "adapted," because we think it is intuitive. Sethi and Lehoczky (1981) provided an interesting comparison of the Ito integral with the Stratonovich integral when applied to finance theory.

We touch on martingales only briefly. For more on martingales, semi-martingales, and/or their relationship to stochastic integration, the reader is referred to Chung (1982), Elliot (1982), Protter (1990), and Billingsley (1995).

McKean's (1969) influence on the presentation of Ito's lemma is transparent. Besides McKean, Arnold (1974) and Friedman (1975) have detailed proofs for Ito's lemma. For the historical development of Ito integral and Ito's lemma, the reader is referred to Malliaris and Brock (1982).

The solutions of linear stochastic differential equations are known. See, for example, Arnold (1974, Chapter 8) and Karatzas and Shreve (1991, Chapter 5). We solve two of the most well-known stochastic differential equations: geometric Brownian motion and the Ornstein–Uhlenbeck process. The presentation of Euler's homogeneous differential equation follows Birkhoff and Rota (1978) and Hartman (2002), although most differential equation textbooks have a nice treatment of the subject. Our discussion on the heat equation, however, follows the setting in Marsden and Tromba (1976, p. 389). We make up the transformations so as to pave the way for a better understanding of the Black–Scholes option pricing formula.

The stochastic Solow equation was first developed by Merton (1975); related issues were addressed in Chang and Malliaris (1987) and Chang

(1988). There are many good texts for Black–Scholes formulation; we recommend Duffie (2001). The presentation here follows Black and Scholes's original *Journal of Political Economy* paper. Their economic argument for forming a risk-free portfolio is of fundamental importance to economics. As an illustration, we present the valuation of the opportunity to invest and the value of an investment project. For more on irreversible investment, the reader is referred to Dixit and Pindyck (1994) for a comprehensive coverage.

The budget equation for the consumption–portfolio rule is based on Merton (1971). However, we do not follow his derivation, because it implicitly assumes Ito's lemma. We give two derivations, one of which is borrowed from Karatzas and Shreve (1991).

4

Stochastic Dynamic Programming

4.1 Introduction

To solve a static, constrained optimization problem, we typically employ the Lagrange multiplier method. The solution to the problem is characterized by the first-order conditions of the Lagrange problem. To solve a stochastic, intertemporal optimization problem, the optimal control policy is characterized by the first-order conditions of the Bellman equation. In this chapter we shall introduce this method of dynamic optimization under uncertainty. One of the objectives is to make the reader feel as comfortable using the Bellman equation in dynamic models as using the Lagrange multiplier method in static models.

The chapter begins with a one-sector optimal growth model. We go through the derivation of the corresponding Bellman equation step by step to convey the mathematical reasoning behind this powerful tool using a real economic problem, not an abstract mathematical formulation. Then we examine the mathematical structure of the stochastic optimization problem, including the existence of the optimal control, the differentiability of the value function, the transversality condition, and the verification theorem. More importantly, we summarize the Bellman equation in a cookbook fashion to make it easy to use. To illustrate, we apply the Bellman equation to several well-known models, such as portfolio selection, index bonds, exhaustible resources, adjustment costs, and life insurance. To make the presentation self-contained, we provide a brief introduction to each topic.

Then, we extend the method from time-additive utility functions with a constant discount rate to a class of recursive utility functions. This class of utility functions has the characteristic that the discount factor is a function of past consumption. It is included in the presentation

113

because the corresponding Bellman equation is just as easy to use as the constant-discount-rate case. It broadens the applicability of the method. To illustrate its usefulness, we present a steady state analysis of a deterministic optimal growth model with recursive preferences. Through the phase diagram, we can see clearly how the recursivity (the degree of impatience) affects the steady state analysis.

4.2 Bellman Equation

4.2.1 Infinite-Horizon Problems

An Optimal Growth Problem

We begin with a one-sector neoclassical growth model in the tradition of Solow (1956). Let the per capita production function $f(k)$ be twice continuously differentiable, strictly increasing, and concave in k. As shown in the previous chapter, the stochastic Solow equation is

$$dk_t = \left[f(k_t) - c_t - \left(n - \sigma^2 \right) k_t \right] dt - \sigma k_t \, dz_t. \tag{4.1}$$

It states that the capital–labor ratio k_t (the state process) evolves according to a stochastic differential equation, once the consumption pattern c_t (the control law) is chosen. For a different control law, the state process follows a different law of motion. A stochastic differential equation that admits control variables in the drift or the variance is called a *controlled stochastic differential equation*, and the corresponding state process is called a *controlled diffusion process*. The control process is a feedback control in the sense that $c_t = c(t, k_t)$. The formal definition of an admissible control will be given later. For the moment, we assume that $c(t, k_t)$ is continuous.

If the uncertainty is due to technology, not population growth, then the corresponding Solow equation can be derived as follows. Assume population growth is nonstochastic, following $dL/L = n\,dt$, and the technical progress is Harrod-neutral (labor-augmenting), so that the efficiency unit of labor is $L^*(t) = A(t)L(t)$. Assume further that $A(t)$ follows a geometric Brownian motion

$$dA = aA\,dt + bA\,dz,$$

where a and b are constants. Then the dynamics of the efficiency unit of labor is

$$dL^* = L\,dA + A\,dL = (a+n)\,L^*\,dt + bL^*\,dz.$$

Let $k^* = K/L^*$ be the capital per efficiency unit of labor and $c^* = C/L^*$ be the consumption per efficiency unit of labor. Then the stochastic Solow equation becomes

$$dk_t^* = \left[f\left(k_t^*\right) - c_t^* - \left(a+n-b^2\right)k_t^* \right]dt - bk_t^*dz_t. \qquad (4.2)$$

Notice that the maintenance requirement is $(a+n-b^2)k^*$, whereas the maintenance requirement for (4.1) is $\left(n-\sigma^2\right)k$. Except for changing parameters and interpretations, there is no structural difference between equations (4.2) and (4.1).

Let $U(c)$ be the instantaneous utility function, which is of class C^2, and ρ be the discount rate. The optimal growth problem is

$$\max_{\{c_t\}} E \int_0^\infty e^{-\rho t}U(c_t)\,dt \qquad \text{s.t. (4.1)}, \ \text{with } k_0 = k \text{ given.} \qquad (4.3)$$

A similar problem can be formulated if the underlying dynamics is (4.2). For the purpose of exposition, we shall only work on (4.1) in what follows.

It is useful to introduce some notation that will greatly simplify the presentation. The operator $E_{s,k}^c$ stands for the conditional expectation given that $k_s = k$ and the control $\{c_t\}$ is used over the time interval of interest. In fact, we shall denote it by $E_{s,k}$, if the control $\{c_t\}$ and the underlying dynamics remain unchanged throughout the time interval (assuming there is no danger of confusion). If $s = 0$, then we further simplify it to E_k.

Let the *current value* of the indirect utility function (or the value function) at time s be

$$J(s,k) = \max_{\{c_t\}} E_{s,k} \int_s^\infty e^{-\rho(t-s)}U(c_t)\,dt \qquad \text{s.t. (4.1)}.$$

Lemma 4.1 *The value function* $J(s, k)$ *is independent of time* s, *and depends only on the initial condition* k.

Proof. By the change of variables $\tau = t - s$. Subject to (4.1),

$$J(s, k) = \max_{\{c_t\}} E_{s,k} \int_s^\infty e^{-\rho(t-s)} U(c_t)\, dt = \max_{\{c_{s+\tau}\}} E_k \int_0^\infty e^{-\rho\tau} U(c_{s+\tau})\, d\tau$$

$$= \max_{\{c_\tau\}} E_k \int_0^\infty e^{-\rho\tau} U(c_\tau)\, d\tau = J(0, k),$$

where the third equality is obtained by relabeling $\{c_{s+\tau}\}$ as $\{c_\tau\}$. ∎

The lemma says that the value function (in current value form) depends only on the initial condition $k_s = k$. Subsequently, the (current) value function is simplified to $J(k)$.

Derivation of the Bellman Equation

Recall that the fundamental concept in control theory is the *principle of optimality*, which usually appears in the form of a *recurrence equation*. For intertemporal optimization problem (4.3), the principle of optimality states that

$$J(k) = \max_{\substack{\{c_t\} \\ 0 \le t \le \Delta t}} E_k \left\{ \int_0^{\Delta t} e^{-\rho t} U(c_t)\, dt \right.$$

$$\left. + \max_{\substack{\{c_t\} \\ \Delta t \le t < \infty}} E_{\Delta t, k + \Delta k} \int_{\Delta t}^\infty e^{-\rho t} U(c_t)\, dt \right\}, \qquad (4.4)$$

where $k + \Delta k = k(\Delta t)$. Using the intermediate value theorem, the first integral of (4.4) can be simplified as, w.p.1,

$$\int_0^{\Delta t} e^{-\rho t} U(c_t)\, dt = e^{-\rho\theta\Delta t} U(c_{\theta\Delta t})\, \Delta t, \qquad (4.5)$$

where $\theta = \theta(\omega)$ and $0 \le \theta \le 1$ such that $\theta \Delta t \in [0, \Delta t]$ and $c_{\theta\Delta t} \to c$ as $\Delta t \to 0$. Using the change of variables $s = t - \Delta t$, the second integral of (4.4) becomes

$$\max_{\substack{\{c_t\} \\ \Delta t \le t < \infty}} E_{\Delta t, k+\Delta k} \int_{\Delta t}^{\infty} e^{-\rho t} U(c_t) \, dt$$

$$= \max_{\substack{\{c_{s+\Delta t}\} \\ 0 \le s < \infty}} E_{k+\Delta k} \int_{0}^{\infty} e^{-\rho(s+\Delta t)} U(c_{s+\Delta t}) \, ds$$

$$= e^{-\rho \Delta t} \max_{\substack{\{c_s\} \\ 0 \le s < \infty}} E_{k+\Delta k} \int_{0}^{\infty} e^{-\rho s} U(c_s) \, ds = e^{-\rho \Delta t} J(k + \Delta k).$$

The second equality of the above equation is obtained by relabeling $\{c_{s+\Delta t}\}$ as $\{c_s\}$. Now we can rewrite (4.4) as

$$0 = \max_{\substack{\{c_t\} \\ 0 \le t \le \Delta t}} E_k \left\{ e^{-\rho \theta \Delta t} U(c_{\theta \Delta t}) \Delta t + e^{-\rho \Delta t} J(k + \Delta k) - J(k) \right\}.$$

$$(4.6)$$

For sufficiently small Δt, we have $e^{-\rho \Delta t} = 1 - \rho \Delta t + o(\Delta t)$. Thus,

$$e^{-\rho \Delta t} J(k + \Delta k) - J(k)$$

$$= (1 - \rho \Delta t) J(k + \Delta k) - J(k) + o(\Delta t)$$

$$= [J(k + \Delta k) - J(k)] - \rho \, \Delta t \, J(k + \Delta k) + o(\Delta t).$$

Notice that if the value function is of class C^2, then, by Ito's lemma,

$$J(k + \Delta k) - J(k) = J'(k) \, \Delta k + \tfrac{1}{2} J''(k)(\Delta k)^2 + o(\Delta t).$$

Taking the conditional expectation, we have

$$E_k \left[J(k + \Delta k) - J(k) \right]$$

$$= \left\{ J'(k)[f(k) - c - (n - \sigma^2)k] + \tfrac{1}{2} J''(k) \sigma^2 k^2 \right\} \Delta t + o(\Delta t). \quad (4.7)$$

We first divide (4.6) by Δt, and then let $\Delta t \to 0$. Since, w.p.1, we have $k + \Delta k \to k$, $e^{-\rho \theta \Delta t} \to 1$, and $c_{\theta \Delta t} \to c$ as $\Delta t \to 0$, (4.6) is simplified as the following Bellman equation:

$$0 = \max_{c} \left\{ U(c) - \rho J(k) + [f(k) - c - (n - \sigma^2)k] J'(k) \right.$$

$$\left. + \tfrac{1}{2} \sigma^2 k^2 J''(k) \right\},$$

or, simply

$$0 = \max_{c}\{U(c) - \rho J(k) + \mathcal{A}^c J(k)\}, \qquad (4.8)$$

where $\mathcal{A}^c$ is the backward operator for a given c:

$$\mathcal{A}^c J(k) = \frac{1}{dt} E\left[J'(k)\, dk + \frac{1}{2} J''(k)(dk)^2\right].$$

In short, we have proved the following:

Theorem 4.2 *Assume the value function $J(k)$ exists and is of class C^2. Then a solution to (4.3) is a solution to the Bellman equation (4.8).*

The Bellman equation of a well-defined discounted infinite-horizon maximization problem such as (4.3) can be written down directly as follows. First, we write down the objective function $U(c)$. Next, we add $-\rho J(k)$. Then, we apply the backward operator to $J(k)$, where Ito's lemma is employed. Finally, we maximize the entire expression over all feasible control c and set the resulting value equal to zero. This yields the Bellman equation of a discounted infinite-horizon maximization problem.

Remark 4.1 *A neat result about continuous-time models under uncertainty is that the Bellman equation is, in effect, a deterministic differential equation because the expectation operator disappears. As a result, we are solving a (nonstochastic) differential equation. By contrast, in a discrete-time model under uncertainty, the Bellman equation for optimality is*

$$J(k_t) = \max_{c_t} E_{t,k_t}\left\{U(c_t) + \max_{\{c_{t+s}\}} E_{t+1,k_{t+1}} \sum_{s=1}^{\infty} \beta^s U(c_{t+s})\, dt\right\}$$

$$- \max_{c_t}\{U(c_t) + E_{t+1}\beta J(k_{t+1})\}, \qquad (4.9)$$

where β is the discount factor. This Bellman equation is a stochastic difference equation. In general we cannot get rid of the conditional expectation operator in (4.9).

General Formulation

Two factors are responsible for equation (4.8). One is the very nature of continuous time, which enables us to take the limit as $\Delta t \to 0$, i.e., w.p.1,

$$\frac{1}{\Delta t} \int_0^{\Delta t} e^{-\rho t} U(c_t)\, dt \to U(c) \qquad \text{as } \Delta t \to 0.$$

The argument is valid if c_t and $U(\cdot)$ are continuous. The other factor is equation (4.7) (and, implicitly, Ito's lemma), which enables us to *get rid of the conditional expectation operator* E_k, since

$$\frac{1}{\Delta t} E_k\left[J(k + \Delta k) - J(k)\right] \to \mathcal{A}^c J(k) \qquad \text{as } \Delta t \to 0$$

if $J(k)$ is of class C^2. These two factors remain valid when we move to higher-dimensional problems.

Based on the aforementioned two factors, we can extend our Bellman equation in two directions. First, we allow the law of motion governing the dynamics of the problem to be multidimensional, since the underlying reasoning is the application of Ito's lemma. Specifically, we let

$$d\mathbf{k}_t = \boldsymbol{\mu}(\mathbf{k}_t, \mathbf{c}_t)\, dt + \Sigma(\mathbf{k}_t, \mathbf{c}_t)\, d\mathbf{z}_t, \tag{4.10}$$

i.e., both the drift and the covariance matrix are functions of $\mathbf{k}_t$ and $\mathbf{c}_t$. Second, we allow the objective function to be a function of the state variable and the control variable, i.e., it is of the form $F(\mathbf{k}_t, \mathbf{c}_t)$, where $\mathbf{k}_t$ is the state variable, and $\mathbf{c}_t$ is the control variable. We also assume it is time-homogeneous, i.e., $F(\mathbf{k}_t, \mathbf{c}_t)$ does not depend on time t. Usually, $F(\mathbf{k}_t, \mathbf{c}_t)$ is assumed to be continuous and integrable, i.e.,

$$E_\mathbf{k} \int_0^\infty e^{-\rho t} F(\mathbf{k}_t, \mathbf{c}_t)\, dt < \infty.$$

However, economists tend to make $F(\mathbf{k}_t, \mathbf{c}_t)$ smoother. Then a typical infinite-horizon optimization problem can be formulated as

$$\max_{\{\mathbf{c}_t\}} E_\mathbf{k} \int_0^\infty e^{-\rho t} F(\mathbf{k}_t, \mathbf{c}_t)\, dt \qquad \text{s.t. (4.10).} \tag{4.11}$$

Similar to the backward operator defined in Chapter 3, let the backward operator of a given feedback control $\{\mathbf{c}_t\}$ be

$$
\mathcal{A}^{\mathbf{c}} = \sum_{i=1}^{n} \mu^i \left(\mathbf{k}, \mathbf{c}\right) \frac{\partial}{\partial k^i} + \frac{1}{2} \sum_{i=1}^{n} \sum_{j=1}^{n} \sigma^{ij} \left(\mathbf{k}, \mathbf{c}\right) \frac{\partial^2}{\partial k^i \partial k^j}.
$$

Theorem 4.3 *Assume the value function* $J\left(\mathbf{k}\right)$ *exists and is of* C^2. *Then a solution to* (4.11) *is a solution to the Bellman equation*

$$
0 = \max_{\mathbf{c}} \left\{ F\left(\mathbf{k}, \mathbf{c}\right) - \rho J\left(\mathbf{k}\right) + \mathcal{A}^{\mathbf{c}} J\left(\mathbf{k}\right) \right\}. \tag{4.12}
$$

Proof. See, for example, Kushner (1971, pp. 336–337). ∎

There are two main questions that need to be answered: When is the value function $J(\mathbf{k})$ of class C^2? When is the solution to (4.12) a solution to (4.11)? These questions and the transversality condition at infinity (TVC$_\infty$) will be discussed along with the verification theorem in the next two subsections.

Dynkin's Formula
Let

$$
\Phi\left(k\right) = E_k \int_0^{\infty} e^{-\rho t} U\left(c_t\right) dt
$$

be the discounted expected utility of a given control policy $\{c_t\}$ subject to (4.1). Note that $\Phi\left(k\right)$ may not be the optimal expected utility. Assume $\Phi\left(k\right) \in C^2$. Applying Ito's lemma to $\Phi\left(k\right)$, we have

$$
d\Phi = \left\{ [f(k) - c^* - (n - \sigma^2) k] \Phi'(k) + \frac{\sigma^2}{2} k^2 \Phi''(k) \right\} dt - \sigma k \Phi'(k) dz
$$

$$
= \mathcal{A}^c \Phi\left(k\right) dt - \sigma k \Phi'\left(k\right) dz.
$$

Integrating both sides of the above equation from 0 to t and then taking the conditional expectation, E_k, we arrive at

$$
E_k \Phi\left(k_t\right) - \Phi\left(k\right) = E_k \int_0^t \left\{ \mathcal{A}^c \Phi\left(k_s\right) \right\} ds. \tag{4.13}
$$

Equation (4.13) is the well-known Dynkin's formula, in current value form (at time t). The significance of the formula is that we can replace the average at a fixed time, $E_k \Phi(k_t)$, by the average over a fixed time interval, the right-hand side of (4.13).

The present value form of Dynkin's formula can be derived as follows. Since the present value of the expected utility is $e^{-\rho s} \Phi(k_s)$,

$$d[e^{-\rho s} \Phi(k_s)] = e^{-\rho s} [d\Phi(k_s) - \rho \Phi(k_s) ds].$$

Integrating both sides from time 0 to t, and taking conditional expectation E_k, we have

$$E_k[e^{-\rho t} \Phi(k_t)] - \Phi(k) = E_k \int_0^t e^{-\rho s} \{\mathcal{A}^c \Phi(k_s) ds - \rho \Phi(k_s)\} ds.$$

Notice that a discount factor $e^{-\rho s}$ applies to the right-hand side. On the left-hand side, the expected value of $\Phi(k_t)$ is discounted by a factor of $e^{-\rho t}$. Notice also that an extra term, $-\rho \Phi(k)$, is added to the right-hand side of the formula. If $\Phi(k) = J(k)$ the optimal discounted expected utility, then we have

$$E_k[e^{-\rho t} J(k_t)] - J(k) = E_k \int_0^t e^{-\rho s} \{\mathcal{A}^c J(k_s) ds - \rho J(k_s)\} ds.$$

In this case Dynkin's formula provides us a formula to compute the discounted expected utility at time t, $E_k[e^{-\rho t} J(k_t)]$.

Theorem 4.4 *(Dynkin's formula) Let*

$$\Phi(\mathbf{k}) = E_\mathbf{k} \int_0^\infty e^{-\rho t} F(\mathbf{k}_t, \mathbf{c}_t) dt$$

for a given control $\{\mathbf{c}_t\}$ subject to (4.10), and $\Phi(\mathbf{k})$ be of class C^2. Then

$$E_\mathbf{k}[e^{-\rho t} \Phi(\mathbf{k}_t)] - \Phi(\mathbf{k}) = E_\mathbf{k} \int_0^t e^{-\rho s} [\mathcal{A}^c \Phi(\mathbf{k}_s) - \rho \Phi(\mathbf{k}_s)] ds.$$

$$(4.14)$$

Proof. For a formal proof, see, for example, Knight (1981, p. 53) and Fleming and Soner (1993, p. 146) ∎

4.2.2 Verification Theorem

The first-order condition for (4.8) is

$$U'(c) = J'(k). \tag{4.15}$$

That is, in current values, the marginal utility of instantaneous consumption equals to the marginal utility of the capital–labor ratio. Most important, consumption is a function of wealth, i.e., $c^* = c^*(k)$. The conditions under which such an optimal control $\{c_t^*\}$ exists will be discussed later.

For the moment, we assume $\{c_t^*\}$ exists. Given this optimal control, we can find the value function through the differential equation

$$0 = U(c^*) - \rho J(k) + J'(k)[f(k) - c^* - (n - \sigma^2)k] + \frac{1}{2}J''(k)\sigma^2 k^2. \tag{4.16}$$

Since $c^* = c^*(k)$, equation (4.16) is a differential equation in k.

The Solution to (4.16) is the Expected Utility

As shown before, Dynkin's formula (4.13) is

$$E_k J(k_t) - J(k) = E_k \int_0^t \left\{ \mathcal{A}^{c^*} J(k_s) \right\} ds$$

$$= E_k \int_0^t \left[\rho J(k_s) - U(c_s^*) \right] ds,$$

where the last equality is obtained by using equation (4.16). Define a new function $V(t) = E_k J(k_t)$. Then the above equation becomes

$$V(t) - V(0) = \int_0^t \left[\rho V(s) - E_k U(c_s^*) \right] ds,$$

which is an integral equation. Convert the integral equation into a differential equation:

$$\frac{dV}{dt} = \rho V(t) - E_k U(c_t^*). \tag{4.17}$$

Equation (4.17) is a first-order ordinary differential equation whose solution (by the method of separation of variables) is of the form

$$V(t) = e^{\rho t} V(0) - e^{\rho t} \int_0^t e^{-\rho s} E_k U(c_s^*) \, ds.$$

Therefore, $V(0)$ satisfies

$$V(0) = e^{-\rho t} V(t) + \int_0^t e^{-\rho s} E_k U(c_s^*) \, ds.$$

This is true for all t. It must be true for $t \to \infty$, i.e.,

$$V(0) = \lim_{t \to \infty} e^{-\rho t} V(t) + \lim_{t \to \infty} \int_0^t e^{-\rho s} E_k U(c_s^*) \, ds,$$

if the limits exist. Assume TVC_∞,

$$\lim_{t \to \infty} E_k[e^{-\rho t} J(k_t)] = \lim_{t \to \infty} e^{-\rho t} V(t) = 0,$$

is satisfied. Then

$$V(0) = E_k \int_0^\infty e^{-\rho s} U(c_s^*) \, ds.$$

By definition, $V(0) = E_k J(k) = J(k)$. Thus, we have

$$J(k) = E_k \int_0^\infty e^{-\rho s} U(c_s^*) \, ds.$$

That is, the solution to (4.16) is indeed the optimal expected utility. This finding serves as a prelude to the verification theorem.

Verification Theorem

This theorem concerns the sufficiency of optimality for (4.11). The question is this: Suppose we have solved the Bellman equation (4.12) and obtained an optimal consumption path $\{c_t^*\}$. How do we verify that the consumption function thus obtained is indeed the optimal control policy for the control problem (4.11)? In the process of verification, we are also asking another question: How do we know that the solution to the differential equation (4.12) is the maximal expected utility? The answer to these questions is the verification theorem, which involves, among other things, TVC_∞:

$$\lim_{t \to \infty} E_{\mathbf{k}} \left[e^{-\rho t} J (\mathbf{k}_t) \right] = 0. \tag{4.18}$$

Theorem 4.5 *(Verification Theorem – Infinite-Horizon Case) Let $J(\mathbf{k})$, which is of class C^2, be the solution to (4.12) satisfying the transversality condition (4.18). Then:*

(a) For any admissible feedback control $\{\mathbf{c}_t\}$, we have

$$J (\mathbf{k}) \geq E_{\mathbf{k}} \int_0^\infty e^{-\rho t} F (\mathbf{k}_t, \mathbf{c}_t) \, dt.$$

(b) If there exists an admissible feedback control $\{\mathbf{c}_s^*\}$ such that

$$\mathbf{c}_s^* \in \arg \max_{\mathbf{c}_s} \{ F (\mathbf{k}_s, \mathbf{c}_s) - \rho J (\mathbf{k}_s) + \mathcal{A}^{\mathbf{c}} J (\mathbf{k}_s) \}$$

for all s, then

$$J (\mathbf{k}) = E_{\mathbf{k}} \int_0^\infty e^{-\rho t} F \left(\mathbf{k}_t, \mathbf{c}_t^* \right) dt.$$

Thus, $\{\mathbf{c}_t^*\}$ is optimal.

Proof. From Dynkin's formula, we have

$$E_k[e^{-\rho t} J(\mathbf{k}_t)] - J (\mathbf{k}) = E_k \int_0^t e^{-\rho s} \left[\mathcal{A}^c J (\mathbf{k}_s) - \rho J (\mathbf{k}) \right] ds.$$

Since $F (\mathbf{k}_s, \mathbf{c}_s) - \rho J (\mathbf{k}_s) + \mathcal{A}^{\mathbf{c}} J (\mathbf{k}_s) \leq 0$ for any admissible $\{\mathbf{c}_s\}$, we have

$$J (\mathbf{k}) \geq E_k \int_0^t e^{-\rho s} F (\mathbf{k}_s, \mathbf{c}_s) \, ds + E_k \left[e^{-\rho t} J (\mathbf{k}_t) \right]. \tag{4.19}$$

Then (a) follows from (4.18).

To prove (b), we note that, by the definition of $\mathbf{c}_s^*$,

$$F \left(\mathbf{k}_s, \mathbf{c}_s^* \right) - \rho J (\mathbf{k}_s) + \mathcal{A}^{\mathbf{c}^*} J (\mathbf{k}_s) = 0 \qquad \forall s. \tag{4.20}$$

Then Dynkin's formula implies that

$$J(\mathbf{k}) = E_{\mathbf{k}} \int_0^t e^{-\rho s} F\left(\mathbf{k}_s, \mathbf{c}_s^*\right) ds + E_k[e^{-\rho t} J(\mathbf{k}_t)].$$

Again, (4.18) implies (b). ∎

Thus, to ascertain that a control is optimal, three conditions are to be verified: that there is a solution to the Bellman equation (4.12), and that the equality (4.20) and the transversality condition (4.18) are satisfied. In other words, the verification theorem reduces the optimal stochastic control problem to two other problems and one assumption. The first problem is to solve the differential equation (4.12) for $J(\mathbf{k})$, and the second is to find the optimal control $\mathbf{c}_t^*$ so that equality (4.20) holds. The latter is usually obtained from the first-order conditions of the Bellman equation. The assumption is TVC_∞. Note that TVC_∞ is *sufficient*, but *not necessary* for optimality. Making it a necessary condition has been one of the major research goals in the area. See, for example, Benveniste and Scheinkman (1982), which makes TVC_∞ a necessary condition in the deterministic case. See also Michel (1982, 1990), Leung (1991), and Kamihigashi (2001).

4.2.3 Finite-Horizon Problems

Now suppose the problem is of the form

$$\max_{\{c_t\}} E \int_0^T e^{-\rho t} U(c_t)\, dt + B(T, k_T) \qquad \text{s.t. (4.1), with } k_0 = k \text{ given,}$$

where T is the planning horizon and $B(T, k_T)$ stands for the *bequest function* at the end of the planning horizon T.

The derivation of the Bellman equation mimics the infinite-horizon case. Let the *present* value of the indirect utility function at time t be

$$J(t, k_t) = \max_{\{c_s\}} E_{t,k_t} \int_t^T e^{-\rho s} U(c_s)\, ds + B(T, k_T) \qquad \text{s.t. (4.1).}$$

The nice result in an infinite-horizon model (that the value function of the optimization problem is independent of t, and depends only on the initial stock) is no longer valid in the finite-horizon case. This is because changing variables will also change the length of the horizon. In fact, some texts prefer the notation $J(T - t, k)$ for the value function, because it emphasizes the actual length of the horizon, $T - t$. See, for example, Kushner (1971, Chapter 11).

Again, invoking the principle of optimality, we have, in present value

$$J(t, k_t) = \max_{\substack{\{c_{t+s}\} \\ 0 \leq s < \Delta t}} E_{t,k_t} \left\{ \int_t^{t+\Delta t} e^{-\rho s} U(c_s) \, ds \right.$$

$$+ \max_{\substack{\{c_{t+s}\} \\ \Delta t \leq s \leq T - t}} E_{t+\Delta t, k_t + \Delta k} \int_{t+\Delta t}^T e^{-\rho s} U(c_s) \, ds + B(T, k_T) \left. \right\}.$$

Using the intermediate value theorem

$$\int_t^{t+\Delta t} e^{-\rho s} U(c_s) \, ds = e^{-\rho(t+\theta \Delta t)} U(c_{t+\theta \Delta t}) \, \Delta t,$$

we arrive at

$$0 = \max_{\substack{\{c_{t+s}\} \\ 0 \leq s \leq \Delta t}} E_{t,k_t} \left\{ e^{-\rho(t+\theta \Delta t)} U(c_{t+\theta \Delta t}) \, \Delta t \right.$$

$$+ J(t + \Delta t, k_t + \Delta k) - J(t, k_t) \left. \right\}. \qquad (4.21)$$

By Ito's lemma,

$$J(t + \Delta t, k_t + \Delta k) - J(t, k_t)$$

$$= J_t \Delta t + J_k \Delta k + \frac{1}{2} J_{kk} (\Delta k)^2 + o(\Delta t),$$

where J_t, J_k, and J_{kk} are partial derivatives of $J(t, k_t)$. Substituting the above equation into (4.21), dividing (4.21) by Δt, and then letting $\Delta t \to 0$, we have

$$0 = \max_{c_t} \{ e^{-\rho t} U(c_t) + J_t(t, k_t) + \mathcal{A}^c J(t, k_t) \}. \qquad (4.22)$$

The counterpart of TVC_∞ is the boundary condition

$$J(T, k_T) = B(T, k_T).$$

In the absence of a bequest motive, the model assumes $J(T, k_T) = 0$.

Remark 4.2 *It may appear that the only difference between the finite-horizon Bellman equation and the infinite-horizon Bellman equation is that J_t replaces $-\rho J$ in the infinite-horizon case. The truth is more subtle than that. To solve the optimization problem, we have to solve the corresponding Bellman equation. Notice that equation (4.22) is a partial differential equation, while equation (4.8) is an ordinary differential equation. It is generally harder to find a closed-form solution to a partial differential equation than an ordinary differential equation. If solvability is an issue, then an infinite-horizon model may be preferred. On the other hand, a discrete-time finite-horizon model makes backward induction possible, but an infinite-horizon model does not. For example, the classical demand for life insurance à la Fischer (1973) is obtained by using backward induction.*

The general formulation of a finite-horizon problem goes as follows. Let the controlled diffusion process be

$$d\mathbf{k}_t = \boldsymbol{\mu}(t, \mathbf{k}_t, \mathbf{c}_t)\, dt + \Sigma(t, \mathbf{k}_t, \mathbf{c}_t)\, d\mathbf{z}_t, \qquad (4.23)$$

i.e., both the drift and the covariance matrix are functions of time. Let the time-dependent backward operator of a given feedback control $\{\mathbf{c}_t\}$ be

$$\mathcal{A}^{\mathbf{c}}(s) = \sum_{i=1}^{n} \mu^i(s, \mathbf{k}_s, \mathbf{c}_s) \frac{\partial}{\partial k^i} + \frac{1}{2} \sum_{i=1}^{n} \sum_{j=1}^{n} \sigma^{ij}(s, \mathbf{k}_s, \mathbf{c}_s) \frac{\partial^2}{\partial k^i \partial k^j}.$$

Then the finite-horizon optimization problem becomes

$$\max_{\{\mathbf{c}_s\}} E_{t,\mathbf{k}_t} \int_t^T F(s, \mathbf{k}_s, \mathbf{c}_s)\, ds + B(T, \mathbf{k}_T) \qquad \text{s.t. (4.23), (4.24)}$$

where the objective function $F(t, \mathbf{k}_t, \mathbf{c}_t)$ is continuous in all variables and is integrable. The fact that the time component enters $F(t, \mathbf{k}_t, \mathbf{c}_t)$ allows the model to go beyond the case of a constant subjective discount rate.

Theorem 4.6 *Assume the value function $J(t, \mathbf{k}_t)$ exists and is of class $C^{1,2}$. Then a solution to (4.24) is a solution to the Bellman equation*

$$0 = \max_{\mathbf{c}_t}\{F(t, \mathbf{k}_t, \mathbf{c}_t) + J_t(t, \mathbf{k}_t) + \mathcal{A}^{\mathbf{c}}(t) J(t, \mathbf{k}_t)\}. \qquad (4.25)$$

Proof. See Kushner (1971, p. 334). ∎

Theorem 4.7 *(Dynkin's Formula) For a given control* $\{c_t\}$*, let*

$$\Phi(t, \mathbf{k}_t) = E_{t, \mathbf{k}_t} \int_t^T F(s, \mathbf{k}_s, \mathbf{c}_s)\, ds + B(T, \mathbf{k}_T)$$

subject to (4.10), and $\Phi(t, \mathbf{k})$ *be of class* $C^{1,2}$*. Then, for* $s < t$*,*

$$E_{s, \mathbf{k}} \Phi(t, \mathbf{k}_t) - \Phi(s, \mathbf{k}) = E_{s, \mathbf{k}} \int_s^t [\Phi_\tau(\tau, \mathbf{k}_\tau) + \mathcal{A}^c(\tau)\Phi(\tau, \mathbf{k}_\tau)]\, d\tau.$$

Proof. For a formal proof, see, for example, Knight (1981, p. 53) and Fleming and Soner (1993, p. 128), or do it as an exercise. ∎

Theorem 4.8 *(Verification Theorem – Finite-Horizon Case) Let* $J(t, \mathbf{k}_t)$*, which is of class* $C^{1,2}$*, be the solution to (4.24) satisfying* $J(T, \mathbf{k}_T) = B(T, \mathbf{k}_T)$*. Then:*

(a) For any admissible feedback control $\{c_t\}$*, we have*

$$J(t, \mathbf{k}_t) \geq E_{t, \mathbf{k}_t} \int_t^T F(s, \mathbf{k}_s, \mathbf{c}_s)\, dt + B(T, \mathbf{k}_T).$$

(b) If there is an admissible feedback control $\{c_s^*\}$ *such that*

$$\mathbf{c}_s^* \in \arg\max_{\mathbf{c}_s}\{F(s, \mathbf{k}_s, \mathbf{c}_s) + J_s(s, \mathbf{k}_s) + \mathcal{A}^c(s)J(s, \mathbf{k}_s)\} \qquad \forall s,$$

then

$$J(t, \mathbf{k}_t) = E_{t, \mathbf{k}_t} \int_t^T F\big(s, \mathbf{k}_s, \mathbf{c}_s^*\big)\, ds + B(T, \mathbf{k}_T).$$

Thus, $\{c_t^*\}$ *is optimal.*

Proof. See Fleming and Rishel (1975, pp. 159–160). ∎

4.2.4 Existence and Differentiability of the Value Function

Admissible Controls

To set up a static optimization problem, the set of choice variables must be specified so that we can choose the "best" solution within the set. For example, in the consumer problem we have the budget set. The optimal solution and the indirect utility function would be different if the budget sets were different. Similarly, to set up a control problem, we need to specify the set of admissible controls such that the stochastic differential equation (4.23) (or (4.10) if autonomous) has a solution.

Definition 4.9 *A function* $f(\mathbf{x})$ *is called Lipschitzian on a subset S of* $\mathbb{R}^n$ *if there is a constant M such that for all* $\mathbf{x}, \mathbf{y} \in S$

$$|f(\mathbf{x}) - f(\mathbf{y})| \leq M |\mathbf{x} - \mathbf{y}|.$$

By definition, a Lipschitzian function is continuous. A differentiable function with bounded derivatives always satisfies the Lipschitz condition. However, a Lipschitzian function may not be differentiable. The best-known example is $f(x) = |x|$.

Theorem 4.10 *(Ito) Suppose that the stochastic differential equation*

$$d\mathbf{X}_t = \mu(t, \mathbf{X}_t)\,dt + \sigma(t, \mathbf{X}_t)\,dz_t \tag{4.26}$$

with an initial distribution $\mathbf{X}_0 = a$ *is given, where* $\mu(t, \mathbf{X}_t)$ *and* $\sigma(t, \mathbf{X}_t)$ *satisfy the following two properties: there exists a constant M such that*

(a) $\forall t \in [0, T]$, $\forall \mathbf{x} \in \mathbb{R}^n$, *and* $\forall \mathbf{y} \in \mathbb{R}^n$,

$$|\mu(t, \mathbf{x}) - \mu(t, \mathbf{y})| + |\sigma(t, \mathbf{x}) - \sigma(t, \mathbf{y})| \leq M |\mathbf{x} - \mathbf{y}|,$$

(b) $\forall t \in [0, T]$ *and* $\forall \mathbf{x} \in \mathbb{R}^n$,

$$|\mu(t, \mathbf{x})|^2 + |\sigma(t, \mathbf{x})|^2 \leq M(1 + |\mathbf{x}|^2).$$

Then equation (4.26) has, on $[0, T]$, *a unique solution* $\mathbf{x}_t$, *which is continuous w.p.1 and satisfies the initial condition* $\mathbf{x}_0 = a$. *It is unique in the sense that any other solution would have the same continuous sample paths w.p.1.*

Proof. See Arnold (1974, pp. 106–111). ∎

Conditions (a) in Ito's theorem is a Lipschitz condition, while condition (b) is called the *growth condition*. The latter assumption bounds $\mu(t, \mathbf{x})$ and $\sigma(t, \mathbf{x})$ uniformly with respect to $t \in [0, T]$ and allows at most linear increase of these functions with respect to $\mathbf{x}$. In the case of an autonomous stochastic differential equation, Ito's theorem is valid if

$$|\mu\,(\mathbf{x}) - \mu\,(\mathbf{y})| + |\sigma\,(\mathbf{x}) - \sigma\,(\mathbf{y})| \leq M\,|\mathbf{x} - \mathbf{y}|,$$

i.e., we need only the Lipschitz condition. (See Arnold (1974, Corollary 6.3.5)).

Before we formally define an admissible control, we need the following setting. Let $(\Omega,\,\mathcal{F},\,P)$ be a filtered probability space with filtration $\{\mathcal{F}_t\}$. Assume the state variables take values in $G \subset \mathbb{R}^n$ and assume the control variables take values in $U \subset \mathbb{R}^m$. The state process is such that $\mathbf{k}_t$ is adapted to $\{\mathcal{F}_t\}$, that the sample paths of $\mathbf{k}_t$ are right-continuous and have left-hand limit, and that $\mathbf{k}_0 = \mathbf{k}$.

Definition 4.11 *A control process* $\mathbf{c}_t = \mathbf{c}\,(t,\mathbf{k}_t)$ *is admissible if it is adapted to* $\{\mathcal{F}_t\}$ *and satisfies a Lipschitz condition on the closure of* $[0,\,T] \times G$.

Let $\mathcal{V}$ be the class of admissible controls. It is shown in Fleming and Rishel (1975, p. 156) that, for a given admissible control, the controlled stochastic differential equation (4.23) (or (4.10) if autonomous) with $\mathbf{k}_0 = \mathbf{k}$ has a unique solution. Formally, our optimization problems discussed earlier should be maximized over $\{\mathbf{c}_t\} \in \mathcal{V}$.

One-Dimensional Controlled Processes
One-dimensional controlled processes deserve a special mention. Mathematically, taking advantage of the specific nature of one-dimensional processes, we have stronger results than in the multidimensional case. Economically, many applied models are set in one dimension. These stronger results should be useful.

Let $\mu\,(k,\mathbf{c})$, $\sigma\,(k,\mathbf{c})$, and $F\,(k,\mathbf{c})$ be real-valued functions with $\mathbf{c} \in U$ and $k \in (-\infty,\infty)$. Assume $\mu\,(k,\mathbf{c})$, $\sigma\,(k,\mathbf{c})$, and $F\,(k,\mathbf{c})$ are *bounded* and satisfy a Lipschitz condition. In addition, the controlled process is uniformly nondegenerate, i.e., $\sigma\,(k,\mathbf{c}) \geq \delta$ on $\mathbb{R} \times U$ for some constant $\delta > 0$. Then we have the following theorem.

Theorem 4.12 *Suppose the initial condition* $k \in [a,b]$. *Under the aforementioned assumptions, the value function* $J\,(k)$ *exists and is of class* $C^2\,[a,b]$, *and* $J''\,(k)$ *satisfies a Lipschitz condition on* $[a,b]$. *For all*

$k \in [a, b]$, *the Bellman equation*

$$0 = \max_{\mathbf{c}} \left\{ F(k, \mathbf{c}) - \rho J(k) + \mu(k, \mathbf{c}) J'(k) + \tfrac{1}{2} \sigma(k, \mathbf{c}) J''(k) \right\}$$

$$(4.27)$$

is satisfied. Furthermore, $J(k)$ is the unique solution of (4.27) *in the class of functions $C^2[a, b]$.*

Proof. See Krylov (1980, pp. 24–32). ∎

It should be emphasized that the control variable is included in the instantaneous variance $\sigma(k, \mathbf{c})$. The only requirement is that $\sigma(k, \mathbf{c})$ be nondegenerate. This result does not extend to higher-dimensional cases, especially $n \geq 3$. The problem arises from the solvability of higher-dimensional differential equations. For details and references, see Krylov (1980, p. 43).

The condition $\sigma(k, \mathbf{c}) \geq \delta$ on $\mathbb{R} \times U$ is employed to ensure that the coefficient of $J''(k)$ is bounded away from zero, so that the Bellman equation (4.27) is nondegenerate, i.e., there is no singularity. Thus, the theorem has its limits. For example, a geometric Brownian motion would fail this condition. In that case, we cannot quote the theorem directly, but must derive the value function using other methods, as we shall see in the next chapter.

Multidimensional Controlled Processes
Let $Q = [0, T] \times G$, $Q_0 = [0, T] \times \mathbb{R}^n$, and $\bar{Q}$ stand for the closure of Q. The major assumptions are:

(1) G is *bounded*, and its boundary is a manifold of class C^2.
(2) U is *compact*.
(3) The objective function $F(t, \mathbf{k}_t, \mathbf{c}_t)$ is of class $C^1(\bar{Q}_0 \times U)$.
(4) The bequest function $B(T, \mathbf{k}_T)$ is of class $C^2(\bar{G})$.
(5) The drift $\mu(t, \mathbf{k}_t, \mathbf{c}_t)$ is of class $C^1(\bar{Q}_0 \times U)$.
(6) The covariance matrix $\Sigma(t, \mathbf{k}_t)$ is of class $C^{1,2}(\bar{Q}_0)$ and is *invertible* for all $(t, \mathbf{k})$ in $\bar{Q}_0$.

Theorem 4.13 *Under assumptions (1)–(6), the value function $J(t, \mathbf{k})$ exists uniquely and is of class $C^{1,2}(Q)$ and continuous on $\bar{Q}$. Moreover,* *there exists an optimal feedback control law* $\mathbf{c}^*$ *satisfying*

$$\mathbf{c}_t^* \in \arg\max_{\mathbf{c}_t}\{F(t, \mathbf{k}_t, \mathbf{c}_t) + J_t(t, \mathbf{k}_t) + \mathcal{A}^{\mathbf{c}}(t) J(t, \mathbf{k}_t)\} \qquad \forall t$$

almost everywhere in Q.

Proof. See Fleming and Rishel (1975, Chapter 6, Theorem 6.1 and Theorem 6.3). ■

Most economic models assume the underlying parameters are smooth. In that context, assumptions (3)–(6) are mild. On the other hand, assumptions (1) and (2) are problematic. In financial economics, the assumption that the control variables take values in a compact set is a big issue. This is because the capital market is assumed *frictionless* in the sense that there are no transactions costs and no taxes and an investor can buy or sell as many shares as she pleases. In other words, the control variable is unbounded, which violates the compactness of U. To overcome this difficulty, Cox and Huang (1989) developed a martingale representation method that transforms the portfolio problem into a static optimization problem. The interested reader is referred to their paper.

As in the one-dimensional case, condition (6) ensures that the coefficient of the second-order term of $\mathcal{A}^{\mathbf{c}}(t) J(t, \mathbf{k})$ is bounded away from zero, so that the differential equation (4.25) has no singularity. Notice that the diffusion coefficient of (4.25), $\Sigma(t, \mathbf{k}_t)$, is assumed *not* to depend on the control variable $\mathbf{c}_t$. In other words, *the control variable enters the drift only*. This means that if your economic model has more than two state variables, and if the control variable also appears in the variance term, then you can *not* be sure that the value function with the desired properties actually exists.

Finally, we note that the control $\mathbf{c}_t$ in Theorem 4.13 may be discontinuous, which presents problems for economists, especially when we try to do comparative dynamics. To ensure continuity, we need additional assumptions:

(7) The set U is *convex*.
(8) The drift is *linear* in $\mathbf{c}_t$:

$$\mu(t, \mathbf{k}_t, \mathbf{c}_t) = \mathbf{a}(t, \mathbf{k}_t) + b(t, \mathbf{k}_t)_{n \times m}\, \mathbf{c}_t.$$

(9) The objective function $F(t, \mathbf{k}_t, \mathbf{c}_t)$ is of class C^2, and the eigenvalues of the Hessian matrix of $F(t, \mathbf{k}_t, \mathbf{c}_t)$ with respect to $\mathbf{c}_t$ are bounded from above by some constant $-\gamma$, where $\gamma > 0$.

Theorem 4.14 *Let $Q' = [0, T'] \times G'$, where $T' < T$ and G' is bounded, and $J(t, \mathbf{k})$ be of class $C^{1,2}(\bar{Q}')$. Under assumptions (1)–(9), the optimal feedback control $\mathbf{c}(t, \cdot)$ satisfies a Lipschitz condition on $\bar{G}'$, uniformly for $t \in [0, T']$.*

Proof. See Fleming and Rishel (1975, Chapter 6, Theorem 6.4). ∎

The constant γ in condition (9) plays two roles in the proof. First, it says that the Hessian matrix is negative definite because it has only negative eigenvalues. This implies that the objective function is strictly concave. Second, it is shown to be a component of the Lipschitz constant for $\mathbf{c}(t, \mathbf{k})$. It is interesting to note that many economic problems, either by nature or by design, do satisfy the conditions that U is convex and that the drift is linear in the control variables. Therefore, this result is quite natural to economists as long as Theorem 4.13 holds. For more mathematical details, the reader is referred to the discussion in Fleming and Rishel (1975, p. 172).

4.3 Economic Applications

In what follows we concentrate on the application of the Bellman equation to various economic problems. Questions related to the functional form of the value function, however, are deferred to the next chapter.

4.3.1 Consumption and Portfolio Rules

An Infinite-Horizon Model
This is based on Merton (1971). The presentation here, however, is set in an infinite-horizon framework. Assume there are $n - 1$ risky assets and one risk-free asset. The risk-free asset pays a constant rate r, while the the return of i-th risky asset follows a geometric Brownian motion

$$dP_i = \mu_i P_i \, dt + \sigma_i P_i \, dz_i, \qquad i = 1, 2, \ldots, n - 1,$$

with $(dz_i)(dz_j) = 0$ if $i \neq j$. Let s_i be the share of wealth invested in the i-th risky asset. As shown in Chapter 3, the consumer's budget equation is

$$dW = \left[\sum_{i=1}^{n-1} s_i (\mu_i - r) W + (rW - c) \right] dt + \sum_{i=1}^{n-1} s_i \sigma_i W dz_i. \quad (4.28)$$

Then the consumer–investor's problem is

$$\max_{\{c,s_i\}} E \int_0^\infty e^{-\rho t} U(c_t) dt \qquad \text{s.t. (4.28) with } W_0 = W \text{ given.}$$

Denote the current value of the value function by $J(W)$. The Bellman equation is

$$0 = \max_{c,s_i} \left\{ U(c) - \rho J(W) + \left[\sum_{i=1}^{n-1} s_i (\mu_i - r) W + (rW - c) \right] J'(W) \right.$$
$$\left. + \frac{1}{2} \sum_{i=1}^{n-1} s_i^2 \sigma_i^2 W^2 J''(W) \right\}.$$

It should be noted that if μ_i or σ_i are functions of P_i, i.e., $\mu_i = \mu_i(P)$ or $\sigma_i = \sigma_i(P)$, then the value function is a function of $(W, P_1, \ldots, P_{n-1})$. In that case, more terms will be added to the Bellman equation.

The optimal consumption/portfolio rules are governed by

$$U'(c) = J'(W) \qquad (4.29)$$

and

$$(\mu_i - r) W J'(W) + s_i \sigma_i^2 W^2 J''(W) = 0, \qquad i = 1, 2, \ldots, n-1.$$

The first equation says that consumption is so chosen that, in current values, the marginal utility of consumption equals the marginal utility of wealth, which is a standard result. The second equation determines the optimal ratio for each risky asset:

$$s_i = \frac{\mu_i - r}{\sigma_i^2} \left[-\frac{J'(W)}{W J''(W)} \right], \qquad i = 1, 2, \ldots, n-1. \quad (4.30)$$

The term in the bracket is the reciprocal of the Arrow–Pratt relative risk aversion. Thus, the equation says that, if the *indirect* utility function has a constant relative risk aversion, then the optimal share of wealth invested in the risky asset is constant over time. We shall study in the next chapter if and when the indirect utility function exhibits constant relative risk aversion.

Wealth Effect

Is consumption an increasing function of wealth? To answer this question, we need the following

Lemma 4.15 *If $U(c)$ is concave in c, then $J(W)$ is concave in W.*

Proof. This mimics the proof in the basic consumer theory, because the budget equation is linear in the state and control variables. However, it is easier to use the budget equation

$$dW(t) = \sum_{i}^{n} N_i(t) dP_i(t) - c(t) dt$$

than (4.28). Let $(\{c^j(t)\}, \{N_i^j(t)\})$ be the optimal solution to the portfolio problem when the initial wealth is W^j, $j = 1, 2$. For $0 \leq \lambda \leq 1$, let $W^\lambda = \lambda W^1 + (1 - \lambda)W^2$. Since $(\{c^j(t)\}, \{N_i^j(t)\})$, $j = 1, 2$, is a solution to a portfolio problem, it satisfies the budget equation

$$d(W^j(t)) = \sum_{i=1}^{n} N_i^j(t) dP_i(t) - c^j(t) dt.$$

Let $c^\lambda(t) = \lambda c^1(t) + (1 - \lambda)c^2(t)$ and $N_i^\lambda(t) = \lambda N_i^1(t) + (1 - \lambda)N_i^2(t)$. Then the control variables $(c^\lambda(t), \{N_i^\lambda(t)\})$ satisfy the budget equation

$$dW^\lambda(t) = \sum_{i=1}^{n} N_i^\lambda(t) dP_i(t) - c^\lambda(t) dt.$$

Therefore,

$$E \int_0^\infty e^{-\rho t} U\left(\lambda c_t^1 + (1 - \lambda) c_t^2\right) dt \leq J(W^\lambda) = J(\lambda W^1 + (1 - \lambda)W^2).$$

Since $U(c)$ is concave,

$$U\left(\lambda c_t^1 + (1 - \lambda) c_t^2\right) \geq \lambda U\left(c_t^1\right) + (1 - \lambda) U\left(c_t^2\right).$$

It follows that

$$J(\lambda W^1 + (1-\lambda)W^2) \geq E \int_0^\infty e^{-\rho t} \left[\lambda U\left(c_t^1\right) + (1-\lambda) U\left(c_t^2\right) \right] dt$$

$$= \lambda J(W^1) + (1-\lambda)J(W^2).$$

This proves the concavity of $J(W)$. ∎

Then, from (4.29), we have

$$U''(c)\frac{\partial c}{\partial W} = J''(W).$$

The concavity of $J(W)$ implies that $\partial c/\partial W > 0$: consumption is positively related to wealth. From (4.30), the wealth effect on the share of each risky asset is zero if the indirect utility function exhibits constant absolute risk aversion. It becomes positive if the indirect utility function exhibits decreasing absolute risk aversion.

Mutual Fund Theorem

More can be said about the optimal portfolio $(s_1, s_2, \ldots, s_n)$. From $\sum s_i = 1$ we know that $(s_1, s_2, \ldots, s_n)$ lies in a hyperplane in $\mathbb{R}^n$. If, in addition, the indirect utility function exhibits constant relative risk aversion α, then we can prove a *mutual fund theorem*. Let $g_i = (\mu_i - r)/\sigma_i^2$. Then equation (4.30) becomes

$$s_i = (1/\alpha) g_i, \qquad i = 1, 2, \ldots, n-1.$$

By definition,

$$s_n = 1 - \sum_{i=1}^{n-1} s_i = 1 - \frac{1}{\alpha}\sum_{i=1}^{n-1} g_i.$$

Then the algebraic identity

$$(s_1, s_2, \ldots, s_n) = (0, 0, \ldots, 0, 1) + \frac{1}{\alpha}\left(g_1, g_2, \ldots, g_{n-1}, -\sum_{i=1}^{n-1} g_i \right),$$

tells us that the vector $(s_1, s_2, \ldots, s_n)$ is spanned by two linearly independent vectors $e_n = (0, \ldots, 0, 1)$ and $(g_1, g_2, \ldots, g_{n-1}, -\sum_{i=1}^{n-1} g_i)$. In other words, $(s_1, s_2, \ldots, s_n)$ lies in a two-dimensional plane! Since each vector is a mixture of assets, it is a mutual fund. The finding says that the optimal portfolio can be formed from a linear combination of only *two* funds.

4.3.2 Index Bonds

This is based on Fischer (1975). The issue Fischer raised was that, at that time, no index bonds were available in the United States. Inflation-indexed bonds provide insurance against sharp surges in prices. In the decade of high inflation rates, the absence of index bonds in the U.S. market is puzzling. To explain this phenomenon, it seems appropriate to study the demand for index bonds. It should be noted that, in the 1990s, inflation-indexed bonds were offered in the U.S. In the presentation, we focus on a positive quantity of index bonds, in contrast to Fischer's analysis, which assumes the optimal demand for index bonds was zero. A major question is this: Is it true that index bonds, as insurance against inflation, command a premium over nominal bonds?

A Three-Asset Model
Assume the consumer can invest in three assets: index bonds, equity, and nominal bonds. The general price level follows a geometric Brownian motion

$$\frac{dP}{P} = \pi \, dt + \sigma_1 \, dz_1. \tag{4.31}$$

The index bond (asset 1, indexed by Q_1) guarantees a real rate of return r_1 so that the nominal rate of return is

$$\frac{dQ_1}{Q_1} = r_1 + \frac{dP}{P} = (r_1 + \pi) \, dt + \sigma_1 \, dz_1 = R_1 \, dt + \sigma_1 \, dz_1,$$

where $R_1 = r_1 + \pi$ is the *expected* nominal rate of return. Assume the nominal return on equity (asset 2, indexed by Q_2) follows

$$\frac{dQ_2}{Q_2} = R_2 \, dt + \sigma_2 \, dz_2,$$

with $(dz_1)(dz_2) = \lambda \, dt$, where λ is the correlation coefficient of dz_1 and dz_2. Finally, assume the nominal return on nominal bonds (asset 3, indexed by Q_3 with a specified nominal rate R_3) follows

$$\frac{dQ_3}{Q_3} = R_3 \, dt.$$

By Ito's lemma,

$$d\left(\frac{Q_3}{P}\right) = \frac{Q_3}{P}\frac{dQ_3}{Q_3} - \frac{Q_3}{P}\frac{dP}{P} - \frac{Q_3}{P}\frac{dP}{P}\frac{dQ_3}{Q_3} + \frac{Q_3}{P}\left(\frac{dP}{P}\right)^2,$$

which implies, using $(dP)(dQ_3) = 0$,

$$\frac{d(Q_3/P)}{Q_3/P} = \frac{dQ_3}{Q_3} - \frac{dP}{P} + \left(\frac{dP}{P}\right)^2 = \left(R_3 - \pi + \sigma_1^2\right)dt - \sigma_1 dz_1.$$

In other words, the real rate of return to nominal bonds is

$$r_3 = R_3 - \pi + \sigma_1^2.$$

Note that the real rate of return is *not* just the difference between the nominal rate and the inflation rate, $R_3 - \pi$.

Let s_i, $i = 1, 2$, be respectively the shares of wealth invested in the index bonds and in equity. Then the consumer's budget equation becomes

$$dW = \left[\sum_{i=1}^{2} s_i(R_i - R_3)W + R_3 W - Pc\right]dt + \sum_{i=1}^{2} s_i \sigma_i W dz_i.$$

$$(4.32)$$

And the consumer–investor's problem is

$$\max_{\{c, s_i\}} E \int_0^\infty e^{-\rho t} U(c_t)\, dt \quad \text{s.t. (4.31) and (4.32), with } W_0 = W \text{ given.}$$

Let the indirect utility function be $J(W, P)$. Then the Bellman equation is

$$0 = \max_{c, s_i} \left\{ U(c) - \rho J(W, P) + \left(\sum_{i=1}^{2} s_i(R_i - R_3)W + R_3 W - PC\right)\right.$$

$$\times J_W + \pi P J_P + \tfrac{1}{2}\left(s_1^2 \sigma_1^2 + 2\lambda s_1 s_2 \sigma_1 \sigma_2 + s_2^2 \sigma_2^2\right) W^2 J_{WW}$$

$$\left. + \tfrac{1}{2}\sigma_1^2 P^2 J_{PP} + \left(s_1 \sigma_1^2 + \lambda s_2 \sigma_1 \sigma_2\right) W P J_{WP}\right\}.$$

The first-order conditions are

$$U'(c) = PJ_W(W, P),$$

$$(R_1 - R_3)J_W + (s_1\sigma_1^2 + \lambda s_2\sigma_1\sigma_2)WJ_{WW} + \sigma_1^2 PJ_{WP} = 0, \quad (4.33)$$

and

$$(R_2 - R_3)J_W + (s_2\sigma_2^2 + \lambda s_1\sigma_1\sigma_2)WJ_{WW} + \sigma_1\sigma_2\lambda PJ_{WP} = 0.$$
$$(4.34)$$

Optimal Portfolio Rules

To work out the portfolio rules, we notice that, even though the indirect utility function is a function of nominal wealth W and price level P, the indirect utility function should be a function of real wealth W/P, i.e., there is no money illusion. In other words, it is economics, not mathematics, that enables us to argue that the indirect utility function should be homogeneous of degree zero in W and P. Then Euler's theorem implies

$$WJ_W + PJ_P = 0.$$

Differentiating this with respect to W, we have

$$J_W + WJ_{WW} + PJ_{WP} = 0,$$

or

$$PJ_{WP} = -J_W - WJ_{WW}.$$

Substituting it into (4.33) and (4.34), we obtain

$$(R_1 - R_3 - \sigma_1^2)J_W + (s_1\sigma_1^2 + s_2\sigma_1\sigma_2\lambda - \sigma_1^2)WJ_{WW} = 0$$

and

$$(R_2 - R_3 - \sigma_1\sigma_2\lambda)J_W + (s_2\sigma_2^2 + s_1\sigma_1\sigma_2\lambda - \sigma_1\sigma_2\lambda)WJ_{WW} = 0.$$

The solutions to this pair of equations are

$$s_1 = 1 + \frac{1}{\alpha}\left[\frac{R_1 - R_3}{\sigma_1^2(1 - \lambda^2)} - \frac{\lambda(R_2 - R_3)}{\sigma_1\sigma_2(1 - \lambda^2)} - 1\right]$$

and

$$s_2 = \frac{1}{\alpha} \left[\frac{R_2 - R_3}{\sigma_2^2(1 - \lambda^2)} - \frac{\lambda(R_1 - R_3)}{\sigma_1\sigma_2(1 - \lambda^2)} \right],$$

where $\alpha = -W J_{WW}/J_W$ is the Arrow–Pratt relative risk aversion. The reader should refer to Fischer (1975) for more detailed implications.

In the next chapter, we shall prove, using the method of symmetry, that there is indeed no money illusion if the utility function $U(c)$ exhibits constant relative risk aversion.

Insurance Premium

Is it reasonable to assume that there is a premium for index bonds in the sense that the expected real rate of return to index bonds is smaller than the expected real rate of nominal bonds, $r_1 < r_3$? To answer this question, we concentrate on the case that $\lambda = 0$. If the model has a solution, then $0 \le s_1 \le 1$, which means

$$\sigma_1^2(1 - \alpha) \le R_1 - R_3 \le \sigma_1^2.$$

Therefore,

$$-\alpha\sigma_1^2 \le r_1 - r_3 \le 0, \tag{4.35}$$

i.e., there is indeed an insurance premium $r_1 \le r_3$. It is interesting to point out that the opposite may occur for nominal rates: $R_1 > R_3$ if $0 < \alpha < 1$.

Our result is a special case. The assumption $\lambda = 0$ is stringent but not totally out of line. If we take the position that inflation is a monetary phenomenon, i.e., dz_1 is a monetary shock, and that the shock to equity (dz_2) is a real shock, then it is conceivable that these two shocks are independent.

Exercise 4.3.1 *Show that the real rate of return to equity is*

$$\frac{d(Q_2/P)}{Q_2/P} = \left(R_2 - \pi + \sigma_1^2 - \sigma_1\sigma_2\lambda\right) dt - \sigma_1 \, dz_1 + \sigma_2 \, dz_2.$$

In particular, $r_2 \ne R_2 - \pi$. Even if $\lambda = 0$ (the two sources of uncertainty are independent), the expected real rate of return to equity is $R_2 - \pi + \sigma_1^2$, which still depends on σ_1^2.

Exercise 4.3.2 *Show that*

$$\lim_{\Delta t \to 0} \frac{1}{\Delta t} E \left\{ \frac{(Q_3/P)(t + \Delta t) - (Q_3/P)(t)}{(Q_3/P)(t + \Delta t)} \middle| \mathcal{F}_t \right\} = R_3 - \pi.$$

This result shows that the expected rate of return, in backward-looking computation, is the difference between the nominal rate and the inflation rate.

Hint. Use the example in Chapter 3 on forward-looking vs. backward-looking computation.

4.3.3 Exhaustible Resources

The problem of exhaustible resources was first studied by Hotelling (1931). It became popular in the 1970s due to the energy crisis. The *Review of Economic Studies* in 1974 devoted a special issue to the subject, Symposium on the Economics of Exhaustible Resources. We begin with reviewing a standard but much simplified model of Dasgupta and Heal (1974) focusing on the rate of extraction. Then we extend it to the stochastic case. Finally, we discuss the published paper by Pindyck (1980).

Dasgupta and Heal (1974)
Dasgupta and Heal (1974) used the Hamiltonian method to solve the deterministic exhaustible resources problem. We, however, shall use the Bellman equation to derive the costate equation.

Let $R(t)$ be the proved reserves (or published estimates) of an exhaustible resource, and $c(t)$ be the consumption (or the rate of extraction) at time t. Then the planning problem is

$$\max_{\{c(t)\}} \int_0^\infty e^{-rt} u(c(t)) \qquad \text{s.t. } \dot{R}(t) = -c(t) \text{ with } R(0) = R.$$

The Bellman equation is

$$0 = \max_c \{ u(c) - rJ(R) - cJ'(R) \}.$$

The first-order condition is

$$u'(c) = J'(R).$$

The optimal extraction rule satisfies

$$u(c) - rJ(R) - cJ'(R) = 0$$

and hence (by the envelope theorem)

$$-rJ'(R) - cJ''(R) = 0. \qquad (4.36)$$

Define the costate variable $p = J'(R)$, which is the shadow price of exhaustible resources, or the spot price of consumption. Then we have the costate equation

$$\dot{p} = J''(R)\,\dot{R} = -cJ''(R) = rJ'(R) = rp, \qquad (4.37)$$

where the third equality is obtained by using (4.36). It follows immediately that

$$p(t) = p(0)\,e^{rt} :$$

the spot price of consumption grows exponentially at the rate of interest.

Next, we derive the Euler equation as follows. From $p = u'(c)$ and the costate equation (4.37), we have

$$u''(c)\,\dot{c} = \dot{p} = rp = ru'(c),$$

which becomes the following Euler equation:

$$\frac{\dot{c}}{c} = -r\left[-\frac{u'(c)}{cu''(c)}\right] = -\frac{r}{\alpha(c)} < 0, \qquad (4.38)$$

where $1/\alpha(c) > 0$ is the elasticity of intertemporal substitution. Clearly, consumption declines with time.

If the utility function exhibits a constant elasticity of intertemporal substitution, $\alpha(c) = \alpha$, then consumption declines exponentially with time

$$c(t) = c(0)\,e^{-(r/\alpha)t}.$$

The reserve at time t is

$$R(t) = R - \int_0^t c(s)\,ds = R + \frac{\alpha c(0)}{r}\left(e^{-(r/\alpha)t} - 1\right).$$

The condition $\lim_{t \to \infty} R(t) = 0$ provides a guide to the choice of the initial consumption, $c(0) = (r/\alpha) R$. This is their Proposition 3. There are two immediate implications. First, an increase in the initial estimate R increases $c(0)$ and raises the entire consumption profile $\{c(t)\}$. Second, an increase in r (or $1/\alpha$) increases the initial consumption $c(0)$ and makes the downward-sloping consumption profile $\{c(t)\}$ steeper.

Stochastic Extension

Suppose the reserves at time t, $R(t)$, follow

$$dR = -qR\,dt + \sigma R\,dz, \tag{4.39}$$

where q stands for the *rate* of extraction. Formulate the exhaustible resource problem as

$$\max_{\{q\}} E\left\{ \int_0^\infty e^{-rt} u(qR)\,dt \right\} \qquad \text{s.t. (4.39), with } R(0) = R \text{ given.}$$

Then the Bellman equation is

$$0 = \max_q \{ u(qR) - rJ(R) - qRJ'(R) + (\sigma^2/2)R^2 J''(R) \}.$$

Clearly, the first-order condition is that the marginal utility of consumption is equal to the marginal utility of reserves:

$$u'(qR) = J'(R).$$

Assume the utility function exhibits constant relative risk aversion

$$u(x) = \frac{x^{1-\alpha}}{1-\alpha}, \qquad 0 < \alpha < 1.$$

Assume also that we know the value function is of the form

$$J(R) = \frac{aR^{1-\alpha}}{1-\alpha},$$

for some constant a. (The method will be discussed in the next chapter.) The first-order condition implies

$$a = q^{-\alpha}.$$

Substituting it into the Bellman equation, the optimal extraction rate is given by

$$q = \frac{r}{\alpha} + \frac{\sigma^2}{2}(1 - \alpha),$$

which is constant over time. Clearly,

$$\frac{\partial q}{\partial r} > 0, \qquad \frac{\partial q}{\partial \alpha} < 0, \quad \text{and} \quad \frac{\partial q}{\partial \sigma^2} > 0.$$

The first two effects are the natural stochastic extension of the deterministic case. (When $\sigma^2 = 0$, we have $q = r/\alpha$ and $c(0) = qR = (r/\alpha)R$.) It is interesting to point out that the extraction rate rises with the uncertainty.

Since q is independent of R, the stochastic process of reserves (4.39) is a geometric Brownian motion, and so is qR. This proves that $R(t) > 0$ and $c(t) = qR(t) > 0$ for all $t > 0$. Furthermore, the instantaneous expected growth rate of consumption is

$$\lim_{\Delta t \to 0} \frac{1}{\Delta t} E_t \left[\frac{qR(t + \Delta t) - qR(t)}{qR(t)} \right] = -q < 0,$$

which is reduced to (4.38) when $\sigma^2 \to 0$. Thus, expected consumption declines over time as before. Here, we obtain a new result: that the expected growth rate of consumption is negatively related to σ^2.

The Model in Pindyck (1980)

In addition to the shocks to resources, there is another source of uncertainty in this paper: demand shock. Another difference is that the paper focuses on profit-maximizing firms, not the representative consumer. We shall address only the extraction rules and the price dynamics. The reader should refer to Pindyck's paper for other issues addressed therein.

The Model. Let $R(t)$ be the proved reserves (or published estimates) of an exhaustible resource, and $x(t)$ be the extraction at time t. Assume the total extraction cost is linear in x of the form $C(R)x(t)$, where $C(R)$ is a function of the proved reserves satisfying $C'(R) < 0$. As such, $C(R)$ is the average cost and the marginal cost of extraction. We shall also assume $C''(R) > 0$, so that the marginal cost of extraction, as a function of the proved reserves, is decreasing and convex in R. The inverse demand for exhaustible resources is given by $y(t)p(x)$ such that

$p(x) > 0$, $p'(x) \leq 0$, and y satisfies

$$dy = \mu y \, dt + \sigma_1 y \, dz_1, \qquad (4.40)$$

where z_1 is a Wiener process. Since the shock to the inverse demand is multiplicative, the inverse demand is positive w.p.1. Assume reserves are subject to fluctuation over time according to

$$dR = -x \, dt + \sigma_2 \, dz_2, \qquad (4.41)$$

where z_2 is another Wiener process satisfying $(dz_1)(dz_2) = 0$. Then the problem of optimal extraction is

$$\max_{\{x\}} E \int_0^\infty e^{-rt} \left[y(t) p(x) x - C(R) x \right] dt$$

s.t. (4.40), (4.41) with $R(0) = R > 0$ and $y(0) = y$ given.

It should be mentioned that Pindyck's original model is set in a finite horizon.

Comments on the Modeling. Notice that equation (4.41) has a solution

$$R(t) = R(0) - \int_0^t x(s) \, ds + \sigma_2 z_2(t).$$

As mentioned in Chapter 3, we know that reserves could be *negative* with a positive probability. In contrast, our equation (4.39) ends up with $R(t) > 0$ for all $t > 0$. One might think that changing (4.41) to $dR = -x \, dt + \sigma_2 R \, dz_2$ will help. While $dR = \sigma_2 R \, dz_2$ has a positive solution w.p.1, adding the term $-x \, dt$ could still lower the value of R from positive to negative, unless $x = 0$ at all times; but then there is no extraction at all. A stopping time $\tau = \min\{t : R(t) = 0\}$ may be needed to ensure $R(t) \geq 0$. However, we shall follow Pindyck by ignoring this complication in what follows.

Solution to the Problem. Let $J(y, R)$ be the current value of the value function of the extraction problem. Then, the Bellman equation is

$$0 = \max_x \left\{ y(t) p(x) x - C(R) x - rJ + \mu y J_y - x J_R + \frac{\sigma_1^2}{2} y^2 J_{yy} \right.$$

$$\left. + \frac{\sigma_2^2}{2} J_{RR} \right\}.$$

The first-order condition is

$$y(t) p(x) - C(R) + xy(t) p'(x) - J_R = 0.$$

Let $\varepsilon = -\frac{p}{x}\frac{\partial x}{\partial p}$ = demand elasticity. Then the optimal extraction rule is

$$J_R = y(t) p(x)\left(1 - \frac{1}{\varepsilon}\right) - C(R).$$

The first term on the right-hand side is the marginal revenue of extraction; the second term is the marginal cost of extraction. Thus, the optimal extraction rule says that the shadow price of the exhaustible resource, J_R, equals the marginal profit of extraction.

Price Dynamics. Note that if the market is competitive, i.e., $p(x) = \bar{p}$ and $\varepsilon = \infty$, then the Bellman equation is linear in x and therefore we may have indeterminacy. Following Pindyck's argument (p. 1208), if $J_R < y(t)\bar{p} - C(R)$, then all firms will produce at the maximal capacity; if $J_R > y(t)\bar{p} - C(R)$, then they will produce nothing. Thus, market clearing implies that $J_R = y(t)\bar{p} - C(R)$ as well.

The price dynamics for the competitive case is given by

$$d\tilde{p}(t) = \bar{p}\, dy(t) = \mu y \bar{p}\, dt + \sigma_1 y \bar{p}\, dz_1,$$

where $\tilde{p}(t) = y(t)\bar{p}$. To compute the drift of the price dynamics, we proceed as follows. Let x be the solution to the Bellman equation, so that

$$0 = y(t)\bar{p}x - C(R)x - rJ + \mu y J_y - x J_R + \frac{\sigma_1^2}{2}y^2 J_{yy} + \frac{\sigma_2^2}{2}J_{RR}.$$

Differentiate this equation with respect to R and use the envelope theorem to obtain

$$-C'(R)x - rJ_R + \mu y J_{yR} - x J_{RR} + \frac{\sigma_1^2}{2}y^2 J_{yyR} + \frac{\sigma_2^2}{2}J_{RRR} = 0.$$

From $J_R = y(t)\bar{p} - C(R)$, we have $J_{yR} = \bar{p}$, $J_{RR} = -C'(R)$, $J_{yyR} = 0$, and $J_{RRR} = -C''(R)$. Then the above equation reduces to

$$-r[\tilde{p}(t) - C(R)] + \mu y \bar{p} - \frac{\sigma_2^2}{2}C''(R) = 0.$$

Therefore, the drift of the price dynamics is [his equation (15)]

$$\lim_{\Delta t \to 0} \frac{1}{\Delta t} E\left[d\widetilde{p}(t)\right] = \mu y \bar{p} = r\left[\widetilde{p}(t) - C(R)\right] + \frac{\sigma_2^2}{2} C''(R). \quad (4.42)$$

This method of differentiating the Bellman equation with respect to the state variable R and then applying the envelope theorem will be repeatedly used in other examples.

Equation (4.42) says that, given a positive marginal profit $\widetilde{p}(t) - C(R) > 0$, prices are expected to rise over time. It also says that the drift of the price dynamics is positively related to the interest rate, the marginal profit, and the variance of the proved reserves. The last dependence says that the expected price increase is larger if the reserves are subject to a greater fluctuation. This is an interesting result. Another interesting result is that the term σ_1^2 does not enter equation (4.42).

Exercise 4.3.3 *(Monopoly Case) Show that the dynamics of the marginal revenue,* $\mathrm{MR} = y(t)\, p(x)\left(1 - \frac{1}{\varepsilon}\right)$, *satisfies*

$$\lim_{\Delta t \to 0} \frac{1}{\Delta t} E\left[d\left(\mathrm{MR}\right)\right] = r\left[\mathrm{MR} - C(R)\right] + \frac{\sigma_2^2}{2} C''(R).$$

4.3.4 Adjustment Costs and (Reversible) Investment

The significance of introducing adjustment costs in the theory of supply is best articulated in Lucas (1967). Basically, the traditional Viner–Wong cost curve, which we teach in undergraduate courses, cannot explain the size distribution of firms. Moreover, firms do not respond to demand change in a one-shot adjustment; rather, the adjustment is staggered. For example, it takes time to learn, to coordinate after installing new machines. In other words, there are *adjustment* costs beyond the purchase price. The early contributions are by Lucas (1967), Gould (1968), and Treadway (1969, 1970). Nickell (1978, Chapter 3) has a nice presentation on the subject. Hayashi (1982) provides a good theoretical piece that links the theory of adjustment costs to Tobin's q-theory of investment.

User Cost
In the theory of the firm, we show that the true cost of investing one dollar in capital is $r + \delta$, where r is the interest rate and δ is the depreciation

rate. Thus, if the purchase price of one unit of capital is v, then the *user cost* of capital is $v(r + \delta)$. Let $q = F(K, L)$ be the production function with inputs: capital K and labor L. If the wage rate is w and the inverse demand is $p = p(q)$, then the firm's problem is

$$\max_{K,L} \{p(q)q - wL - v(r + \delta)K\}.$$

The first-order conditions are

$$\frac{\partial [p(q)q]}{\partial L} = w \quad \text{and} \quad \frac{\partial [p(q)q]}{\partial K} = v(r + \delta),$$

i.e., the marginal revenue product of labor equals the wage rate, and the marginal revenue product of capital equals the user cost. This is standard.

Dynamic Model without Adjustment Costs

In a dynamic and deterministic model, the firm's capital evolves according to

$$dK = (I - \delta K)dt, \tag{4.43}$$

and the problem is

$$\max_{\{L,I\}} \int_0^\infty e^{-rt} [p(q)q - wL - vI]dt \qquad \text{s.t. (4.43)}.$$

The corresponding Bellman equation is

$$0 = \max_{L,I} \{p(q)q - wL - vI - rJ + (I - \delta K)J'(K)\}.$$

Hence, the demand for labor and the demand for investment are, respectively,

$$\frac{\partial [p(q)q]}{\partial L} = w \quad \text{and} \quad J'(K) = v.$$

The question is this: What is the optimal investment rule in the steady state? Using the method developed earlier, i.e., differentiating the Bellman equation with respect to K and applying the envelope theorem, we have, for optimal q,

$$0 = \frac{\partial [p(q)q]}{\partial K} - (r + \delta)J'(K) + (I - \delta K)J''(K).$$

At the steady state $\dot{k} = 0$, or $I - \delta K = 0$, we have

$$\frac{\partial [p(q)q]}{\partial K} = (r + \delta) J'(K) = v(r + \delta).$$

This dynamic problem without adjustment costs is equivalent to the static user cost problem. A simple static user cost model will be sufficient for this purpose.

Adjustment Costs

Adjustment costs can be introduced in two ways. The first to introduce an *installation function* $G(K, I)$ that measures the *effective* capital stock out of gross investment I. That is, only $G(K, I)$ units of capital stock are derived from I. We assume $G(K, I)$ satisfies $G(K, 0) = 0$, $G_I(K, I) > 0$ and $G_{II}(K, I) \leq 0$. Then the problem is

$$\max_{\{L,I\}} \int_0^\infty e^{-rt} [p(q)q - wL - vI] \, dt \qquad \text{s.t. } \dot{K} = G(K, I) - \delta K.$$

The corresponding first-order conditions are

$$\frac{\partial [p(q)q]}{\partial L} = w \quad \text{and} \quad G_I(K, I) J'(K) = v.$$

Recall that Tobin's marginal q is defined as $J'(K)/v$. Therefore, Tobin's marginal q equals $1/G_I$.

The second is to introduce an adjustment cost function $C(I)$, as a function of gross investment I, satisfying $C(0) = 0$, $C'(I) > 0$, $C''(I) > 0$, in a dynamic, deterministic model as follows:

$$\max_{\{L,I\}} \int_0^\infty e^{-rt} [p(q)q - wL - vI - C(I)] \, dt \qquad \text{s.t. (4.43)}.$$

This is the one we shall follow. The presentation basically follows Gould (1968). The difference is that we take the Bellman equation approach, not the Hamiltonian method.

The Bellman equation for the adjustment cost problem is

$$0 = \max_{L,I} \{ p(q)q - wL - vI - C(I) - rJ + (I - \delta K) J'(K) \}.$$

The first-order conditions are

$$\frac{\partial [p(q)q]}{\partial L} = w \quad \text{and} \quad J'(K) = v + C'(I).$$

Using the same method developed earlier, the optimal L and I satisfies

$$0 = \frac{\partial [p(q)q]}{\partial K} - (r+\delta)J'(K) + (I - \delta K)J''(K).$$

Let $\lambda = J'(K)$ be the costate variable. Then the costate equation is

$$\dot{\lambda} = (r+\delta)\lambda - \frac{\partial [p(q)q]}{\partial K}, \qquad (4.44)$$

and the Euler equation (derived from $v + C'(I) = J'(K)$) is

$$C''(I)\dot{I} - (r+\delta)C'(I) - (r+\delta)v + \frac{\partial [p(q)q]}{\partial K} = 0.$$

This Euler equation is in general not a linear differential equation.

Assume quadratic adjustment cost function $C(I) = a_1 I + a_2 I^2$. The corresponding Euler equation becomes linear:

$$\dot{I} - (r+\delta)I + \frac{1}{2a_2}\left[\frac{\partial [p(q)q]}{\partial K} - (r+\delta)(a_1 + v)\right] = 0.$$

Thus, the gross investment grows at the rate $r+\delta$. Gould examined an interesting case of constant prices and linearly homogeneous production function $q = F(K, L)$ for a competitive firm. In this case, the optimal quantity of labor satisfies

$$w = pF_L(K, L) = pF_L(K/L, 1),$$

i.e., K/L is a function of w/p. Denote it by $K/L = \phi(w/p)$. It follows that

$$\frac{\partial [p(q)q]}{\partial K} = pF_K(K, L) = pF_K(K/L, 1) = pF_K(\phi(w/p), 1),$$

which is a constant given constant prices. Then the Euler equation is simplified to

$$\dot{I} - (r+\delta)I + \frac{1}{2a_2}[pF_K(\phi(w/p), 1) - (r+\delta)(a_1 + v)] = 0.$$

Assuming the transversality condition, Gould found that the solution to this first-order differential equation is a constant

$$I(t) = \frac{pF_K(\phi(w/p), 1) - (r + \delta)(a_1 + v)}{2a_2(r + \delta)}.$$

In other words, the competitive firm's optimal investment rule is *constant* over time, if prices are constant over time and the production function is linearly homogeneous.

The Model in Pindyck (1982)

Now assume there are adjustment costs and the source of uncertainty is demand shock. Suppose the inverse demand facing a firm is given by $p = p(q, \theta) > 0$, where q is output produced and θ is a stochastic element, satisfying $p_\theta > 0$ and $p_q \leq 0$. If the firm is a competitive firm, $p_q = 0$ and the inverse demand becomes $p = p(\theta)$. Let the adjustment cost function be $C(I)$ with $C'(I) > 0$, $C''(I) > 0$, where I is the gross investment. Obviously, $C(I)$ includes the quadratic cost function as a special case. The law of motion for capital is (4.43). Assume the stochastic element follows

$$d\theta = \sigma(\theta)dz. \tag{4.45}$$

Then the investment problem of the firm is

$$\max_{\{L,I\}} E \int_0^\infty e^{-rt}[p(q, \theta)q - wL - vI - C(I)]dt,$$
s.t. (4.43) and (4.45) with $K(0) = K$.

Let $J(K, \theta)$ be the value function of the investment problem. Then the Bellman equation is

$$0 = \max_{L,I} \left\{ p(q, \theta)q - wL - vI - C(I) - rJ \right.$$

$$\left. + (I - \delta K)J_K + \frac{[\sigma(\theta)]^2}{2}J_{\theta\theta} \right\}.$$

Denote by $\varepsilon = -\frac{p}{q}\frac{\partial q}{\partial p}$ the elasticity of demand for output. The first-order conditions are

$$\frac{\partial[p(q, \theta)q]}{\partial L} = p\left(1 - \frac{1}{\varepsilon}\right)F_L = w$$

and

$$v + C'(I) = J_K.$$

The former says that the marginal revenue product of labor equals the wage rate, while the latter says that the marginal cost of investment, $v + C'(I)$, equals the marginal benefit of investment (the return to capital, J_K). To derive more results, we need an explicit functional form for $J(K, \theta)$, which will be discussed in the next chapter.

4.3.5 Uncertain Lifetimes and Life Insurance

In a finite-horizon model, the terminal date T is given. If we treat the terminal date as the age of death and let it be stochastic, then we have an uncertain lifetime. In this case, the age of death becomes a random variable, $\widetilde{T}$. In the literature, it is usually assumed that there is a maximal date, $\overline{T}$, beyond which no one will live. As mentioned in Chapter 1, allowing $\overline{T} \to \infty$ may be more desirable. What we shall show is that, with the aid of a survival function, the problem of uncertain lifetimes can be greatly simplified.

Survival Function
Assume the probability that one dies at age t is $\pi(t)$. Clearly, $\int_0^{\overline{T}} \pi(t) \, dt = 1$. The distribution function $F(t)$ is the probability that one dies before age t. Let the survival function at time t, i.e., the probability that one lives t years or more, be

$$S(t) = \int_t^{\overline{T}} \pi(t) \, dt = 1 - F(t).$$

By definition, $S(0) = 1$, $S(\overline{T}) = 0$, and $S'(t) < 0$. The *hazard rate* (*intensity rate, instantaneous failure rate* or *force of mortality*) is defined as

$$\lambda(t) = \frac{\pi(t)}{S(t)} = -\frac{d}{dt} \log S(t).$$

Thus, the survival function is of the form

$$S(t) = \exp\left\{ -\int_0^t \lambda(s) \, ds \right\}.$$

Within this framework, the expected utility from consumption can be written as

$$E \int_0^{\widetilde{T}} e^{-\rho t} u\,(c_t)\,dt = \int_0^{\overline{T}} \pi\,(t) \left[\int_0^t e^{-\rho s} u\,(c_s)\,ds \right] dt,$$

where ρ is the discount rate derived from factors other than lifetime uncertainty. Using integration by parts and $S'\,(t) = -\pi\,(t)$, we have

$$E \int_0^{\widetilde{T}} e^{-\rho t} u\,(c_t)\,dt$$

$$= -S\,(t) \left[\int_0^t e^{-\rho s} u\,(c_s)\,ds \right] \bigg|_{t=0}^{t=\overline{T}} + \int_0^{\overline{T}} S(t)\,e^{-\rho t} u(c_t)\,dt$$

$$= \int_0^{\overline{T}} S(t)\,e^{-\rho t} u(c_t)\,dt$$

$$= \int_0^{\overline{T}} \exp\left\{ -\rho t - \int_0^t \lambda(s)\,ds \right\} u(c_t)\,dt. \tag{4.46}$$

In the case that there is no maximal date of life, we have

$$E \int_0^{\widetilde{T}} e^{-\rho t} u\,(c_t)\,dt = \int_0^{\infty} \exp\left\{ -\rho t - \int_0^t \lambda\,(s)\,ds \right\} u\,(c_t)\,dt$$

if

$$\lim_{t \to \infty} S\,(t) \left[\int_0^t e^{-\rho s} u\,(c_s)\,ds \right] = 0.$$

From (4.46), the total discount factor at time t is $\exp\{-\rho t - \int_0^t \lambda(s)\,ds\}$, and the survival function plays the role of a discount factor due to lifetime uncertainty. If $\lambda\,(s) = \lambda$ for all s, i.e., if the distribution is exponential with Poisson parameter λ, then the total discount factor becomes $e^{-(\rho+\lambda)t}$ and the total discount rate is $\rho + \lambda$.

Example 4.16 *(Life Expectancy) Assume $\overline{T} = \infty$. Let the distribution be Weibull, i.e., the survival function is $S\,(t) = e^{-\lambda t^{\gamma}}$, $\gamma \geq 1$. To compute* *the life expectancy, we recall that the gamma function is defined by*

$$\Gamma(\alpha) = \int_0^\infty x^{\alpha-1} e^{-x} dx,$$

which satisfies

$$\Gamma(\alpha) = (\alpha - 1)\Gamma(\alpha - 1).$$

Using the change of variables: $x = \lambda t^\gamma$, the life expectancy becomes

$$E[\widetilde{T}] = \int_0^\infty S(t)\, dt = \int_0^\infty e^{-x} \left(\frac{1}{\lambda\gamma}\right) \left(\frac{x}{\lambda}\right)^{\frac{1}{\gamma}-1} dx$$

$$= \left(\frac{1}{\gamma}\right) \left(\frac{1}{\lambda}\right)^{\frac{1}{\gamma}} \int_0^\infty x^{\frac{1}{\gamma}-1} e^{-x} dx = \left(\frac{1}{\gamma}\right) \left(\frac{1}{\lambda}\right)^{\frac{1}{\gamma}} \Gamma\left(\frac{1}{\gamma}\right)$$

$$= \Gamma\left(1 + \frac{1}{\gamma}\right) \left(\frac{1}{\lambda}\right)^{\frac{1}{\gamma}}.$$

A reduction in λ increases life expectancy. When $\gamma = 1$, the distribution is exponential and

$$E[\widetilde{T}] = \Gamma(2)\left(\frac{1}{\lambda}\right) = \frac{1}{\lambda},$$

since $\Gamma(n) = (n-1)!$ for integer n.

Is More Information Better? An Anecdote

Consider two regimes: regime 1, in which all individuals are born with a common probability density that determines the length of life; and regime 2, in which individuals are informed at birth of a specific length of life that is drawn from the same distribution. Which is better? In other words, will the knowledge of one's length of life before birth make one better off?

To make the story simple, let $A > 0$ be the asset endowed at birth, and let the interest rate and the subjective discount rate be zero, $r = \rho = 0$. We further assume one's earnings over time are constant, denoted by y, and that the annuity market is perfect so that one's expected expenditure equals expected earnings. Then the individual in regime 1 solves

$$\max_{\{c_t\}} \int_0^{\overline{T}} S(t)\, u(c_t)\, dt \qquad \text{s.t.} \int_0^{\overline{T}} S(t)\, c_t = A + \int_0^{\overline{T}} S(t)\, y.$$

The first-order condition ($u'(c_t)$ is a constant for all t) implies that

$$c_t = y + A/E[\widetilde{T}] \qquad \forall t,$$

using $\int_0^{\overline{T}} S(t)\,dt = E[\widetilde{T}]$. Thus, the maximized expected utility in regime 1 is

$$E[\widetilde{T}]u(y + A/E[\widetilde{T}]).$$

In regime 2, if an individual's announced lifetime is T, then that individual solves

$$\max_{\{c_t\}} \int_0^T u(c_t)\,dt \qquad \text{s.t.} \int_0^T c_t = A + \int_0^T y = A + Ty.$$

It is easy to verify that the optimal consumption is $c_t = y + A/T$ for all t and the maximized utility is

$$U(T) = Tu\left(y + \frac{A}{T}\right).$$

Ex ante, the individual can expect

$$E[U(\widetilde{T})] = \int_0^{\overline{T}} S(T)U(T)\,dT.$$

Now we are ready to compare the two regimes. Notice that the maximized expected utility in regime 1 can be written as $U[E(\widetilde{T})]$. Since

$$U''(T) = -u''\left(y + \frac{A}{T}\right)\frac{A^2}{T^3} > 0,$$

$U(T)$ is convex in T. By Jensen's inequality,

$$U[E(\widetilde{T})] \geq E[U(\widetilde{T})].$$

Conclusion: Ignorance is preferred. As pointed out by Barro and Friedman (1977), the key element that produces this interesting result is that the consumer's ability to buy insurance gives her the same expected lifetime utility as she would have if her lifetime were known with certainty to be of length $E(\widetilde{T})$. On the other hand, they also pointed out that there are "planning benefits," with regard to human capital investment, that derive from knowledge of the time of death. Then the consumer *could* be made better off with more information. The interested reader should consult their paper for this result.

Life Insurance

As in most standard models, the demand for life insurance is derived from a bequest function. First, we assume there is a risky asset and a risk-free asset as in Merton's model. However, the budget equation has to be modified due to the presence of life insurance. Let the insurance premium for age t be θ_t per dollar of coverage. If the amount of insurance purchased is Q, then the insurance premium is θQ. Then the budget dynamics becomes

$$dW_t = [s_t (\mu - r) W_t + (r W_t - c_t) - \theta_t Q_t] dt + s_t \sigma W_t \, dz_t. \quad (4.47)$$

Should one die at age t, the wealth left behind plus life insurance will go to heirs. Assume the bequest function is of the form $B(t, Z_t)$, where

$$Z_t = W_t + Q_t.$$

Extending this formulation to the case of $n - 1$ risky assets is straightforward and is left as an exercise.

Given an uncertain lifetime $\widetilde{T}$, with a density function $\pi(t)$, the consumer's expected utility is

$$\int_0^{\widetilde{T}} \pi(t) \left[\int_0^t e^{-\rho s} u(c_s) \, ds + B(t, Z_t) \right] dt.$$

Using integration by parts as before, we can formulate the problem as

$$\max_{\{c_t, s_t, Q_t\}} \int_0^{\widetilde{T}} \left[e^{-\rho t} S(t) u(c_t) + \pi(t) B(t, Z_t) \right] dt \qquad \text{s.t. (4.47).}$$

Notice that there are two different sources of uncertainty in this problem, one comes from the risky asset and the other comes from lifetime uncertainty.

For easy computation, let the value function be of the form $S(t) J(t, W_t)$. Since $\pi(t) = \lambda(t) S(t)$, the Bellman equation is

$$0 = \max_{c_t, s_t, Q_t} \left\{ e^{-\rho t} u(c_t) + \lambda(t) B(t, Z_t) + J_t - \lambda(t) J \right.$$

$$\left. + [s_t(\mu - r) W_t + (r W_t - c_t) - \theta_t Q_t] J_W + (\sigma^2/2) s_t^2 W_t^2 J_{WW} \right\}.$$

Then the first-order conditions are

$$e^{-\rho t} u'(c_t) = J_W(t, W_t),$$

$$s_t W_t = \frac{\mu - r}{\sigma^2} \left[-\frac{J_W}{W_t J_{WW}} \right],$$

and

$$\lambda(t) B_Z(t, Z_t) = \theta(t) J_W. \qquad (4.48)$$

Clearly, the optimal consumption and portfolio rules remain the same as in Merton. The new result is equation (4.48). In the next chapter, we shall show how to find the value function given the functional form of the utility function and the bequest function.

4.4 Extension: Recursive Utility

So far we have assumed the discount rate is constant over time. This assumption of a fixed rate of impatience can have strange results. According to Hicks (1965), successive consumption units are supposed to be complementary. An additively separable (in time) utility function implies that the marginal rate of substitution between lunch and dinner is independent of the type of breakfast one had that morning or expects to have the next morning. See Wan (1970, p. 274).

Additive separability also blurs the distinction between risk aversion and intertemporal substitution. See Epstein and Zin (1989) for the discrete-time case and Duffie and Epstein (1992) for the continuous-time case. For example, if $U(c) = c^{1-\alpha}$, then α is the degree of relative risk aversion and $1/\alpha$ is the elasticity of intertemporal substitution. The effect of α on the optimal policy c, $\partial c / \partial \alpha$, has two different economic interpretations.

Last but not least, if the rate of interest is constant, as typically assumed, then a consumer with a constant subjective discount rate will save without limit or borrow without limit unless the two rates are identical. Furthermore, when there are heterogeneous agents, then, *in the long run,* the most patient consumer (the one with the smallest discount rate) will own all the capital, while all other agents consume nothing and pay back their debts with all their labor income. See Becker (1980).

One way to avoid this problem is to allow the discount factor to change with the underlying consumption path $\{c_t : t \geq 0\}$. The basic concepts of recursive preferences are easier to understand in a discrete-time setting. Let $C = (c_1, c_2, \dots)$ be a consumption profile, S be the (right) shift operator so that $SC = (c_2, c_3, \dots)$, and $V(C)$ be the utility of the consumption profile C. The notion of recursive utility is that the utility of the profile C is a function of the utility of current consumption, $U(c_1)$, and the utility of future consumption, $V(SC)$. Formally,

$$V(C) = V(c_1, SC) = W(U(c_1), V(SC)),$$

where $W(c, y)$ is called the aggregator.

For example, if

$$W(c, y) = U(c_1) + \beta y,$$

where β is the discount factor, then

$$V(C) = U(c_1) + \beta V(SC) = U(c_1) + \beta[U(c_2) + \beta V(S^2 C)] = \cdots$$

$$= \sum_{t=1}^{\infty} \beta^{t-1} U(c_t),$$

which is the constant-discount-rate case. If

$$W(c, y) = -(1 - y) \exp\{-\rho(c)\},$$

then

$$V(C) = -(1 - V(SC))e^{-\rho(c_1)} = -\left\{1 + [1 - V(S^2 C)]e^{-\rho(c_2)}\right\} e^{-\rho(c_1)}$$

$$= -e^{-\rho(c_1)} - e^{-[\rho(c_1)+\rho(c_2)]} + V(S^2 C)e^{-[\rho(c_1)+\rho(c_2)]} = \cdots$$

$$= -\sum_{t=1}^{\infty} \exp\left\{-\sum_{i=1}^{t} \rho(c_i)\right\},$$

which is the Epstein–Hynes (1983) functional. If

$$W(c, y) = U(c) + y \exp\{-\rho(c)\},$$

then

$$V\left(C\right) = U\left(c_1\right) + V\left(SC\right)e^{-\rho(c_1)}$$
$$= U\left(c_1\right) + \left[U\left(c_2\right) + V(S^2C)e^{-\rho(c_2)}\right]e^{-\rho(c_1)} = \cdots$$
$$= \sum_{t=1}^{\infty} \exp\left\{-\sum_{i=1}^{t-1}\rho\left(c_i\right)\right\} U\left(c_t\right).$$

What we are interested in is the continuous-time version of this class of functions, which is obtained by changing summations to integrals, i.e.,

$$\int_0^{\infty} \exp\left\{-\int_0^t \rho\left(c_s\right)ds\right\} U\left(c_t\right)dt.$$

This class includes as special cases the constant-discount-rate case ($\rho\left(c_s\right) = \rho$) and Epstein–Hynes functionals ($U\left(c_t\right) = -1$). It also includes Uzawa (1968) functionals if $\rho\left(c_t\right)$ is a monotonically increasing, strictly convex transformation of $U\left(c_t\right)$.

Define the discount factor $D(t)$ at time t as

$$D\left(t\right) = \exp\left\{-\int_0^t \rho\left(c_s\right)ds\right\},$$

where $\rho\left(c_s\right) \geq 0$, $\rho'\left(c_s\right) > 0$, and $\rho''\left(c_s\right) < 0$. The strict inequality $\rho'\left(c_s\right) > 0$ is referred to as *increasing marginal impatience* in the literature. See, for example, Lucas and Stokey (1984) and Epstein (1983). The discount factor thus defined clearly depends on the underlying consumption path $\{c_t : t \geq 0\}$. Moreover, $D\left(t\right)$ is *decreasing in time* with values in (0, 1], since

$$D'\left(t\right) = -D\left(t\right)\rho\left(c_t\right) < 0. \tag{4.49}$$

Clearly, $D\left(0\right) = 1$ and $D'\left(0\right) = -\rho\left(c_0\right)$. Notice that $\rho\left(c_s\right)$ must have a dimension of "per unit of time" to make $D\left(t\right)$ a bona fide discount factor. Then the objective function is $D\left(t\right)U\left(c_t\right)$, and the optimal growth problem with a recursive preference is

$$\max_{\{c_t\}} E_k \int_0^{\infty} D\left(t\right)U\left(c_t\right)dt \quad \text{s.t. (4.1)}. \tag{4.50}$$

4.4.1 Bellman Equation with Recursive Utility

Again, we invoke the principle of optimality

$$J(k) = \max_{\substack{\{c_t\} \\ 0 \leq t \leq \Delta t}} E_k \left\{ \int_0^{\Delta t} D(t) U(c_t) dt \right.$$

$$\left. + \max_{\substack{\{c_t\} \\ \Delta t \leq t < \infty}} E_{\Delta t, k+\Delta k} \int_{\Delta t}^{\infty} D(t) U(c_t) dt \right\}.$$

Using the property of the exponential function, for any given consumption path $\{c_t : t \geq 0\}$ and small $\Delta t > 0$, we can decompose the discount factor $D(t)$, $t \geq \Delta t$, as

$$D(t) = D(\Delta t) \exp \left\{ - \int_{\Delta t}^t \rho(c_s) ds \right\}.$$

Since $D(\Delta t)$ is $\mathcal{F}_{\Delta t}$-measurable,

$$\max_{\substack{\{c_t\} \\ \Delta t \leq t < \infty}} E_{\Delta t, k+\Delta k} \int_{\Delta t}^{\infty} D(t) U(c_t) dt$$

$$= D(\Delta t) \max_{\substack{\{c_t\} \\ \Delta t \leq t < \infty}} E_{\Delta t, k+\Delta k} \int_{\Delta t}^{\infty} \exp \left\{ - \int_{\Delta t}^t \rho(c_s) ds \right\} U(c_t) dt$$

$$= D(\Delta t) J(k + \Delta k).$$

The above equation shows that past consumption, $\{c_t : t \leq \Delta t\}$, while affecting future decisions through the discount factor, can be factored out and separated from future consumption. Then Bellman's principle of optimality can be written as

$$0 = \max_{\substack{\{c_t\} \\ 0 \leq t \leq \Delta t}} E_k \left\{ \int_0^{\Delta t} D(t) U(c_t) dt + D(\Delta t) J(k + \Delta k) - J(k) \right\},$$

$$(4.51)$$

which is similar to (4.6). Equation (4.51) highlights the fact that the optimization problem (4.50) retains the analytic tractability of a constant-discount-rate model as developed earlier.

Formally, when $\Delta t \to 0$, one has

$$\frac{1}{\Delta t} E_k \int_0^{\Delta t} D(t) U(c_t) dt \to D(0) U(c) = U(c),$$

by the intermediate value theorem and $c_0 = c$. Next, we note the algebraic identity

$$D(\Delta t) J(k + \Delta k) = [D(\Delta t) - 1] J(k + \Delta k) + J(k + \Delta k).$$

By the mean-value theorem, $[D(\Delta t) - 1] = D'(\theta \Delta t) \Delta t$, where $\theta = \theta(\omega)$ and $0 \le \theta \le 1$. Then, using (4.49),

$$\frac{1}{\Delta t} E_k\{ [D(\Delta t) - 1] J(k + \Delta k)\} = E_k [D'(\theta(\omega) \Delta t) J(k + \Delta k)]$$

$$\to D'(0) J(k) = -\rho(c) J(k),$$

since $k + \Delta k \to k$. Finally, by Ito's lemma,

$$\frac{1}{\Delta t} E_k [J(k + \Delta k) - J(k)] \to \mathcal{A}^c J(k).$$

Thus, the Bellman equation for the optimal growth problem with recursive utility (4.50) is

$$0 = \max_c \{U(c) - \rho(c) J(k) + \mathcal{A}^c J(k)\}. \tag{4.52}$$

Equation (4.52) differs from (4.8) in that the constant discount rate ρ is replaced by the variable discount function $\rho(c)$.

The first-order condition of (4.52) is

$$U'(c) - \rho'(c) J(k) - J'(k) = 0. \tag{4.53}$$

The extra term, $\rho'(c) J(k)$, requires some explanation. An increase in consumption would increase the discount rate by a factor of $\rho'(c)$. Since the indirect utility was $J(k)$, the change in the total utility due to a change in consumption is $\rho'(c) J(k)$ at the margin. Therefore, the *full* cost of current consumption $U'(c)$ is the marginal utility of wealth *plus* the loss in utility due to future discounting arising from current consumption. In the constant-discount-rate case, $\rho'(c) = 0$, and there is no loss in utility due to consumption.

4.4.2 Effects of Recursivity: Deterministic Case

How does the introduction of recursivity affect the optimal consumption path? In what follows we shall concentrate on the deterministic case, $\sigma = 0$, so that we can use the phase diagram analysis and compare the results with the well-known phase diagram when $\rho(c) = \rho$.

Costate Equation

With $\sigma = 0$, equation (4.52) is reduced to

$$0 = \max_c \{U(c) - \rho(c) J(k) + [f(k) - c - nk] J'(k)\}. \qquad (4.54)$$

Let c be the optimal consumption, which satisfies

$$U(c) - \rho(c) J(k) + [f(k) - c - nk] J'(k) = 0.$$

By the envelope theorem,

$$[f'(k) - n - \rho(c)]J'(k) + [f(k) - c - nk] J''(k) = 0. \qquad (4.55)$$

Let the costate variable be $p = J'(k)$. Then we have

$$\dot{p} = \frac{dp}{dt} = \frac{dJ'(k)}{dt} = J''(k)\dot{k} = [f(k) - nk - c] J''(k),$$

where the last equality is obtained from the state equation

$$\dot{k} = f(k) - c - nk, \qquad (4.56)$$

Using (4.55), we have the costate equation

$$\dot{p} = -p[f'(k) - n - \rho(c)]. \qquad (4.57)$$

Remark 4.3 *This is a good place to derive the costate equation using the Hamiltonian method, because the problem is general enough. Let the Hamiltonian function be*

$$H(k, c, t) = D(t) U(c) + D(t) p(t) [f(k) - c - nk].$$

Then the costate equation is

$$\frac{d}{dt}[D(t) p(t)] = -\frac{\partial H}{\partial k} = -D(t) p(t) [f'(k) - n].$$

Since $D'(t) = -D(t)\rho(c)$, we arrive at (4.57).

Exercise 4.4.1 *Use the Hamiltonian method to verify costate equations* (4.37) *and* (4.44).

Euler Equation

Typically, the phase diagram of an optimal growth model is analyzed through the state equation and the Euler equation, not the costate equation. To this end, we differentiate $p = U'(c) - \rho'(c) J(k)$ with respect to t to obtain

$$\frac{\dot{p}}{p} = \frac{\frac{d}{dt}\left[U'(c) - \rho'(c) J(k)\right]}{U'(c) - \rho'(c) J(k)} = \frac{U''(c) - \rho''(c) J(k)}{U'(c) - \rho'(c) J(k)}\dot{c} - \rho'(c)\dot{k}.$$

Using the costate equation (4.57), we arrive at the following Euler equation

$$b(k, c)\frac{\dot{c}}{c} = f'(k) - n - \rho(c) - \rho'(c)[f(k) - c - nk], \qquad (4.58)$$

where

$$b(k, c) = -\frac{c[U''(c) - \rho''(c) J(k)]}{U'(c) - \rho'(c) J(k)}.$$

To ensure that the coefficient $b(k, c)$ is always positive so that (4.58) would be nondegenerate, we assume the second-order *sufficient* condition of (4.54), $U''(c) - \rho''(c) J(k) < 0$, is satisfied. Then $b(k, c) > 0$, because the denominator is the shadow price p, which is positive. Notice that the sign of the change in consumption (the sign of $\dot{c}$) is independent of the utility function $U(c)$. Typically, we use equations (4.56) and (4.58) to study the steady state.

In the event that $\rho(c) = \rho$, we have $b(k, c) = -cU''(c)/U'(c)$ and the classical Euler equation for growth models,

$$\left[-\frac{cU''(c)}{U'(c)}\right]\frac{\dot{c}}{c} = f'(k) - n - \rho. \qquad (4.59)$$

If $U(c) = -1$, then $b(k, c) = -c\rho''(c)/\rho'(c)$ and the Euler equation becomes

$$\left[-\frac{c\rho''(c)}{\rho'(c)}\right]\frac{\dot{c}}{c} = f'(k) - n - \rho(c) - \rho'(c)[f(k) - c - nk].$$

Phase Diagram

First, we briefly review the phase diagram analysis of the optimal growth model with a constant discount rate ρ. The steady state analysis is obtained by studying the pair of equations (4.56) and (4.59) in the (k, c)-plane. Let $\bar{k}$ be the maximal sustainable capital–labor ratio, i.e., $f(\bar{k}) = n\bar{k}$, and let (k_0, c_0) be the steady state solution to the growth problem satisfying $\dot{k} = \dot{c} = 0$, i.e.,

$$f(k) - c - nk = 0 \qquad (4.60)$$

and

$$f'(k) - n - \rho = 0. \qquad (4.61)$$

The curve defined by (4.60), denoted by $\dot{k} = 0$, is of inverted-U shape with k-axis intercepts 0 and $\bar{k}$. The curve defined by (4.61) is a vertical line with $f'(k_0) = n + \rho$. Since $f(k)$ is strictly concave in k, we have $\dot{c} < 0$ if $k > k_0$, and $\dot{c} > 0$ if $k < k_0$. This determines the vertical arrows in the entire phase diagram. Similarly, if c is above $\dot{k} = 0$, i.e., $c > f(k) - nk$, then $\dot{k} < 0$, and if c is below $\dot{k} = 0$, then $\dot{k} > 0$. This determines the horizontal arrows in the entire phase diagram. Combining them, we have Figure 4.1.

Now we return to the recursive utility case. The steady state, if it exists, is denoted by (k^*, c^*). By definition, (k^*, c^*) satisfies $\dot{k} = \dot{c} = 0$,

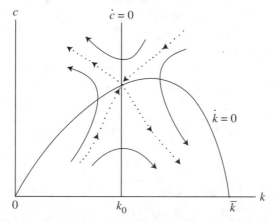

Figure 4.1: Steady state: constant-discount-rate case.

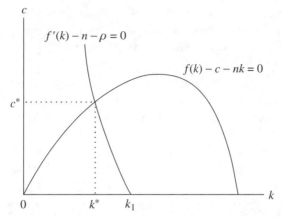

Figure 4.2: Existence of steady state: recursive utility case.

i.e., (4.60) and

$$f'(k) - n - \rho(c) = 0. \tag{4.62}$$

The curve defined by (4.60) is of inverted-U shape with k-axis intercepts 0 and $\bar{k}$, which is the same as the constant-discount-rate case. The curve defined by (4.62) satisfies $dc/dk < 0$ due to the strict concavity of f and $\rho'(c) > 0$. Its k-axis intercept is $(f')^{-1}(n + \rho(0)) = k_1$. The intersection of the two curves defines (k^*, c^*). See Figure 4.2. If the constant discount rate ρ is defined as $\rho(0)$, then $k^* < k_1 = k_0$ and $c^* < c_0$. That is, the steady state consumption and capital for recursive utility are lower than the ones for constant discount rate.

The phase diagram can be obtained as follows. The horizontal arrows are the same as in the constant-discount-rate case, i.e., if c is above $\dot{k} = 0$, then $\dot{k} < 0$, and if c is below $\dot{k} = 0$, then $\dot{k} > 0$. It remains to characterize the vertical arrows.

Let the curve defined by $\dot{c} = 0$ be $R(k, c) = 0$, where

$$R(k, c) = f'(k) - n - \rho(c) - \rho'(c)[f(k) - c - nk].$$

By the implicit function theorem, *k is a function of c* and has a derivative

$$\frac{dk}{dc} = -\frac{R_c}{R_k} = \frac{\rho''(c)[f(k) - c - nk]}{f''(k) - \rho'(c)[f'(k) - n]}.$$

Note that we treat k as a function of c, rather than c as a function of k, mainly for ease in characterizing the curve $\dot{c} = 0$. Specifically, since the denominator is negative on $k \leq \bar{k}$ and since $\rho''(c) < 0$, the "slope" of the curve $R(k, c) = 0$, dk/dc, has the same sign as $f(k) - c - nk$ or $\dot{k}$. That is, k is decreasing in c in the region $\dot{k} < 0$ and is increasing in c in the region $\dot{k} > 0$; in particular, $dk/dc = 0$ at c^*. Thus, the curve $\dot{c} = R(k, c) = 0$ is of inverted-C shape and is tangent to the line $k = k^*$ at (k^*, c^*).

Now we are ready to determine the vertical arrows of the phase diagram. Since $R_k(k, c) < 0$ on $k \leq \bar{k}$, we have $\dot{c} = R(k, c) > 0$ in the region to the left of the curve $R(k, c) = 0$, and $\dot{c} = R(k, c) < 0$ in the region to the right of $R(k, c) = 0$. Hence, c is increasing in the region to the left of $\dot{c} = 0$, and c is decreasing in the region to the right of $\dot{c} = 0$ on $k \leq \bar{k}$. Combining all arrows, a complete phase diagram is drawn in Figure 4.3.

The differences between the two cases are obvious. In the constant-discount-rate case, $\dot{c} = 0$ is a vertical line, whereas in the recursive utility case, $\dot{c} = 0$ is of inverted-C shape. The direction of vertical arrows and that of horizontal arrows remain unchanged. Thus, the steady state of optimal growth with a recursive utility is a saddle point, which can still be reached either by accumulating or by decumulating both capital and consumption.

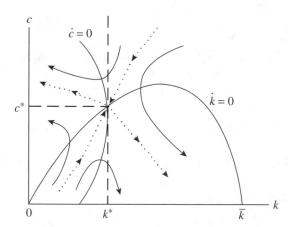

Figure 4.3: Steady state: recursive utility case.

Exercise 4.4.2 *Show that an increase in recursivity, defined as replacing* $\rho(c)$ *by* $\rho(c) + \rho_1(c)$ *with* $\rho_1(c) \geq 0$ *for all c, lowers the steady state consumption and the steady state capital–labor ratio.*

Exercise 4.4.3

(1) Show that a decrease in the population growth rate or Hicks-neutral technical progress increases the steady state consumption, but the effect on the steady state capital–labor ratio is ambiguous.

(2) Compare the results in (1) with the standard constant-discount-rate case.

4.5 Notes and Further Readings

The derivation of the Bellman equation evolves from Chang (1988) with supplements from Kushner (1971) and Krylov (1980). Most of the mathematical texts derive the Bellman equation through a cost minimization problem. In that setting, the Bellman equation has the minimum or infimum, not the maximum or supremum, in its formulation. We stay with a maximization problem throughout to make it easy for economic applications. Dynkin's formula is standard in most mathematics texts. For more on this subject, the reader is referred to Knight (1981) and Fleming and Soner (1993).

The section on the verification theorem draws heavily from Fleming and Rishel (1975) and Fleming and Soner (1993). The transversality condition in those books is weaker than the one we used, equation (4.18), which assumes the limit exists. In contrast, they require only liminf or limsup in the formulation. We assume the stronger version to make it easy to use.

We define admissible controls by way of the Lipschitz condition for its simplicity and for the reason that economists often assume smoothness in the model. There are other, weaker conditions. The interested reader should refer to Fleming and Rishel (1975, p. 156) and Fleming and Soner (1993) for more details. We mention that a Lipschitzian function is continuous but not always differentiable. It should also be mentioned that it is a well-known mathematical fact that a locally Lipschitzian function is differentiable at almost every interior point of its domain. See Fleming and Rishel (1975, p. 85).

The existence of the value function comes from existence theorems from the theory of second-order partial differential equations. Fleming and Soner (1993) refer to them as "classical solutions" as opposed to a more powerful solution technique known as the "viscosity" solution, which will be discussed in Chapter 6.

The portfolio model by Merton (1971) has become a standard example in stochastic analysis. It even appears in several mathematics books, e.g., Fleming and Rishel (1975), Karatzas and Shreve (1991), and Fleming and Soner (1993). The original paper has some typos, which were corrected in Merton (1973) and in Merton (1990). Karatzas, Lehoczky, Sethi, and Shreve (1986) provides, perhaps, the most complete study of this portfolio problem. There are many extensions of this model. In Chapter 6, we shall study Vila and Zariphopoulou (1997), which extends Merton's model to one with borrowing constraints.

Borch (1990, Chapter 4) provides a nice review of the early development of life insurance since the Middle Ages. Life insurance in its current form started about the 16th century. The uncertain-lifetime discussion is based on Chang (1991); the anecdote is based on Barro and Friedman (1977), while the demand for life insurance is from Richard (1975). The technique of reducing an uncertain-lifetime problem to a deterministic model by way of a survival function is standard. For more on survival functions, the reader is referred to Elandt-Johnson and Johnson (1980).

Our discussion on discrete-time recursive utility follows Becker and Boyd (1997), a comprehensive text on the subject. The class of recursive utility functions discussed in this chapter and the corresponding Bellman equation are available in Krylov (1980). Our presentation is based on Chang (1994). The Bellman equation for a more general class of recursive functions is shown in Duffie and Epstein (1992). Finally, the phase diagram of the optimal growth with a constant discount rate is standard. See, for example, Intriligator (1971, p. 441).

5

How to Solve it

5.1 Introduction

We have shown in Chapter 4 that the Bellman equation enables us to derive the equations that govern the optimal control policies. However, to have a better understanding of these behavioral functions we often need to know the functional form of the value function. For example, if the indirect utility function is of constant relative risk aversion in Merton's consumption and portfolio model, then we have shown that the share of wealth invested in each risky asset is constant over time. In this chapter we study the methods that determine the functional form of the value function of a stochastic, intertemporal optimization problem.

By definition, the value function depends on the specification of the objective function and the underlying controlled diffusion process. Changing the objective function or the controlled diffusion process would change the functional form of the value function and, hence, the optimal control.

We shall divide economic problems into four different classes of problems. The first class is the one in which the diffusion equation is linear in both state and control variables and the objective function is quadratic. This is the so-called linear–quadratic problem in control theory. The second class is the one in which the controlled diffusion process is linear in both state and control variables and the objective function exhibits hyperbolic absolute risk aversion (HARA). This class of functions contains most of the commonly employed objective functions and therefore deserves a special mention. The third class is the one in which the controlled diffusion process remains linear in state and control variables, but the objective function is concave and generally not of HARA form. The fourth class is the one in which the controlled diffusion process is not linear and the objective function is concave. The best-known example is the optimal growth problem.

We begin the chapter with a discussion on HARA functions. Then we introduce several methods of finding the closed-form representation of the value function. We illustrate each solution method with examples from the aforementioned four classes of problems. We also include the inverse optimum methodology in the discussion, because it is the functional form of the behavioral function (the optimal control) that is of interest to economists, not necessarily the specific functional form of the underlying utility functions.

5.2 HARA Functions

5.2.1 The Meaning of Each Parameter

We now consider a class of utility functions frequently used in economics. By definition, a HARA function, $U(c)$, is one whose absolute risk aversion is hyperbolic, i.e.,

$$-\frac{U''(c)}{U'(c)} = \frac{1}{ac+b} > 0 \qquad \text{for some constants } a \text{ and } b. \quad (5.1)$$

In the financial economics literature, the reciprocal of the absolute risk aversion is called the risk tolerance. Therefore, HARA functions are linear risk tolerance functions. In what follows we shall assume $c \geq 0$, since we are not interested in negative consumption. This additional assumption makes our formulation different from that in Merton (1971). However, it makes the classification simpler, as we shall see next.

From (5.1) we have

$$\frac{d}{dc}\left(-\frac{U''(c)}{U'(c)}\right) = \frac{-a}{(ac+b)^2}.$$

Since $ac + b > 0$, the sign of the derivative is the same as the sign of $-a$. In the event $a < 0$ (necessarily $b > 0$) we have the class of increasing absolute risk aversion (IARA) functions. When $a = 0$ (necessarily $b > 0$), we have the class of constant absolute risk aversion (CARA) functions with constant $1/b$. Similarly, if $a > 0$, then we have the class of decreasing absolute risk aversion (DARA) functions. In short, the sign of the parameter $-a$ determines the rising or falling of absolute risk aversion.

The relative risk aversion of a HARA function is defined as

$$-\frac{cU''(c)}{U'(c)} = \frac{c}{ac+b}.$$

If $a = 0$ (necessarily $b > 0$), then we have the class of increasing relative risk aversion (IRRA). If $a \neq 0$, then we shall rewrite the relative risk aversion as

$$-\frac{cU''(c)}{U'(c)} = \frac{1}{a} - \frac{b}{a^2c + ab}.$$

If $b > 0$, then we have IRRA functions. (Note that the sign of a does not matter as long as $ac + b > 0$.) If $b < 0$ (necessarily $a > 0$), then we have the class of decreasing relative risk aversion (DRRA) functions. If $b = 0$ (necessarily $a > 0$), then we have the class of constant relative risk aversion (CRRA) functions with constant $1/a$. In short, the sign of the parameter b determines the rising or falling of relative risk aversion.

In summary, the HARA functions are classified as follows:

$b \backslash a$	$+$	0	$-$
$+$	DARA & IRRA	CARA & IRRA	IARA & IRRA
0	DARA & CRRA	Undefined	Undefined
$-$	DARA & DRRA	Undefined	Undefined

It is obvious from the table that, if the utility function does not exhibit DARA, then the utility function must exhibit IRRA, i.e., if $a \leq 0$, then $b > 0$. Similarly, if the utility function does not exhibit IRRA, then the utility function must exhibit DARA, i.e., if $b \leq 0$, then $a > 0$.

5.2.2 Closed-Form Representations

Solving the differential equation (5.1) for $U'(c)$, the general form is found to be

$$U'(c) = \begin{cases} A\,(ac+b)^{-1/a}, & A > 0 \text{ constant} \quad \text{if } a \neq 0, \\ Ae^{-c/b}, & A > 0 \text{ constant} \qquad\quad \text{if } a = 0. \end{cases}$$

Thus, the general form for HARA functions is, unique up to a linear transformation,

$$U(c) = \frac{1}{a-1}(ac+b)^{1-\frac{1}{a}} \qquad \text{if } a \neq 0 \text{ and } a \neq 1, \qquad (5.2)$$

$$U(c) = -be^{-c/b} \qquad \text{if } a = 0, \qquad (5.3)$$

or

$$U(c) = \log(c+b) \qquad \text{if } a = 1. \qquad (5.4)$$

Equation (5.3) is a CARA function with absolute risk aversion $1/b$. As a reference, Merton (1971) presented his equivalent of (5.2) as

$$U(c) = \frac{1-\gamma}{\gamma}\left(\frac{\beta c}{1-\gamma} + \eta\right)^{\gamma}, \qquad \beta > 0, \quad \gamma \neq 0, \quad \gamma \neq 1.$$

Some comments on the class of IARA functions ($b > 0$) are in order. From (5.2), we have

$$U(0) = \frac{1}{a-1}b^{1-\frac{1}{a}} \neq 0$$

and

$$U'(0) = b^{-1/a} < \infty.$$

Such a function implies that we can still derive positive utility if $a > 1$ by consuming nothing ($c = 0$) and that the Inada condition $U'(0) = \infty$ is violated. This could present problems for some economic models, because we cannot rule out the possibility that zero consumption ($c = 0$) is a choice. Then it is possible that the optimal consumption path may include an extended period of zero consumption, particularly when one's wealth is running low. This becomes an issue if lifetime uncertainty is involved, because we typically model death as the state of zero consumption.

DARA and IRRA ($a > 0, b > 0$)
This class of functions presents an interesting case. Its risk aversion is decreasing in wealth in one measure, but is increasing in another. It renders the term risk aversion ambiguous unless we clarify whether it is the absolute measure or the relative measure that is involved. This

class of functions was made popular by Arrow (1965) in his portfolio selection model. Specifically, a risk-averse investor with initial wealth w is choosing between investing in a risk-free asset with a constant rate of return $r \geq 0$, and in a risky asset with a random rate of return ε. Let a be the amount of wealth invested in the risky asset, so that the value of the portfolio becomes

$$\widetilde{w} = (w - a)(1 + r) + a(1 + \varepsilon) = (1 + r)w + a(\varepsilon - r).$$

The investor's problem is

$$\max_{a} E\left[u(\widetilde{w})\right].$$

Arrow showed that the risky asset is a normal good ($da/dw > 0$) if the utility function exhibits DARA. This is a standard example in many of the first-year graduate texts in price theory. Arrow also showed that if the utility function exhibits IRRA, then the wealth elasticity of the risk-free asset is greater than unity:

$$\frac{w}{w - a}\frac{d(w - a)}{dw} > 1. \tag{5.5}$$

Thus, the risk-free asset is a luxury good. In other words, "security is a luxury good" if the utility function exhibits IRRA.

Exercise 5.2.1 *Prove the inequality (5.5).*
   Hint. See Arrow (1965) or Arrow (1984, Chapter 9).

CARA ($a = 0, b > 0$) – Exponential Utility Functions
Functions of the form (5.3) are CARA (and IRRA) with a absolute risk aversion $1/b$. The exponential utility function is popular because we can take advantage of its functional form. For example, in a static model, if wealth W is normally distributed with mean μ and variance σ^2, then the utility of wealth $U(W) = -(1/\gamma)e^{-\gamma W}$ is lognormally distributed. As shown before, the expected value of a lognormal distribution becomes

$$E\left[U(W)\right] = -(1/\gamma)\exp\{-\gamma\mu + \gamma^2\sigma^2/2\}.$$

Thus, the expected utility reduces to a mean–variance form, and the problem is greatly simplified. The shortcoming of this function in our dynamic setting is that the first-order condition could imply negative consumption, as we shall see later.

IARA and IRRA $(a < 0, b > 0)$
For this class of functions, $ac + b > 0$ implies that $c < b/(-a)$. A typical example is the popular *quadratic utility function*

$$U(c) = -(b - c)^2/2, \qquad 0 \le c \le b. \tag{5.6}$$

Without this upper bound $c \le b$, the function would violate the nonsatiation assumption in price theory. This function is employed often because its marginal utility is linear in consumption, which makes the model more tractable whenever the expected utility is involved. This is especially true in discrete-time models. In this case

$$E_t[U'(c_{t+1})] = b - E_t c_{t+1},$$

and the Euler equation of marginal utilities can be translated directly into an equation of consumption.

CRRA $(a > 0, b = 0)$
This class of CRRA (and DARA) functions with a constant relative risk aversion α can be written (up to a linear transformation) as

$$U(c) = \begin{cases} \frac{1}{1-\alpha} c^{1-\alpha} & \text{if } \alpha > 0, \\ \log c & \text{if } \alpha = 1. \end{cases} \tag{5.7}$$

This class of utility functions is perhaps the most commonly employed in the literature. As we pointed out in the previous chapter, α is the degree of relative risk aversion and $1/\alpha$ is the elasticity of intertemporal substitution.

DARA and DRRA $(a > 0, b < 0)$
For this class of functions, $ac + b > 0$ implies that $c > (-b)/a > 0$. In other words, there is a "subsistence" level of consumption for these functions. They are usually written in the form

$$U(c) = \frac{1}{1-\alpha}(c - h)^{1-\alpha}, \qquad c > h, \quad \alpha > 0, \quad \alpha \ne 1.$$

Exercise 5.2.2 *Show that if $U(c)$ is of class C^3 and exhibits DARA, then* $U'''(c) > 0$.

Hint. Show that $U'''(c) U'(c) > [U''(c)]^2$.

5.3 Trial and Error

The essence of this approach is to guess a functional form for the value function. From this guesswork we can derive a closed-form solution for the optimal control policy. To see whether we have guessed correctly, we must verify that the hypothesized value function and the associated optimal controls indeed satisfy the Bellman equation. If they do not, we try again. Over the years, researchers have found some classes of utility functions that do have closed-form solutions. How do we know which function will work? In general, it comes from trial and error guided perhaps by "immortal hand or eye" or, as Professor William A. Brock called it, "divine revelation."

5.3.1 Linear–Quadratic Models

This is a commonly employed model in which the dynamics is linear in state and control variables and the objective function is quadratic. Let x be the state variable and c be the control variable. For positive constants a, b, and σ, the problem is

$$\max_{\{c_t\}} E_x \int_0^\infty e^{-\rho t} \left[-ax_t^2 - bc_t^2 \right] dt \qquad \text{s.t. } dx_t = c_t \, dt + \sigma x_t \, dz_t.$$

Then the Bellman equation is

$$0 = \max_c \left\{ -ax^2 - bc^2 - \rho J(x) + cJ'(x) + \frac{\sigma^2}{2} x^2 J''(x) \right\}.$$

We shall try

$$J(x) = Ax^2, \qquad A < 0.$$

If there is a solution for the parameter A such that the trial function solves the Bellman equation, then this $J(x)$ is a solution. Given this functional form, the Bellman equation is simplified to

$$0 = \max_c \{ -ax^2 - bc^2 - \rho Ax^2 + 2Axc + A\sigma^2 x^2 \}.$$

The first-order condition is

$$c = \frac{A}{b}x,$$

i.e., the control variable is *linear* in the state variable. The second-order condition of the Bellman equation is $-2b < 0$. Substituting $c = (A/b)x$ into the Bellman equation, we have the following quadratic equation

$$\frac{1}{b}A^2 + (\sigma^2 - \rho)A - a = 0.$$

Since $(\sigma^2 - \rho)^2 + 4a/b > 0$, both roots are real. Then we choose the coefficient A to be the negative (real) root of the quadratic equation.

The most commonly employed example of linear–quadratic model is in the theory of consumption functions. It is employed mainly for its tractability. Specifically, we assume the utility function is of the quadratic form (5.6). Then the consumer's problem is

$$\max_{\{c_t\}} E_W \int_0^\infty e^{-\rho t} U(c_t)\, dt \qquad \text{s.t. } dW_t = (rW_t - c_t)\, dt + \sigma W_t\, dz_t.$$

Guess that the functional form of $J(W)$ is

$$J(W) = -\frac{2r + \sigma^2 - \rho}{2}\left[\left(\frac{b}{r+\sigma^2} - W\right)^2 + \frac{\sigma^2}{\rho}\left(\frac{b}{r+\sigma^2}\right)^2\right].$$

The first-order condition becomes

$$(2r + \sigma^2 - \rho)\left(\frac{b}{r+\sigma^2} - W\right) = b - c,$$

or

$$c = (2r + \sigma^2 - \rho)W - \frac{b}{r+\sigma^2}(r - \rho).$$

To ensure $c'(W) > 0$, or $J''(W) < 0$, we need

$$2r + \sigma^2 - \rho > 0.$$

Given the standard assumption that $r \geq \rho$, we need a relatively large initial wealth to ensure $c > 0$. When $r = \rho$, the optimal consumption is $c = (r + \sigma^2) W > 0$ if $W > 0$. If, in addition, $\sigma^2 = 0$, then $c = rW$, which is consistent with the permanent-income theory.

There are, however, serious problems with this immensely popular model. Under the assumption of $r = \rho$, the condition $b - c \geq 0$ implies

$$W \leq \frac{b}{r + \sigma^2},$$

i.e., wealth is bounded from above. On the other hand, the dynamics of wealth is a geometric Brownian motion

$$dW = -\sigma^2 W dt + \sigma W dz,$$

which is always positive and unbounded from above w.p.1. The model is thus self-contradictory, and its applicability is certainly limited.

Exercise 5.3.1 *Find the value function of the following linear–quadratic problem:*

$$\max_c E_x \left\{ \int_0^\infty e^{-\rho t} \left[-\alpha x_t^2 - \beta c_t^2 - \gamma \right] dt \right\}$$
$$s.t. \ dx_t = (\delta x_t + \eta c_t) dt + \sigma x_t \, dz_t,$$

where $\alpha, \beta, \gamma, \delta, \eta$ are all positive constants.

Hint. Try $J(x) = A_0 + A_1 x + A_2 x^2$, and then try to solve for A_0, A_1, and A_2. Verify that $A_1 = 0$. Or guess

$$J(x) = Ax^2 - \frac{\gamma}{\rho}.$$

Then find A.

5.3.2 Linear–HARA models

We shall use Merton's (1971) consumption–portfolio model presented in the previous chapter as our example. For simplicity, assume there is a risk-free asset with interest rate r. Assume the price of the risky asset i, $i = 1, 2, \ldots, n - 1$, follows a geometric Brownian motion, i.e.,

$$dP_t^i = \mu_i P_t^i \, dt + \sigma_i P_t^i \, dz_t^i, \qquad i = 1, 2, \ldots, n - 1, \qquad (5.8)$$

with $(dz_t^i)(dz_t^j) = 0$ if $i \neq j$. Let s_i be the share of wealth allocated to asset i. Recall that the consumer's wealth follows the controlled diffusion process

$$dW = \left[\sum_{i=1}^{n-1} s_i (\mu_i - r) W + (rW - c)\right] dt + \sum_{i=1}^{n-1} s_i \sigma_i W dz^i, \quad (5.9)$$

and the consumer's problem is formulated as

$$\max_{\{c, s_i\}} E \int_0^{\infty} e^{-\rho t} U(c_t) dt \qquad \text{s.t. (5.9)}, \text{ with } W_0 = W. \qquad (5.10)$$

Then the Bellman equation of the problem (5.10) is

$$0 = \max_{c, s_i} \left\{ U(c) - \rho J(W) + \left[\sum_{i=1}^{n-1} s_i(\mu_i - r)W + (rW - c)\right] J'(W) \right.$$

$$\left. + \frac{1}{2} \sum_{i=1}^{n-1} s_i^2 \sigma_i^2 W^2 J''(W) \right\} \quad (5.11)$$

From the first-order conditions of (5.11), we have

$$U'(c) = J'(W) \qquad (5.12)$$

and

$$s_i = \frac{\mu_i - r}{\sigma_i^2} \left[-\frac{J'(W)}{W J''(W)}\right], \qquad i = 1, 2, \ldots, n - 1. \qquad (5.13)$$

Utility Function of the Form (5.2)

If the utility function is of the form (5.2), then the marginal utility function is of the form $U'(c) = (ac + b)^{-1/a}$, if $a \neq 0$. Try

$$J(W) = A \left(\frac{a}{a-1}\right)(W + b')^{1-\frac{1}{a}}, \qquad (5.14)$$

where A and b' are to be determined. Clearly,

$$J'(W) = A(W + b')^{-\frac{1}{a}}.$$

Then (5.12) and (5.13) imply that

$$ac + b = A^{-a}(W + b')$$

and

$$s_i W = \left(\frac{\mu_i - r}{\sigma_i^2} \right) a \, (W + b').$$

This shows that, if (5.14) is a value function, then c and each $s_i W$ are linear functions of W.

It remains to find A and b' so that (5.14) is a solution to the Bellman equation. To this end, we notice that

$$s_i \, (\mu_i - r) \, W J'(W) = \left(\frac{\mu_i - r}{\sigma_i} \right)^2 A a \, (W + b')^{1-\frac{1}{a}}$$

$$= \left(\frac{\mu_i - r}{\sigma_i} \right)^2 A^a a \, (ac + b)^{1-\frac{1}{a}}$$

and

$$s_i^2 \sigma_i^2 W^2 J''(W) = - \left(\frac{\mu_i - r}{\sigma_i} \right)^2 A a \, (W + b')^{1-\frac{1}{a}}$$

$$= - \left(\frac{\mu_i - r}{\sigma_i} \right)^2 A^a a \, (ac + b)^{1-\frac{1}{a}}$$

are opposite in sign. In fact, all terms in the Bellman equation, except possibly the term $(r W - c) J'(W)$, have a common factor $(ac + b)^{1-\frac{1}{a}}$. Since $J'(W)$ is of order $(ac + b)^{-1/a}$, it suggests that we should choose b' in such a way that $r W - c$ is proportional to $ac + b$. To this end, we choose $b' = b/(ar)$ so that

$$r W - c = r \, (W + b') - r b' - c = r A^a (ac + b) - \frac{1}{a} (ac + b).$$

Substituting them into the Bellman equation and dividing it by $(ac + b)^{1-\frac{1}{a}}$, the Bellman equation is of the form $\Psi A^a + \Phi = 0$, viz.,

$$\frac{1}{a-1} - \frac{1}{a} + \left[-\frac{\rho}{a-1} + \frac{1}{2} \sum_{i=1}^{n-1} \left(\frac{\mu_i - r}{\sigma_i} \right)^2 + \frac{r}{a} \right] a A^a = 0.$$

If there is a solution for A to the above equation, then we are done. To ensure its existence, however, we need $\Psi \Phi < 0$. Additional restrictions on the parameters are thus needed. Since that is rather straightforward, we shall leave it as an exercise.

CARA Utility Functions

Assume the utility function is of the form (5.3). For notational convenience, we shall denote it by

$$U(c) = -(1/\alpha) e^{-\alpha c}, \qquad \alpha > 0,$$

with the degree of absolute risk aversion α. An educated guess would be that the value function is also of constant absolute risk aversion,

$$J(W) = -(A/\alpha) e^{-r\alpha W}, \qquad A > 0,$$

because consumption c should be related to permanent income rW. This value function has a constant absolute risk aversion αr. Then, from (5.12), the optimal consumption is

$$c = rW - (1/\alpha) \log(rA), \tag{5.15}$$

and, from (5.13), the optimal portfolio rule is

$$s_i W = \left(\frac{\mu_i - r}{\sigma_i^2} \right) \left(\frac{1}{\alpha r} \right). \tag{5.16}$$

It is interesting to point out that it is the *absolute* amount, $s_i W$, not the relative share of wealth invested in the risky asset, that is constant. Substituting (5.15) and (5.16) into the Bellman equation and dividing it by $(Ar/\alpha) \exp\{-r\alpha W\}$, we have

$$\log(rA) - 1 + \frac{\rho}{r} + \frac{1}{2} \sum_{i=1}^{n-1} \left(\frac{\mu_i - r}{\sigma_i} \right)^2 \left(\frac{1}{r} \right) = 0.$$

This determines the constant A, i.e.,

$$A = \frac{1}{r} \exp \left\{ 1 - \frac{\rho}{r} - \frac{1}{2} \sum_{i=1}^{n-1} \left(\frac{\mu_i - r}{\sigma_i} \right)^2 \left(\frac{1}{r} \right) \right\} > 0.$$

Since $\log(rA) \neq 0$ in general, it is possible that, from (5.15), negative consumption may occur. This will happen, for example, if W is very small and $\log(rA) > 0$. It is interesting to note that if $r = \rho$, then $\log(rA) < 0$ and there is no danger of negative consumption.

CRRA Utility Functions

Let the utility function be of CRRA, as represented by (5.7). This class of utility function is frequently employed in the literature and hence deserves a discussion by itself. As with (5.14), we shall try the following value function:

$$J(W) = \frac{A^{-\alpha}}{1-\alpha} W^{1-\alpha}, \qquad A > 0,$$

i.e., $J(W)$ is also isoelastic. From (5.13),

$$s_i = \frac{\mu_i - r}{\alpha \sigma_i^2},$$

i.e., each s_i is a constant. From equation (5.12), we have

$$c = AW,$$

i.e., consumption is proportional to wealth. It remains to determine the parameter A. Substituting c and s_i into the Bellman equation and dividing it by $A^{-\alpha} W^{1-\alpha}$, we have

$$\frac{A}{1-\alpha} - \frac{\rho}{1-\alpha} + r - A + \frac{1}{2} \sum_{i=1}^{n-1} \frac{(\mu_i - r)^2}{\alpha \sigma_i^2} = 0.$$

Thus, the Bellman equation is satisfied if we choose

$$A = \frac{\rho}{\alpha} - \frac{1-\alpha}{\alpha} \left[r + \frac{1}{2} \sum_{i=1}^{n-1} \frac{(\mu_i - r)^2}{\alpha \sigma_i^2} \right]. \tag{5.17}$$

To ensure that $A > 0$, we need

$$\rho > (1-\alpha) \left[r + \frac{1}{2} \sum_{i=1}^{n-1} \frac{(\mu_i - r)^2}{\alpha \sigma_i^2} \right]. \tag{5.18}$$

This equation is also needed in Merton's finite-horizon model. (See his equation (47).)

Logarithmic Utility Functions

Now suppose $U(c) = \log c$ as a special case of (5.4). The degree of relative risk aversion is 1, i.e., $\alpha = 1$. Then we choose

$$J(W) = (1/A) \log W + B.$$

Notice that we have two coefficients A and B to be determined. In this case, the share of each risky asset, $s_i = (\mu_i - r)/\sigma_i^2$, is still a constant, and consumption, $c = AW$, is still linear in wealth. Substituting c and s_i into the Bellman equation, we have

$$\log A + \log W - \left(\frac{\rho}{A}\right) \log W - \rho B$$

$$+ \frac{1}{A}\left[\frac{1}{2}\sum_{i=1}^{n-1}\frac{(\mu_i - r)^2}{\sigma_i^2} + r - A\right] = 0.$$

Clearly, we should choose $A = \rho$ to get rid of $\log W$ terms, and

$$B = \frac{1}{\rho}\left\{\log \rho + \frac{1}{\rho}\left[\frac{1}{2}\sum_{i=1}^{n-1}\frac{(\mu_i - r)^2}{\sigma_i^2} + r - \rho\right]\right\}.$$

Exercise 5.3.2 *Show that, if there is only one risky asset, then $U(c)$ is of HARA class if and only if c and sW are linear in W.*

Hint. See Merton (1971).

5.3.3 Linear–Concave Models

The best example of a linear law of motion and a strictly concave objective function is the model of adjustment costs discussed in Chapter 4. The value function of the adjustment cost model as set up in Pindyck (1982) has no known closed-form solution. In order to obtain such a solution, we examine a special case in which the market is competitive and the production function is of Cobb–Douglas form. This example is due to Abel (1983). Our presentation, however, is based on Chang (1993).

Competitive Firm

Suppose the inverse demand follows

$$dp = \sigma p\, dz, \tag{5.19}$$

i.e., the price follows a geometric Brownian motion with zero drift. Thus $p > 0$ w.p.1 at all times. The investment equation is

$$dK = (I - \delta K)\,dt. \tag{5.20}$$

Let $F(K, L) = K^{1-\alpha}L^\alpha$, $0 < \alpha < 1$. Then the problem is

$$\max_{\{L,I\}} E \int_0^\infty e^{-rt}\left[pK^{1-\alpha}L^\alpha - wL - vI - C(I)\right]dt$$

$$\text{s.t. (5.19) and (5.20)}.$$

The corresponding Bellman equation is

$$0 = \max_{L,I}\left\{pK^{1-\alpha}L^\alpha - wL - vI - C(I) - rJ(K, p)\right.$$

$$\left. + (I - \delta K)J_K(K, p) + \tfrac{1}{2}\sigma^2 p^2 J_{pp}(K, p)\right\}.$$

The first-order conditions are

$$J_K(K, p) = v + C'(I) \tag{5.21}$$

and

$$w = p\alpha (K/L)^{1-\alpha},$$

which implies

$$L = \left(\frac{p\alpha}{w}\right)^{\frac{1}{1-\alpha}} K.$$

Then the maximized short-run profit is

$$pK^{1-\alpha}L^\alpha - wL = (1 - \alpha)\,p^{\frac{1}{1-\alpha}}\left(\frac{\alpha}{w}\right)^{\frac{\alpha}{1-\alpha}} K = hp^{\frac{1}{1-\alpha}}K,$$

where

$$h = (1 - \alpha)\left(\frac{\alpha}{w}\right)^{\frac{\alpha}{1-\alpha}}.$$

And the Bellman equation can be simplified as

$$0 = \max_{I} \left\{ hp^{\frac{1}{1-\alpha}} K - vI - C(I) - rJ(K, p) \right.$$

$$\left. + (I - \delta K)J_K(K, p) + \tfrac{1}{2}\sigma^2 p^2 J_{pp}(K, p) \right\}.$$

How to Guess the Solution

Mussa (1977, p. 171) showed that the market value of a competitive firm is a linear function of the firm's current capital stock if the production function is linearly homogeneous in capital and labor. In other words, the value function of the adjustment cost problem is linear in K, that is, the shadow price of capital is independent of the level of the capital. This suggests that an educated guess for the value function in the stochastic case should have a similar form:

$$J(K, p) = G(p)K + H(p), \tag{5.22}$$

so that $J_K(K, p)$ is independent of the level of capital, K. It has the interpretation that the expected market value of a firm is the expected return from the existing capital, $G(p)K$, plus the expected value of the firm's capacity to create newly installed capital, $H(p)$. The presence of price uncertainty, on the other hand, affects only the shadow price of capital, $J_K = G(p)$, and the expected value of new installment, $H(p)$.

Substituting (5.22) into the Bellman equation and comparing terms (those with K and those without K), we obtain

$$hp^{\frac{1}{1-\alpha}} - (r + \delta)G(p) + \frac{1}{2}\sigma^2 p^2 G''(p) = 0 \tag{5.23}$$

and

$$IG(p) - vI - C(I) - rH(p) + \frac{1}{2}\sigma^2 p^2 H''(p) = 0. \tag{5.24}$$

The equation made up of the last two terms of equation (5.23) is

$$(r + \delta)G(p) + \frac{1}{2}\sigma^2 p^2 G''(p) = 0. \tag{5.25}$$

Equation (5.25) takes the form of an Euler's homogeneous equation whose solutions are of the power function form. Moreover, since $J_K > 0$, we must have $G(p) > 0$ for all p. This suggests that a particular solution to (5.23) should be of the form

$$G(p) = ahp^{\frac{1}{1-\alpha}},$$

for some constant $a > 0$. It is easy to verify that a satisfies, from (5.23),

$$1 - (r + \delta)a + a\left(\frac{\sigma^2}{2}\right)\left(\frac{1}{1-\alpha}\right)\left(\frac{1}{1-\alpha} - 1\right) = 0.$$

That is,

$$\frac{1}{a} = r + \delta - \frac{\sigma^2}{2}\frac{\alpha}{(1-\alpha)^2}.$$

Some comments are in order. Since $G(p) > 0$, we must have $a > 0$ or

$$r + \delta > \frac{\sigma^2}{2}\frac{\alpha}{(1-\alpha)^2}.$$

Equivalently, σ^2 has an upper bound. Though we have obtained a closed-form solution, the model may not be applicable if the environment is very volatile, i.e., if the variance is very large. We shall, however, assume this inequality is valid in what follows.

Implications

An interesting implication of this closed-form solution is the effect of uncertainty on investment. Specifically, from (5.21),

$$C''(I)\frac{\partial I}{\partial \sigma^2} = \frac{\partial G(p)}{\partial \sigma^2} = hp^{\frac{1}{1-\alpha}}\left(\frac{\partial a}{\partial \sigma^2}\right) > 0.$$

Since $C''(I) > 0$, we have $\partial I/\partial \sigma^2 > 0$. We conclude that investment rises with the degree of uncertainty. Another result is that our guess $J_{KK}(K, p) = 0$ implies

$$I = (C')^{-1}(G(p) - v) = (C')^{-1}\left(ahp^{\frac{1}{1-\alpha}} - v\right).$$

Clearly, the optimal investment, I, is independent of K. Moreover, under the assumption of constant prices, I is constant over time. Thus, we have reestablished Gould's result shown in Chapter 4.

To find an explicit solution for $H(p)$, we need to spell out the functional form of $C(I)$. Once $C(I)$ is given, we can solve for the optimal investment, I, in terms of $G(p)$. For example, if $C(I) = I^{1+\beta}/(1+\beta)$, $\beta > 0$, then $I = [G(p) - v]^{1/\beta}$. Substituting $G(p) = ahp^{\frac{1}{1-\alpha}}$ into (5.24), we can in principle find a solution for $H(p)$.

Exercise 5.3.3 *Show that if* $C(I) = \gamma I^\beta$, $\beta > 1$, *and* $v = 0$, *then*

$$H(p) = \frac{(\beta - 1)\gamma \left(\frac{G(p)}{\beta\gamma}\right)^{\beta/(\beta-1)}}{r - \frac{\beta(1-\alpha+\alpha\beta)\sigma^2}{2(1-\alpha)^2(\beta-1)^2}}.$$

5.3.4 Nonlinear–Concave Models

A closed-form solution for the value function for this class of problems is generally difficult to obtain because of the nonlinearity of the controlled diffusion process. The best example in this class is the optimal growth model.

An Optimal Growth Model

To present this method, we have to be more specific about the concave utility function and the concave production function. Let the utility function be of the form

$$U(c) = \frac{1}{1-\alpha}c^{1-\alpha}, \qquad 0 < \alpha < 1,$$

and the production function be of Cobb–Douglas form such that

$$f(k) = Ak^\alpha, \qquad A > 0.$$

Notice that the production elasticity is the same as the degree of risk aversion. Recall that the stochastic Solow equation is

$$dk_t = [f(k_t) - c_t - (n - \sigma^2)k_t]\,dt - \sigma k_t\,dz_t, \qquad (5.26)$$

which is nonlinear. Then the Bellman equation becomes

$$0 = \max_{c} \left\{ \tfrac{1}{1-\alpha} c^{1-\alpha} - \rho J(k) + \left[Ak^{\alpha} - c - (n - \sigma^2)k \right] J'(k) \right.$$

$$\left. + \tfrac{1}{2}\sigma^2 k^2 J''(k) \right\}$$

How to Guess the Solution

The first-order condition of the Bellman equation is

$$c^{-\alpha} = J'(k). \tag{5.27}$$

Then the Bellman equation

$$0 = \frac{\alpha}{1-\alpha}[J'(k)]^{-\frac{1-\alpha}{\alpha}} - \rho J(k) + [f(k) - (n - \sigma^2)k]J'(k)$$

$$+ \frac{1}{2}\sigma^2 k^2 J''(k) \tag{5.28}$$

involves $J(k)$ and its derivatives. Suppose we remove the production function $f(k)$ from (5.28), i.e., suppose we look at the following equation:

$$0 = \frac{\alpha}{1-\alpha}[J'(k)]^{-\frac{1-\alpha}{\alpha}} - \rho J(k) - (n - \sigma^2)kJ'(k) + \frac{1}{2}\sigma^2 k^2 J''(k). \tag{5.29}$$

The homogeneous component of (5.29) is Euler's homogeneous equation, whose solution is a power function of k. It is easy to verify that $a^{-1}k^{1-\alpha}$, for some constant a, is a solution to (5.29). The presence of the production function may still be manageable if the term $f(k)J'(k)$ is a constant. This suggests that the problem can be solved if the production function has a constant production elasticity α.

Indeed, we shall guess the value function to be of the form

$$J(k) = (1 - \alpha)^{-1} a^{-1} k^{1-\alpha} + b. \tag{5.30}$$

Then (5.27) implies that the optimal consumption is *linear* in the capital–labor ratio, i.e.,

$$c = a^{1/\alpha}k.$$

It remains to show that the value function (5.30) is legitimate. Since $J'(k) = a^{-1}k^{-\alpha}$ and $J''(k) = -\alpha a^{-1}k^{-\alpha-1}$, every term in the Bellman equation is either of the form $k^{1-\alpha}$ or of the form k^0. A straightforward calculation shows that the coefficients for $k^{1-\alpha}$ and k^0 are, respectively, governed by

$$\frac{\alpha}{1-\alpha}a^{(1-\alpha)/\alpha} - \frac{1}{1-\alpha}\rho a^{-1} - (n - \sigma^2)a^{-1} - \frac{\sigma^2}{2}\alpha a^{-1} = 0$$

and

$$Aa^{-1} - \rho b = 0.$$

Therefore,

$$a = \left\{\frac{1-\alpha}{\alpha}\left(n - \sigma^2 + \frac{\sigma^2}{2}\alpha\right) + \frac{\rho}{\alpha}\right\}^{\alpha}$$

and

$$b = \rho^{-1}Aa^{-1}.$$

This example is obviously a very special case. Even a mild modification of the model may not have known solutions. For example, if the production function is still of Cobb–Douglas form but the production elasticity is different from the degree of relative risk aversion, then equation (5.30) can not be a solution to the problem. As mentioned earlier, it is the nonlinearity of the Solow equation that makes the problem hard.

5.4 Symmetry

What is a symmetry? Loosely speaking, it is a transformation so that the transformed geometric object is the same as the original object. For example, given a square, a rotation of 90°, 180°, 270°, ... about its center will leave the square invariant. Any of these transformations is a symmetry. Similarly, any rotation of a circle about its center is a symmetry. A sine curve is invariant under a translation of $2k\pi$, where k is an integer. Higher-dimensional geometric objects also have their symmetries, e.g., a rotation of a sphere about its axis.

A typical intertemporal optimization problem has two components: the objective function and the law of motion governing the dynamics of the model. In stochastic control problems, the dynamics is summarized by a controlled diffusion process. The set of solutions to the controlled diffusion process is a geometric object in the space of the state and control variables. A transformation (change of variables) of the original control problem changes the objective function and the dynamics, and gives rise to a new value function. However, some changes of variables may have left the dynamics invariant. Such a transformation, if it exists, is a symmetry, because it represents the same law of motion. If the objective function is preserved in some ways, then the new value function can be related to the original value function. Then it is possible to ascertain the functional form of the value function.

It would be instructive to apply this idea to some well-known results in standard consumer theory. A typical consumer problem has two components: tastes and opportunities. The former is described by the preference structure and the latter is characterized by the budget equation. The budget equation represents the budget line, the geometric object in this problem. By definition, the indirect utility function is

$$V\left(\mathbf{P}, I\right) = \max_{\mathbf{X}} \left\{ U\left(\mathbf{X}\right) : \mathbf{P} \cdot \mathbf{X} = I \right\}.$$

Suppose $U\left(\mathbf{X}\right)$ is homogeneous of degree $\alpha > 0$ in $\mathbf{X}$. We shall show that the indirect utility function is homogeneous of degree α in I, using the symmetry method. The symmetry we are looking for is

$$\Phi\left(\mathbf{P}, I, \mathbf{X}\right) = \left(\mathbf{P}, \gamma I, \gamma \mathbf{X}\right), \qquad \gamma > 0,$$

because the budget line $\{\mathbf{X} : \mathbf{P} \cdot \mathbf{X} = I\}$ is identical to $\{\mathbf{X} : \mathbf{P} \cdot (\gamma \mathbf{X}) = \gamma I\}$. While the budget equation remains unchanged, the objective function is changed into $U\left(\gamma \mathbf{X}\right) = \gamma^{\alpha} U\left(\mathbf{X}\right)$. Therefore, the new value function $V\left(\mathbf{P}, \gamma I\right)$ is related to the original $V\left(\mathbf{P}, I\right)$ by a factor of γ^{α}, i.e., we have the equation

$$V\left(\mathbf{P}, \gamma I\right) = \gamma^{\alpha} V\left(\mathbf{P}, I\right).$$

Hence, $V\left(\mathbf{P}, I\right)$ is homogeneous of degree α in I. Incidentally, this proposition is often used to illustrate the law of diminishing marginal utility of income if $\alpha < 1$.

It is useful to compare this symmetry argument with the standard proof in price theory for this proposition. The standard proof goes as follows.

Using the change of variables, $\mathbf{Y} = \gamma \mathbf{X}$,

$$V(\mathbf{P}, \gamma I) = \max_{\mathbf{Y}} \{U(\mathbf{Y}) : \mathbf{P} \cdot \mathbf{Y} = \gamma I\} = \max_{\mathbf{X}} \{U(\gamma \mathbf{X}) : \mathbf{P} \cdot (\gamma \mathbf{X}) = \gamma I\}$$

$$= \gamma^{\alpha} \max_{\mathbf{X}} \{U(\mathbf{X}) : \mathbf{P} \cdot \mathbf{X} = I\} = \gamma^{\alpha} V(\mathbf{P}, I).$$

This makes the point that the method of symmetry is not new to economists, and certainly is not a "fearful" one.

Exercise 5.4.1

(1) Suppose $U(\mathbf{X})$ is homogeneous of degree α in $\mathbf{X}$. Show that $V(\mathbf{P}, I)$ is homogeneous of degree $-\alpha$ in $\mathbf{P}$.

Hint. The symmetry is

$$\Phi(\mathbf{P}, I, \mathbf{X}) = (\gamma \mathbf{P}, I, (1/\gamma)\mathbf{X}).$$

(2) Suppose $U(\mathbf{X})$ is homogeneous of degree α in $\mathbf{X}$. Show that $V(\mathbf{P}, I)$ is homogeneous of degree zero in $(\mathbf{P}, I)$.

Hint. The symmetry is

$$\Phi(\mathbf{P}, I, \mathbf{X}) = (\gamma \mathbf{P}, \gamma I, \mathbf{X}).$$

5.4.1 Linear–Quadratic Model Revisited

This is the simplest case. The law of motion is

$$dx = c\, dt + \sigma x\, dz.$$

If we change the state variable from x to γx, for some $\gamma > 0$, and change the control variable from c to γc, the law of motion remains unchanged. In other words, the transformation

$$\Phi(x, c) = (\gamma x, \gamma c)$$

is the symmetry we are looking for. Then, the transformed objective function is

$$E \int_0^{\infty} e^{-\rho t}[-a(\gamma x)^2 - b(\gamma c)^2]\, dt = \gamma^2 E \int_0^{\infty} e^{-\rho t}[-ax^2 - bc^2]\, dt.$$

This says that the indirect utility function satisfies the following equation:

$$J(\gamma x) = \gamma^2 J(x), \qquad \gamma > 0. \tag{5.31}$$

It is well known that a real-valued function that is homogeneous of degree 2 must be of the form

$$J(x) = Ax^2,$$

as shown earlier. The constant A can also be solved as follows. Substituting $\gamma = 1/x$ in (5.31), we have $J(1) = (1/x)^2 J(x)$, which implies $J(x) = J(1) x^2$. Thus, the constant A has the economic meaning $J(1)$.

There is a new result using this approach. Under "divine revelation," we try $J(x) = Ax^2$, and it works. Thus $J(x) = Ax^2$ is a solution. Under symmetry, however, we show that the value function has to be of this form. Hence, $J(x) = Ax^2$ is *the* solution in the class of C^2 functions. The constant A is uniquely determined by the Bellman equation, as demonstrated before.

5.4.2 Merton's Model Revisited

Merton's consumption and portfolio selection model provides a nice contrast between the symmetry method and the "divine revelation" method of the previous section.

CRRA Utility Functions

Let $U(c) = \frac{1}{1-\alpha} c^{1-\alpha}$, $\alpha > 0$, $\alpha \neq 1$. For a symmetry to be useful, we have to be able to exploit the nature of this utility function, specifically, that it raises consumption to its $(1 - \alpha)$-th power. It suggests that the symmetry will be in some multiplicative form. Suppose we double wealth *at all times*. Intuition tells us that consumption at all times should also be doubled. Suppose that is the case. Now look at the budget equation (5.9). If all wealth and consumption are doubled, and *if* the share of the risky asset remains unchanged, then the new budget equation becomes

$$d(\gamma W) = \left[\sum_{i=1}^{n-1} s_i (\mu_i - r)(\gamma W) + r(\gamma W) - \gamma c \right] dt$$
$$+ \sum_{i=1}^{n-1} s_i \sigma_i (\gamma W) dz^i. \tag{5.32}$$

Notice that equation (5.32) is the same as equation (5.9) multiplied by γ. Then both equations should describe the same dynamics. In other words, the transformation

$$\Phi(W, c, s_1, \ldots, s_{n-1}) = (\gamma W, \gamma c, s_1, \ldots, s_{n-1}) \qquad (5.33)$$

is a symmetry.

Using this symmetry, the transformed utility is

$$U(\gamma c_t) = \frac{1}{1-\alpha}(\gamma c_t)^{1-\alpha} = \gamma^{1-\alpha} U(c_t).$$

We can pull the factor $\gamma^{1-\alpha}$ outside the maximization problem. What remains then is a problem that maximizes the original utility function subject to a law of motion, which is identical to the original law of motion. Other than the extra term $\gamma^{1-\alpha}$, the rest is the same as the problem (5.10). Therefore, the value function associated with the initial wealth γW, $J(\gamma W)$, can be equated to the value function associated with (5.10) as follows:

$$J(\gamma W) = \gamma^{1-\alpha} J(W). \qquad (5.34)$$

This says that the value function is homogeneous of degree $1 - \alpha$. Setting $\gamma = 1/W$, we have

$$J(W) = J(1) W^{1-\alpha}.$$

Again, this is *the* only functional form for the problem. The determination of $J(1)$ will proceed as before.

Let $U(c) = \log c$. A major property of logarithmic functions is that the logarithm of the product equals the sum of the logarithms, i.e., $\log ab = \log a + \log b$. This again suggests that the symmetry we are looking for is also of multiplicative form. Indeed, it is similarly verified that transformation (5.33) is a symmetry. Using this symmetry, the transformed utility is

$$U(\gamma c) = \log(\gamma c) = \log \gamma + U(c).$$

Then the objective function becomes

$$E \int_0^\infty e^{-\rho t} U(\gamma c_t)\, dt = E \int_0^\infty e^{-\rho t} U(c_t)\, dt + \frac{1}{\rho} \log \gamma.$$

Thus, we have

$$J(\gamma W) = J(W) + (1/\rho)\log\gamma. \qquad (5.35)$$

Setting $\gamma = 1/W$, equation (5.35) leads us to

$$J(W) = (1/\rho)\log W + J(1).$$

The constant $J(1)$ can be determined as before.

CARA Utility Functions

Let the utility function be of constant absolute risk aversion, $U(c) = -e^{-\alpha c}$. It should be obvious to the reader that the symmetry (5.33) does not work in this case. This is because we cannot separate $U(c) = -e^{-\alpha c}$ from $U(\gamma c) = -e^{-\alpha\gamma c} = -(e^{-\alpha c})^{\gamma}$ in an additive or a multiplicative form. We must look for a different symmetry. In contrast to the case of logarithmic utility function, the exponential functions satisfy that the exponential of a sum is the product of exponentials, $e^{a+b} = e^{a}e^{b}$. This suggests that the desired symmetry is of additive form.

Suppose wealth goes up by γ at all times. Assume c_t is transformed to c'_t and s_t is transformed into s'_t. Then we have a new budget equation

$$d(W+\gamma) = \left[\sum_{i=1}^{n-1} s'_i(\mu_i - r)(W+\gamma) + r(W+\gamma) - c'\right] dt$$

$$+ \sum_{i=1}^{n-1} s'_i\sigma_i(W+\gamma)\,dz^i. \qquad (5.36)$$

The left-hand side of (5.36) satisfies $d(W_t + \gamma) = dW_t$. For the budget equation (5.36) to be the same as the budget equation (5.9), we need the following two equations:

$$\sum_{i=1}^{n-1} s'_i(\mu_i - r)(W+\gamma) + r(W+\gamma) - c'$$

$$= \sum_{i=1}^{n-1} s_i(\mu_i - r)W + rW - c \qquad (5.37)$$

and

$$\sum_{i=1}^{n-1} s'_i \sigma_i (W + \gamma) = \sum_{i=1}^{n-1} s_i \sigma_i W. \qquad (5.38)$$

Equation (5.38) is satisfied if

$$s'_i = \frac{s_i W}{W + \gamma}, \qquad i = 1, 2, \ldots, n - 1. \qquad (5.39)$$

Substituting (5.39) into (5.37), we have

$$c' = c + r\gamma. \qquad (5.40)$$

Equation (5.40) is actually quite intuitive. It says that if wealth goes up by an amount γ, then consumption will go up by the corresponding permanent income $r\gamma$. To summarize, the symmetry we are looking for is

$$\Phi(W, c, s_1, \ldots, s_{n-1}) = \left(W + \gamma, c + r\gamma, \frac{s_1 W}{W + \gamma}, \ldots, \frac{s_{n-1} W}{W + \gamma} \right). \qquad (5.41)$$

Using this symmetry, the utility function is

$$U(c_t + r\gamma) = -e^{-\alpha(c_t + r\gamma)} = e^{-\alpha r\gamma} U(c_t),$$

and the value function satisfies the equation

$$J(W + \gamma) = e^{-\alpha r\gamma} J(W).$$

Setting $\gamma = -W$, we arrive at

$$J(W) = J(0) e^{-\alpha r W}, \qquad J(0) < 0.$$

It shows that the value function has a constant absolute risk aversion αr. Using this value function, the optimal consumption is

$$c = rW - (1/\alpha) \log [-rJ(0)],$$

which is (5.15), except that the constant A may be interpreted as $-J(0)$. Similarly, the share of wealth invested in the risky asset is given by (5.16). The determination of $J(0)$ is straightforward.

5.4.3 Fischer's Index Bond Model

This example shows that sometimes we have to use more than one symmetry to solve the problem. As mentioned in the previous chapter, there are three assets in this model: index bonds (asset 1), equity (asset 2), and nominal bonds (asset 3). Recall that the general price level follows a geometric Brownian motion

$$\frac{dP}{P} = \pi \, dt + \sigma_1 \, dz. \qquad (5.42)$$

Let s_1, s_2 be the share of wealth invested in index bonds and equity respectively, and let R_i be the nominal return to asset i, $i = 1, 2, 3$. Then the budget equation is

$$dW = \left\{ \sum_{i=1}^{2} s_i (R_i - R_3)W + R_3 W - Pc \right\} dt + \sum_{i=1}^{2} s_i \sigma_i W \, dz^i. \qquad (5.43)$$

Assume the utility function is of constant relative risk aversion, $U(c) = c^{1-\alpha}/(1-\alpha)$, $\alpha > 0$. Then the consumer's problem is

$$\max_{\{c, s_1, s_2\}} E_W \int_0^\infty e^{-\rho t} \frac{c^{1-\alpha}}{1-\alpha} dt \qquad \text{s.t. (5.42) and (5.43)}.$$

The first symmetry is similar to the one from Merton's model,

$$\Phi_1 (W, P, c, s_1, s_2) = (\gamma W, P, \gamma c, s_1, s_2).$$

Under this symmetry, the value function satisfies

$$J(\gamma W, P) = \gamma^{1-\alpha} J(W, P).$$

This equation says that the value function is homogeneous of degree $1 - \alpha$ in W. Thus, we may write

$$J(W, P) = J(1, P) W^{1-\alpha}. \qquad (5.44)$$

An immediate corollary is that $J(W, P)$ exhibits constant relative risk aversion in wealth.

There is another symmetry

$$\Phi_2 (W, P, c, s_1, s_2) = (\gamma W, \gamma P, c, s_1, s_2).$$

Under this symmetry, the value function satisfies

$$J(\gamma W, \gamma P) = J(W, P). \qquad (5.45)$$

This equation says that the value function is a function of *real* wealth, not nominal wealth. Moreover,

$$J(1, P) W^{1-\alpha} = J(W, P) = J(\gamma W, \gamma P) = J(1, \gamma P) \gamma^{1-\alpha} W^{1-\alpha},$$

implies that

$$J(1, \gamma P) \gamma^{1-\alpha} = J(1, P).$$

Setting $\gamma = 1/P$, we have

$$J(1, P) = J(1, 1)(1/P)^{1-\alpha}.$$

Consequently, the value function is of the form

$$J(W, P) = J(1, 1)(W/P)^{1-\alpha}. \qquad (5.46)$$

This value function should come in handy in solving for the demand for the index bond problem. Recall that, in the previous chapter, we *assumed* that the value function is homogeneous of degree zero in W and P, based on the assumption of no money illusion. Here we *proved* that there is indeed no money illusion.

Exercise 5.4.2 *Let the utility function be logarithmic, $U(c) = \log c$. Show that the indirect utility function for Fischer's index bond problem is of the form $J(W, P) = J(1, 1) + \log(W/P)$.*

5.4.4 Life Insurance

As discussed in Chapter 4, we can convert an uncertain-lifetime problem into a deterministic optimization problem by using the survival function $S(t) = \int_t^{\overline{T}} \pi(t) \, dt$. Assume there is only one risky asset, and recall that the budget dynamics is

$$dW_t = [s_t(\mu - r)W_t + (rW_t - c_t) - \theta_t Q_t] \, dt + s_t \sigma W_t \, dz_t, \qquad (5.47)$$

where θ_t is the insurance premium per dollar of coverage, and Q_t is the amount of insurance purchased at age t. Let the bequest function be of the form $B(t, Z_t)$, where $Z_t = W_t + Q_t$ is the contingent bequest. Then the problem of life insurance purchase is

$$\max_{\{c_t, s_t, Q_t\}} \int_0^{\overline{T}} \left[e^{-\rho t} S(t) u(c_t) + \pi(t) B(t, Z_t) \right] dt \qquad \text{s.t. (5.47)}.$$

Recall that, for easy computation, we have set the value function to be of the form $S(t) J(t, W_t)$ with hazard rate $\lambda(t) = \pi(t) / S(t)$.

To apply the symmetry method, let both the utility function and the bequest function be isoelastic with the same elasticity α, i.e., for $\alpha > 0$,

$$u(c) = \frac{1}{1 - \alpha} c^{1 - \alpha}$$

and

$$B(t, Z) = \frac{1}{1 - \alpha} e^{-\rho t} Z^{1 - \alpha}.$$

Then

$$\Phi(W_t, c_t, s_t, Q_t) = (\gamma W_t, \gamma c_t, s_t, \gamma Q_t)$$

is a symmetry. Thus, the value function satisfies

$$J(t, \gamma W) = \gamma^{1 - \alpha} J(t, W).$$

Then the value function is of the form

$$S(t) J(t, W) = \frac{1}{1 - \alpha} S(t) J(t, 1) W^{1 - \alpha},$$

where $J(t, 1)$ is to be determined from the Bellman equation. From the Bellman equation

$$0 = \max_{c_t, s_t, Q_t} \left\{ e^{-\rho t} u(c_t) + \lambda(t) B(t, Z_t) + J_t - \lambda(t) J \right.$$
$$+ \left[s_t (\mu - r) W_t + (r W_t - c_t) - \theta_t Q_t \right] J_W$$
$$+ \left. (\sigma^2 / 2) s_t^2 W_t^2 J_{WW} \right\},$$

the first-order conditions are

$$e^{-\rho t} u'(c_t) = J_W,$$

$$s_t W_t = \left(\frac{\mu - r}{\sigma^2}\right) \frac{1}{\alpha} \qquad \forall t,$$

and

$$\lambda(t) B_Z(t, Z_t) = \theta_t J_W.$$

Thus, the optimal consumption is

$$c(t) = \left[\frac{e^{-\rho t}}{J(t, 1)}\right]^{\frac{1}{\alpha}} W(t),$$

and the optimal quantity of bequest is

$$Z(t) = \left[\frac{\lambda(t)}{\theta_t} \frac{e^{-\rho t}}{J(t, 1)}\right]^{\frac{1}{\alpha}} W(t).$$

In addition to the standard results from Merton's model that consumption is linear in wealth and the share of wealth invested in the risky asset is constant, we also have the result that the optimal quantity of contingent bequest is proportional to wealth. This is in line with the standard result on life insurance à la Fischer (1973). Richard (1975) noted that in the case of $Z(t) < W(t)$, the consumer becomes the seller, not the buyer, of life insurance.

5.5 The Substitution Method

The essence of this method is this: Since the first-order conditions enable us to express all control variables as functions of state variables, a direct substitution will turn the Bellman equation into a differential equation in state variables alone. Then the value function can be solved for, at least in principle, through this differential equation. To do so, we assume the value function is smooth enough to have continuous n-th order derivatives if necessary.

To illustrate, we return to the optimal growth model. Recall that the stochastic optimal growth problem is

$$\max_{\{c_t\}} E_k \int_0^\infty e^{-\rho t} U(c_t)\, dt \qquad \text{s.t. (5.26)},$$

and the Bellman equation is

$$0 = \max_c \left\{ U(c) - \rho J(k) + [f(k) - c - (n - \sigma^2)k]J'(k) \right.$$
$$\left. + \frac{\sigma^2 k^2 J''(k)}{2} \right\}. \tag{5.48}$$

The corresponding first-order condition is

$$U'(c) = J'(k), \tag{5.49}$$

which implies

$$c = (U')^{-1}(J'(k)). \tag{5.50}$$

Substituting this c into the Bellman equation, we have the following equation:

$$U\big((U')^{-1}(J'(k))\big) - \rho J(k) + \big[f(k) - (U')^{-1}(J'(k)) - (n - \sigma^2)k\big]J'(k)$$
$$+ \tfrac{1}{2}\sigma^2 k^2 J''(k) = 0. \tag{5.51}$$

Notice that equation (5.51) is a second-order, nonlinear ordinary differential equation in $J(k)$. The presence in it of $f(k)J'(k)$, $U\big((U')^{-1}(J'(k))\big)$, and $(U')^{-1}(J'(k))J'(k)$ makes it difficult to find a closed-form solution. Thus, numerical estimation may be useful after an honest attempt has been made. In addition, we need some initial conditions to ensure the uniqueness of the solution.

On the other hand, if the utility function is of isoelastic form, $U(c) = c^{1-\alpha}/(1-\alpha)$, then $U'(c) = c^{-\alpha}$ and hence $(U')^{-1}(x) = x^{-1/\alpha}$. Then

$$U\big((U')^{-1}(J'(k))\big) = \frac{1}{1-\alpha}[J'(k)]^{-(1-\alpha)/\alpha},$$

and

$$(U')^{-1}(J'(k))J'(k) = [J'(k)]^{-(1-\alpha)/\alpha}.$$

Hence, equation (5.51) can be simplified to (5.28). As shown before, we can find a closed-form solution to this equation.

5.6 Martingale Representation Method

The method of martingale representation is to change the probability measure so that the original problem is transformed into something more manageable. This is another change-of-variables method. However, the emphasis is on transforming the probability measure, whereas the emphasis of the symmetry method is on keeping the underlying dynamics invariant.

The method was developed by Cox and Huang (1989, 1991). Recall that the existence theorem for an optimal policy requires that the admissible set of controls be a compact set. For the consumption–portfolio problem in which the purchase of securities is supposedly without limit, this compactness condition could be problematic. At the very least, it makes the existence of a solution an issue, if we employ the dynamic programming method. Their objective was to find an alternative way of solving a more general consumption–portfolio problem. A by-product is an alternative way of finding the value function, to which we now turn.

Recall that in calculus, when transforming one vector-valued function to another, we pay attention to the Jacobian matrix, which represents its vector-valued derivative. There is a similar result in transforming probability measures. The derivative in question is called a Radon–Nikodym derivative. Formally, a probability measure Q is *absolutely continuous* with respect to another measure P (alternatively, Q is *dominated* by P) if for each $A \in \mathcal{F}$, $P(A) = 0$ implies $Q(A) = 0$. According to the Radon–Nikodym theorem, if Q is dominated by P, then there exists a measurable function (Radon–Nikodym derivative), denoted by dQ/dP, such that

$$Q(A) = \int_A \frac{dQ}{dP}\, dP(\omega).$$

The Girsanov transformation to be discussed below shows us how to identify dQ/dP.

5.6.1 Girsanov Transformation

To motivate the Girsanov transformation, we begin with the following stochastic differential equation:

$$dX = -\left(\theta^2/2\right) dt + \theta \, dz,$$

where θ is a measurable, adapted process to be formally defined later. Ito's lemma shows that

$$de^X = e^X dX + \frac{1}{2} e^X (dX)^2 = e^X \theta \, dz.$$

In integral form, if we assume $X(0) = 0$, then

$$e^{X(t)} = 1 + \int_0^t e^{X(s)} \theta(s) \, dz.$$

If $\theta(t)$ is w.p.1 uniformly bounded, as assumed in Cox and Huang (1991), then $\theta(s) e^{X(s)}$ is square integrable satisfying the zero expectation property of the Ito integral. Hence,

$$E\left[e^{X(t)}\right] = 1 + E\left[\int_0^t e^{X(s)}\theta(s) \, dz\right] = 1 \qquad \forall t \leq T.$$

The line of reasoning extends to

$$E\left[e^{X(t)} \,\middle|\, \mathcal{F}_s\right] = E\left\{\exp\left\{\int_s^t \left(-\frac{\theta^2}{2}\right) dt + \theta \, dz\right\} \,\middle|\, \mathcal{F}_s\right\} = 1,$$

$$0 \leq s \leq t \leq T,$$

if $X(s) = 0$.

Let

$$\eta(t, \theta) = \exp\left\{\int_0^t -\left(\theta^2/2\right) dr + \theta \, dz\right\}. \tag{5.52}$$

Then

$$E\left[\eta(t,\theta)\,|\,\mathcal{F}_s\right]$$

$$= E\left[\exp\left\{\int_0^s\left(-\frac{\theta^2}{2}\right)dr+\theta\,dz\right\}\exp\left\{\int_s^t\left(-\frac{\theta^2}{2}\right)dr+\theta\,dz\right\}\Bigg|\,\mathcal{F}_s\right]$$

$$= \eta(s,\theta)\,E\left[\exp\left\{\int_s^t\left(-\frac{\theta^2}{2}\right)dr+\theta\,dz\right\}\Bigg|\,\mathcal{F}_s\right]=\eta(s,\theta).$$

That is, $\{\eta(t,\theta)\}$ is a martingale.

The above heuristic argument is valid under certain conditions. Formally, if $\theta(t)$ is a measurable, adapted process satisfying (i) $\theta(t)\in M_0([0,T],\Omega)$, i.e.,

$$P\left[\int_0^T\theta(t)^2\,dt<\infty\right]=1,\qquad 0\le T<\infty,$$

and (ii) the Novikov condition

$$E\left[\exp\left\{\frac{1}{2}\int_s^t\theta(r)^2\,dr\right\}\right]<\infty,$$

then $\{\eta(t,\theta)\}$ defined in (5.52) is a martingale. See Karatzas and Shreve (1991, section 3.5).

Define a new probability measure by

$$Q(A)=E\left[\eta(T,\theta)\,1_A\right]=\int_A\eta(T,\theta)\,dP(\omega),$$

i.e.,

$$dQ(\omega)=\eta(T,\theta)\,dP(\omega).$$

Thus, the Girsanov transformation plays the role of dQ/dP.

Once the probability measure is changed from P to Q, we define a new stochastic process

$$dz^*=dz-\theta\,dt. \tag{5.53}$$

It can be shown that z^* is a standard Wiener process with respect to the new probability measure, Q. See Karatzas and Shreve (1991, p. 191).

5.6.2 Example: A Portfolio Problem

The relevance of the Girsanov transformation can be seen from the following reformulation of the consumption–portfolio problem. The objective function is the standard

$$E \int_0^T e^{-\rho t} u\left(c\left(t\right)\right) dt + e^{-\rho T} V\left(W\left(T\right)\right), \qquad (5.54)$$

which is similar to the life-cycle theory of consumption with bequest motive. The interesting part is the budget equation.

To keep the presentation simple, we consider only two assets: one risky, the other risk-free. The risky asset carries dividends, which have an instantaneous return $\delta\left(S, t\right)$. More precisely, if $S\left(t\right)$ is the price of the risky asset (security) at time t, then the dividend at time t is

$$D\left(t\right) = \int_0^t \delta\left(S, s\right) ds.$$

Assume $S\left(t\right) + D\left(t\right) = G\left(t\right)$ follows a diffusion process (not necessarily a geometric Brownian motion)

$$dG = dS + \delta\left(t\right) dt = \mu\left(S, t\right) dt + \sigma\left(S, t\right) dz. \qquad (5.55)$$

We shall refer to $G\left(t\right)$ as a *gain process*. It is useful to note that if $\delta\left(t\right) = 0$, $\mu\left(S, t\right) = \mu S$, and $\sigma\left(S, t\right) = \sigma S$ for all t, then $G(t) = S(t)$ is a geometric Brownian motion, the case we have covered before.

In contrast, the price of the risk-free asset (bond) follows the simple equation

$$dB\left(t\right) = r\left(t\right) B\left(t\right) dt.$$

The gain process measured in units of bonds is $G^*\left(t\right) = G\left(t\right)/B\left(t\right)$. If we consider the standard case that $r\left(t\right) = r \quad \forall t \leq T$, then $B\left(t\right) = e^{rt}$ and $G^*\left(t\right) = e^{-rt} G\left(t\right)/B\left(0\right)$. If, in addition, we use the period 0 bond price as the numeraire, i.e., $B\left(0\right) = 1$, then we have $G^*\left(t\right) = e^{-rt} G\left(t\right)$, which is the discounted gain process.

Let α and β be, respectively, the number of shares of bonds and of the risky asset. By construction, the wealth at time t is

$$W\left(t\right) = \alpha\left(t\right) B\left(t\right) + \beta\left(t\right) G\left(t\right).$$

Similar to Merton's model discussed in Chapter 3, the wealth equation is

$$dW(t) = \alpha(t)\,dB(t) + \beta(t)\,dG(t) - c(t)\,dt, \qquad (5.56)$$

with initial wealth $W(0) = \alpha(0)\,B(0) + \beta(0)\,S(0)$. In integral form,

$$\alpha(t)\,B(t) + \beta(t)[S(t) + D(t)] + \int_0^t c(s)\,ds$$

$$= \alpha(0)\,B(0) + \beta(0)\,S(0) + \int_0^t [\alpha(s)\,r(s)\,B(s) + \beta(s)\,\mu(S, s)]\,ds$$

$$+ \int_0^t \beta(s)\,\sigma(S, s)\,dz. \qquad (5.57)$$

The left-hand side of (5.57) is the value of the portfolio at time t plus the accumulated consumption *up to time* t, while the right-hand side is the initial value of the portfolio plus the accumulated capital gains (or losses). This is related to the consumer's budget equation. To complete the budget constraint, we note that the boundary condition for time T is

$$W(T) = \alpha(T)\,B(T) + \beta(T)\,S(T). \qquad (5.58)$$

This last equation is needed because the sample functions are right-continuous with left limit. It ensures that borrowing to consume without paying back is not admissible.

In summary, the problem is

$$\max_{\{\alpha(t), \beta(t), c(t), W(T)\}} E_{W_0} \int_0^T e^{-\rho t} u(c(t))\,dt + e^{-\rho T} V(W(T))$$

s.t. (5.57) and (5.58).

The consumption–wealth pair $(c(t), W(t))$ in (5.57) and (5.58) is said to be *financed by the trading strategy* $(\alpha(t), \beta(t))$.

5.6.3 Which θ to Choose?

By Ito's lemma, the normalized gain process satisfies

$$dG^*(t) = d\left(\frac{G}{B}\right)(t) = \frac{dG(t)}{B(t)} - \frac{G(t)\,dB(t)}{B(t)^2}$$

$$= \frac{1}{B(t)}[\mu(S, t) - r(t)\,G(t)]\,dt + \frac{\sigma(S, t)}{B(t)}\,dz. \qquad (5.59)$$

We choose our $\theta(t)$ to be the mean–variance ratio of the above equation,

$$\theta(t) = -\sigma(S, t)^{-1}[\mu(S, t) - r(t)G(t)]. \qquad (5.60)$$

The factor $\sigma(S, t)^{-1}$ stands for the reciprocal of $\sigma(S, t)$. It goes without saying that in the case of multiple risky assets, $\sigma(S, t)^{-1}$ is understood as the inverse matrix.

It is useful to observe that if $\delta(t) = 0$, $\mu(S, t) = \mu S$, and $\sigma(S, t) = \sigma S$ for all t, then $G(t) = S(t)$, and

$$\theta(t) = -\frac{\mu S - r S}{\sigma S} = -\frac{\mu - r}{\sigma}$$

is constant over time. Thus, (5.60) is a natural extension of the simple case.

Now we are ready to study the dynamics of $G^*(t)$. From (5.59),

$$dG^*(t) = d\left(\frac{G}{B}\right)(t) = -\frac{\theta(t)\sigma(S, t)}{B(t)}dt + \frac{\sigma(S, t)}{B(t)}dz$$

$$= \frac{\sigma(S, t)}{B(t)}[dz - \theta(t)dt] = \frac{\sigma(S, t)}{B(t)}dz^*,$$

by (5.53). This is the most interesting result, because *the drift is zero*, i.e., the "denominated" gain process $G^*(t)$ is "detrended" with respect to the probability measure Q.

While dG^* has zero drift, the drift of dG is nonzero. Again from (5.59),

$$dG = B(t)dG^* + \frac{G(t)dB(t)}{B(t)} = \sigma(S, t)dz^* + G(t)r(t)dt$$

$$= \sigma(S, t)dz^* + [\mu(S, t) + \theta(t)\sigma(S, t)]dt,$$

using (5.60). Thus, if we denote

$$\mu^*(S, t) = \mu(S, t) + \theta(t)\sigma(S, t),$$

then

$$dG = \mu^*(S, t)dt + \sigma(S, t)dz^*.$$

Mathematically, this is known as Girsanov's theorem. By changing the probability measure, we can convert a given Ito process into another

Ito process with an arbitrary drift. Put differently, if we consider the gain process under two different probability measures as two different stochastic processes, they must have the same sample functions. This last part is important because we want to change the probability measure without changing the underlying gain process.

5.6.4 A Transformed Problem

Now we shall convert this dynamic optimization problem into a static one. Using (5.53), (5.55), (5.56), (5.59), (5.60), and Ito's lemma, we have

$$
d\left(\frac{W(t)}{B(t)}\right)
$$

$$
= \frac{dW(t)}{B(t)} - \frac{W(t)\,dB(t)}{B(t)^2}
$$

$$
= \frac{\alpha(t)\,dB(t) + \beta(t)\,dG(t) - c(t)\,dt}{B(t)}
$$

$$
- \frac{[\alpha(t)B(t) + \beta(t)G(t)]\,r(t)\,dt}{B(t)}
$$

$$
= \beta(t)\left[\frac{\mu(S,t)\,dt + \sigma(S,t)\,dz}{B(t)}\right] - \frac{c(t)}{B(t)}dt - \beta(t)\frac{r(t)G(t)}{B(t)}dt
$$

$$
= \frac{\beta(t)[\mu(S,t) - r(t)G(t)]\,dt}{B(t)} + \frac{\beta(t)\sigma(S,t)\,dz}{B(t)} - \frac{c(t)}{B(t)}dt
$$

$$
= -\frac{\beta(t)\theta(t)\sigma(S,t)\,dt}{B(t)} + \frac{\beta(t)\sigma(S,t)\,dz}{B(t)} - \frac{c(t)}{B(t)}dt
$$

$$
= \frac{\beta(t)\sigma(S,t)}{B(t)}dz^* - \frac{c(t)}{B(t)}dt.
$$

In integral form,

$$
\frac{W(t)}{B(t)} + \int_0^t \frac{c(s)}{B(s)}ds = \alpha(0) + \frac{\beta(0)S(0)}{B(0)} + \int_0^t \frac{\beta(s)\sigma(S,s)}{B(s)}dz^*.
$$

This is a budget equation measured in units of bonds. Taking the expectation of the above equation with respect to the transformed probability measure Q, and denoting it by E^*, we have

$$E^* \left\{ \frac{W(T)}{B(T)} + \int_0^T \frac{c(s)}{B(s)} \, ds \right\} = \alpha(0) + \frac{\beta(0) S(0)}{B(0)} = \frac{W(0)}{B(0)}. \quad (5.61)$$

Notice that the control variables $\alpha(t)$ and $\beta(t)$ are not in the equation. Then the problem becomes

$$\max_{\{c(t)\}, W(T)} E^* \int_0^T e^{-\rho t} u(c(t)) \, dt + e^{-\rho T} V(W(T)) \qquad \text{s.t. (5.61).}$$
$$(5.62)$$

According to Bayes's rule, the expectation with respect to the transformed probability measure can be transformed back to an expectation with the old measure. See Karatzas and Shreve (1991, Lemma 5.3, p. 193). That is, equation (5.61) can be written as

$$E \left\{ \frac{\eta(T, \theta) W(T)}{B(T)} + \int_0^T \frac{\eta(t, \theta) c(t)}{B(t)} \, dt \right\} = \frac{W(0)}{B(0)}. \quad (5.63)$$

Then the value function $J(W_0)$ for the optimization problem

$$\max_{\{c(t)\}, W(T)} E_{W_0} \int_0^T e^{-\rho t} \eta(t, \theta) u(c(t)) \, dt + e^{-\rho T} \eta(T, \theta) V(W(T))$$
$$\text{s.t. (5.63)} \quad (5.64)$$

is the same as the value function for (5.62). The problem (5.64) is a standard Arrow–Debreu uncertainty problem, which in principle is much easier to solve.

For easy reference, the commonly employed special case of $r(t) = r \quad \forall t \leq T$ and $B(0) = 1$ would simplify equation (5.61) to

$$E^* \left\{ e^{-rT} W(T) + \int_0^T e^{-rs} c(s) \, ds \right\} = W(0). \quad (5.65)$$

Then Bayes's rule implies

$$E \left\{ e^{-rT} \eta(T, \theta) W(T) + \int_0^T e^{-rt} \eta(t, \theta) c(t) \, dt \right\} = W(0).$$

Example 5.1 *Consider the case* $\delta(t) = 0$, $\mu(S, t) = \mu S$, $\sigma(S, t) = \sigma S$, $B(0) = 1$, *and* $r(t) = r$ *for all* t. *Then* $G(t) = S(t)$, *and* $\theta(t) = \theta = -(\mu - r)/\sigma$ *is constant over time. Then the Girsanov transformation is*

$$\eta(t, \theta) = \exp\left\{\int_0^t \left(-\frac{\theta^2}{2}\right) dr + \theta \, dz\right\} = \exp\left\{-\frac{\theta^2}{2}t + \theta z(t)\right\},$$

and the budget equation (5.63) *becomes*

$$E\left\{e^{-(r+\theta^2/2)T} e^{\theta z(T)} W(T) + \int_0^T e^{-(r+\theta^2/2)t} e^{\theta z(t)} c(t) \, dt\right\} = W(0).$$

Clearly,

$$\Phi(W, c) = (\lambda W, \lambda c)$$

is a symmetry. Therefore, if $u(c(t))$ *and* $V(W(T))$ *are isoelastic, then so is the value function* $J(W_0)$. *This is consistent with Merton's result.*

5.7 Inverse Optimum Method

The methods mentioned above have a common theme: Given the preference structure and the budget equations, we try to find the value function, from which we can ascertain the observable policy functions. These observed behavioral functions are then put to empirical tests or used to derive policy implications. The goal of solving an optimization problem is to enhance our understanding of the observed behavioral functions.

There is another way to better understand these behavioral functions. Any constrained optimization problem has three components: an objective function, constraints, and policy functions. The standard optimization can be described as: given the first two (objective function and constraints), find the third (policy functions). The inverse optimum method is the "inverse" of the standard approach in the sense that given the third and one of the first two, we find the other one. If there is a solution to this inverse problem, then we can say that the given behavioral functions are consistent with the economic theory of optimizing behavior. This approach can also be used to check compatibility among the three components.

A good example of an inverse optimum problem is the integrability problem in consumer theory, which can be stated as follows. Suppose we have a system of demand functions in hand. The question then is this: Can we find a utility function such that the solution to the utility maximization problem (subject to the budget constraint) is indeed the given system of demand functions? In other words, we are to find the preference structure given the policy functions and the budget equation.

The dynamic version of the integrability problem in the context of optimal growth is called the *inverse optimal problem* by Kurz (1969). Formally stated, given an observed saving function and the Solow equation, we are to find a preference structure (a utility function and a discount rate) such that the observed saving function is the optimal policy function of an optimal growth problem. Our presentation, however, follows Chang (1988), which covers both deterministic and stochastic cases.

The economic significance of the solvability of the inverse optimal problem is related to the equivalence principle (the dynamic equivalent of welfare theorems). The equivalence principle says that a perfect-foresight competitive equilibrium solves the optimal growth problem, and conversely, the solution to the optimal growth problem is supported by a perfect-foresight competitive equilibrium. Then, the solvability of the inverse optimal problem ensures us that the observed policy function is supported by a perfect-foresight competitive equilibrium.

5.7.1 The Inverse Optimal Problem: Certainty Case

Assume we observe $c = c(k)$, which is a continuously differentiable function of k with $c'(k) > 0$. If this observed consumption function is an optimal policy function of the optimal growth problem, then it satisfies the Bellman equation,

$$0 = U(c) - \rho J(k) + [f(k) - nk - c] J'(k).$$

Differentiating the Bellman equation with respect to k, we have

$$0 = [f'(k) - (n + \rho)] U'(c) + [f(k) - nk - c] c'(k) U''(c), \quad (5.66)$$

by using the first-order condition

$$U'(c) = J'(k) \qquad \text{for } k > 0$$

and

$$U''(c)c'(k) = J''(k) \qquad \text{for } k > 0.$$

The solution to (5.66) solves the inverse optimal problem with two degrees of freedom: the choice of $U(c_0)$ and $U'(c_0)$. It simply says that we need two initial conditions; that is, the optimal policy function is invariant under a linear transformation of the utility function.

The solution to the one-dimensional, deterministic inverse optimal problem is well known and is summarized in the next two propositions.

Proposition 5.2 *Assume there is no steady state to the Solow equation $\dot{k} = f(k) - nk - c$. Then the inverse optimal problem for any continuously differentiable consumption function satisfying $c'(k) > 0$ is solvable if and only if $f'(k) > n$ for all k.*

Proof. Sufficiency: Since there is no steady state, $\dot{k} > 0$. Then (5.66) can be written as

$$U''(c) + g(k)U'(c) = 0, \tag{5.67}$$

where

$$g(k) = \frac{f'(k) - (n + \rho)}{[f(k) - nk - c]c'(k)}.$$

Equation (5.67) is a first-order differential equation with solution

$$U'(c) = U'(c_0)\exp\left\{-\int_{c_0}^{c} g(c^{-1}(x))\,dx\right\}. \tag{5.68}$$

The exponential form of $U'(c)$ says that $U'(c) > 0$ if $U'(c_0) > 0$. To ensure $U''(c) < 0$, we need $g(k) > 0$ for all k. The stated condition, $f'(k) > n$ for all k, will be sufficient. In this case, we choose any ρ satisfying $0 \le \rho < f'(k) - n$ for all k.

Necessity: If there exists $\rho \ge 0$ and a concave utility function $U(c)$ such that a C^1-class consumption function $c = c(k)$ with $c'(k) > 0$ is the optimal policy function, then (5.66) (and (5.67)) is satisfied. Since $U' > 0, U'' < 0, c'(k) > 0$, and $\dot{k} > 0$, it must be the case that $g(k) > 0$, i.e., $f'(k) > n + \rho \ge n$. ∎

This proposition says that, in the case of no steady state, the inverse optimal problem is solvable if and only if the production function never crosses the population maintenance line ($f'(k) > n$). The next proposition deals with the case when there is a nontrivial steady state k^*. At k^*, $\dot{k} = f(k) - nk - c = 0$. Then the coefficient of the $U''(c)$ term in (5.66) vanishes at k^*. In this case, equation (5.66) has a singularity at k^*. However, this singular point is a *removable singularity* and can be made a *regular singular point*. Consequently, the problem can still be solved.

Proposition 5.3 *Assume there is a steady state, k^*, to the Solow equation $\dot{k} = f(k) - nk - c$. Then the inverse optimal problem for any continuously differentiable consumption function satisfying $c'(k) > 0$ is solvable if and only if $n \leq f'(k^*) < n + c'(k^*)$.*

Proof. Sufficiency: Suppose there is a steady state k^* and an observed continuously differentiable consumption function $c = c(k)$ satisfying $c'(k) > 0$. Recall that the costate equation is

$$\dot{p} = -p[f'(k) - (n + \rho)].$$

At the steady state, $\dot{p} = 0$, $f'(k^*) = n + \rho$. The stated condition, $n \leq f'(k)$, enables us to choose $\rho = f'(k^*) - n \geq 0$. It remains to find a concave $U(c)$.

Since $\dot{k} = 0$ at k^*, equation (5.66) has a *singular point of order one* at k^*. However, we shall turn this singular point into a regular singular point. To this end, we first factor out $k - k^*$ from (5.66) to obtain

$$G(k)c'(k)U''(c) + H(k)U'(c) = 0, \tag{5.69}$$

where

$$G(k) = \frac{f(k) - nk - c}{k - k^*} \qquad \text{for } k \neq k^*$$

and

$$H(k) = \frac{f'(k) - (n + \rho)}{k - k^*} \qquad \text{for } k \neq k^*.$$

Next, we define $G(k^*)$ and $H(k^*)$. By l'Hôpital's rule, we define $G(k^*) = f'(k^*) - n - c'(k^*)$ and $H(k^*) = f''(k^*) < 0$, so that $G(k)$ and $H(k)$ are continuous for all k. Then equation (5.69) is defined for all k. It is straightforward to verify that $H(k) < 0$ for all k. To ensure a concave $U(c)$, we must have $G(k) < 0$ for all k.

The stated condition, $f'(k^*) < n + c'(k^*)$, implies that $G(k^*) < 0$, and hence the concavity of $U(c)$ *in the neighborhood* of k^*. In that neighborhood, $\dot{k} > 0$ for $k < k^*$ and $\dot{k} < 0$ for $k > k^*$. Since k^* is unique, this local property ($\dot{k} > 0$ for $k < k^*$ and $\dot{k} < 0$ for $k > k^*$) is also global, which implies that $G(k) < 0$ for all k. Hence, $U(c)$ is concave for all k. Then we set $g(k) = H(k)/[G(k)c'(k)]$ and choose $U(c)$ by way of (5.68).

Necessity: Suppose the solution to the inverse optimal problem ($\rho \geq 0$ and concave $U(c)$) is given. Since k^* is the steady state, $f'(k^*) = n + \rho \geq n$. The concavity of $f(k)$ implies $H(k) < 0$ for all k. Then, from (5.69), $G(k) < 0$ for all k, by the concavity of $U(c)$. In particular, $0 > G(k^*) = f'(k^*) - n - c'(k^*)$. ∎

It is best to decompose $n \leq f'(k^*) < n + c'(k^*)$ into two inequalities. The first is $n \leq f'(k^*)$, that the marginal product at the steady state is not less than the population growth rate. This is quite obvious. The second is

$$f'(k^*) - c'(k^*) < n,$$

which says that, at the steady state k^*, the savings function, $f(k) - c(k)$, crosses the population maintenance requirement line $m = nk$ from above.

5.7.2 The Inverse Optimal Problem: Stochastic Case

Assume we observe $c = c(k)$, which is a twice continuously differentiable function in k with $c'(k) > 0$. If this observed consumption function is an optimal policy function of the optimal growth problem, then it satisfies the Bellman equation,

$$0 = U(c) - \rho J(k) + \left[f(k) - c - (n - \sigma^2)k\right]J'(k) + \tfrac{1}{2}\sigma^2 k^2 J''(k).$$

In particular, the control variable is a function of the state variable $c = c(k)$ through the first-order condition (5.49). Our objective is to find a utility function $U(c)$ and a discount rate ρ (and implicitly the value function $J(k)$) that satisfy the above equation.

The problem will become more manageable if we can express the above equation exclusively in terms of $U(c)$ (or $J(k)$) and its derivatives.

To this end, we differentiate the Bellman equation with respect to the state variable, using the first-order condition (5.49) and the envelope theorem, to arrive at

$$0 = \gamma(k)J'(k) + M(k)J''(k) + \tfrac{1}{2}\sigma^2 k^2 J'''(k), \qquad (5.70)$$

where

$$\gamma(k) = f'(k) - (n + \rho - \sigma^2)$$

and

$$M(k) = f(k) - c(k) - (n - 2\sigma^2)k.$$

Notice that (5.70) is an *ordinary, linear* differential equation of the second order (in $J'(k)$).

Exercise 5.7.1 *Show that the fundamental equation, expressed exclusively in terms of $U(c)$ and its derivatives, is*

$$0 = \gamma(k)U'(c) + \{M(k)c'(k) + \tfrac{1}{2}\sigma^2 k^2 c''(k)\}U''(c)$$
$$+ \tfrac{1}{2}\sigma^2 k^2 [c'(k)]^2 U'''(c). \qquad (5.71)$$

Hint. Use the first-order condition (5.49) and its derivatives

$$J''(k) = U''(c)c'(k) \quad and \quad J'''(k) = U'''(c)[c'(k)]^2 + U''(c)c''(k).$$

Notice that equation (5.71) is expressed in terms of variables c and k instead of expressing k as a function of c. That is to remind the reader that the production function $f(k)$, the consumption function $c(k)$, and their derivatives are exogenously given in this inverse optimal problem. Once these observed functions are substituted in the equation, the entire equation is expressed exclusively in terms of c. When $\sigma = 0$, equation (5.71) is reduced to (5.66).

Existence Theorem
The theorem has lots of technical details. For expository purposes, we shall only outline the structure.

Issues. First, we have to make sure that equation (5.70) has no singularities, i.e., $k \neq 0$. In fact, we need that the capital–labor ratio will never degenerate to zero ($k(t) > 0$ for all t). This problem will be addressed in the next chapter. For now we shall assume that is the case. That is, we assume $f'(0) < \infty$, $c'(0) < \infty$, and

$$f'(\infty) = \lim_{k \to \infty} f'(k) < n - \sigma^2/2, \qquad (5.72)$$

so that equation (5.70) is well defined on $(0, \infty)$. Notice that $n > \sigma^2/2$ follows from (5.72).

Second, we need to know when equation (5.70) has a solution. The answer is a well-known mathematical fact: that a second-order linear differential equation such as (5.70) has a unique solution if the coefficients are continuous and two initial conditions are given. It is the so-called *initial value problem*. This part is trivial from an economic perspective.

Third, while it is true that the solution exists, the mathematical theorem does not guarantee that the solution $U(c)$ or $J(k)$ acquires the desired concavity of the preference structure. The concavity of $U(c)$ is essential because the second-order necessary condition of (5.48) requires $U''(c) \leq 0$. More structural restrictions are in order. This is the main focus of the existence theorem.

How to Find ρ. Assume

$$f'(0) - c'(0) > n - \sigma^2/2. \qquad (5.73)$$

This says that the savings function, $f(k) - c(k)$, is sufficiently steep at the origin so that the marginal propensity to save is greater than the slope of the maintenance line $m = (n - \sigma^2/2)k$. Choose the discount rate ρ such that

$$c'(0) < \rho \leq c'(0) + \sigma^2/2.$$

This choice of ρ ($\rho \leq c'(0) + \sigma^2/2$) implies

$$\gamma(0) = f'(0) - (n + \rho - \sigma^2) \geq f'(0) - c'(0) - (n - \sigma^2/2) > 0.$$

Notice that the assumptions (5.73), $c'(0) < \infty$, and $f'(0) < \infty$ together imply that the savings function, $f(k) - c(k)$, has a finite and positive slope at $k = 0$. The condition $c'(0) < \rho$ is used to show $M'(0) > 0$ in the proof.

$J(k)$ *is Concave.* Suppose the solution to (5.70) is obtained. Let us plot the solution in the $(J'(k),\ J''(k))$-plane, the so-called Poincaré phase-plane. Our goal is to show that the solution lies in the fourth quadrant and never crosses the axes, if the initial point is in that quadrant. Then $J'(k) > 0$ and $J''(k) < 0$ for all k, and we are done. To this end, we shall transform the second-order equation (5.70), through a new function, $v(k) = -J''(k)/J'(k)$, to a first-order, but nonlinear, differential equation

$$v'(k) = [v(k)]^2 - \left(\frac{2}{\sigma^2}\right)\frac{M(k)}{k}\frac{v(k)}{k} + \left(\frac{2}{\sigma^2}\right)\frac{\gamma(k)}{k^2}. \qquad (5.74)$$

Equation (5.74) is a *Riccati equation.* Note that this is a first-order differential equation in the absolute risk aversion function $v(k)$. It suffices to show that the solution of the Riccati equation satisfies $v(k) > 0$ on $(0, \infty)$. In other words, the absolute risk aversion must be positive at all k.

Finally, we need

$$f'(\infty) - c'(\infty) < n - 2\sigma^2. \qquad (5.75)$$

This says that the savings function is sufficiently flat at infinity that it crosses from above *another* maintenance line, $m = (n - 2\sigma^2)k$. When $\sigma = 0$, the two maintenance lines become one, $m = nk$. If, in addition, the saving rate is constant, then inequalities (5.73) and (5.75) become the well-known Solow conditions $(sf'(0) > n,\ sf'(\infty) < n)$ in the deterministic growth model, which ensure a nontrivial steady state.

The main theorem of the inverse optimal problem can be stated as follows.

Theorem 5.4 *Let the production technology $f(k)$ and the consumption function $c(k)$ be twice continuously differentiable and monotonically increasing with $f'(0) < \infty$ and $c'(0) < \infty$. Under the assumptions (5.72), (5.73), and (5.75), the inverse optimal problem under uncertainty has a solution.*

Proof. See Chang (1988, pp. 157–160). ∎

Unlike the deterministic case, the conditions imposed in Theorem 5.4 are only sufficient. More importantly, unlike the deterministic case, the solution to the inverse optimal problem has more than two degrees of freedom. More precisely, besides $U(c_0)$, $U'(c_0)$ we also have the choice of $U''(c_0)$. But we do not have three full degrees of freedom either, because $U''(c_0)$ must be constrained to ensure the concavity of $U(c)$. This plethora of solutions emerges as a result of applying Ito's lemma.

The required condition $f'(0) < \infty$ in the existence theorem outlaws Cobb–Douglas production functions in the stochastic inverse optimal problem. The next two examples allow $f'(0) = \infty$.

Example 5.5. Keynesian Consumption Function

Let $c(k) = (1 - s) f(k)$, where $s < 1$ is a constant representing the savings rate. The term Keynesian refers to the fact that consumption is a function of current income $y = f(k)$. Then the fundamental equation (5.71) becomes

$$\left(\frac{\sigma^2}{2}\right)\left(\frac{kf'}{f}\right)^2 c^2 U'''(c) + \left\{\left[\frac{sf}{k} - (n - 2\sigma^2)\right]\left(\frac{kf'}{f}\right)\right.$$

$$\left. + \left(\frac{\sigma^2}{2}\right)\left(\frac{k^2 f''}{f}\right)\right\} cU''(c) + [f'(k) - (n + \rho - \sigma^2)]U'(c) = 0.$$

$$(5.76)$$

A Special Case with $f'(0) = \infty$. The intuition is this. If the consumption function is Keynesian, then $f'(0) = \infty$ implies that the marginal propensity to save at $k = 0$ is ∞. It takes a utility function with $U'(0) = \infty$ to prevent the consumption path from degenerating to zero in finite time.

Assume further that the production function is of Cobb–Douglas form, $f(k) = Ak^\alpha$, with $\alpha < 1$, $A > 0$. Then equation (5.76) is simplified as

$$\frac{\sigma^2}{2}\alpha^2 c^2 U'''(c) + \left\{[sAk^{\alpha-1} - (n - 2\sigma^2)]\alpha + \frac{\sigma^2}{2}\alpha(\alpha - 1)\right\} cU''(c)$$

$$+ [\alpha Ak^{\alpha-1} - (n + \rho - \sigma^2)]U'(c) = 0. \quad (5.77)$$

The strategy to solve this equation is to break it into two parts. The first part is related to the production technology:

$$s\alpha Ak^{\alpha-1} cU''(c) + \alpha Ak^{\alpha-1}U'(c) = 0,$$

which can be simplified as

$$scU''(c) + U'(c) = 0. \tag{5.78}$$

The second part is independent of the technology:

$$\frac{\sigma^2}{2}\alpha^2 c^2 U'''(c) + \left\{ -(n - 2\sigma^2)\alpha + \frac{\sigma^2}{2}\alpha(\alpha - 1) \right\} cU''(c)$$

$$- \left(n + \rho - \sigma^2\right) U'(c) = 0. \tag{5.79}$$

Equation (5.78) suggests that the utility function should be of constant relative risk aversion, $-cU''(c)/U'(c) = 1/s > 1$. Equation (5.79) is an Euler's homogeneous differential equation whose solution has a constant relative risk aversion. If we choose $-cU''(c)/U'(c) = 1/s > 1$ and

$$\rho = \frac{n(\alpha - s)}{s} + \frac{(\alpha - s)(\alpha - 2s)\sigma^2}{2s^2},$$

then the inverse optimal problem is solved. The coefficient $\rho > 0$, if $2s \le \alpha$; when $\sigma = 0$, we need only $s < \alpha$. Notice that the family of utility functions thus obtained is invariant under linear transformations.

Compatibility. The utility function obtained above has a constant relative risk aversion greater than unity. How restrictive is this? Could logarithmic functions, which are of unit relative risk aversion, be solutions too? After all, they also satisfy Euler's homogeneous differential equation (5.79). It is interesting to point out that the Keynesian consumption function $c(k) = (1 - s)f(k)$ is *not* supported by *any* logarithmic utility function if the production function is of Cobb–Douglas form. To see this, let $U(c) = B_1 \log c + B_2$, where B_1, B_2 are constants. Then equation (5.77) becomes

$$(1 - s)\alpha k^{\alpha - 1} + \text{constant terms} = 0.$$

Since $\alpha > 0$ and $s < 1$, the above equation has no solution for any $k > 0$. In other words, the *Keynesian consumption function, Cobb–Douglas production function, and logarithmic utility function are not compatible*.

Caveat. The aforementioned example highlights the difference between continuous-time models and discrete-time models. Normally, we connect the two models by letting the time intervals shrink to zero. Some economists treat them as if they were always equivalent and the choice of continuous-time or discrete-time models were more a matter of personal taste than anything else. That is not so in this example. In a discrete-time Ramsey problem, a logarithmic utility function together with a Cobb–Douglas production function implies that the optimal consumption function is indeed a function of current income. See Mirman and Zilcha (1975) for a popular example in the macroeconomic literature. However, that is not true in continuous time.

Example 5.6. Consumption is Linear in k

The intuition is similar to Example 5.5. The marginal propensity to save at $k = 0$ is ∞ if $f'(0) = \infty$. Thus, we are once again looking for a utility function with $U'(0) = \infty$ to prevent the consumption path from degenerating to zero in finite time.

By assumption, $c = c(k) = bk$ for some $b > 0$. Clearly, $c''(k) = 0$, and equation (5.71) is simplified as

$$0 = [f'(k) - (n + \rho - \sigma^2)]U'(c) + \left[\frac{f(k)}{k} - (n + b - 2\sigma^2)\right] cU''(c)$$

$$+ (\sigma^2/2)c^2 U'''(c).$$

Using the separation method, we divide the above equation into two equations: the one with production,

$$-\frac{cU''(c)}{U'(c)} = \frac{kf'(k)}{f(k)},$$

and the one without,

$$(\sigma^2/2)c^2 U'''(c) - (n + b - 2\sigma^2)cU''(c) - (n + \rho - \sigma^2)U'(c) = 0.$$

The first equation suggests that, if the production function is of Cobb–Douglas form, i.e., $f(k) = k^\alpha$, $0 < \alpha < 1$, then we should choose (up to a linear transformation)

$$U(c) = c^{1-\alpha}.$$

This functional form works for the second equation as well. Moreover, the choice of ρ is given by

$$\rho = (\sigma^2/2)(1 - \alpha)(2 - \alpha) + [b\alpha - (1 - \alpha)n].$$

Note that $\rho \geq 0$ if and only if

$$b \geq \left[\frac{1-\alpha}{\alpha}\right]\left[n - \frac{\sigma^2 (2-\alpha)}{2}\right] > 0.$$

The constant $(1-\alpha)/\alpha$ is the ratio of wage share to rental share, $F_L L / F_K K$. The problem is solvable if $n > \sigma^2 (2-\alpha)/2$.

Exercise 5.7.2 *Show that the Keynesian consumption function, logarithmic production function, and logarithmic utility function are not compatible.*

Hint. Show that equation (5.76) is simplified to

$$n + \rho - \sigma^2 = \frac{1-s}{k} + (function\ of\ \log k).$$

Exercise 5.7.3 *Solve the inverse optimal problem when the production function is of Cobb–Douglas form and the consumption function is the Cambridge consumption function, $c(k) = f(k) - kf'(k)$, i.e., one consumes all wage income.*

Hint. The Cambridge consumption function is a Keynesian consumption function when the production technology is Cobb–Douglas.

5.7.3 Inverse Optimal Problem of Merton's Model

Classical Formulation

The inverse optimal problem of Merton's (1971) consumption and portfolio rules can be stated as follows. Assume the price of each risky asset follows a geometric Brownian motion (5.8). Given the observed consumption function and the observed percentage of wealth invested in each risky asset s_i, find a utility function $U(c)$ and a discount rate ρ such that the observed policy functions mentioned above are the solution to the associated optimization problem (5.10).

The solution method is similar to that for the inverse optimal problem. If these policy functions are optimal, then they satisfy the maximized Bellman equation (5.11),

$$0 = \left\{ U(c) - \rho J(W) + \left[\sum_{i=1}^{n-1} s_i (\mu_i - r) W + (rW - c)\right] J'(W) \right.$$

$$\left. + \frac{1}{2}\sum_{i=1}^{n-1} s_i^2 \sigma_i^2 W^2 J''(W) \right\}.$$

Recall that these policy functions are functions of the state variable W. Differentiating the above equation with respect to W, we have

$$0 = \left[\sum_{i=1}^{n-1} s_i (\mu_i - r) + r - \rho\right] J'(W)$$

$$+ \left[\sum_{i=1}^{n-1} \left(s_i (\mu_i - r) + s_i^2 \sigma_i^2\right) W + (rW - c)\right] J''(W)$$

$$+ \frac{1}{2} \sum_{i=1}^{n-1} s_i^2 \sigma_i^2 W^2 J'''(W). \tag{5.80}$$

Solving this fundamental equation, we have a value function $J(W)$ from which the utility function can be derived.

For example, assume the consumption function is linear in wealth, $c = AW$, $A > 0$, and the share of wealth invested in each risky asset, s_i, is constant. Then equation (5.80) is an Euler differential equation, and hence the solution is of CRRA. Write $J'(W) = W^{-\alpha}$, for some $\alpha > 0$. Then equation (5.80) implies

$$\rho = (1 - \alpha)\left[\sum_{i=1}^{n-1} s_i (\mu_i - r) + r - \frac{1}{2}\alpha \sum_{i=1}^{n-1} s_i^2 \sigma_i^2\right] + \alpha A.$$

If $s_i = (\mu_i - r)/(\alpha \sigma_i^2)$, then the above equation is simplified to (5.17). Notice that logarithmic functions can be solutions if $\alpha = 1$. In that case $J'(W) = 1/W$ and $\rho = A$.

General Formulation

He and Huang (1994) present a more general form of the inverse optimal problem of Merton's consumption and portfolio rules. Assume that there is only one risky asset. First, they relax the assumption that the price of the risky asset follows a geometric Brownian motion, because accumulating empirical evidence does not support it. They replace (5.8) with a more general diffusion process

$$dP_t = \mu_t(P_t)P_t\, dt + \sigma_t(P_t)P_t\, dz_t. \tag{5.81}$$

The classic case is the one in which $\mu_t(P_t) = \mu$ and $\sigma_t(P_t) = \sigma$, for some constants μ and σ. They assume that stochastic differential equation (5.81) has a solution, which requires among other things that the drift and the instantaneous variance of (5.81) satisfy a linear growth condition and a local Lipschitz condition. They also *assume* that this general price process maintains the nice property that $P_t > 0$ *with probability one*.

Next, they assume the consumption function $c_t(W, P)$ and the *absolute* amount of wealth invested in the risky asset $a_t(W, P)$ are continuously differentiable functions of two state variables W and P. At each period, the consumer allocates her wealth between the risky asset and the risk-free asset. Then the consumer's wealth follows the following controlled diffusion process:

$$dW_t = \{a_t(W_t, P_t)[\mu_t(P_t) - r] + rW_t - c_t(W_t, P_t)\} dt$$
$$+ a_t(W_t, P_t)\sigma_t(P_t) dz_t. \tag{5.82}$$

Some regularity conditions, such as smoothness of the value function, are imposed on (5.82) so that the budget equation has a unique solution. Suppressing the subscripts and recognizing that $c = c(W, P)$, $a = a(W, P)$, $\mu = \mu(P)$, $\sigma = \sigma(P)$, the associated Bellman equation is

$$0 = \max_{c,a}\{U(c) - \rho J + [a(\mu - r) + rW - c]J_W + \mu P J_P$$
$$+ \tfrac{1}{2}a^2\sigma^2 J_{WW} + a\sigma^2 P J_{WP} + \tfrac{1}{2}\sigma^2 P^2 J_{PP}\}. \tag{5.83}$$

For given policy functions c and a, the tastes (represented by a utility function and a discount rate) and opportunities (represented by budget equations) must *jointly* satisfy the Bellman equation, (5.83). It says that only some preferences and some opportunity sets will be solutions to the inverse optimal problem. They presented a set of necessary and sufficient conditions for the inverse optimal problem with given $c(W, P)$ and $a(W, P)$. For more details, the reader should consult their paper.

An Explicit Example
In this example, we are to ascertain the price dynamics given the utility function and the observed consumption–portfolio rules.

Suppose the utility function is of constant relative risk aversion $U'(c) = c^{-\alpha}$, $\alpha > 0$. Suppose the observed behavioral functions are such that the marginal propensity to consume is linearly proportional to the stock price, in addition to being proportional to wealth, and that the amount of investment in the risky asset is a decreasing function of the stock price. More precisely, suppose we have

$$c(W, P) = \gamma P W$$

and

$$a(W, P) = \left[A_3 - \frac{r}{\alpha\sigma^2} - \sqrt{A_1 + A_2 P} \right] W, \qquad (5.84)$$

where $\gamma > 0$, $\sigma > 0$, $A_1 \geq 0$, $A_2 > 0$ are all constants. If, in addition,

$$A_3 > \frac{r}{\alpha\sigma^2} + \sqrt{A_1},$$

then $a(W, P) > 0$ when the stock price is low, and $a(W, P) < 0$ when the stock price is high. In the latter case, the investor short-sells the risky asset.

What can we say about the budget equation and the price process, (5.81)? The constancy of σ in (5.84) suggests that we should take $\sigma(P) = \sigma$. It remains to determine $\mu(P)$.

The demand for the optimal investment in the risky asset is given by

$$a = \left(\frac{\mu(P) - r}{\sigma^2} \right) \left(-\frac{J_W}{J_{WW}} \right) - \frac{P J_{WP}}{J_{WW}}. \qquad (5.85)$$

From the functional form of the utility, we have $J_W(W) = U'(c) = c^{-\alpha}$. It follows that

$$-\frac{J_W}{J_{WW}} = \frac{c}{\alpha c_W} = \frac{c}{\alpha\gamma P} = \frac{W}{\alpha},$$

which implies that the indirect utility function has a constant relative risk aversion α, and that

$$-\frac{P J_{WP}}{J_{WW}} = -\frac{P c_P}{c_W} = -\frac{P \gamma W}{\gamma P} = -W.$$

Thus, from (5.85), a is linearly proportional to wealth, i.e.,

$$a(W, P) = \left[\frac{\mu(P) - r}{\alpha \sigma^2} - 1 \right] W.$$

Comparing this equation to (5.84), we have

$$\frac{\mu(P) - r}{\alpha \sigma^2} - 1 = A_3 - \frac{r}{\alpha \sigma^2} - \sqrt{A_1 + A_2 P}.$$

Hence, we conclude that the price process is

$$dP_t = \alpha \sigma^2 \left[A_3 + 1 - \sqrt{A_1 + A_2 P_t} \right] P_t \, dt + \sigma P_t \, dz_t.$$

Exercise 5.7.4 *Formulate an inverse optimal problem for a profit-maximizing firm with adjustment costs.*

Hint. Suppose we have observed the demand for labor (L) and the investment function I. Find the installation function $G(K, I)$.

5.8 Notes and Further Readings

The HARA class of functions was introduced by Merton (1971). We rewrite this class of function so that each parameter has its economic interpretation. The simple portfolio selection model of Arrow (1965) is standard in the price theory texts. See, for example, Varian (1992) and Jehle and Reny (2001).

The method of symmetry on which our presentation is based is due to Boyd (1990). The idea of symmetry is germane to the conservation theorems in the theory of differential equations. For applications of symmetry principles to sciences, the reader is referred to Rosen (1983). It should be mentioned that the applicability of symmetry method is broader in discrete-time models. The interested reader should consult Boyd (1990).

The martingale representation method basically follows Cox and Huang (1989, 1991) with the help from Karatzas and Shreve (1991). Their emphasis is different from ours, as discussed in the text. The subject is somewhat mathematically involved. Instead of proving every lemma and losing the flow of argument, we outline the main results by invoking mathematical theorems wherever appropriate. The quoted theorems are followed immediately by references.

The inverse optimum method is based on Chang (1988). The issues had been discussed extensively by many, in particular, Hahn (1968) and Kurz (1968, 1969). Kurz (1969) solved the deterministic inverse optimal problem using the Hamiltonian method. In a related study, Brock (1975) found necessary and sufficient conditions for dynamic integrability problems. In solving the deterministic inverse optimal problem, we employed a technique in differential equations for removing singular points. For more on singular points, especially regular singular points, the reader is referred to Birkhoff and Rota (1978) and Hartman (2002).

6

Boundaries and Absorbing Barriers

6.1 Introduction

In this chapter we shall discuss some issues related to the *boundaries* of a stochastic optimization problem. We begin with the important issue of the nonnegativity constraint, which is usually overlooked in the literature. Mathematically, the controlled stochastic differential equation that represents the law of motion is defined on the whole real line. The solution to such an equation cannot rule out the possibility that the state variables and/or the control variables are negative at some times on a set of positive probability. Economically, these variables typically represent consumption, stocks of capital, capital–labor ratio, or exhaustible resources. It makes no sense to have negative values for these variables. Since the nonnegativity constraint is not part of the mathematical solutions, more work needs to be done.

To address this issue, we use the optimal growth problem as our example. Our question is this: Is it possible that, with positive probability, the solution to the stochastic Solow equation explodes in finite time or has a negative capital–labor ratio at some point in time? We point out the major difficulties of this problem, and then discuss some methods to tackle it. Among them, we include the *comparison theorem*, which enables us to compare the solution of one differential equation with the solution of another differential equation that has some nice properties. Then we introduce a *reflection method* developed by Chang and Malliaris (1987) to solve this nonnegativity problem of optimal growth. Finally, we extend the discussion to include constraints on state and control variables in dynamic optimization problems. Specifically, we work out a portfolio problem with borrowing constraints. We discuss the associated Kuhn–Tucker conditions and the related *viscosity solution* technique.

On the other hand, there are economic problems in which the boundary should actually be reached. We use the transactions demand for money to exemplify this class of problems. We first extend Baumol and Tobin's static money demand model to an infinite-horizon optimization problem in which money is replenished once it is reduced to a certain level. Then we point out that the amount of money holding dictates the timing of visits to the bank, and conversely. Under uncertainty, the choice of timing is an *optimal stopping time* problem. Another example in which the boundary should be reached is the classical rotation problem, in which the timing to cut (and replant) a tree is chosen to maximize the discounted net gain. Again, we point out that the choice of cutting time is the choice of cutting size, given the pattern of tree growth. Naturally, its stochastic version is an optimal stopping time problem. Finally, we work out the optimal investment timing problem when the project value follows a geometric Brownian motion. We show that this problem is essentially a tree-cutting problem.

As we shall see, the key to these stopping time problems is the expected discounted factor of a stopping time. We shall go through the mathematics of how to compute these expected discounted factors in as much detail as possible. Furthermore, these economic problems usually do not have a closed-form solution. The method of doing comparative dynamics of an implicit function will also be discussed in this chapter.

6.2 Nonnegativity Constraint

6.2.1 Issues and Problems

Let us return to the stochastic optimal growth problem. Recall that the stochastic Solow equation is

$$dk_t = [f(k_t) - c_t - (n - \sigma^2)k_t]dt - \sigma k_t\, dz_t, \qquad (6.1)$$

and the problem is

$$\max_{\{c_t\}} E_k \int_0^\infty e^{-\rho t} U(c_t)\, dt \qquad \text{s.t. (6.1)}. \qquad (6.2)$$

When solving an optimization problem such as (6.2), it is imperative that the constraint set be nonempty. From the first-order condition $U'(c) = J'(k)$, it is obvious that consumption per capita is a function of the capital–labor ratio, i.e., $c = (U')^{-1}(J'(k)) = c(k)$. Thus, the stochastic Solow equation (6.1) is a stochastic differential equation in k. To ensure that the constraint set is nonempty, we must show that equation (6.1) with $c = c(k)$ has a solution. A standard existence theorem is Ito's theorem, which was discussed in Chapter 4. It requires among other things the Lipschitz condition and the growth condition. Even if these conditions are satisfied, there is still another problem.

Is $k_t > 0$ for all $t > 0$ w.p.1?
Although the solution to (6.1) exists, it is defined on the whole real line. In other words, while this mathematical theorem assures us a solution, it also allows for the possibility of *negative* capital–labor ratios at some times on a set of positive probability. But, we are only interested in the nonnegative capital–labor ratios. Therefore, the theorem is not directly applicable.

Standard Approach
Traditionally, we approach this problem by first ignoring the nonnegativity constraint and proceeding to solve the problem. Once we obtain the optimal control of the problem, we substitute it into the Bellman equation and verify that the solution to the Bellman equation (in state variables) is indeed nonnegative. If so, the nonnegativity constraint is no longer binding and the problem is taken care of.

For example, consider Merton's model of consumption and portfolio rules. Since short selling is allowed, there is no nonnegativity constraint on shares. However, there is such a constraint on consumption. As long as the optimal consumption is proportional to wealth ($C = aW$) and the optimal portfolio is constant over time, the dynamics of wealth follows a geometric Brownian motion. In that case wealth is positive at all times w.p.1, and so is consumption.

Unfortunately, this approach does not work for the stochastic optimal growth problem. To see this, and to set up the notation, define the savings rate (as a function of k) by $s(k) = 1 - c(k)/f(k)$. Assume $0 \leq s(k) \leq 1$ or $f(k) \geq c(k) \geq 0$. The admissible control in this case, instead of the usual consumption function $c(k)$, is the savings rate $s(k)$. Then the saving function is $s(k)f(k) = f(k) - c(k)$, and (6.1) becomes

$$dk = [s(k)f(k) - (n - \sigma^2)k]\,dt - \sigma k\,dz. \qquad (6.3)$$

This is an autonomous stochastic differential equation in k. Since $f(k)$ is strictly concave, the saving function is in general not linear in wealth. Therefore, the trick of converting the equation to a geometric Brownian motion does not apply.

A natural approach to tackle the nonnegativity problem is to transform equation (6.3) into another equation so that the solution to the new equation, if it exists, will imply positive capital–labor ratios. Specifically, we shall make the transformation $x = \log k$. Using Ito's lemma, the transformed equation is

$$dx = -\left[\left(n - \frac{\sigma^2}{2}\right) - \frac{s\left(e^x\right)f\left(e^x\right)}{e^x}\right]dt - \sigma\,dz. \qquad (6.4)$$

Then the solution to this equation, $x \in \mathbb{R}$, implies that $k = e^x > 0$, which should take care of the complexities. Still, there is a problem.

The problem arises from the fact that not all standard growth models satisfy the growth condition for (6.4). For example, any model with a Cobb–Douglas production function and a *constant* savings rate $s\left(e^x\right) = s$ (known as Denison's law) will violate this condition. To see this, let

$$f(k) = bk^{\alpha}, \qquad b > 0, \qquad 0 < \alpha < 1.$$

Then the growth condition for (6.4) is

$$\left[\left(n - \frac{\sigma^2}{2}\right) - \frac{sf\left(e^x\right)}{e^x}\right]^2 + \sigma^2 \leq M\left(1 + x^2\right)$$

for some constant M. It is obvious that this condition can never be satisfied, because of the term

$$\frac{sf\left(e^x\right)}{e^x} = sbe^{(\alpha - 1)x} \to \infty \qquad \text{as } x \to -\infty.$$

There is no way Ito's theorem is applicable. The capital–labor ratio may explode in finite time or become negative with positive probability.

In the counterexample, the growth condition fails because $sf(k)/k \to \infty$ as $k \to 0$. The issue here concerns the behavior of the saving function at $k = 0$. It suggests that the solution to the stochastic Solow equation might exist if the saving function is reasonably well behaved at $k = 0$. There are two ways to handle this problem. One is to solve the equation case by case, taking advantage of a specific functional form of production and employing other mathematical theorems. See, for example, Jensen and Wang (1999). Another is to find a sufficient condition for the existence of the solution that applies to many cases without an explicit functional form of production. It is the latter approach that we shall take.

Some Useful Theorems

For one-dimensional, autonomous stochastic differential equations with continuously differentiable drifts and variances, there are more powerful theorems than the Ito theorem. We shall conclude this subsection with two such theorems, one of which will be used later. Let $\mu(x), \sigma(x) \in C^1(\mathbb{R})$, which are standard assumptions in many economic models.

Theorem 6.1 *(Bounded Slope Theorem) If μ and σ are of bounded slope, i.e., $\|\mu'\|_\infty < \infty$ and $\|\sigma'\|_\infty < \infty$, then*

$$dX_t = \mu(t, X_t)dt + \sigma(t, X_t)dz_t \tag{6.5}$$

has a unique solution for $t \geq 0$.

Proof. See McKean (1969, section 3.2). ∎

Theorem 6.2 *(Nonexplosive Theorem) If there exists a constant b such that*

$$\mu^2 + \sigma^2 \leq b(1 + x^2), \tag{6.6}$$

then (6.5) has a unique solution for $t \geq 0$.

Proof. See McKean (1969, section 3.3). It is obtained by combining his theorem in section 3.3 and Problem 1 of that section. His theorem in section 3.3 states that (6.5) has a unique solution up to the explosion time. Recall that if $\tau_n = \min\{t : |k_t| = n\}$, then the explosion time is $\tau_\infty = \lim_{n \to \infty} \tau_n$. His Problem 1 of that section states that (6.6) implies that $\tau_\infty = \infty$ w.p.1. ∎

6.2.2 Comparison Theorems

To motivate, we return to the inverse optimal problem. Recall that the absolute risk aversion function $v(k) = -J''(k)/J'(k)$ satisfies a Riccati equation. To complete the proof, we need to find conditions to ensure that $v(k) > 0$ for all $k > 0$ given $v(k_0) > 0$. In other words, we must show that the boundary $v = 0$ cannot be reached. However, solving the Riccati equation is no simple matter. When a differential equation cannot be solved in terms of elementary functions, a common technique is to compare the unknown solution of a given equation with the known solution of another. Results of this type are referred to as comparison theorems; they are sometimes discussed under the heading of *differential inequalities*. This comparison theorem is another tool to handle the boundary problem.

Ordinary Differential Equation

Proposition 6.3 *Let F satisfy a Lipschitz condition on any closed subinterval of $x \geq a$. If f satisfies the differential inequality*

$$f'(x) \leq F(x, f(x)) \qquad \text{for all } x \geq a,$$

and if g is a solution of

$$y' = F(x, y)$$

satisfying the initial condition $g(a) \geq f(a)$, then $g(x) \geq f(x)$ for all $x \geq a$.

Proof. See Chang (1988, p. 157) or Birkhoff and Rota (1978, p. 26). ■

The intuition is this: A head start and a consistently higher speed will keep one ahead at all times. Put differently, for any two functions, one that is endowed with a larger initial condition *and* a larger slope must have a larger functional value than the other everywhere to the right of the initial point.

An immediate corollary of this proposition is the next one.

Proposition 6.4 *Let F satisfy a Lipschitz condition on any closed interval $[b, a]$, where $0 < b < a$. If f satisfies the differential inequality*

$$f'(x) \leq F(x, f(x)) \qquad \text{on } (0, a],$$

and if g is a solution of

$$y' = F(x, y)$$

satisfying the condition $g(a) < f(a)$, then $g(x) \leq f(x)$, on $(0, a]$.

Proof. See Chang (1988, p. 157). ∎

It is easier to understand this proposition by regarding the condition $g(a) < f(a)$ as the *terminal* condition at point a, and interpreting the slope to the left of point a as the rate of reduction if we move the coordinate leftward. Then the intuition is this: At the terminal point, the one running faster, yet still behind, must have started behind. Put differently, given any two functions, the one that is endowed with a higher value at point a and a smaller rate of reduction must have a higher value than the other everywhere to the left of a.

These two propositions provide us comparison theorems to the left and to the right of a given point. They were used to prove $v(k) > 0$ given $v(k_0) > 0$. For details, the reader is referred to Chang (1988, pp. 157–160).

The propositions just mentioned are tailored for the inverse optimal problem. A standard mathematics theorem, however, is the following:

Theorem 6.5 *(Comparison Theorem). Let f and g be solutions of the differential equations*

$$y' = F(x, y) \quad and \quad z' = G(x, z)$$

respectively, where $F(x, y) \leq G(x, y)$ in the strip $a \leq x \leq b$, and F or G satisfies a Lipschitz condition. Let also $f(a) = g(a)$. Then $f(x) \leq g(x)$ for all $x \in [a, b]$.

Proof. See Birkhoff and Rota (1978, pp. 26–27). ∎

Corollary 6.6 *In Theorem 6.5, assume that F, as well as G, satisfies a Lipschitz condition and, instead of $f(a) = g(a)$, that $f(a) < g(a)$. Then $f(x) < g(x)$ for all $x \geq a$.*

Proof. See Birkhoff and Rota (1978, p. 27). ∎

Stochastic Differential Equation
There is a similar comparison theorem for one-dimensional stochastic differential equations (SDEs).

Theorem 6.7 *(Comparison Theorem for SDEs). Let $(\Omega, \mathcal{F}, P)$ be a filtered probability space with a filtration $\{\mathcal{F}_t\}$, and let z_t be the standard Wiener process. Suppose we have two stochastic differential equations*

$$dX_t^i = \mu_i\left(t, X_t^i\right) dt + \sigma\left(t, X_t^i\right) dz_t, \qquad 0 \le t < \infty,$$

for $i = 1, 2$. We assume that

(i) the coefficients $\sigma(t, x)$ and $\mu_i(t, x)$ are continuous, real-valued functions on $[0, \infty) \times \mathbb{R}$,
(ii) the coefficient $\sigma(t, x)$ satisfies the inequality

$$|\sigma(t, x) - \sigma(t, y)| \le h(|x - y|)$$

for every $0 \le t < \infty$ and $x, y \in \mathbb{R}$, where $h : [0, \infty) \to [0, \infty)$ is a strictly increasing function with $h(0) = 0$ and

$$\int_{(0,\varepsilon)} \frac{1}{[h(u)]^2} du = \infty \qquad \forall \varepsilon > 0,$$

(iii) $X_0^1 \le X_0^2$ w.p.1,
(iv) $\mu_1(t, x) \le \mu_2(t, x) \ \forall t \in [0, \infty), \ x \in \mathbb{R}$, and
(v) either $\mu_1(t, x)$ or $\mu_2(t, x)$ satisfies a uniform (in time) Lipschitz condition, i.e., there exists a constant K such that

$$|\mu_i(t, x) - \mu_i(t, x)| < K|x - y|.$$

Then $X_t^1 \le X_t^2$ for all $0 \le t < \infty$, w.p.1.

Proof. See Karatzas and Shreve (1991, pp. 293–294). ■

Most of the conditions are nothing but smoothness, which is typically assumed in economic models. The only concern is the function $h(u)$. According to Karatzas and Shreve (1991), we may take h to be $h(u) = u^\alpha$ with $\alpha \ge 1/2$. In our growth model, $\sigma(t, x) = \sigma x$. We may simply take $h(u) = \sigma u$.

It should be emphasized that the two stochastic differential equations under comparison must have *identical variance function*. The difference between them can only come from the drift component, just as in the deterministic case. If nonnegativity is at issue, then we may want to compare the equation with a geometric Brownian motion or an equation like $dX_t = \frac{1}{4}dt + \sqrt{X_t}\,dz_t$, as shown in Chapter 3.

Corollary 6.8 *Theorem 6.7 remains valid under the same conditions except that condition (v) is dropped and condition (iv) is strengthened to strict inequality.*

Proof. See Karatzas and Shreve (1991, p. 294). ∎

Exercise 6.2.1 *Show that the solution to the stochastic differential equation*

$$dX = (aX + b)\,dt + \sigma X dz,$$

with $b > 0$ and given $X_0 > 0$, uniquely exists and w.p.1 has only positive values.

Exercise 6.2.2 *Show that the solution to the stochastic differential equation*

$$dX = \left(a + \tfrac{1}{4}\right)dt + \sigma\sqrt{X}dz,$$

with $a > 0$ and given $X_0 > 0$, uniquely exists and w.p.1 has only positive values.

6.2.3 Chang and Malliaris's Reflection Method

This method (Chang and Malliaris, 1987) applies to any economic problem in which the (economic) variable is defined only on the set of nonnegative real numbers. We continue to use the optimal growth problem as our example.

Extending (6.3) to the Whole Real Line
Recall that equation (6.3) is defined only on $k \geq 0$. We propose to extend it to the whole real line by reflection. However, care must be taken to ensure the coefficients of the extended equation are of class $C^1(\mathbb{R})$ so that the nonexplosive theorem is applicable. To this end, we first extend the production function $f(k_t)$ to a new function defined on the whole

real line as

$$\widetilde{f}(k_t) = \begin{cases} f(k_t) & \text{if } k_t \geq 0, \\ -f(-k_t) & \text{if } k_t < 0. \end{cases}$$

In other words, $\widetilde{f}(k_t)$ is obtained by first reflecting $f(k_t)$ with respect to the vertical axis and then reflecting the image with respect to the horizontal axis. Then $\widetilde{f}(k_t)$ is an *odd function* defined on $\mathbb{R}$, which is invariant under a $180°$ rotation with respect to the origin. Next, we extend the saving function $s(k)$ to the whole real line by setting

$$\widetilde{s}(k_t) = \begin{cases} s(k_t) & \text{if } k_t \geq 0, \\ s(-k_t) & \text{if } k_t < 0. \end{cases}$$

In other words, $\widetilde{s}(k_t)$ is obtained by reflecting $s(k_t)$ with respect to the vertical axis. Then $\widetilde{s}(k_t)$ is an *even function*. Let

$$F(k_t) = \widetilde{s}(k_t)\,\widetilde{f}(k_t) - \left(n - \sigma^2\right)k_t,$$

$$G(k_t) = -\sigma k_t.$$

By definition, F and G are odd functions on $\mathbb{R}$. Clearly, $G(k_t)$ is of class $C^1(\mathbb{R})$.

If $s(k)$ and $f(k)$ are continuously differentiable on $k \geq 0$, then $F(k)$ is of class $C^1(\mathbb{R})$, except possibly at the origin. Since $F(k)$ is an odd function, we must have $F(0) = 0$ to maintain continuity at the origin. For this purpose we shall assume $f(0) = 0$. We also need a finite slope of $F(k)$ at $k = 0$ to make the reflection possible. Formally, we need $f'(0) < \infty$ and

$$n - \sigma^2 < \lim_{k \to 0^+} \frac{d}{dk}[s(k)f(k)] < \infty. \tag{6.7}$$

Then the value of $F'(0)$ is determined by the one-sided limit

$$F'(0) = \lim_{k \to 0} F'(k) = \lim_{k \to 0^+} \frac{d}{dk}[s(k)f(k)] - (n - \sigma^2)$$

with $0 < F'(0) < \infty$, because $F(k_t)$ is an odd function. Therefore, the stochastic differential equation

$$dk_t = F(k_t)\,dt + G(k_t)\,dz_t \qquad \text{with } k_0 \text{ given} \tag{6.8}$$

is an *extension* of equation (6.1) in the sense that any solution to (6.8) with $k_t \geq 0$ for all $t \geq 0$ is a solution to equation (6.1) and that any solution to (6.1) solves (6.8).

Existence and Uniqueness Theorem
In what follows we shall first demonstrate the existence and uniqueness of the solution to equation (6.8). Then we show that the solution thus obtained is everywhere positive ($k_t > 0$ for all $t \geq 0$) if the initial condition is positive ($k_0 > 0$). Therefore, equation (6.1) has a unique solution.

Theorem 6.9 *(Existence and Uniqueness). If the production function $f(k)$ is strictly concave and continuously differentiable on $[0, \infty)$ and satisfies $f(0) = 0$, $f'(0) < \infty$, (6.7), and $\lim_{k \to \infty} f'(k) < 1$, then there is a unique solution to (6.1).*

Proof. First, we extend (6.1) to (6.8). Since $f(k)$ is strictly concave, $f(0) = 0$, and $\lim_{k \to \infty} f'(k) < 1$, there exists $k_1 \neq 0$ that solves the equation $f(k) = k$, unless $f(k) < k$ for all $k > 0$. Then, the boundedness of the savings rate, $0 \leq s(k) \leq 1$, implies that there exists a constant $B_0 > 0$ such that

$$\left| \widetilde{s}(k) \, \widetilde{f}(k) \right| \leq \begin{cases} B_0 & \text{for } |k| \leq k_1, \\ |k| & \text{for } |k| > k_1. \end{cases}$$

Then

$$\left| \widetilde{s}(k) \, \widetilde{f}(k) \right|^2 \leq B_0^2 + |k|^2 \qquad \forall k \geq 0.$$

Notice that if k_1 does not exist, i.e., $f(k) < k$ for all $k > 0$, then the above inequality is automatically satisfied. Choose

$$B = \max \left\{ 2B_0^2, 6(n - \sigma^2)^2, 3\sigma^2, 6 \right\}.$$

Using a standard algebraic formula, $(a - b)^2 \leq 2[a^2 + b^2]$, we have

$$\begin{aligned}
F^2 + G^2 &= \left[\widetilde{s}(k_t) \, \widetilde{f}(k_t) - (n - \sigma^2)k_t \right]^2 + \sigma^2 k_t^2 \\
&\leq 2 \left\{ \left[\widetilde{s}(k_t) \, \widetilde{f}(k_t) \right]^2 + \left[(n - \sigma^2)k_t \right]^2 \right\} + \sigma^2 k_t^2 \\
&\leq 2B_0^2 + 2k_t^2 + 2(n - \sigma^2)^2 k_t^2 + \sigma^2 k_t^2 \\
&\leq B + \frac{B}{3}k_t^2 + \frac{B}{3}k_t^2 + \frac{B}{3}k_t^2 \leq B\left(1 + k_t^2\right).
\end{aligned}$$

Thus, the solution to (6.8) exists and is unique by the nonexplosive theorem.

It remains to show that the solution thus obtained is positive w.p.1. To this end, we note that the Solow equation without saving,

$$dk = -(n - \sigma^2)k\,dt - \sigma k\,dz \qquad (6.9)$$

is a geometric Brownian motion, whose solution is of the form

$$k_t = k_0 \exp\{-(n - \sigma^2)t - \sigma z_t\} > 0 \qquad \text{w.p.1,} \qquad (6.10)$$

since the initial condition is $k_0 > 0$. The addition of $\widetilde{s}(k_t)\,\widetilde{f}(k_t)\,dt$, when $k_t > 0$, to (6.9) will simply shift the stochastic process (6.10) upward. Consequently, a zero capital–labor ratio is an inaccessible boundary, and hence, the solution to (6.8) is everywhere positive provided $k_0 > 0$. ∎

The condition $f'(0) < \infty$ rules out Cobb–Douglas production functions. However, CES (constant elasticity of substitution) production functions with the elasticity of substitution *less than unity* would satisfy $f(0) = 0$, $f'(0) < \infty$, and $\lim_{k\to\infty} f'(k) < 1$ in Theorem 6.9. This is because for any CES production function

$$F(K, L) = A\,[\alpha K^{-\gamma} + (1 - \alpha)L^{-\gamma}]^{-1/\gamma},$$

where A, α, and γ are constants with $A > 0$, $0 < \alpha < 1$, $\gamma > -1$, and $\gamma \neq 0$, we have

$$f(k) = A\,[(1 - \alpha) + \alpha k^{-\gamma}]^{-1/\gamma}.$$

Note that the elasticity of substitution is $\sigma = (1 + \gamma)^{-1}$. It is understood that the Cobb–Douglas case is associated with $\gamma = 0$ (and $\sigma = 1$). Then, from

$$f(k) = A\left[\frac{k^\gamma}{\alpha + (1 - \alpha)\,k^\gamma}\right]^{1/\gamma}$$

and

$$f'(k) = A\alpha\left[\frac{1}{\alpha + (1 - \alpha)\,k^\gamma}\right]^{1+1/\gamma},$$

we see that if $\gamma > 0$ (or $\sigma < 1$), then $f(0) = 0$, $\lim_{k\to\infty} f'(k) = 0$, and $f'(0) = A\alpha^{-1/\gamma} < \infty$. Those CES functions with $\sigma > 1$ are ruled out because when $\sigma > 1$ (or $\gamma < 0$) we have $f(0) = A(1-\alpha)^{-1/\gamma} > 0$, which violates the assumption $f(0) = 0$. In summary, we have

Corollary 6.10 *There is a unique solution to* (6.1) *for all CES functions with elasticity of substitution less than unity.*

For easy reference, we set $\alpha = 1/2$ and $A = 1$ to obtain

$$
\begin{aligned}
\gamma &= -1 \ (\text{or } \sigma = \infty) & f(k) &= \tfrac{1}{2}(1+k) \\
\gamma &= -\tfrac{1}{2} & f(k) &= \tfrac{1}{4}\big(1+\sqrt{k}\big)^2 \\
\gamma &= 0 \ (\text{or } \sigma = 1) & f(k) &= \sqrt{k} \\
\gamma &= 1 & f(k) &= 2k/(1+k) \\
\gamma &= \infty \ (\text{or } \sigma = 0) & f(k) &= \min\{1, k\}
\end{aligned}
$$

Exercise 6.2.3 *The condition* (6.7) *is not listed in the existence theorem of the inverse optimal problem. Why not?*

Hint. Notice that $(d/dk)[s(k)f(k)] = f'(k) - c'(k)$. *The conditions required for solving the inverse optimal problem include* $f'(0) - c'(0) > n - \sigma^2/2$.

6.2.4 Inaccessible Boundaries

From the proof of the theorem, we can see that $k_t = 0$ is not accessible, because $k_t > 0$ for all t. Thus, the theorem demonstrates that the solution to (6.3) will not degenerate to zero in finite time. We have also shown (indirectly) that $k_t = \infty$ is not an accessible boundary. To see this, we first recall that the boundary $k_t = \infty$ is accessible if there is a positive probability of the capital–labor ratio k_t exploding (i.e., $k_t = \infty$) in finite time. If $k_t = \infty$ is accessible, then equation (6.3) is not defined after the explosion time. Our proof shows that the nonexplosive theorem is valid, which suggests that the explosion time τ_∞ is ∞ and hence $k_t = \infty$ cannot be an accessible boundary. In short, the nonexplosive theorem and the reflection method together imply that $k_t = 0$ and $k_t = \infty$ are inaccessible boundaries.

In contrast, Merton (1975) formally proved the inaccessibility of boundaries $k_t = 0$ and $k_t = \infty$ by way of the existence of a steady state distribution. It involves several conditions, and the proof is much more complicated. One of those conditions, however, deserves a special mention. Recall that, in a deterministic growth model, the condition $f'(\infty) = \lim_{k \to \infty} f'(k) < n$ ensures the existence of a maximal sustainable capital–labor ratio, and hence the steady state. Similarly, under uncertainty, we need a condition that relates the production function to the population dynamics to ensure the capital–labor ratio will not, with positive probability, go to infinity in finite time. Specifically, we need the following assumption on the maintenance requirement:

$$f'(\infty) < n - \sigma^2/2. \tag{6.11}$$

Since $f'(\infty) \geq 0$, (6.11) implies $n - \sigma^2/2 > 0$, which is one of the sufficient conditions for the existence of a steady state in Merton (1975, p. 379). This observation is particularly useful in that it is a restriction only on the dynamics of population growth and is independent of the preference structure. Furthermore, equation (6.10) helps us see that $n - \sigma^2/2 \geq 0$ is *necessary* for the existence of a steady state distribution; otherwise, $n < \sigma^2/2$, the drift of (6.9) is positive, and, from (6.10), k_t grows exponentially with time.

When $\sigma = 0$, (6.11) is the deterministic condition discussed above. Furthermore, given a production function, the population growth rate, n, must be greater than $f'(\infty) + \sigma^2/2$. That is, in comparison with the certainty case, we need a *larger* expected population growth rate to balance shocks (i.e., $n > \sigma^2/2$) if the Inada condition $f'(\infty) = 0$ is assumed.

6.3 Other Constraints

The standard method for a static constrained optimization problem is to apply the Kuhn–Tucker conditions to solve the problem. Is there something similar for dynamic models? What would happen if we "mechanically" include the constraints in the formulation of a continuous-time stochastic optimization problem? Can we derive a similar Bellman equation with the associated constraints? Can we be sure that the solution to the constrained Bellman equation is the value function, i.e., can we be sure that the verification theorem holds? In what follows we shall use concrete examples to discuss these issues.

6.3.1 A Portfolio Problem with Borrowing Constraints

General Setting

Recall Merton's consumption–portfolio model with two assets, one of which is risk-free. Let W_t, c_t, s_t, r, μ, and σ^2 be, respectively, wealth, consumption, the share of wealth invested in the risky asset at time t, the return to the risk-free asset, the expected rate of return to the risky asset, and the instantaneous variance of the risky asset satisfying $\mu > r$. As shown before, the budget equation is

$$dW_t = [s_t (\mu - r) W_t + (r W_t - c_t)] \, dt + \sigma s_t W_t \, dz_t. \qquad (6.12)$$

Now we impose nonnegativity constraints on the state and control variables: $W_t \geq 0$, $c_t \geq 0$, and $s_t \geq 0$. The last nonnegativity constraint is, of course, the no-short-sale constraint. To make the discussion more interesting, we include a borrowing constraint:

$$s_t W_t \leq W_t + L, \qquad \text{or} \qquad s_t \leq 1 + L/W_t,$$

where $L > 0$ is a given constant. The product $s_t W_t$ represents the absolute magnitude of investment in the risky asset, whereas L represents the absolute maximum a person can borrow at any time. Notice that when $L = 0$ (or $s_t \leq 1$), no borrowing is allowed, and when $L = \infty$, the problem is exactly Merton's model in which you are allowed to have unlimited borrowing.

Let $\mathbb{R}_+ = (0, \infty)$. The utility function $U(c)$ is of class $C^3 (\mathbb{R}_+)$, strictly increasing and strictly concave in c. In addition, $\lim_{c \to 0} U'(c) = \infty$ and $\lim_{c \to \infty} U'(c) = 0$. Then the consumer's problem can be formulated as

$$\max_{\substack{\{c_t, s_t\} \\ c_t \geq 0, 0 \leq s_t \leq 1 + L/W_t}} E_W \int_0^\infty e^{-\rho t} U(c_t) \, dt \qquad \text{s. t. (6.12) and } W_t \geq 0.$$

$$(6.13)$$

This problem differs from the one discussed in the previous chapters in that the admissible set of controls is different and that the state variable has a nonnegativity constraint. Let the value function of this problem be $J(W)$.

Properties of the Value Function. Several properties of the value function $J(W)$ of this constrained optimization problem (6.13) can be easily derived.

(1) As in the proof in Chapter 4, we can show that $J(W)$ is strictly concave in W.

(2) Since $(c, s) = (r W, 0)$ is admissible, the value function is bounded from below: $J(W) \geq U(r W)/\rho$.

(3) Let $J^\infty(W)$ be the value function associated with Merton's model. Since the set of admissible controls for the problem (6.13) is smaller than the set for Merton's problem, the value function is bounded from above by $J(W) \leq J^\infty(W)$, provided $J^\infty(W) < \infty$. An obvious example of $J^\infty(W) < \infty$ is when the utility function is of HARA class. In what follows we shall assume $J^\infty(W) < \infty$, so that the value function $J(W)$ is bounded.

(4) The value function $J(W)$ is uniformly continuous on $[0, \infty)$, and is strictly increasing in W. In particular, $J(0) = U(0)/\rho$. The proof is in Zariphopoulou (1994, p. 63).

Major Difficulty. What makes this portfolio problem difficult is that the value function $J(W)$ may not be smooth because of the presence of the constraints. A few comments are in order. We have just shown that $J(W)$ is strictly concave. As pointed out in Howe (1982), a concave function is differentiable almost everywhere, i.e., it is differentiable everywhere except for a set of measure zero. In addition, he showed that any concave function can be approximated arbitrarily closely by a smooth (even analytic) concave function. (Functions that have power-series expansions about all points in the domain are called analytic. By definition, an analytic function is a C^∞ function.) Even with these results, it turns out that proving $J(W) \in C^2(\mathbb{R}_+)$ is a major task, which will be discussed later. An immediate corollary of $J(W)$ being of class $C^2(\mathbb{R}_+)$ is that under the assumption of $\mu > r$, the no-short-sale constraint $s_t \geq 0$ is no longer binding and can thus be removed.

Bellman Equation. Following the lines of derivation in Chapter 4, if $J(W)$ is of class $C^2(\mathbb{R}_+)$, then the Bellman equation (on suppressing the subscripts) is, for $W > 0$,

$$0 = \max_{c \geq 0, s \leq 1 + L/W} \{U(c) - \rho J(W) + [s(\mu - r)W + (rW - c)]J'(W)$$
$$+ \tfrac{1}{2}s^2\sigma^2 W^2 J''(W)\} \quad (6.14)$$

with $J(0) = u(0)/\rho$. This Bellman equation looks familiar except for the constraints. We shall see that its economic implications are quite novel.

The Bellman equation (6.14) can be rewritten for $W > 0$, as

$$\rho J(W) = \max_{s \leq 1 + L/W} \{s(\mu - r)WJ'(W) + \tfrac{1}{2}\sigma^2 s^2 W^2 J''(W)\}$$
$$+ \max_{c \geq 0}\{U(c) - cJ'(W)\} + rWJ'(W), \quad (6.15)$$

with $J(0) = u(0)/\beta$. The first is a *static* constrained maximization problem with borrowing constraint $s \leq 1 + L/W$. The second is another static maximization problem, with nonnegativity constraint $c \geq 0$. In short, the problem (6.13) is reduced to two static constrained optimization problems. Thereupon, Kuhn–Tucker conditions are readily applicable.

Kuhn–Tucker Conditions. Let λ be the Lagrange multiplier for the first constrained maximization problem. Then the Kuhn–Tucker conditions are

$$(\mu - r)WJ'(W) + \sigma^2 s W^2 J''(W) - \lambda = 0,$$

$$\lambda(1 + L/W - s) = 0,$$

$$\lambda \geq 0,$$

and

$$1 + L/W - s \geq 0.$$

If $s < 1 + L/W$, then $\lambda = 0$ and

$$-\frac{\mu - r}{\sigma^2} \frac{J'(W)}{WJ''(W)} = s < 1 + L/W.$$

If $s = 1 + L/W$, then

$$(\mu - r)WJ'(W) + s\sigma^2 W^2 J''(W) = \lambda \geq 0,$$

which can be written as

$$-\sigma^2 W^2 J''(W) \left\{ -\frac{\mu - r}{\sigma^2} \frac{J'(W)}{WJ''(W)} - s \right\} \geq 0.$$

It follows that

$$1 + \frac{L}{W} = s \leq -\frac{\mu - r}{\sigma^2} \frac{J'(W)}{WJ''(W)}.$$

Thus, we have

$$s = \min\left\{ -\frac{\mu - r}{\sigma^2} \frac{J'(W)}{WJ''(W)}, 1 + \frac{L}{W} \right\}. \tag{6.16}$$

This last equation reflects the effect of the borrowing constraint on portfolio selection.

Similarly, the second optimization problem's Kuhn–Tucker condition is simplified to

$$U'(c) - J'(W) = 0,$$

because of the assumption $\lim_{c \to 0} U'(c) = \infty$. Thus, the optimal consumption is

$$c(W) = (U')^{-1}[J'(W)]. \tag{6.17}$$

To summarize, the solutions to the consumption and portfolio selection problem with borrowing constraints are given by (6.16) and (6.17).

Example: CRRA Utility Functions

Let $U(c) = c^{1-\alpha}/(1-\alpha)$, $\alpha > 0$, $\alpha \neq 1$. The coefficient α is the degree of relative risk aversion. As shown in Chapter 5, if there is no borrowing limit ($L = \infty$), then

$$c = AW,$$

$$s = \frac{\mu - r}{\alpha \sigma^2},$$

and

$$J(W) = \frac{A^{-\alpha}}{1 - \alpha} W^{1-\alpha}, \qquad A > 0,$$

provided that

$$\rho > (1 - \alpha)\left[r + \frac{1}{2}\frac{(\mu - r)^2}{\alpha \sigma^2} \right],$$

which ensures

$$A = \frac{\rho}{\alpha} - \frac{1 - \alpha}{\alpha}\left[r + \frac{1}{2}\frac{(\mu - r)^2}{\alpha \sigma^2} \right] > 0.$$

Now suppose $L = 0$ (no borrowing is allowed). As long as $s < 1$ or $\mu - r < \alpha \sigma^2$, the borrowing constraint is not binding and the solution derived in Chapter 5 remains valid. The interesting question raised by Vila and Zariphopoulou (1997) is this: What if $\mu - r > \alpha \sigma$?

From (6.16),

$$s = \min\left\{\frac{\mu - r}{\alpha\sigma^2}, 1\right\} = 1.$$

It can be verified that the optimal consumption function is

$$c = BW$$

and the value function is

$$J(W) = \frac{B^{-\alpha}}{1 - \alpha}W^{1-\alpha}, \qquad B > 0, \tag{6.18}$$

where

$$B = \frac{\rho}{\alpha} - \frac{1 - \alpha}{\alpha}\left(\mu - \frac{\alpha\sigma^2}{2}\right) > 0.$$

Again, we need

$$\rho > (1 - \alpha)\left(\mu - \frac{\alpha\sigma^2}{2}\right)$$

to ensure that $B > 0$.

Exercise 6.3.1 *Verify that the value function is of the form* (6.18) *and the optimal consumption is* $c = BW$, *when the utility function is of CRRA class.*

Hint. Since $s = 1$, *the Bellman equation becomes*

$$0 = \max_c\left\{U(c) - \rho J(W) + (\mu W - c)J'(W) + \tfrac{1}{2}\sigma^2 W^2 J''(W)\right\}.$$

Exercise 6.3.2 *Find the value function and the optimal policy functions for the portfolio problem when there is no borrowing* $(L = 0)$ *and* $U(c) = \log c$.

6.3.2 Viscosity Solutions

In our derivation and application, we assume that the value function $J(W)$ is of class $C^2(\mathbb{R}_+)$. In fact, $J(W)$ is the unique $C^2(\mathbb{R}_+)$ solution to the Bellman equation (6.15), which is the central result of Zariphopoulou (1994) and Vila and Zariphopoulou (1997). So, what are the mathematical issues?

To begin with, the value function $J(W)$ as defined by the problem (6.13) may not be smooth enough to satisfy the Bellman equation. As we have discussed in Chapter 4, the instantaneous variance term must be uniformly nondegenerate, i.e., $\frac{1}{2}s^2\sigma^2 W^2 \geq \delta$ for some constant δ, to ensure that the value function $J(W)$ as defined by (6.13) is of class C^2 satisfying the Bellman equation. Because $\frac{1}{2}s^2\sigma^2 W^2$ may become zero, this theorem is not directly applicable to our problem. Obviously, we have to show that sW is bounded away from zero in $\mathbb{R}_+$.

The method taken by Vila and Zariphopoulou (1997) is the so-called viscosity solution technique. This concept was first proposed by Crandall and Lions (1983) for deterministic Bellman equations. "The name refers to the 'vanishing viscosity' method used in the existence results, and was chosen for want of a better idea" [Crandall and Lions (1983, footnote 2)]. Lions (1983) introduced the viscosity solution technique for optimal control of diffusion processes and the Bellman equations. The idea is to introduce a more general solution concept, which makes the classical solution, i.e., $J(W) \in C^2(\mathbb{R}_+)$, a special case.

To introduce the definition, we begin with a second-order differential equation

$$F\left(W, J, J', J''\right) = 0. \tag{6.19}$$

For example, if we define

$$
\begin{aligned}
F&\left(W, J, J', J''\right)\\
&= \max_{c \geq 0, s \leq 1+L/W} \left\{U(c) - \rho J(W) + [s(\mu - r)W + (rW - c)]J'(W)\right.\\
&\qquad\qquad \left. + \tfrac{1}{2}s^2\sigma^2 W^2 J''(W)\right\},
\end{aligned}
\tag{6.20}
$$

then solving the Bellman equation becomes solving the differential equation (6.19). Crandall and Lions (1983) gave a nice motivation for the definition of a viscosity solution for first-order equations $F(W, J, J') = 0$. The interested reader should consult their paper. The following definition for the second-order equations (6.19), however, is taken from Vila and Zariphopoulou (1997).

Definition 6.11 *Suppose* $F : [0, \infty) \times \mathbb{R} \times \mathbb{R} \times \mathbb{R} \to \mathbb{R}$ *is a continuous function and is decreasing in its last argument. A continuous function* $J : [0, \infty) \to \mathbb{R}$ *is a viscosity solution of the equation* (6.19) *if and only if for every* C^2 *function* ϕ *the following conditions hold:*

(i) *for each local maximum point* W_0 *of* $J - \phi$, *we have*

$$F(W_0, J(W_0), \phi'(W_0), \phi''(W_0)) \leq 0, \qquad (6.21)$$

(ii) *for each local minimum point* W_0 *of* $J - \phi$, *we have*

$$F(W_0, J(W_0), \phi'(W_0), \phi''(W_0)) \geq 0. \qquad (6.22)$$

We first show that *every classical solution is a viscosity solution.* Suppose W_0 is a local maximum point of $J - \phi$. Then $J'(W_0) - \phi'(W_0) = 0$, and $J''(W_0) - \phi''(W_0) \leq 0$. Since $J(W)$ is a classical solution of (6.19), we have

$$F(W_0, J(W_0), J'(W_0), J''(W_0)) = 0.$$

Substituting $\phi'(W_0)$ for $J'(W_0)$ and $\phi''(W_0)$ for $J''(W_0)$, and using the fact that F is decreasing in the last argument, we have (6.21). Similarly, (6.22) can be proved. Thus, viscosity solutions generalize classical solutions.

A natural question is this: When is a viscosity solution a classical solution? The answer: *Every* C^2 *viscosity solution is a classical solution.* To see this, we choose $\phi = J$ so that $J - \phi \equiv 0$ in the whole domain. Then every W is a maximizer and a minimizer of $J - \phi$, and therefore (6.21) and (6.22) are satisfied for all W. Consequently, $F(W, J(W), J'(W), J''(W)) = 0$.

When a more general solution concept is introduced, the uniqueness of the solution is often an issue. As pointed out in Crandall and Lions (1983), however, one of the advantages of the viscosity solutions is that they have the uniqueness theorem as well as the existence theorem. Moreover, there is a stability theorem, which says roughly that, if J_ε, $\varepsilon > 0$, is a viscosity solution of $F_\varepsilon(W, J_\varepsilon, J'_\varepsilon, J''_\varepsilon) = 0$, and if $F_\varepsilon \to F$ and $J_\varepsilon \to J$, as $\varepsilon \to 0$, on compact subsets of the domain of F, then J is a viscosity solution of $F(W, J, J', J'') = 0$. In short, the limit of viscosity solutions is also a viscosity solution. See Lions (1983, Proposition I.3).

Vila and Zariphopoulou (1997) solved the portfolio problem with borrowing constraint by approximating the problem (6.13) with a sequence of optimization problems such that the Bellman equation of each problem in the sequence is nondegenerate. The value function of each constructed problem in the sequence is well behaved and is the viscosity solution to the corresponding Bellman equation. Then, using the stability theorem and the uniqueness theorem of viscosity solutions, they prove that $J(W)$ is the unique $C^2(\mathbb{R}_+)$ solution of the Bellman equation (6.14). The proof is quite elaborate, and the interested reader should consult their paper for more details.

There is no doubt that the viscosity solution technique is a powerful tool for solving dynamic optimization problems. It has been shown that the technique is quite useful for extending Merton's portfolio problem to the ones with various constraints. For example, Fleming and Zariphopoulou (1991) solved the portfolio problem when the borrowing rate is greater than the lending rate; Duffie, Fleming, Soner, and Zariphopoulou (1997) solved the portfolio problem when the investor is endowed with stochastic income. See the references cited therein for other extensions. Unfortunately, as pointed out in Vila and Zariphopoulou (1997), there is *no* general framework for this class of problems, and each case requires a specific analysis. Given that these extensions are somewhat technical, collaboration between the two professions, mathematics and economics, is highly recommended.

6.4 Stopping Rules – Certainty Case

6.4.1 The Baumol–Tobin Model

Square-Root Rule

Baumol and Tobin used the well-known inventory model to determine the elasticities of money demand. Their model is static and is described as follows. Assume an economic agent, be that a business firm or a household, that spreads out its purchases over time from a fixed income. For simplicity, the rate of spending is constant over the period. Except at the end of the period, it holds some asset, the yet unspent portion of its income, which has an opportunity cost of foregone interest earnings, say from bonds. On the other hand, going to the bank to get cash incurs a transactions cost of exchanging bonds for cash. The agent faces two different types of costs: foregone interest earnings and the transactions cost. The problem is how much cash it should hold, or how many trips to the bank it should make, so that the total cost is minimized. Notice that the time path of money holding follows a sawtooth pattern.

Let M, r, C, and Y be, respectively, the money holding, the interest rate, the transactions cost, and the income in a given period. The average money holding between trips is $M/2$, and therefore, the foregone interest is $r(M/2)$. The number of trips to the bank is Y/M, so that the transactions cost is $C(Y/M)$. Then the problem is

$$\min_{M} \left\{ r\left(\frac{M}{2}\right) + C\left(\frac{Y}{M}\right) \right\}.$$

The first-order condition implies the well-known square-root rule,

$$M = \sqrt{\frac{2CY}{r}}.$$

In this case the income elasticity, the transactions-cost elasticity, and the absolute value of the interest elasticity of the money demand are all $1/2$.

Optimal Scheduling

Why is the classical sawtooth pattern of demand for money optimal? The argument goes as follows. Suppose we plan to make n trips to the bank. We shall show that the timing for transactions should be *evenly spaced* over the given time period. Then the problem is reduced to finding the optimal number of trip as we just did. The following argument is based on Tobin (1956).

Let Y be the income in a given period $[0, 1]$, which comes in cash. This income will be exhausted at the end of the period. Since income is dispersed at a constant rate, the available income for transactions at time $t \in [0, 1]$ is $T(t) = (1 - t)Y$. The optimal scheduling can be obtained as follows. Since the number of trips is exogenous, the total transactions cost is given. Therefore, the scheduling should be the one that gives rise to the maximal interest earnings. Let the scheduling be $\{t_1, t_2, \ldots, t_n\}$ with the understanding that $0 \leq t_1 < t_2 < \cdots < t_n < t_{n+1} = 1$. At t_1, the economic agent goes to the bank and purchases $T(t_2)$ dollars of bonds and begins to earn interests. At each following t_{i-1}, $i \geq 3$, the economic agent goes to the bank and converts from bonds to cash. In other words, at time t_{i-1}, $i \geq 2$, the economic agent holds $T(t_i)$ dollars in bonds, and $T(t_{i-1}) - T(t_i) = (t_i - t_{i-1})Y$ in cash. The interest earning from t_{i-1}

to t_i is

$$r\left(t_i - t_{i-1}\right) T\left(t_i\right) = r\left(t_i - t_{i-1}\right)\left(1 - t_i\right) Y,$$

where r is the interest rate. Then the optimal scheduling is the solution to the problem

$$\max_{\{t_i\}} \sum_{i=2}^{n} r\left(t_i - t_{i-1}\right)\left(1 - t_i\right) Y = rY \max_{\{t_i\}} \sum_{i=2}^{n} \left(t_i - t_{i-1}\right)\left(1 - t_i\right).$$

The first-order conditions for optimal scheduling are

$$\left(1 - t_i\right) - \left(t_i - t_{i-1}\right) - \left(1 - t_{i+1}\right) = 0, \qquad i = 2, 3, \ldots, n - 1,$$

and

$$\left(1 - t_n\right) - \left(t_n - t_{n-1}\right) = 0.$$

They can be formulated as (recalling $t_{n+1} = 1$)

$$2t_i = t_{i-1} + t_{i+1}, \qquad i = 2, 3, \ldots, n.$$

It means that each t_i, except t_1, is the midpoint of the two adjacent points. That is, the transaction times are evenly spaced. Formally,

$$t_i = t_1 + \frac{i - 1}{n}\left(1 - t_1\right), \qquad i = 2, 3, \ldots, n.$$

It follows that

$$t_i - t_{i-1} = \frac{1}{n}\left(1 - t_1\right), \qquad i = 2, 3, \ldots, n,$$

and the total interest earning is

$$rY \sum_{i=2}^{n} \left(t_i - t_{i-1}\right)\left(1 - t_i\right) = rY \sum_{i=2}^{n} \frac{n - i + 1}{n^2}\left(1 - t_1\right)^2.$$

Hence, $t_1 = 0$ is necessary for maximizing interest earnings.

Integer Constraint?

In the Baumol–Tobin model, the number of trips to the bank is Y/M. What happens to the theory if it is not an integer? Barro (1976) provided an answer to this question. However, the problem can be looked at from a different angle. Since the choice of the length of time is arbitrary, why choose one month or one year? Why not make the problem truly dynamic? In the next subsection, we shall examine this possibility.

6.4.2 A Dynamic Model of Money Demand

Let the money demand at time t be M_t. Assume money is spent at a constant rate μ, i.e.,

$$dM_t = -\mu\, dt, \tag{6.23}$$

or $M_t = M_0 - \mu t$, where $M_0 > 0$ is the initial money holding. The parameter μ represents the rate of disbursement or cash expenditure and has units of dollars per unit of time. It is related to the volume of transactions in the Baumol–Tobin model. If the dynamic model of money demand is obtained from extending the Baumol–Tobin model to infinite horizon, then the time path of money should go as follows. When $t = M_0/\mu$, the stock of money is exhausted and another M_0 is replenished. After the first adjustment, money holding continues to follow equation (6.23) until time $t = 2(M_0/\mu)$. The replenishment takes place again and the process continues. This gives rise to the usual sawtooth profile of money depletion.

Optimal Scheduling

Is this sawtooth profile of money demand optimal? Let M_{t_i} be the amount of money replenished at time t_i, where $t \in \{t_0, t_1, t_2, \dots\}$, with the understanding that $t_0 = 0$ and M_0 is the initial holding. Our objective is to show that $\triangle t_i = t_{i+1} - t_i$ is a constant, for $i = 0, 1, 2, \dots$.

By definition, $M_{t_i} = \mu\,(t_{i+1} - t_i) = \mu\,\triangle t_i$. This says that the choice of the timing for transactions dictates the extent of money holding, and conversely. At any $t \in [t_i, t_{i+1})$, the money holding is

$$M_t = M_{t_i} - \mu\,(t - t_i) = \mu\,(t_{i+1} - t).$$

The foregone interest of holding money in time interval $[t_i, t_{i+1})$ discounted to time t_i (i.e., in current value) is

$$\int_{t_i}^{t_{i+1}} e^{-r(t-t_i)} r M_t \, dt = \int_{t_i}^{t_{i+1}} e^{-r(t-t_i)} r \mu \, (t_{i+1} - t) \, dt.$$

Using integration by parts and the change of variables $s = t - t_i$, we have

$$\int_{t_i}^{t_{i+1}} e^{-r(t-t_i)} r M_t \, dt$$

$$= \int_0^{\Delta t_i} e^{-rs} r \mu \, (\Delta t_i - s) \, ds$$

$$= -e^{-rs} \mu \, (\Delta t_i - s) \Big|_0^{\Delta t_i} - \int_0^{\Delta t_i} \mu e^{-rs} \, ds$$

$$= \mu \Delta t_i + \left(\frac{\mu}{r} \right) e^{-rs} \Big|_0^{\Delta t_i} = \mu \Delta t_i - \left(\frac{\mu}{r} \right) (1 - e^{-r \Delta t_i})$$

$$= M_{t_i} - \left(\frac{\mu}{r} \right) \left[1 - \exp \left\{ - \left(\frac{r}{\mu} \right) M_{t_i} \right\} \right].$$

Thus, the *current value* of foregone interest of holding money is a function of $M_{t_i} = \mu \, \Delta t_i$. Denote it by

$$I \left(M_{t_i} \right) = I \left(\mu \, \Delta t_i \right) = \int_{t_i}^{t_{i+1}} e^{-r(t-t_i)} r M_t \, dt.$$

By definition, $I(0) = 0$. The total cost of money holding has two components: adjustment cost and foregone interest earnings. Assume the interest rate $r > 0$ is constant and, for the moment, the adjustment cost (the brokerage fee), $C > 0$, is also constant. Then the problem is to minimize the present value of the total cost:

$$\min_{\{t_i\}} \sum_{i=0}^{\infty} e^{-r t_i} \left[I \left(\mu \, \Delta t_i \right) + C \right]. \tag{6.24}$$

Lemma 6.12 *At optimum*, $t_i = i t_1$, $i = 2, 3, \ldots$.

Proof. Let $t_1 = \Delta t_0$ (or M_0) be optimally chosen. Using the change of variables $s_{i-1} = t_i - t_1$ (which satisfies $s_0 = 0$ and $\Delta s_{i-1} = \Delta t_i$) and $j = i - 1$, the *current value* of the total cost of money holding from t_1 onward is

$$\min_{\{t_i\}} \sum_{i=1}^{\infty} e^{-r(t_i - t_1)} [I(\mu \Delta t_i) + C] = \min_{\{s_i\}} \sum_{i=1}^{\infty} e^{-rs_{i-1}} [I(\mu \Delta s_{i-1}) + C]$$

$$= \min_{\{s_j\}} \sum_{j=0}^{\infty} e^{-rs_j} [I(\mu \Delta s_j) + C],$$

which is identical to (6.24). Thus, the corresponding first adjustment time must be the same as that in (6.24), i.e., $s_1 = t_1$. Hence, the optimal t_2 must satisfy $t_2 - t_1 = s_1 = t_1$, or $t_2 = 2t_1$. The lemma is proved by induction. ∎

Formulation of Money Demand

From the lemma we have $M_{t_i} = M_0$ for all i, and $t_1 = M_0/\mu$. It follows that the current value of foregone interest earning in each evenly divided time interval is

$$I(M_0) = M_0 - \frac{\mu}{r}(1 - \lambda),$$

where

$$\lambda = \exp\left\{ -\frac{r M_0}{\mu} \right\} < 1.$$

Note that $\lambda = \exp\{-rt_1\}$ is the discount factor at time $t_1 = M_0/\mu$. Since replenishment takes place at time $t_i = it_1 = i \cdot (M_0/\mu)$, where $i = 1, 2, \ldots$, the present value of the total cost of holding M_0 is

$$G(M_0) = \sum_{i=0}^{\infty} e^{-rt_i} [I(M_0) + C] = [I(M_0) + C] \sum_{i=0}^{\infty} \lambda^i = \frac{I(M_0) + C}{1 - \lambda}$$

$$= \frac{M_0 + C}{1 - \lambda} - \frac{\mu}{r}. \tag{6.25}$$

The dynamic, deterministic transactions demand for money is obtained by choosing an M_0 so that $G(M_0)$ is minimized. That is, the problem becomes

$$\max_{M_0} \left\{ \frac{M_0 + C}{1 - \lambda} - \frac{\mu}{r} \right\}. \tag{6.26}$$

It is instructive to derive (6.25) from another angle. The principle developed here will make the stochastic case easier to follow. Let $G(M_0)$ be the current value of the total cost of holding money. The present value of the total cost of holding money M_0 from the first adjustment time onward is

$$e^{-rt_1} G(M_0) = e^{-r(M_0/\mu)} G(M_0) = \lambda G(M_0).$$

The present value of the total cost of holding money has three components: the initial installment cost, the foregone interest up to the first adjustment and the present value of the total cost from the first adjustment onward, i.e.,

$$G(M_0) = C + I(M_0) + \lambda G(M_0).$$

Simplifying this equation, we have (6.25).

The first-order condition on the money demand is

$$1 - \lambda - (M_0 + C) \left(\frac{r}{\mu} \right) \lambda = 0. \tag{6.27}$$

Define

$$\varsigma = \frac{1}{\lambda} = \exp\left(\frac{r M_0}{\mu} \right).$$

Then the first-order condition can be rewritten as

$$(M_0 + C) \left(\frac{r}{\mu} \right) + 1 = \varsigma = \exp\left(\frac{r M_0}{\mu} \right). \tag{6.28}$$

The optimal demand for money is implicitly defined by (6.28).

Properties of Money Demand
The solution to (6.28) always exists and is unique. The following graphic argument, set in (M_0, y) coordinates, will be helpful. The left-hand side of (6.28) is a straight line with slope r/μ and y-intercept $1 + C(r/\mu) > 1$.

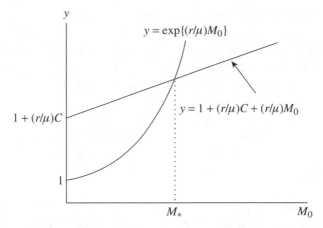

Figure 6.1: Money demand: existence and uniqueness.

The right-hand side of (6.28) is an exponential curve with y-intercept 1. The intersection of the straight line with the exponential curve uniquely determines the optimal demand for money. Denote it by M_*. See Figure 6.1.

From

$$\frac{\partial \lambda}{\partial M_0} = -\left(\frac{r}{\mu}\right)\lambda,$$

it is easy to verify that

$$G''(M_*) = \frac{r/\mu}{1-\lambda} > 0.$$

Since M_* is uniquely determined, the local minimum is also global.

It is easy to see from Figure 6.1 that an increase in C shifts the line $y = (M_0 + C)(r/\mu) + 1$ upward while leaving $y = \exp(r M_0/\mu)$ invariant, and hence $\partial M_*/\partial C > 0$.

The optimal demand for money is a function of three variables: the transactions cost C, the disbursement μ, and the interest rate r. Although the function $M_* = M_*(C, \mu, r)$ may not be readily available in closed form, the central properties of this function are not difficult to obtain from equation (6.28). Specifically, $M_*(C, \mu, r)$ is homogeneous of degree one in the first two variables C and μ, because a doubling of C and μ followed by a doubling of M_* leaves equation (6.28) unchanged.

Similarly, $M_* (C, \mu, r)$ is also homogeneous of degree zero in the last two variable μ and r, since equation (6.28) is invariant under a doubling of μ and r. It is equally straightforward, albeit less obvious, that $M_* (C, \mu, r)$ is homogeneous of degree one in the first variable C and the reciprocal of the last variable, $1/r$. This is because doubling $1/r$ is the same as cutting the interest rate r by half; then, doubling C and $1/r$ followed by a doubling of M_* leaves equation (6.28) unchanged.

Let $\eta (M_*, x)$ be the elasticity of money demand with respect to parameter x. Using Euler's theorem, the above homogeneity conditions are summarized in the following

Proposition 6.13 *Let $\eta (M_*, C)$, $\eta (M_*, r)$, and $\eta (M_*, \mu)$ be respectively the transactions-cost elasticity, the interest elasticity, and the transactions elasticity of demand for money in a dynamic inventory model. Then*

$$\eta (M_*, C) - \eta (M_*, r) = 1,$$

$$\eta (M_*, C) + \eta (M_*, \mu) = 1,$$

$$\eta (M_*, r) + \eta (M_*, \mu) = 0.$$

Notice that, although there are three equations here, any two of them imply the third. Thus, these three elasticities have only one degree of freedom: the determination of one implies the other two. Proposition 6.13 is germane to the sum-of-elasticities property of Milbourne (1988).

The above analysis can be extended to the case in which part of the transactions cost is proportional to the quantity of money handled. That is, the transactions cost is of the form $C + kM_0$, with constant $k > 0$. It is easy to verify that the associated first-order condition is

$$(M_0 + C') \left(\frac{\mu}{r}\right) + 1 = \exp\left\{\frac{r M_0}{\mu}\right\}, \qquad C' = \frac{C}{1 + k}.$$

Substituting C' for C in the analysis, the homogeneity conditions remain valid.

There are many more interesting results of this money demand. However, we shall defer discussing them, since they can be treated as a special case of the stochastic money demand.

What happens if the money stock follows a diffusion process? Clearly, the adjustment time is not $t_1 = M_*/\mu$, but some stopping time τ. An educated guess is that the discounted factor $\lambda = e^{-rt_1}$ will be replaced by some expected discounted factor $E[e^{-r\tau}]$. As we shall see, the stochastic version of the money demand model is indeed obtained by replacing λ with $E[e^{-r\tau}]$ in (6.26).

6.4.3 The Tree-Cutting Problem

The tree-cutting problem is an example of Austrian capital theory. That school of thought is associated with the Swedish economist Wicksell as well as the Austrian economists Böhm-Bawerk and Hayek. Usually known as the tree paradigm, it analyzes the optimal timing of cutting a tree to maximize the net present value of the tree. The paradigm can also be used to address the schooling problem. That is, if we treat human capital like a tree, then the question is this: When is the best time for a student to quit school and enter the job market? If, however, there is replanting after cutting, then the problem is usually known as the rotation problem and is a renewable resources problem. The rotation problem was pioneered by a German forester named Faustmann and made popular through his formula.

Let $X(t)$ be the size of a tree at age t. Assume $X(0) = 0$ (just for convenience; this assumption will be changed in the stochastic case), $X'(t) > 0$, and $X''(t) \leq 0$. The growth of a tree can be represented by a differential equation

$$dX(t) = f(t)\,dt,$$

with $f(t) > 0$ and $f'(t) \leq 0$. This representation will be most useful when we extend the model to the stochastic case. This type of growth is known as the *age-dependent* tree-cutting problem. In contrast, if the growth pattern follows

$$dX(t) = f(X)\,dt,$$

then it is called *size-dependent*. For example, the deterministic Solow equation without consumption satisfies the above equation. We shall, however, discuss mainly age-dependent problems.

Without Rotation

Assume tree-cutting is a one-time business. If we keep the tree, its value will grow. If we cut the tree at a cost $c \geq 0$, we have the opportunity of selling it at a price $p > 0$ and depositing the profit in the bank, where it grows at the rate of interest $r > 0$. The question then is this: When is the best time to cut the tree so that its net present value is maximized? Formally, the problem is

$$\max_{t}\{e^{-rt}\,[pX(t) - c]\}.$$

The first-order condition is

$$X'(t) = r\,[X(t) - c/p].\tag{6.29}$$

It says that, measured in terms of the size of a tree, the marginal benefit of keeping the tree, $X'(t)$, is equal to the marginal cost of keeping the tree, which is measured in terms foregone interest earnings, $r\,[X(t) - c/p]$.

A diagrammatic analysis in (t, y) coordinates will be most helpful. If $X''(t) = 0$, then, plotted against t, $y = X'(t)$ is horizontal, while $y = r\,[X(t) - c/p]$ is linear with slope $r > 0$. They must cross each other. See Figure 6.2.

If $X''(t) < 0$, then, as functions of t, $y = X'(t)$ is downward sloping, while $y = r\,[X(t) - c/p]$ is upward sloping and strictly concave in t. They cross each other unless both are asymptotic to some straight line

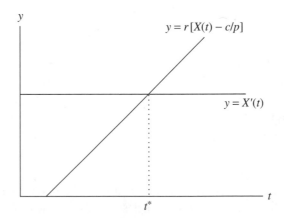

Figure 6.2: Optimal cutting time: linear growth case.

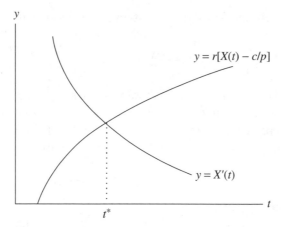

Figure 6.3: Optimal cutting time: concave growth case.

$y = m > 0$. But then $X'(t) > m$ would imply $y = r[X(t) - c/p]$ is rising at a rate greater than m, which is impossible. See Figure 6.3.

In either case, the two curves cross at a unique point, t^*, the optimal time of cutting the tree. The second-order sufficient condition is

$$e^{-rt}\{[pX'(t) - rpX(t) + rc](-r) + pX''(t) - rpX'(t)\}|_{t=t^*}$$
$$= pe^{-rt}[X''(t^*) - rX'(t^*)] < 0.$$

It is straightforward to verify that $X'(t) > 0$ and $X''(t) < 0$ are sufficient for the second-order condition. Since the crossing is unique, this local maximum is also global.

It is straightforward to verify that

$$\frac{\partial t^*}{\partial r} < 0, \qquad \frac{\partial t^*}{\partial c} > 0, \qquad \frac{\partial t^*}{\partial p} < 0.$$

In fact, an increase in r (an increase in p, or a decrease in c) shifts the marginal cost curve $y = r[X(t) - c/p]$ upward, while leaving the marginal benefit curve $y = X'(t)$ unchanged. In other words, we have the following

Proposition 6.14 *An increase in the interest rate, an increase in the price of lumber, or a decrease in the cutting cost lowers the optimal cutting time t^*.*

Alternatively, the first-order condition can be written as

$$\frac{d}{dt} \log [pX(t) - c] = r.$$

It says that the growth rate of the net value of the tree, $\frac{d}{dt} \log [pX(t) - c]$, is equal to the market interest rate r, the opportunity cost of keeping the tree. This representation may be referred to as the Faustmann formula (without rotation). When $X(t) = \mu t$, the optimal cutting size $b = X(t^*)$ satisfies

$$b = \frac{c}{p} + \frac{\mu}{r}. \tag{6.30}$$

With Rotation

Let the initial time be 0. Let c be the cutting and seedling cost. Suppose the cutting times are $\{t_1, t_2, \dots\}$. Then the rotation problem is

$$\max_{\{t_i\}} \sum_{i=1}^{\infty} e^{-rt_i} [pX(t_i - t_{i-1}) - c] \tag{6.31}$$

with the understanding that $t_0 = 0$. As in the proof that money demand follows a sawtooth pattern, we can show that cutting times must be evenly spaced as well, i.e., $t_i = it_1$. Then, the problem is reduced to finding the optimal "first" cutting time t_1. For notational convenience, we shall drop the subscript 1 from t_1. Then the problem (6.31) can be simplified as

$$\max_t \sum_{i=1}^{\infty} e^{-rit} [pX(t) - c] = \max_t \frac{p[X(t) - c/p]e^{-rt}}{1 - e^{-rt}}. \tag{6.32}$$

The first-order condition is

$$\left\{ X'(t)(1 - e^{-rt}) - r[X(t) - c/p] \right\} pe^{-rt}(1 - e^{-rt})^{-2} = 0,$$

which implies

$$X'(t) = \frac{r[X(t) - c/p]}{1 - e^{-rt}}. \tag{6.33}$$

This says that, again measured in terms of the size of a tree, the marginal benefit of keeping a tree, $X'(t)$, must equal to the marginal cost of keeping the tree, which is the present value of all foregone interest earnings from cutting and replanting a tree.

To ensure the existence of a solution, we assume $X'(t)$ satisfies

$$\frac{d}{dt} \log [X(t) - c/p] = \frac{X'(t)}{X(t) - c/p} > e^{-rt} \left(\frac{r}{1 - e^{-rt}} \right),$$

so that the right-hand side of (6.33) is an upward-sloping curve, whereas the left-hand side is obviously downward sloping. That is, if there is a lower bound for the growth rate of the net value of the tree, then the optimal cutting time of a tree with rotation is uniquely determined. Denote it by t^*.

The second-order sufficient condition for the local optimum t^* is

$$\left[X''(t^*) - rX'(t^*) \right] \left(1 - e^{-rt^*} \right) pe^{-rt^*} \left(1 - e^{-rt^*} \right)^{-2} < 0.$$

Clearly, a concave $X(t)$ will suffice. Since t^* is uniquely determined, the optimum is global.

By comparing (6.33) with (6.29), we see immediately that the optimal cutting time is shortened when there are rotations, which is most intuitive. The comparative dynamics are similar to the case of no rotation. An increase in c (or a decrease in p) lowers the marginal cost of keeping a tree; meanwhile the marginal benefit remains invariant. Hence, it will delay the cutting of the tree. Using the fact that

$$e^{rt} > 1 + rt \qquad \forall t \geq 0,$$

we can show that $g(r) = r(1 - e^{-rt})^{-1}$ satisfies

$$g'(r) = (1 - e^{-rt})^{-2}(1 - e^{-rt} - rte^{-rt}) > 0.$$

Hence, an increase in r would raise the marginal cost curve, the right-hand side of (6.33) and hence lower the optimal cutting time. In summary,

$$\frac{\partial t^*}{\partial r} < 0, \qquad \frac{\partial t^*}{\partial p} < 0, \qquad \frac{\partial t^*}{\partial c} > 0.$$

An alternative expression for the first-order condition is

$$\frac{d}{dt} \log [X(t) - c/p] = \frac{X'(t)}{X(t) - c/p} = \frac{r}{1 - e^{-rt}}. \tag{6.34}$$

This is the Faustmann formula. Rewrite (6.34) as

$$X'(t) = r[X(t) - c/p] + \frac{r[X(t) - c/p]}{e^{rt} - 1}.$$

In comparison with (6.29), this equation has an extra term, the second term on the right-hand side. In the literature of forestry, this term is known as the *site value*.

If the tree is growing at a fixed rate, say, $X(t) = \mu t$, then finding the optimal cutting time is the same as finding the optimal cutting size. In fact, the optimal cutting size $b = X(t^*) = \mu t^*$, from (6.34), satisfies

$$b + \left(\frac{\mu}{r}\right) e^{-rb/\mu} = \frac{c}{p} + \frac{\mu}{r}. \tag{6.35}$$

This equation is analogous to (6.30).

Exercise 6.4.1 *For the problem* (6.31), *show that* $t_i = it_1$, $i = 2, 3, \ldots$.
Hint. It is similar to Lemma 6.12.

What happens if the tree growth follows a diffusion process, say,

$$dX = \mu \, dt + \sigma \, dz?$$

A plausible approach is to find the optimal cutting size. But then the corresponding cutting time is a random variable, a stopping time τ. Like the problem of stochastic money demand, the rotation problem under uncertainty could be solved by replacing the discount factor $\lambda = e^{-rt}$ with the expected discounted factor $E[e^{-r\tau}]$ in (6.32). What then is $E[e^{-r\tau}]$?

6.5 The Expected Discount Factor

In this section, we shall formally derive the expected discount factor of a stopping time τ. Since a Wiener process is unbounded, we know the set

$$[\tau < \infty] = \{\omega \in \Omega : \tau(\omega) < \infty\}$$

is of probability one. Our objective is to find $E_x[e^{-r\tau} : \tau < \infty]$ when τ is a stopping time of a stochastic process $\{X_t\}$ with $X_0 = x$. When there is no danger of confusion, we shall abbreviate it as $E_x[e^{-r\tau}]$.

Our approach has three steps. First, we introduce the Wald martingale. Second, by invoking the optional stopping theorem that relates the expected value of a martingale to its initial condition, we can evaluate the expected value of the Wald martingale, from which an equation for $E_x[e^{-r\tau}]$ can be derived. Finally, we present different formula of $E_x[e^{-r\tau}]$ for different types of absorbing barriers.

6.5.1 Fundamental Equation for $E_x[e^{-r\tau}]$

Wald Martingales

Suppose we have a Wiener process $\{X_t\}$ with drift μ and instantaneous variance σ^2. By Ito's lemma, the stochastic process $\{Y_t\} = \{e^{aX_t}\}$, for any dummy variable a, is a geometric Brownian motion

$$dY_t = \left(\mu a + \frac{\sigma^2}{2}a^2\right) Y_t\, dt + \sigma a Y_t\, dz_t = q\,(a)\,Y_t\, dt + \sigma a Y_t\, dz_t,$$

where

$$q\,(a) = \mu a + \frac{\sigma^2}{2}a^2.$$

As shown in Chapter 3, the first moment of a geometric Brownian motion is

$$E\,[Y_t \mid \mathcal{F}_s] = Y_s \exp\{q\,(a)\,(t-s)\}.$$

Then

$$E\left[\frac{Y_t}{\exp\{q\,(a)\,t\}} \,\middle|\, \mathcal{F}_s\right] = Y_s \exp\{-q\,(a)\,s\},$$

and hence

$$E\,[\exp\{aX_t - q\,(a)\,t\} \mid \mathcal{F}_s] = \exp\{aX_s - q\,(a)\,s\}.$$

In other words,

$$V_a\,(t) = \exp\{aX_t - q\,(a)\,t\}$$

is a martingale. Such a martingale is known as a *Wald martingale* with dummy variable a.

Our next step is to evaluate $E_x[V_a(\tau)]$. The objective is obvious. If we know $E_x[V_a(\tau)]$, then we can derive the formula for $E_x[e^{-r\tau}]$. Specifically, if we set $q(a) = r$, then

$$E_x[V_a(\tau)] = E[\exp\{aX_\tau - r\tau\}] = e^{aX_\tau}E_x[e^{-r\tau}],$$

if the value of X_τ is nonstochastic. Then $E_x[e^{-r\tau}]$ can be evaluated if we know the value of $E_x[V_a(\tau)]$. In the case of money demand, the stopping time takes place when money is depleted and therefore $X_\tau = 0$. In that case, $E_x[e^{-r\tau}] = E_x[V_a(\tau)]$.

The method of finding $E_x[V_a(\tau)]$ is well-known in mathematics. In what follows we shall briefly summarize the results.

Optional Stopping Theorem

Recall that a martingale is a fair game, in that the expected return from the gamble is no different from its current return. Can the gambler improve her expected return by suitably choosing the time to quit? If the game is truly fair, we would expect that the answer is negative. This is the essence of the optional stopping theorem.

To formalize the theorem, we define a stopped process $\{X(t \wedge \tau); \ t \geq 0\}$ for a given stopping time τ by

$$X(t \wedge \tau) = \begin{cases} X(t) & \text{if } t < \tau, \\ X(\tau) & \text{if } t \geq \tau. \end{cases}$$

Notice that in our money demand model such a stopped process corresponds to the stochastic version of one sawtooth.

Theorem 6.15 *(Martingale Stopping Theorem). Let $(\Omega, \mathcal{F}, P)$ be a filtered probability space, τ a stopping time on this space, and $X(t)$ a martingale with right-continuous sample paths. Then the stopped process $\{X(t \wedge \tau); \ t \geq 0\}$ is also a martingale.*

Proof. See Harrison (1985). ∎

An immediate corollary of the martingale stopping theorem is the following

Corollary 6.16 *Let* $(\Omega, \mathcal{F}, P)$ *be a filtered probability space, τ a stopping time on this space, and $X(t)$ a martingale with right-continuous sample paths. Then $E[X(t \wedge \tau)] = E[X(0)]$ for any $t > 0$.*

Theorem 6.17 *(Optional Stopping Theorem). Let $(\Omega, \mathcal{F}, P)$ be a filtered probability space, τ a stopping time on this space, and $X(t)$ a martingale with right-continuous sample paths such that*

(i) $P(\tau < \infty) = 1,$
(ii) $E[|X(t)|] < \infty,$ *and*
(iii) $E[X(t \wedge \tau)] \rightarrow E[X(\tau)]$ *as* $t \rightarrow \infty.$

Then

$$E[X(\tau)] = E[X(0)]. \tag{6.36}$$

Proof. See Bhattacharya and Waymire (1990, p. 53) or Harrison (1985, p. 130). ∎

Since $P([\tau < \infty]) = 1$, we have $X(t \wedge \tau) \rightarrow X(\tau)$ w.p.1 as $t \rightarrow \infty$. To satisfy condition (iii), Harrison added a condition that $\{X(t \wedge \tau); \ t \geq 0\}$ is uniformly bounded so that the dominated convergence theorem is applicable. In our case, we shall concentrate on $q(a) \geq 0$. Then $\{V_a(t \wedge \tau); \ t \geq 0\}$ is uniformly bounded. Hence, (6.36) is applicable, i.e.,

$$E_x[V_a(\tau)] = E_x[V_a(0)], \tag{6.37}$$

if the initial state is $X(0) = x > 0$. *Equation (6.37) is the fundamental equation for $E_x[e^{-r\tau}]$.*

6.5.2 One Absorbing Barrier

A boundary that confines a diffusion process is called a *barrier*. The most useful type of barrier for economists is called an *absorbing barrier*. An absorbing barrier is like a black hole – the process is absorbed once it hits the barrier. In what follows we shall work out $E_x[e^{-r\tau}]$ for different types of absorbing barriers.

One Absorbing Barrier: $X(\tau) = 0$

If $X(\tau) = 0$, then the stopping time is the first passage time τ_0, where the subscript stands for the barrier. For notational convenience, however, we shall continue to use τ unless there is confusion or a need to highlight the barrier. From equation (6.37) and $X(0) = x > 0$, we have

$$E_x\left[e^{-q(a)\tau}\right] = e^{ax}.$$

We shall identify $q(a)$ by r and look for the proper a such that $q(a) = r$, or the solution to the equation

$$(\sigma^2/2)\,a^2 + \mu a - r = 0. \tag{6.38}$$

There are two real roots, opposite in sign. Since $E_x[e^{-r\tau}] < 1$, we shall choose the negative one, a_1, where

$$a_1 = \frac{-\mu - \sqrt{\mu^2 + 2r\sigma^2}}{\sigma^2} < 0. \tag{6.39}$$

Then

$$E_x[e^{-r\tau}] = e^{a_1 x}. \tag{6.40}$$

Equation (6.40) will be used to formulate the stochastic money demand model.

Expected Discounted Cost Up to a Stopping Time

Assume $B(x)$ is the instantaneous cost of holding $x > 0$. In the case of money demand it will be the instantaneous foregone interest earning $B(M_t) = r M_t$. Our objective is to evaluate $E_x\left[\int_0^\tau e^{-rt} B(X_t)\,dt\right]$. To facilitate the presentation, let

$$F(X) = \int_0^\infty e^{-rt} B(X_t)\,dt.$$

and

$$h(x) = E_x\left[\int_0^\infty e^{-rt} B(X_t)\,dt\right] = E_x\left[F(X)\right]. \tag{6.41}$$

Proposition 6.18 *Assume X_t follows $dX = \mu \, dt + \sigma \, dz$ with constants μ and σ, $X_0 = x$, $X_\tau = 0$ and any continuous function $B : \mathbb{R} \to \mathbb{R}$ such that $|B|$ is bounded by a polynomial. Then*

$$E_x \left[\int_\tau^\infty e^{-rt} B(X_t) \, dt; \tau < \infty \right] = E_x[e^{-r\tau}; \tau < \infty] h(0), \quad (6.42)$$

and

$$E_x \left[\int_0^\tau e^{-rt} B(X_t) \, dt; \tau < \infty \right] = h(x) - h(0) e^{a_1 x} \quad (6.43)$$

Proof. Note that

$$E_x \left[\int_0^\tau e^{-rt} B(X_t) \, dt \right]$$

$$= E_x \left[\int_0^\infty e^{-rt} B(X_t) \, dt \right] - E_x \left[\int_\tau^\infty e^{-rt} B(X_t) \, dt; \tau < \infty \right].$$

$$(6.44)$$

The first term on the right-hand side of (6.44) is simply $h(x)$. To compute the second term, define a new stochastic process on $[\tau < \infty]$,

$$X_t^* = X_{\tau+t}, \qquad t \geq 0,$$

i.e., X_t^* is a translation of X_t by the random variable τ. By the Dynkin–Hunt theorem, $\{X_t^*\}$ is a Wiener process with starting state $X_0^* = X_\tau = 0$ and is independent of $\mathcal{F}_\tau$. Note that, on $[\tau < \infty]$,

$$\int_\tau^\infty e^{-rt} B(X_t) \, dt = e^{-r\tau} \int_\tau^\infty e^{-r(t-\tau)} B(X_t) \, dt$$

$$= e^{-r\tau} \int_0^\infty e^{-rs} B(X_{\tau+s}) \, ds$$

$$= e^{-r\tau} \int_0^\infty e^{-rs} B(X_s^*) \, ds.$$

Let $P_x(A)$ be the conditional probability of event A when the initial state x is given. Then the second term on the right-hand side of (6.44) is

$$E_x\left[\int_\tau^\infty e^{-rt}B(X_t)\,dt;\tau<\infty\right]$$

$$= E_x\left[e^{-r\tau}\int_0^\infty e^{-rt}B(X_t^*)\,dt;\tau<\infty\right]$$

$$= \int_{[\tau<\infty]}\left[e^{-r\tau}\int_0^\infty e^{-rt}B(X_t^*)\,dt\right]dP_x$$

$$= \int_{[\tau<\infty]}E_x\left[e^{-r\tau}\int_0^\infty e^{-rt}B(X_t^*)\,dt\,\bigg|\,\mathcal{F}_\tau\right]dP_x$$

$$= \int_{[\tau<\infty]}e^{-r\tau}E_x\left[\int_0^\infty e^{-rt}B(X_t^*)\,dt\,\bigg|\,\mathcal{F}_\tau\right]dP_x$$

$$= \int_{[\tau<\infty]}e^{-r\tau}E_x[F(X^*)\mid\mathcal{F}_\tau]dP_x = \int_{[\tau<\infty]}e^{-r\tau}h(X_\tau)\,dP_x$$

$$= h(0)\int_{[\tau<\infty]}e^{-r\tau}dP_x = h(0)E_x[e^{-r\tau};\tau<\infty].$$

This proves (6.42). In the derivation we have used the strong Markov property that

$$E_x\left[F(X^*)\mid\mathcal{F}_\tau\right] = h(X_0^*) = h(X_\tau)\qquad\text{on }[\tau<\infty].$$

Since $E_x[e^{-r\tau}] = e^{a_1 x}$, equation (6.43) follows immediately. ∎

Equation (6.43) will be used to compute the present value of foregone interest of money holding up to the first stopping time.

One Absorbing Barrier: $X(\tau) = b,\ b > x$
If $X(\tau) = b > x$, then the stopping time is the first passage time τ_b. Again, we shall continue to use τ unless there is confusion or a need to highlight the barrier. From equation (6.37) we have

$$E_x\left[e^{-q(a)\tau}\right] = e^{-a(b-x)}.$$

Then we choose the positive root

$$a_2 = \frac{-\mu + \sqrt{\mu^2 + 2r\sigma^2}}{\sigma^2} > 0, \tag{6.45}$$

so that $E_x[e^{-r\tau}] < 1$. Hence

$$E_x[e^{-r\tau}] = e^{-a_2(b-x)}. \tag{6.46}$$

Equation (6.46) will be used to formulate the stochastic rotation problem. It should be noted that in applying this formula we allow the state variable, which follows $dX = \mu\,dt + \sigma\,dz$, to assume negative values at some points in time. In many economic applications, however, this condition could be problematic.

Example 6.19 *Let $\tau = \inf\{t : X(t) = b\}$. If $X(t)$ is a standard Wiener process ($\mu = 0, \sigma = 1$) with $X(0) = 0$, then $a_2 = \sqrt{2r}$ and hence*

$$E_x[e^{-r\tau}] = e^{-b\sqrt{2r}}.$$

Exercise 6.5.1 *State and prove a proposition corresponding to Proposition 6.18 for $X(\tau) = b, b > x$.*

6.5.3 Two Absorbing Barriers

Two Absorbing Barriers 0 and b, with $0 < x < b$
Now consider the case

$$\tau = \tau_0 \wedge \tau_b = \min\{\tau_0, \tau_b\},$$

i.e., the process stops at whichever barrier is hit first. Partition the set $[\tau < \infty]$ by $[\tau_0 < \infty]$ and $[\tau_b < \infty]$. Define

$$E_x[Z; A] = \int_A Z\,dP_x = E_x[Z \mid A]\,P_x(A).$$

By definition,

$$E_x\left[e^{-r\tau}; \tau < \infty\right] = E_x\left[e^{-r\tau_0}; X_\tau = 0\right] + E_x\left[e^{-r\tau_b}; X_\tau = b\right].$$

From (6.37), for any dummy variable a,

$$
\begin{aligned}
e^{ax} &= E_x\left[V_a(0)\right] = E_x\left[V_a(\tau)\right] \\
&= E_x\left[V_a(\tau); X_\tau = 0\right] + E_x\left[V_a(\tau); X_\tau = b\right] \\
&= E_x\left[e^{-r\tau_0}; X_\tau = 0\right] + E_x\left[e^{ab-r\tau_b}; X_\tau = b\right]. \quad (6.47)
\end{aligned}
$$

Replacing a by a_1 and a_2 in (6.47), we have

$$
e^{a_1 x} = E_x\left[e^{-r\tau_0}; X_\tau = 0\right] + e^{a_1 b} E_x\left[e^{-r\tau_b}; X_\tau = b\right]
$$

and

$$
e^{a_2 x} = E_x\left[e^{-r\tau_0}; X_\tau = 0\right] + e^{a_2 b} E_x\left[e^{-r\tau_b}; X_\tau = b\right].
$$

Solving this pair of equations, we have

$$
E_x\left[e^{-r\tau_0}; X_\tau = 0\right] = \frac{e^{a_1 x} - e^{-a_2(b-x)} e^{a_1 b}}{1 - e^{a_1 b} e^{-a_2 b}} \quad (6.48)
$$

and

$$
E_x\left[e^{-r\tau_b}; X_\tau = b\right] = \frac{e^{-a_2(b-x)} - e^{a_1 x} e^{-a_2 b}}{1 - e^{a_1 b} e^{-a_2 b}}. \quad (6.49)
$$

Thus,

$$
\begin{aligned}
&E_x\left[e^{-r\tau}; \tau < \infty\right] \\
&= \frac{e^{-a_2(b-x)} + e^{a_1 x} - e^{a_1 x} e^{-a_2 b} - e^{-a_2(b-x)} e^{a_1 b}}{1 - e^{a_1 b} e^{-a_2 b}}.
\end{aligned}
$$

While the formula is relatively simple, its application to economic problems, especially the comparative dynamics with respect to μ and σ^2, may not be straightforward.

The next example shows that the expected discount factor of a stopping time with two barriers can be quite simple in some special cases.

Example 6.20 Let $\tau = \inf\{t : |X(t)| = b\}$. *Show that if $X(t)$ is a standard Wiener process with $X(0) = 0$, then $E_x[e^{-r\tau}] = 1/\cosh(b\sqrt{2r})$.*
   First, we note that

$$
\tau = \inf\{t : |X(t)| = b\} = \tau_b \wedge \tau_{-b} = \min\{\tau_b, \tau_{-b}\}.
$$

With $\mu = 0$ and $\sigma^2 = 1$, the choice of a for τ_b is $a_2 = \sqrt{2r}$. The choice of a for τ_{-b} is obtained from the equation

$$E_x[e^{-r\tau}] = e^{-a(-b-x)} = e^{a(b+x)}.$$

Clearly, we must choose the negative solution of (6.38), which is $a_1 = -\sqrt{2r}$. Then

$$1 = e^{aX(0)} = E_x[V_a(\tau)]$$

$$= E_x[V_a(\tau); X_\tau = b] + E_x[V_a(\tau); X_\tau = -b]$$

$$= E_x\left[e^{ab-r\tau_b}; X_\tau = b\right] + E_x\left[e^{-ab-r\tau_{-b}}; X_\tau = -b\right].$$

Substituting a_1 and a_2 for a in the above equation, we have

$$1 = e^{b\sqrt{2r}} E_x\left[e^{-r\tau_b}; X_\tau = b\right] + e^{-b\sqrt{2r}} E_x\left[e^{-r\tau_{-b}}; X_\tau = -b\right]$$

and

$$1 = e^{-b\sqrt{2r}} E_x\left[e^{-r\tau_b}; X_\tau = b\right] + e^{b\sqrt{2r}} E_x\left[e^{-r\tau_{-b}}; X_\tau = -b\right].$$

Therefore,

$$\left(e^{b\sqrt{2r}} + e^{-b\sqrt{2r}}\right)\left\{E_x\left[e^{-r\tau_b}; X_\tau = b\right] + E_x\left[e^{-r\tau_{-b}}; X_\tau = -b\right]\right\} = 2.$$

By definition,

$$E_x\left[e^{-r\tau}; \tau < \infty\right] = E_x\left[e^{-r\tau_0}; X_\tau = 0\right] + E_x\left[e^{-r\tau_b}; X_\tau = b\right]$$

$$= \frac{2}{e^{b\sqrt{2r}} + e^{-b\sqrt{2r}}} = \frac{1}{\cosh\left(b\sqrt{2r}\right)}.$$

Expected Discounted Cost with Two Barriers with $0 < x < b$
A result similar to Proposition 6.18 can similarly be derived. First, we decompose

$$E_x\left[\int_\tau^\infty e^{-rt} B(X_t) dt; \tau < \infty\right] = E_x\left[\int_\tau^\infty e^{-rt} B(X_t) dt; X_\tau = 0\right]$$

$$+ E_x\left[\int_\tau^\infty e^{-rt} B(X_t) dt; X_\tau = b\right].$$

Then follow an argument made earlier that

$$
E_x \left[\int_\tau^\infty e^{-rt} B(X_t)\, dt; X_\tau = 0 \right]
$$

$$
= E_x \left[e^{-r\tau} \int_0^\infty e^{-rt} B(X_t^*)\, dt; X_\tau = 0 \right]
$$

$$
= E_x \left[e^{-r\tau} E_x \left\{ \int_0^\infty e^{-rt} B(X_t^*)\, dt \,\middle|\, \mathcal{F}_\tau \right\}; X_\tau = 0 \right]
$$

$$
= E_x \left[e^{-r\tau}; X_\tau = 0 \right] h(0) = \frac{e^{a_1 x} - e^{-a_2(b-x)} e^{a_1 b}}{1 - e^{a_1 b} e^{-a_2 b}} h(0),
$$

where the last equality is obtained by using (6.48) and $h(x)$ is defined in (6.41). Similarly,

$$
E_x \left[\int_\tau^\infty e^{-rt} B(X_t)\, dt; X_\tau = b \right]
$$

$$
= E_x \left[e^{-r\tau}; X_\tau = b \right] h(b) = \frac{e^{-a_2(b-x)} - e^{a_1 x} e^{-a_2 b}}{1 - e^{a_1 b} e^{-a_2 b}} h(b),
$$

where the last equality is obtained by using (6.49). Thus, the expected cost is

$$
E_x \left[\int_\tau^\infty e^{-rt} B(X_t)\, dt; \tau < \infty \right]
$$

$$
= \frac{\left[e^{a_1 x} - e^{-a_2(b-x)} e^{a_1 b} \right] h(0) + \left[e^{-a_2(b-x)} - e^{a_1 x} e^{-a_2 b} \right] h(b)}{1 - e^{a_1 b} e^{-a_2 b}}.
$$

The formula should be helpful in solving two-barrier problems.

6.6 Optimal Stopping Times

6.6.1 Dynamic and Stochastic Demand for Money

Absorbing Barrier

Now assume the depletion of the money stock is stochastic. Instead of having a sawtooth shape, the sample function fluctuates about the old sawtooth path. The money stocks follow a stochastic differential equation

$$
dM_t = -\mu\, dt + \sigma\, dz_t, \tag{6.50}
$$

where $\mu > 0, \sigma > 0$, and M_0 is given. In other words, the money stock at time t is normally distributed with mean $M_0 - \mu t$ and the variance $\sigma^2 t$. With a normal distribution, the probability of hitting $M_t = 0$ at any point of time is positive. Starting from $M_0 > 0$, each sample path will w.p.1 hit $M_t = 0$ in finite time. The time at which the money stock hits zero, $M_t = 0$, is a first passage time of the stochastic process (6.50). Denote it by

$$\tau_0 = \inf\{t \geq 0 : M_t = 0\}.$$

The sample path from the initial time $t = 0$ to the first hitting time τ_0 is a stochastic version of one sawtooth.

Once the absorbing barrier is reached the money stock is replenished. By the strong Markov property, the replenished money stock

$$M_t^* = M_{t+\tau_0} + M_0, \qquad t \geq 0,$$

which is independent of $\mathcal{F}_{\tau_0}$, follows the same Ito process (6.50) until it hits the absorbing barrier again. Call this stopping time τ_0^2. Once again we replenish the money stock, and the process continues. This gives rise to a family of stopping times $\{\tau_0^0, \tau_0^1, \tau_0^2, \ldots\}$, with the convention that $\tau_0^0 = 0$ w.p.1 and $\tau_0^1 = \tau_0$.

The rule that the money stock will be replenished once depleted is a natural stochastic extension of the deterministic case. In the literature, it is known as an (s, S) rule, where s stands for the trigger (a level that triggers response) and S stands for the target. Therefore, it is also called a trigger–target rule. Our demand for money example is a $(0, M_0)$ rule. The problem then is this: What is the optimal level of money stock that minimizes the expected present value of the total cost of holding money?

Formulation of the Demand-for-Money Function
We shall extend our dynamic model of money demand to the stochastic case in the following three steps. First, we must be able to compute the expected foregone interest earnings up to the first passage time τ_0, which is again denoted by $I(M_0)$ for easy reference to the deterministic case. Second, we add the initial cost of installing M_0, which is C. Then $C + I(M_0)$ is the present value of the cost of holding money up to the first passage time. Third, we compute the expected present value of all costs following the first passage time τ_0, i.e., the stochastic version of $\lambda G(M_0)$.

The expected present value of foregone interest earnings due to money holding from $t = 0$ up to the first passage time τ_0, given the interest rate r, is

$$I(M_0) = E_{M_0}\left[\int_0^{\tau_0} e^{-rt} r M_t \, dt\right].$$

This can be obtained by using Proposition 6.18 and $B(M_t) = r M_t$. Specifically, we have

$$h(M_0) = E_{M_0}\left[\int_0^{\infty} e^{-rt} r M_t \, dt\right]. \tag{6.51}$$

By Fubini's theorem, (6.51) becomes

$$h(M_0) = \int_0^{\infty} e^{-rt} r E_{M_0}(M_t) \, dt = \int_0^{\infty} e^{-rt} r (M_0 - \mu t) \, dt = M_0 - \frac{\mu}{r}.$$

Using (6.40) and (6.43), we have

$$I(M_0) = E_{M_0}\left[\int_0^{\tau_0} e^{-rt} r M_t \, dt\right] = M_0 - \frac{\mu}{r} + \left(\frac{\mu}{r}\right) E_{M_0}[e^{-r\tau_0}].$$

For notational convenience, we shall heretofore write $\alpha = E_{M_0}[e^{-r\tau_0}]$.

Let $G(M_0)$ be the expected present value of the total cost of holding M_0 with stopping times $\{\tau_0^0, \tau_0^1, \tau_0^2, \ldots\}$. Then

$$G(M_0) = E_{M_0}\left\{\sum_{i=0}^{\infty} e^{-r\tau_0^i} (I(M_0) + C)\right\}.$$

Since the stochastic process $\{M_t^*\}$ is a Wiener process with initial state M_0 and is independent of $\mathcal{F}_{\tau_0}$, the set of stopping times $\{\tau_0^1 - \tau_0, \tau_0^2 - \tau_0, \ldots\}$ conditional on $\mathcal{F}_{\tau_0}$ is equivalent to $\{\tau_0^0, \tau_0^1, \tau_0^2, \ldots\}$. It follows that

$$G(M_0)$$

$$= I(M_0) + C + E_{M_0} \left\{ E_{M_0} \left[e^{-r\tau_0} \sum_{i=1}^{\infty} e^{-r(\tau_0^i - \tau_0)} (I(M_0) + C) \,\middle|\, \mathcal{F}_{\tau_0} \right] \right\}$$

$$= I(M_0) + C + E_{M_0} \left\{ e^{-r\tau_0} E_{M_0} \left[\sum_{i=1}^{\infty} e^{-r(\tau_0^i - \tau_0)} (I(M_0) + C) \,\middle|\, \mathcal{F}_{\tau_0} \right] \right\}$$

$$= I(M_0) + C + E_{M_0} \left\{ e^{-r\tau_0} G(M_0) \right\}$$

$$= I(M_0) + C + G(M_0) E_{M_0}[e^{-r\tau_0}].$$

Thus,

$$G(M_0) = I(M_0) + C + \alpha G(M_0)$$
$$= M_0 - \frac{\mu}{r} + \left(\frac{\mu}{r}\right)\alpha + C + \alpha G(M_0),$$

or

$$G(M_0) = \frac{M_0 + C}{1 - \alpha} - \frac{\mu}{r}. \tag{6.52}$$

Notice that this objective function is identical to (6.25) if λ is replaced by α.

From

$$E_{M_0}[e^{-r\tau_0}] = e^{-a(0 - M_0)} = e^{aM_0},$$

we must choose the negative solution to the quadratic equation

$$(\sigma^2/2) a^2 - \mu a - r = 0.$$

This equation differs from (6.38) because the drift in (6.50) is $-\mu$, not μ, which accounts for the sign change. The choice of a is

$$a_3 = \frac{\mu - \sqrt{\mu^2 + 2r\sigma^2}}{\sigma^2}.$$

It is interesting to note that $a_3 = -a_2$.

For easy comparison between α and $\lambda = \exp\{-r\,(M_0/\mu)\}$, we shall define

$$\delta = \mu a_2 = \frac{-\mu + \sqrt{\mu^2 + 2r\sigma^2}}{\sigma^2/\mu} > 0. \tag{6.53}$$

Then

$$\alpha = E_{M_0}[e^{-r\tau_0}] = \exp\left\{-\frac{\delta M_0}{\mu}\right\}.$$

Notice that δ plays the role of r in the stochastic case. In fact, δ is the stochastic extension of r in the sense that if σ^2 is arbitrarily small, then δ is approximately r. To see this, we recall Newton's binomial series: For $|x| < 1$, and any real number y,

$$(1+x)^y = 1 + yx + \frac{1}{2!}y\,(y-1)x^2 + \frac{1}{3!}y\,(y-1)\,(y-2)\,x^3 + \cdots.$$

If $x = 2r\sigma^2/\mu^2 < 1$, then

$$\sqrt{\mu^2 + 2r\sigma^2} = \mu\left(1 + \frac{2r\sigma^2}{\mu^2}\right)^{1/2}$$

$$= \mu + \frac{1}{2}\frac{2r\sigma^2}{\mu} - \frac{1}{8}\frac{(2r\sigma^2)^2}{\mu^3} + \frac{1}{16}\frac{(2r\sigma^2)^3}{\mu^5} - \cdots.$$

For given r and μ, we have $2r\sigma^2 < \mu^2$ for arbitrarily small σ^2. Therefore,

$$\delta = \frac{-\mu + \sqrt{\mu^2 + 2r\sigma^2}}{\sigma^2/\mu} = r - \frac{1}{2}\frac{r^2\sigma^2}{\mu^2} + o\left(\sigma^2\right) \to r \qquad \text{as } \sigma^2 \to 0.$$

The firm's problem is to minimize (6.52). Let $\beta = 1/\alpha$. Then the first-order condition can be rewritten as

$$(M_0 + C)\left(\frac{\delta}{\mu}\right) + 1 = \beta = \exp\left(\frac{\delta M_0}{\mu}\right). \tag{6.54}$$

The optimal demand for money is implicitly defined by (6.54). Notice that (6.54) differs from (6.28) only in that δ replaces r. Then, using the same diagram as in Figure 6.1 with r replaced by δ, it becomes obvious that the solution to (6.54) always exists and is unique. In short, (6.54) is a natural extension of the deterministic (6.28).

Properties of the Money Demand

As with other demand functions, we are interested in the elasticities of money demand with respect to exogenous parameters. It is not necessary to have a closed-form money demand function to derive useful results. Here we shall demonstrate that ordinary implicit differentiation and mathematical reasoning can go a long way. Even though the optimal demand for money is only implicitly defined by (6.54), we shall show that the elasticities of money demand can be directly analyzed. In particular, the properties of the interest elasticity enable us to draw conclusions on financial innovations and the efficacy of monetary policies.

Homogeneity. The optimal demand for money is a function of four variables: the transactions cost C, the disbursement μ, the interest rate r, and the uncertainty factor σ^2. Again, even though the closed-form function $M_* = M_*(C, \mu, r, \sigma^2)$ is not known, we can still derive the central properties of this function as before. Specifically,

$$M_*(C, \mu, r, \sigma^2) = M_*\left(C, \mu, \delta\left(\mu, r, \sigma^2\right)\right).$$

Since $\delta(\mu, r, \sigma^2)$ is linearly homogeneous in r and $1/\sigma^2$, and M_* is linearly homogeneous in C and $1/\delta$, we have, for $\theta > 0$,

$$M_*\left(\theta C, \mu, \delta\left(\mu, r/\theta, \theta\sigma^2\right)\right) = M_*\left(\theta C, \mu, (1/\theta)\delta\left(\mu, r, \sigma^2\right)\right)$$
$$= \theta M_*\left(C, \mu, \delta\left(\mu, r, \sigma^2\right)\right).$$

That is, $M_*(C, \mu, \delta(\mu, r, \sigma^2))$ is homogeneous of degree one in $C, 1/r$, and σ^2. Similarly, since $\delta(\mu, r, \sigma^2)$ is linearly homogeneous in all three variables and M_* is homogeneous of degree zero in μ and δ, we have, for $\theta > 0$,

$$M_*\left(C, \theta\mu, \delta\left(\theta\mu, \theta r, \theta\sigma^2\right)\right) = M_*\left(C, \theta\mu, \theta\delta\left(\mu, r, \sigma^2\right)\right)$$
$$= M_*\left(C, \mu, \delta\left(\mu, r, \sigma^2\right)\right),$$

i.e., $M_*(C, \mu, \delta(\mu, r, \sigma^2))$ is homogeneous of degree zero in μ, r, and σ^2. Thus, we have

Proposition 6.21 *Let* $\eta(M_*, \sigma^2)$ *be the uncertainty elasticity of demand for money in a dynamic inventory model. Then*

$$\eta(M_*, C) - \eta(M_*, r) + \eta(M_*, \sigma^2) = 1,$$
$$\eta(M_*, \mu) + \eta(M_*, r) + \eta(M_*, \sigma^2) = 0,$$
$$\eta(M_*, C) + \eta(M_*, \mu) + 2\eta(M_*, \sigma^2) = 1,$$
$$\eta(M_*, C) - \eta(M_*, \mu) - 2\eta(M_*, r) = 1.$$

$$(6.55)$$

Proof. We have already proved the first two. The last two are obtained by algebraic manipulation of the first two. ∎

It is easy to verify that the results of Miller and Orr (1966) and Whalen (1966) that $\eta(M_*, C) = -\eta(M_*, r) = \eta(M_*, \sigma^2) = 1/3$ satisfy the first equation of (6.55), and that the results of Baumol (1952) and Tobin (1956) that $\eta(M_*, C) = -\eta(M_*, r) = \eta(M_*, \mu) = 1/2$ satisfy the last equation of (6.55).

Money Demand as a Function of Transactions Cost. While there are four elasticities of money demand, there are only two degrees of freedom. By homogeneity, the determination of any two elasticities implies the remaining two. Therefore, to study the transactions elasticity and the interest elasticity of money demand, we shall first examine the transactions-cost elasticity and the uncertainty elasticity of money demand. The following proposition shows that, while money demand is defined only implicitly, it does possess nice properties.

Proposition 6.22

(a) As a function of transactions cost, the demand-for-money function satisfies the Inada conditions: $M'_*(C) > 0$, $M''_*(C) < 0$, *with* $M_*(0) = 0$, $\lim_{C \to \infty} M_*(C) = \infty$, $M'_*(0) = \infty$, *and* $\lim_{C \to \infty} M'_*(C) = 0$.

(b) The transactions-cost elasticity of money demand, $\eta(M_*, C)$, *is a decreasing function of C satisfying* $0 < \eta(M_*, C) < 1/2$. *In particular, we have* $\lim_{C \to \infty} \eta(M_*, C) = 0$ *and* $\lim_{C \to 0} \eta(M_*, C) = 1/2$.

Proof. (a) From (6.54), we have (by implicit differentiation)

$$\frac{\partial M_*}{\partial C} = \frac{1}{\beta - 1} > 0, \qquad \frac{\partial^2 M_*}{\partial C^2} = -\frac{(\delta/\mu)\beta}{(\beta - 1)^3} < 0.$$

This proves $M'_*(C) > 0$ and $M''_*(C) < 0$. From Figure 6.1 (with r replaced by δ), an increase in C produces a parallel shift of the line $y = (M_0 + C)(\mu/r) + 1$. Thus, the optimal M_* is obtained by tracing the exponential function $y = \beta = \exp\{(\delta/\mu) M_0\}$. Therefore, $M_*(0) = 0$ and $\lim_{C\to\infty} M_*(C) = \infty$. As $C \to 0$, we have $\beta \to 1$ and $M'_*(C) \to \infty$. As $C \to \infty$, we have $\beta \to \infty$ and $M'_*(C) \to 0$.

To prove (b), we first note that the transactions-cost elasticity is given by

$$\eta(M_*, C) = \frac{C/M_*}{\beta - 1}. \tag{6.56}$$

By differentiating $\eta(M_*, C)$ with respect to C, we see that $\partial\eta(M_*, C)/\partial C < 0$ if the inequality

$$M_*(\beta - 1) < C\left\{1 + \frac{(\delta M_*/\mu)\beta}{\beta - 1}\right\} \tag{6.57}$$

holds. Assume (6.57) is valid for now. Note that

$$\frac{\partial[M_*(\beta - 1)]}{\partial C} = 1 + \frac{\beta \log \beta}{\beta - 1}.$$

By repeatedly applying l'Hôpital's rule to (6.56) and using the facts that $C \to \infty$ implies $\beta \to \infty$ and that $C \to 0$ implies $\beta \to 1$, we have

$$\lim_{C\to\infty} \eta(M_*, C) = \frac{1}{1 + \lim_{\beta\to\infty} \frac{\beta \log \beta}{\beta - 1}} = 0$$

and

$$\lim_{C\to 0} \eta(M_*, C) = \frac{1}{1 + \lim_{\beta\to 1} \frac{\beta \log \beta}{\beta - 1}} = \frac{1}{2}.$$

This proves the range of the elasticity.

Now we return to (6.57). To simplify the notation, let $x = \delta C/\mu$, $y = \delta M_*/\mu$. Then $\beta = e^y$, and the inequality (6.57) can be written as

$$y(e^y - 1) < x\left\{1 + \frac{ye^y}{e^y - 1}\right\}.$$

The first-order condition becomes $x = e^y - y - 1$. Substituting this x into the inequality above, we have

$$(e^y - 1)^2 > y^2 e^y. \tag{6.58}$$

To prove (6.58), we set $g(y) = e^y - 1 - ye^{y/2}$. Since $e^z > 1 + z$ for all $z > 0$, we have $g'(y) = e^{y/2} \left(e^{y/2} - 1 - y/2 \right) > 0$. Thus, $g(y)$ is a strictly increasing function of y. Given the initial value $g(0) = 0$, we have $g(y) > 0$ for all $y > 0$. The inequality (6.58) is obtained when this function $g(y)$ is multiplied by a positive function $e^y - 1 + ye^{y/2}$. ∎

The Interest and Transactions Elasticities. Our ultimate concern is with the interest elasticity and the transactions elasticity. To complete the analysis, we need the following two propositions.

Proposition 6.23 *The transactions-cost elasticity of money demand, $\eta(M_*, C)$, is an increasing function of σ^2.*

Proof. See Chang (1999, pp. 728–729). ∎

Proposition 6.24 *The uncertainty elasticity of money demand, $\eta(M_*, \sigma^2)$, is increasing in C and satisfies $0 < \eta(M_*, \sigma^2) < 1/2$.*

Proof. See Chang (1999, p. 729). ∎

Proposition 6.25
  (a) *The transactions elasticity of money demand, $\eta(M_*, \mu)$, is increasing in C and decreasing in σ^2, and satisfies $0 < \eta(M_*, \mu) < 1$.*
  (b) *The interest elasticity (in absolute value) of money demand, $-\eta(M_*, r)$, is increasing in C and decreasing in σ^2, and satisfies $1/4 < -\eta(M_*, r) < 1$.*

Proof. See Chang (1999, p. 724). ∎

This proposition has some implications for financial innovations. Recall that a rise in the interest elasticity weakens the control of monetary authorities over the financial system and impedes the effectiveness of monetary policy. Does the process of financial innovation hinder the efficacy of monetary policy? New cash management techniques are directed either toward lowering the cash flow uncertainty or toward lowering transactions costs. By Proposition 6.25 (b), the former increases the interest elasticity (in absolute value), while the latter decreases the interest elasticity (in absolute value). The answer to the question thus depends on the types of financial innovation.

Exercise 6.6.1 *Show that, if* $\sigma^2 = 0$, *then* $1/2 < \eta(M_*, \mu) < 1$ *and* $1/2 < -\eta(M_*, r) < 1$.

6.6.2 Stochastic Tree-Cutting and Rotation Problems

Consider the simplest case of linear growth

$$dX = \mu\, dt + \sigma\, dz,$$

where μ and σ are constants. Assume we cut the tree when it grows to the size b. Then the timing of cutting is the first passage time

$$\tau_b = \inf\{t \geq 0 : X(t) = b\}.$$

It should be mentioned that even though the probability of a negative tree size is nonzero in this setting, $dX = \mu\, dt + \sigma\, dz$ is one of the most commonly studied cases. Usually the justification, valid or not, is that we are looking at the forest, not a tree.

Without Rotation
The problem is to maximize the present value of cutting a tree. Assume the initial size of the tree is x and the cost of cutting is c, measured in terms of the value of a tree. Formally, the problem

$$\max_b E_x[(X(\tau_b) - c)\, e^{-r\tau_b}] = \max_b \{(b - c)\, E_x[e^{-r\tau_b}]\}.$$

Since the trigger is $X(\tau_b) = b > x$, the expectation $E_x[e^{-r\tau_b}]$ is defined by (6.46), i.e.,

$$E_x[e^{-r\tau_b}] = e^{-a_2(b-x)},$$

where a_2 is defined in (6.45). The first-order condition is

$$e^{-a_2(b-x)} - (b - c)\, a_2 e^{-a_2(b-x)} = 0,$$

or simply

$$b = c + \frac{1}{a_2} = c + \frac{\sigma^2}{-\mu + \sqrt{\mu^2 + 2r\sigma^2}} = c + \frac{\mu}{\delta},$$

where δ is defined in (6.53). As shown before, $\delta \to r$ when $\sigma^2 \to 0$. Thus the above equation is the stochastic extension of (6.30).

It is straightforward to verify that

$$\frac{\partial b}{\partial r} < 0, \qquad \frac{\partial b}{\partial c} > 0, \qquad \frac{\partial b}{\partial \mu} > 0, \quad \text{and} \quad \frac{\partial b}{\partial \sigma^2} > 0. \qquad (6.59)$$

We note that an increase in the interest rate or a decrease in the cutting cost lowers the cutting size, i.e., lowers the cutting time – a result that is clearly a stochastic extension of the deterministic case. The positive effect of the drift μ upon b means that if the tree is expected to grow faster, then we should not cut the tree until it becomes taller. The uncertainty effect – that an increase in uncertainty may allow the tree to grow taller – is interesting. However, such a positive effect of uncertainty is quite common in stochastic analysis, as we have seen.

Exercise 6.6.2 *Prove the inequalities in* (6.59).
   Hint. The following inequality should come in handy:

$$\mu^2 + r\sigma^2 > \mu\sqrt{\mu^2 + 2r\sigma^2}.$$

With Rotation
With rotation, c stands for the cost of cutting and replanting, sometimes known as the seedling cost. The initial size x is the seedling size. Assume $0 \le x < c$. Let $G(b)$ be the total (current) value of tree-cutting at size b with rotation. Just as in the money demand model, $G(b)$ is the sum of the net value up to the first cutting–replanting time τ_b and the discounted value thereafter. In other words, $G(b)$ must satisfy the following equation:

$$G(b) = E_x[(X(\tau_b) - c)e^{-r\tau_b}] + E_x[e^{-r\tau_b}]G(b).$$

Rearranging terms, we have

$$G(b) = \frac{(b - c)E_x[e^{-r\tau_b}]}{1 - E_x[e^{-r\tau_b}]} = \frac{(b - c)e^{-a_2(b-x)}}{1 - e^{-a_2(b-x)}}.$$

Thus, we can formulate the stochastic rotation problem as

$$\max_b \left\{ \frac{(b-c)\, e^{-a_2(b-x)}}{1 - e^{-a_2(b-x)}} \right\},$$

which is the stochastic version of (6.32).

Using

$$\frac{\partial e^{-a_2(b-x)}}{\partial b} = -a_2 e^{-a_2(b-x)},$$

the first-order condition is simplified as

$$1 + a_2 c - a_2 b = e^{-a_2(b-x)}. \tag{6.60}$$

Again, a diagrammatic analysis set in (b, y) coordinates would be helpful. As a function of b, the left-hand side of (6.60), $y = 1 + a_2 c - a_2 b$, is a straight line with a negative slope $-a_2$ and a positive y-intercept $1 + a_2 c$. In contrast, the right-hand side of (6.60), $y = e^{-a_2(b-x)}$, is decreasing and convex in b and is asymptotic to the b-axis with a positive y-intercept $e^{a_2 x}$. As long as $1 + a_2 c > e^{a_2 x}$, the optimal b^* is uniquely determined. See Figure 6.4.

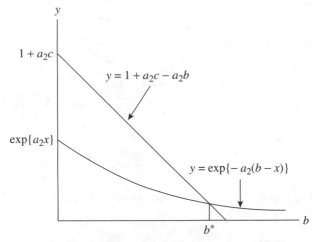

Figure 6.4: Optimal cutting time: stochastic case.

It is straightforward to verify that the second-order condition evaluated at the optimal b is

$$G''(b) = \frac{-e^{-a_2(b-x)}}{1 - e^{-a_2(b-x)}} < 0.$$

Thus, the solution is the maximum, since we have proved that it is unique.

It is instructive to rewrite the first-order condition as

$$b - c = \frac{1}{a_2}\left[1 - e^{-a_2(b-x)}\right].$$

Since $a_2\mu = \delta$, it becomes

$$b + \frac{\mu}{\delta}e^{-\delta(b-x)/\mu} = c + \frac{\mu}{\delta},$$

which is the stochastic version of the Faustmann formula (6.35).

The comparative dynamics of increasing c is straightforward, since it shifts the line $y = 1 + a_2 c - a_2 b$ upward and leaves the other curve $y = e^{-a_2(b-x)}$ unchanged. Thus, an increase in the seedling cost would raise the cutting size, i.e., $\partial b/\partial c > 0$. Formally,

$$\frac{\partial b}{\partial c} = \frac{1}{1 - e^{-a_2(b-x)}} > 0.$$

To study the comparative dynamics of the other three parameters, we note that

$$\frac{\partial a_2}{\partial \mu} = \frac{1}{\sigma^2}\left(-1 + \frac{\mu}{\sqrt{\mu^2 + 2r\sigma^2}}\right) < 0,$$

$$\frac{\partial a_2}{\partial \sigma^2} = \frac{\mu\sqrt{\mu^2 + 2r\sigma^2} - (\mu^2 + r\sigma^2)}{(\sigma^2)^2\sqrt{\mu^2 + 2r\sigma^2}} < 0,$$

and

$$\frac{\partial a_2}{\partial r} = \frac{1}{\sqrt{\mu^2 + 2r\sigma^2}} > 0.$$

Once the sign of $\partial b/\partial a_2$ is determined, so are the signs of $\partial b/\partial r$, $\partial b/\partial \mu$, and $\partial b/\partial \sigma^2$.

Exercise 6.6.3 *Show that $b \to x$ as $c \to x$, and $b \to \infty$ as $c \to \infty$.*

Exercise 6.6.4 *Show that $\partial b / \partial a_2 < 0$. Hence, we have the comparative dynamics*

$$\frac{\partial b}{\partial r} < 0, \qquad \frac{\partial b}{\partial \mu} > 0, \qquad and \qquad \frac{\partial b}{\partial \sigma^2} > 0.$$

Hint. First, show that

$$\frac{\partial b}{\partial a_2} = \frac{c - b + (b - x) e^{-a_2(b-x)}}{a_2 \left[1 - e^{-a_2(b-x)} \right]}.$$

Then, let $f(c) = c - b + (b - x) e^{-a_2(b-x)}$. Show that $f(x) = 0$ and $f'(c) < 0$ to conclude that $f(c) < 0$ for all $c > x$. Compare your results with Miller and Voltaire (1980, p. 139).

Exercise 6.6.5 *There are homogeneity conditions embedded in (6.60). Can you find them?*

6.6.3 Investment Timing

The model of investment timing was first developed by McDonald and Siegel (1986) and was extensively discussed in Dixit and Pindyck (1994, Chapter 5). The problem is this: A firm must decide when to invest in a project, whose value is stochastic, given that the investment cost is a constant I. Assume that the value of the project at time t, $V(t)$, follows a geometric Brownian motion

$$dV = \mu V dt + \sigma V dz, \tag{6.61}$$

where μ and σ are constants, and $V(0) > 0$ is known. For convenience, we shall assume $V(0) = 1$. As we discussed in Chapter 3, the value of investment opportunity is an option, which is governed by a differential equation. Dixit and Pindyck (1994) pointed out that, because of the analogy with financial options, the opportunities to acquire real assets are sometimes called "real options." In fact, they mentioned (p. 7) that their book on irreversible investment could be titled "The Real Options Approach to Investment." They solved this investment timing problem using the real option approach and the dynamic programming method.

We shall solve this problem using the optimal stopping method developed in this chapter. The firm waits for the right time to maximize the expected present value of the project, $E[(V(t) - I)e^{-rt}]$. In this respect, this problem resembles the tree-cutting problem. Finding the optimal time to invest is analogous to finding the optimal time to cut the tree. Therefore, the investment timing problem is to find the critical value of the project such that the firm will invest the first time that value is reached.

Let

$$\tau = \min \{t : V(t) = b\}$$

be the first passage time – the time the value of the project reaches b. Then the problem can be formulation as

$$\max_b E[(V(\tau) - I)e^{-r\tau}] = \max_b (b - I) E[e^{-r\tau}],$$

subject to (6.61).

To apply the formula for $E[e^{-r\tau}]$ developed earlier, it is useful to change variables. Let $X = \log V$. Then (6.61) is transformed to

$$dX = (\mu - \sigma^2/2) dt + \sigma dz, \tag{6.62}$$

with initial condition $x = \log V(0) = 0$. If b is the critical value for V, then $\log b$ is the critical value for X, at which the firm will invest. In other words,

$$\tau = \min \{t : X(t) = \log b\}.$$

The choice of a is to satisfy the equation (recall $x = \log V(0) = 0$)

$$E[e^{-r\tau}] = e^{-a \log b} = b^{-a}.$$

Since $V(0) = 1$ and $b > V(0) = 1$, we shall choose the positive root of

$$(\sigma^2/2) a^2 + (\mu - \sigma^2/2) a - r = 0,$$

i.e., we choose

$$a_4 = \frac{-(\mu - \sigma^2/2) + \sqrt{(\mu - \sigma^2/2)^2 + 2r\sigma^2}}{\sigma^2} > 0. \tag{6.63}$$

Then the investment timing problem becomes

$$\max_{b} \left\{ (b - I) b^{-a_4} \right\}.$$

The first-order condition is

$$b^{-a_4} \left[1 - \frac{a_4}{b} (b - I) \right] = 0.$$

Hence, the critical value of the project is

$$b = \frac{a_4 I}{a_4 - 1} = I + \frac{I}{a_4 - 1}. \tag{6.64}$$

Obviously, we need $a_4 > 1$, or, equivalently, $r > \mu$. Similarly, the expected value of the investment is

$$(b - I) b^{-a_4} = \left(\frac{a_4 I}{a_4 - 1} - I \right) \left(\frac{a_4 I}{a_4 - 1} \right)^{-a_4} = \frac{(a_4 - 1)^{a_4 - 1}}{a_4^{a_4} I^{a_4 - 1}}.$$

The second-order condition, evaluated at the optimal b, is

$$b^{-a_4} \left(-\frac{a_4 I}{b^2} \right) < 0,$$

which is obviously true.

The comparative dynamics of the optimal investing size are done in two steps. First, from (6.64), we have

$$\frac{\partial b}{\partial I} > 0 \quad \text{and} \quad \frac{\partial b}{\partial a_4} < 0,$$

Then, from (6.63), we have

$$\frac{\partial a_4}{\partial \mu} < 0, \qquad \frac{\partial a_4}{\partial r} > 0, \quad \text{and} \quad \frac{\partial a_4}{\partial \sigma^2} < 0.$$

Thus,

$$\frac{\partial b}{\partial r} < 0, \qquad \frac{\partial b}{\partial I} > 0, \qquad \frac{\partial b}{\partial \mu} > 0, \quad \text{and} \quad \frac{\partial b}{\partial \sigma^2} > 0. \tag{6.65}$$

The last inequality is of particular interest. It says that the investment timing is positively related to the volatility of project values. Using numerical analysis, Dixit and Pindyck (1994, p. 153) showed that b indeed increases with σ^2. Here we prove it.

Exercise 6.6.6 *We assumed above that $r > \mu$, or, equivalently, $a_4 > 1$. Show that this is indeed the case. Then explain why the model must have $r > \mu$.*

Hint. $V(t)$ follows a geometric Brownian motion; or see Dixit and Pindyck (1994, p. 138).

Exercise 6.6.7 *Verify* (6.65).

6.7 Notes and Further Readings

The section on the nonnegativity constraint draws from Chang and Malliaris (1987). In constructing an extension of the Solow equation from the half line to the whole real line, we mention odd functions and even functions. Some remarks are in order. A function is odd if $f(-x) = -f(x)$; it is even if $f(-x) = f(x)$. It is well known that all odd functions have Taylor polynomials with only odd terms, and all even functions have Taylor polynomials with only even terms. For example, the Taylor polynomial for the sine contains only odd terms, with alternating signs, while the Taylor polynomial for the cosine contains only even terms, again with alternating signs. See, for example, Hubbard and Hubbard (1999). The discussion of CES functions borrows from Wan (1970, pp. 39–40), which includes a nice geometric representation for each parametric value. There is a "Feller's test for explosions" that can be used to ensure nonnegativity conditions. The interested reader is referred to Karatzas and Shreve (1991, pp. 342–351) for more details.

The discussion on other constraints, especially the portfolio selection problem with borrowing constraints, is based on Zariphopoulou (1994) and Vila and Zariphopoulou (1997). As mentioned in the main text, the difficult part is to prove the smoothness of the value function, which requires the viscosity solution technique. There are many good texts and references on this subject. Besides the references cited in the main text, we also recommend the *User's Guide* by Crandall, Ishii, and Lions (1992), and Fleming and Soner (1993). Since our Bellman equation is autonomous, this type of equations is referred to as *elliptic*. If the model is of finite horizon so that the Bellman equation includes the term J_t, then it is referred to as *parabolic*. To learn more about viscosity solutions of parabolic equations, the reader is referred to Fleming and Soner (1993, Chapters 4 and 5).

We present a simple version of the comparison theorem for *first-order* ordinary differential equations, which is related to our economic models. It should be noted that there are comparison theorems (for example, Strum's theorems) for certain second-order ordinary differential equations. The interested reader should consult Birkhoff and Rota (1978) and Hartman (2002). In contrast, the study of comparison theorems for stochastic differential equations is relatively recent. Karatzas and Shreve (1991, p. 395) provides a brief review of the literature. The reader may also want to consult Protter (1990) for more results.

The stochastic money demand model was first developed by Frenkel and Jovanovic (1980). Their seminal work has generated a literature. Our presentation is based on Chang (1999). We add the deterministic case to make it more intuitive. The mathematical preliminaries for computing $E[e^{-r\tau}]$ draw heavily from Harrison (1985) with the help of Bhattacharya and Waymire (1990). There is a more general optional stopping theorem, sometimes known as the optional sampling theorem, which applies to submartingales as well. For more on this subject, the reader is referred to Bhattacharya and Waymire (1990), Billingsley (1995), and Karatzas and Shreve (1991). For the optimality of the (s, S) policy, the reader is referred to Scarf (1960) for the deterministic case and to Constantinides and Richard (1978) for the stochastic case. In fact, the latter also provide results for two triggers.

Clark (1990) provides a nice review of the tree-cutting problem and the rotation problem. For the stochastic tree-cutting and rotation problems, the reader is referred to Brock, Rothschild, and Stiglitz (1989), Chang (2003), Malliaris and Brock (1982), Miller and Voltaire (1980, 1983), and Willassen (1998). For analyses of age-dependent and size-dependent harvest decisions, the reader is referred to Clarke and Reed (1989) and Reed and Clarke (1990). We use optimal stopping techniques to solve the rotation problem. Willassen (1998) argued that the "impulse control" method would be more powerful because it provides more tools for potentially more results. For more results on the method of solving optimal switching problems, the reader is referred to Brekke and Øksendal (1994).

APPENDIX A

Miscellaneous Applications and Exercises

1. FARMLAND INVESTMENT

A farmer often faces many risks from production, from prices, and from investments. Hertzler (1991) discussed several agricultural economics problems that use stochastic control techniques. In what follows, however, we concentrate only on the investment issue.

A farmer uses farmland L and input x to produce grains. Let $f(x)$ be the nonstochastic production function of grains per hectare. Denote by P_L, P_x, and P, respectively, the price of farmland, the price of input, and the price of output (grains). No physical degradation of farmland is assumed. Then the profit *per hectare* is $Pf(x) - P_x x$. If the farmer invests in L hectares of farmland, then the total profit is

$$\pi(x) = [Pf(x) - P_x x] L.$$

At each point in time, the farmer can invest his wealth W either in bonds B or in farmland, i.e., we have

$$W = B + P_L L.$$

As usual, a bond earns a constant interest rate r, or

$$dB = rB\, dt.$$

The price of farmland, however, is subject to fluctuations. This is the only source of shocks in this model. Assume the price of farmland follows a geometric Brownian motion

$$dP_L = \mu P_L\, dt + \sigma P_L\, dz,$$

288

where μ has the interpretation of the expected appreciation rate of farmland. The objective function of the farmer is the typical

$$E \int_0^\infty e^{-\rho t} u\,(c_t)\,dt,$$

where ρ is the subject discount rate and c_t is the consumption at time t. Let P_c be the price of the consumption good. Then the farmer's problem is to maximize the discounted expected lifetime utility subject to a wealth equation. The wealth equation can be obtained by including the farmer's consumption and the profit from production in the computation. It is achieved in the same way as in the derivation of the wealth equation in Merton's model discussed in Chapter 3.

(1) Show that the wealth equation is

$$dW = \{rW + (\mu - r)\,P_L L + [Pf\,(x) - P_x x]L - P_c c\}\,dt + \sigma P_L L\,dz.$$

(2) Derive the Bellman equation of the farmer's problem.

(3) Find the demand for farmland.

(4) If the utility function $u\,(c_t)$ is of CRRA form, then use the symmetry technique to find the value function.

(5) Find the wealth effect and the increased uncertainty effect of farmland prices on the demand for farmland.

2. FUTURES PRICING

This exercise is based on Brennan and Schwartz (1985).

Most agricultural commodities are produced seasonally by farmers. Oranges are picked during the winter, and potatoes are dug out mainly in the fall. Between harvests the commodities are stored. Since output price fluctuations are substantial in natural resource industries, producers as well as processors who are risk-averse would like to insure against the possibility of a low price. This is accomplished through the medium of a futures contract. A futures contract is a legal commitment to deliver a specified good at a specified future date for a specified price. People who buy or sell futures contracts are called speculators.

There are benefits from holding a physical commodity instead of a futures contract. For example, should there be a sudden drought, the owner of wheat would be able to profit from temporary shortages of wheat. The profit may rise either from the price increase or from the ability to maintain a production process as a result of ownership of an inventory of raw material. The value of this benefit is called the convenience yield of holding a physical unit. A major assumption in Brennan and Schwartz's paper is that the marginal net convenience yield $Y(S)$ depends only on the spot price S of the commodity.

Assume S follows a geometric Brownian motion

$$dS = \mu S \, dt + \sigma S \, dz.$$

Let $F(S, \tau)$, where $\tau = T - t$, be the futures price at time t mature at time T. Another major assumption they made is that the interest rate r is nonstochastic. How do we price $F(S, \tau)$?

(1) Form a portfolio composed of the commodity and its futures contract such that the resulting portfolio is risk-free. Specifically, form $S - nF$. Find n.

(2) Show that, in time interval $[t, t + dt)$, the return to this risk-free portfolio, $dS - n \, dF$, plus the convenience yield $Y(S) \, dt$ should have a return equal to $rS \, dt$, since entering the futures contracts involves no receipt or outlay of funds.

(3) Show that $F(S, \tau)$ is governed by the following differential equation:

$$(\sigma^2/2) S^2 F_{SS}(S, \tau) - F_S(S, \tau)[Y(S) - rS] - F_\tau(S, \tau) = 0.$$

This equation and the boundary condition

$$F(S, 0) = S.$$

Determine the futures price.

(4) Suppose $Y(S)$ is proportional to S, i.e., $Y(S) = aS$. Prove that the closed-form solution for $F(S, \tau)$ is of the form

$$F(S, \tau) = Se^{(r-a)\tau}.$$

Notice that this futures price is independent of the stochastic process of the spot price.

(5) Show that the change in the futures price can be expressed in terms of the convenience yield and the change in spot price:

$$dF = F_S[(\mu - r)S + Y]dt + \sigma F_s S dz.$$

3. HABIT FORMATION AND PORTFOLIO SELECTION

Our problem is based on Sundaresan (1989) and Constantinides (1990). The basic structure is similar to Merton's portfolio selection problem except that the utility function is not additively separable in time. The utility function of the investor at time t, $u(c_t, x_t)$, is dependent not only on current consumption c_t at time t, but also on the weighted average of past consumption, x_t, where $x_0 = x$ and

$$x_t = e^{-at}x + b \int_0^t e^{-a(t-\tau)}c_\tau \, d\tau,$$

for some $a > 0$, $b > 0$. Assume $u_c(c_t, x_t) > 0$, $u_x(c_t, x_t) \le 0$, $u_c(c_t, x_t) + u_x(c_t, x_t) \ge 0$, $u_{cc}(c_t, x_t) < 0$, and $u_{cc}(c_t, x_t)u_{xx}(c_t, x_t) - [u_{cx}(c_t, x_t)]^2 > 0$. Then the problem is to maximize

$$E\left[\int_0^\infty e^{-\rho t}u(c_t, x_t)\,dt\right]$$

subject to the budget equation

$$dW = \left[\sum_{i=1}^{n-1} s_i(\mu_i - r)W + (rW - c)\right]dt + \sum_{i=1}^{n-1} s_i\sigma_i W dz_i,$$

given the initial wealth W and the initial past consumption x. As usual, $(dz_i)(dz_j) = \lambda_{ij} dt$.

(1) Show that x_t satisfies

$$dx_t = (bc_t - ax_t)dt.$$

Verify that Merton's model corresponds to $a = b = 0$.
(2) Derive the Bellman equation.
(3) Find the first-order conditions.

(4) Suppose that there is only one risky asset and that

$$u(c_t, x_t) = (c_t - x_t)^\alpha / \alpha, \qquad \text{where } \alpha < 1.$$

The utility function is defined only on $c_t > x_t$. The past consumption x_t represents the subsistence level of consumption, or the "floor" level as Sundaresan (1989) called it. Assume $r + a > b$ and

$$W > \frac{x}{r + a - b}.$$

Show that the value function is of the form

$$J(W, x) = B \left(W - \frac{x}{r + a - b} \right)^\alpha,$$

for some constant B.

(5) Show that the optimal policy functions are

$$c = x + A \left(W - \frac{x}{r + a - b} \right),$$

$$sW = \frac{\mu - r}{(1 - \alpha)\sigma^2} \left(W - \frac{x}{r + a - b} \right),$$

for some constant A. Determine the constant A. In contrast to Merton's model, the optimal consumption c under habit formation is a linear combination of current wealth W and past consumption x. The share of risky asset s converges to a constant if wealth W converges to infinity. Find that constant, and compare it with Merton's model.

(6) Show that, if $a = b$, then x_t satisfies

$$\frac{dx_t}{dt} = b(c_t - x_t) > 0.$$

This is an interesting result in that it shows that the subsistence level is endogenous, increasing with time and rising with wealth.

4. MONEY AND GROWTH

Rebelo and Xie (1999) extended the classical model of money and growth by Brock (1974) to the stochastic case. Their objective is to show that interest rate smoothing is optimal: the optimal monetary policy requires a constant nominal interest rate. In addition to capital k and the corresponding Solow equation, there are other assets in their model. Money is introduced through a cash-in-advance constraint. The agent would invest her nominal wealth W in bonds B, which yield a nominal interest rate r (i.e., $dB = rB\,dt$), and in money holdings M. Let P be the general price level, which is *conjectured* to follow a geometric Brownian motion

$$\frac{dP}{P} = \pi\,dt - \sigma\,dz.$$

Notice that the coefficient for dz term is negative. Assume money supply expands at a constant rate μ. Let v be the lump sum transfer in real terms. Then the budget constraint in real terms is

$$dk + \frac{dM}{P} + \frac{dB}{P} = (Ak - c)\,dt + k\sigma\,dz + v\,dt + \frac{rB}{P}\,dt.$$

At any point in time, the real wealth is

$$w = \frac{W}{P} = k + \frac{M}{P} + \frac{B}{P}.$$

The change in the agent's real wealth is, by definition,

$$dw = d\left(\frac{W}{P}\right) = dk + d\left(\frac{M}{P}\right) + d\left(\frac{B}{P}\right).$$

The objective function of the agent is

$$E \int_0^\infty e^{-\rho t} \frac{c_t^{1-\lambda}}{1 - \lambda}\,dt, \qquad \rho > 0, \quad \lambda > 0.$$

(1) Use Ito's lemma to derive, in real terms, the budget equation for dw. Specifically, let $s_1 = k/w$ and $s_2 = (B/P)/w$ be, respectively, the share of capital and bonds in wealth, all in real terms. Show that the budget equation is

$$dw = \left[As_1 w - c + (1 - s_1)\,w\left(-\pi + \sigma^2\right) + v + rs_2 w\right]dt + \sigma w\,dz,$$

and the cash-in-advance is

$$c = (1 - s_1 - s_2)\,w.$$

(2) Keep in mind that there is an evolution of per capita wealth in the economy, $\bar{w}$, which is outside the control of an individual agent. Assume

$$d\bar{w} = g(\bar{w}) dt + h(\bar{w}) dz.$$

Formulate the agent's problem, and derive the corresponding Bellman equation. Make sure that the state variables are w and $\bar{w}$ and the control variables are s_1 and s_2.

(3) Find the first-order conditions for the Bellman equation. The optimal $s_i = s_i(w, \bar{w})$ are functions of $(w, \bar{w})$. Then show that $r = A + \pi - \sigma^2$.

(5) Let the Solow equation be

$$dk = (Ak^\alpha - c) dt + k\sigma \, dz.$$

Find the value function and the solution to the optimal growth problem.

Note. Rebelo and Xie (1999) went on to conjecture a *closed-form* representation of the value function:

$$J(w, \bar{w}) = \frac{b(w + \beta\bar{w})^{1-\lambda}}{1 - \lambda},$$

for some constants b and β, and

$$g(\bar{w}) = As(\bar{w}, \bar{w})\bar{w} - (1 - s(\bar{w}, \bar{w}))\bar{w}(1 + \pi - \sigma^2) + v,$$
$$h(\bar{w}) = \sigma\bar{w}.$$

Then by comparing the coefficients of w and $\bar{w}$ in the Bellman equation they arrived at, in equilibrium, a relationship between π and μ:

$$A + \pi - \sigma^2 - \mu = \frac{\rho - (1 - \lambda)A}{\lambda} + \frac{1}{2}(1 - \lambda)\sigma^2.$$

It shows that whenever the rate of money growth μ is constant, the nominal interest rate is also a constant. The interested reader should consult their paper for these results.

5. A STOCHASTICALLY GROWING MONETARY MODEL

In a stochastically growing monetary model, Grinols and Turnovsky (1998) address the problem whether the government debt should be financed by short-term bonds or long-term bonds. In so doing, they set up a four-asset model, similar to Fischer's three-asset model, to study the demand for assets. The four assets are: money, M; short-term bonds, B_S; long-term bonds, B_L; and equity claims on capital, K. Money has a zero nominal return; short-term bonds pay a nominal return i, i.e., $dB_S = i B_S dt$; and long-term bonds pay a fixed coupon of one unit of one dollar over the instant dt. The general price level, P, is assumed to follow a geometric Brownian motion

$$dP = \pi P \, dt + \sigma_1 P \, dz_1.$$

Suppose the price of long-term bonds at time t is P_L, which follows

$$dP_L = \eta(t) P_L \, dt + \sigma_2 P_L \, dz_2,$$

with $\rho_{12} = (dz_1)(dz_2)$. The flow of new output, dY, is produced from capital by means of a stochastic constant-returns-to-scale technology

$$dY = \alpha K \, dt + \alpha K \sigma_3 \, dz_3,$$

with $\rho_{23} = (dz_2)(dz_3)$ and $\rho_{13} = (dz_1)(dz_3)$. The government tax income is

$$dT = \tau \, dY$$

from the consumer in period $[t, t + dt)$, where τ represents the tax rate. The wealth at time t is derived from investment in these four assets in the time interval $[t - dt, t)$:

$$W(t) = \frac{M(t)}{P(t)} + \frac{B_S(t)}{P(t)} + \frac{P_L(t) B_L(t)}{P(t)} + Y(t).$$

The objective function of the consumer is the money-in-utility function in the tradition of Brock (1974):

$$E \int_0^\infty e^{-\rho t} U\left(C, \frac{M}{P}\right) dt.$$

Our question is a partial equilibrium exercise of their model.

(1) Show that the rate of return to the long-term bonds is

$$\frac{dB_L}{B_L} = \frac{1}{P_L} dt.$$

Then show that the real rates of return on money, on short-term bonds, and on long-term bonds are, respectively,

$$\frac{d(M/P)}{M/P} = \left(-\pi + \sigma_1^2\right) dt - \sigma_1 dz_1,$$

$$\frac{d(B_S/P)}{B_S/P} = \left(i - \pi + \sigma_1^2\right) dt - \sigma_1 dz_1,$$

and

$$\frac{d(P_L B_L/P)}{P_L B_L/P} = \left(\frac{1}{P_L} + \eta(t) - \pi + \rho_{12}\sigma_1\sigma_2 + \sigma_1^2\right) dt$$
$$+ \sigma_2 dz_2 - \sigma_1 dz_1.$$

(2) Derive the wealth equation after including consumption and tax. More precisely, from

$$dW = d\left(\frac{M}{P}\right) + d\left(\frac{B_S}{P}\right) + d\left(\frac{P_L B_L}{P}\right) + dY - C\,dt - dT,$$

come up with an equation of the form

$$dW = (\psi W - C)\,dt + \psi_1 W dz_1 + \psi_2 W dz_2 + \psi_3 W dz_3.$$

Specify ψ and ψ_i, $i = 1, 2, 3$, in terms of the exogenous parameters. Make sure that the variables

$$s_1 = \frac{M/P}{W}, \qquad s_2 = \frac{B_S/P}{W}, \qquad s_3 = \frac{P_L B_L/P}{W}, \qquad s_4 = \frac{K}{W}$$

are in your formulation.

(3) Formulate the consumer's problem. Be specific about the state and control variables.

(4) Find the Bellman equation.

(5) Find the demand for each asset.

(6) If the utility function is of the form

$$U\left(C(t), \frac{M(t)}{P(t)}\right) = \theta \log C(t) + (1 - \theta) \log\left(\frac{M(t)}{P(t)}\right),$$

then find the value function of the consumer problem. In this case the symmetry technique ought to be applicable. Specifically, show that the value function satisfies

$$J(\lambda W) = J(W) + \frac{1}{\rho} \log \lambda.$$

Also simplify the demand for each asset.

Note. The interested reader should consult Grinols and Turnovsky (1998) to see how they close the model, determine the macroeconomic equilibrium, and analyze the effects of debt financing.

6. GROWTH AND TRADE

This exercise is based on Jensen and Wang (1999). It is a two-factor, two-sector growth model in which a small country trades in both commodities. Assume commodity 1 is an investment good, and commodity 2 is a consumption good. The question is this: What is the corresponding Solow growth equation?

Let K_i, L_i and Y_i be, respectively, the capital, labor employed, and output produced in sector i, $i = 1, 2$. The production function in each sector is $F_i(K_i, L_i) = Y_i$, which exhibits constant returns to scale. Denote by $k_i = K_i/L_i$ and $\ell_i = L_i/L$. Then we have

$$y_i = \frac{Y_i}{L_i} = \frac{F_i(K_i, L_i)}{L_i} = F_i\left(\frac{K_i}{L_i}, 1\right) = f_i(k_i).$$

Assume $f_i(k_i)$ is a strictly increasing and strictly concave function. Let P_i be the price of output i, $i = 1, 2$. Assume full employment of factors so that

$$K = K_1 + K_2, \qquad L = L_1 + L_2,$$

be the total capital and labor in the country. Assume the relative price $p = P_1/P_2$ is confined to the zero-profit price interval. Let δ be the depreciation rate of capital, $s = P_1 Y_1 / Y$ be the expenditure share of investment good, and $y = Y/L$ be per capita output. Then the capital accumulation equation is

$$dK = (Y_1 - \delta K)\, dt = [Ls\,(y/P_1) - \delta K]\, dt.$$

To motivate the Solow equation, we begin with the deterministic case. Assume population grows geometrically, i.e., $dL/L = n\, dt$.

(1) Show that, if $k = K/L$, then

$$\dot{k} = s\,[y_1 \ell_1 + (y_2/p)\,\ell_2] - (n + \delta)k.$$

(2) Now consider the stochastic case. There are two sources of uncertainty. First, assume L follows geometric Brownian motion:

$$dL = nL\, dt + \sigma_1 L\, dz_1.$$

Then assume there is a shock to the depreciation rate so that the capital accumulation equation is

$$dK = [Ls\,(y/P_1) - \delta K]\, dt - \sigma_2 K dz_2,$$

where $(dz_1)(dz_2) = \rho\, dt$. Show that the stochastic differential equation for dk satisfies

$$dk = \left\{ s\,[y_1 \ell_1 + (y_2/p)\,\ell_2] - \left[n + \delta - \left(\sigma_1^2 + \rho\sigma_1\sigma_2\right)\right] k \right\} dt$$
$$- \sigma_1 k\, dz_1 - \sigma_2 k\, dz_2.$$

(3) Show that the equation without savings component,

$$dk = -\left[n + \delta - \left(\sigma_1^2 + \rho\sigma_1\sigma_2\right)\right] k\, dt - \sigma_1 k\, dz_1 - \sigma_2 k\, dz_2,$$

satisfies $k > 0$ w.p.1.

Note. For the nonnegativity of k with savings, the interested reader is referred to Jensen and Wang (1999).

7. INTEGRABILITY PROBLEM OF ASSET PRICES

The problem is this: given asset prices, can we find a subjective discount rate and a concave utility function such that the corresponding optimization model reproduces the asset price in equilibrium? This exercise is based on Wang (1993), which combines Lucas's (1978) discrete-time asset pricing model with the solution technique of Chang (1988). In the tradition of Lucas (1978), the optimal consumption is only an intermediate variable that links the asset price with consumer preferences in equilibrium.

Before we solve the inverse optimal problem, we shall briefly describe the optimal problem. Consider a closed economy with one asset and one consumption good. The asset pays dividends. Let y_t be the dividend at time t. Assume y_t follows

$$dy_t = \mu(y_t) y_t \, dt + \sigma(y_t) y_t \, dz_t.$$

The asset price is a function of y_t, and is denoted by $p(y_t)$. The gains from holding one unit of the asset from time 0 to time t is

$$G_t = p(y_t) + \int_0^t y_s \, ds.$$

Let θ_t be the number of asset held at time t. Then the wealth at time t is $W_t = p(y_t)\theta_t$, and the wealth equation is

$$d[p(y_t)\theta_t] = \theta_t \, dG_t - c_t \, dt.$$

The representative consumer's problem is to maximize

$$E \int_0^\infty e^{-\rho t} u(c_t) \, dt,$$

subject to the wealth equation and

$$\lim_{t \to \infty} E[p(y_t)\theta_t] = 0,$$

by choosing $\{(c_t, \theta_t)\}$.

For simplicity, let the supply of asset share be unity. In equilibrium, $c_t = y_t$ and the wealth is $p(y_t)$. Under certain conditions, Wang showed that the equilibrium asset price is given by

$$p(y_t) = E_t \left[\int_t^\infty e^{-\rho(s-t)} \frac{u'(y_s)}{u'(y_t)} y_s \, ds \right].$$

Now, given the asset price $p(y_t)$ as defined above, find the preference structure that implies $p(y_t)$. The method is similar to the one used for the inverse optimal problem discussed in Chapter 5: converting the problem to a differential equation problem.

(1) Let

$$\varphi(y) = E_y \left[\int_t^\infty e^{-\rho(s-t)} u'(y_s) y_s \, ds \right],$$

with $y_t = y$. Find Dynkin's formula for $E_y [\varphi(y_s)]$, $s > t$.

(2) Show that the solution to the equation

$$0 = \frac{1}{2} \sigma^2(y) y^2 \varphi''(y) + \mu(y) y \varphi'(y) - \rho \varphi(y) + u'(y) y$$

is $\varphi(y)$ defined in (1). You should assume the transversality condition is satisfied.

(3) Let $\varphi(y) = p(y) u'(y)$. Show that, if $p \in C^2$ and $u \in C^3$, then

$$0 = \frac{1}{2} \sigma^2(y) y^2 u'''(y) + \left[\mu(y) + \frac{y p'(y)}{p(y)} \sigma^2(y) \right] y u''(y)$$

$$+ \left[\frac{1}{2} \frac{y^2 p''(y)}{p(y)} \sigma^2(y) + \frac{y p'(y)}{p(y)} \mu(y) + \frac{y}{p(y)} - \rho \right] u'(y).$$

This is a second-order ordinary differential equation in $u'(y)$, which is linear in $u'(y)$ given $p(y)$.

(4) Show that the solution to the differential equation in (3) exists.

(5) Find the conditions under which the solution to the differential equation in (3) is increasing and concave.

Note. Part (5) is nontrivial. The interested reader is referred to Wang (1993) for details.

8. ENTRY AND EXIT

In undergraduate textbooks, the entry and exit of competitive, profit-maximizing firms are dictated by the crossing of the marginal cost curve with the average cost curve and with the average variable cost curve—the so-called zero-profit point and the shutdown point. Dixit (1989) used the real options theory to provide a better explanation.

An idle firm can become active by paying a lump sum k, from which it can produce one unit of output with a variable cost w. An active firm can suspend the operation and exit the market by paying a lump sum exit cost ℓ. Once exited, the firm has to pay another k to reenter. Let ρ be the firm's discount rate. Assume the market price for the output produced is P, which follows a geometric Brownian motion

$$dP = \mu P\, dt + \sigma P\, dz.$$

If the firm is active, then the problem is when to exit. Similarly, if the firm is idle, then the problem is when to enter.

Let $V_0(P)$ be the value of the idle firm poising to enter, if optimal policies are followed. Similarly, let $V_1(P)$ be the value of the active firm poising to exit, if optimal policies are followed. What then are the optimal policies?

(1) Start with the idle firm. Show that the expected capital gain $E[V_0(P + dP) - V_0(P)]$ in the period $[t, t + dt)$ must equal $\rho V_0(P)\, dt$.

(2) Derive the differential equation governing $V_0(P)$:

$$(\sigma^2/2)\, P^2 V_0''(P) + \mu P V_0'(P) - \rho V_0(P) = 0,$$

which is an Euler's homogeneous equation.

(3) Now consider the active firm. Show that the expected capital gain plus dividend, $E[V_1(P + dP) - V_1(P)] + (P - w)\, dt$, in period $[t, t + dt)$ must equal $\rho V_1(P)\, dt$.

(4) Derive the differential equation governing $V_1(P)$:

$$(\sigma^2/2)\, P^2 V_1''(P) + \mu P V_1'(P) - \rho V_1(P) = w - P.$$

The homogeneous part is again an Euler's homogeneous equation.

(5) Solve the two equations in (2) and (4), keeping in mind that $V_0(P) > 0$ and $V_1(P) > 0$ and that we can get rid of one of the

homogeneous solutions by economic reasoning. Let B be the coefficient for the homogeneous solution of $V_0(P)$, and A be that of $V_1(P)$.

(6) Let P_H be the entry price and P_L be the exit price. At P_H, the firm pays k and receives $V_1(P_H)$. Thus, we have the so-called value-matching condition

$$V_0(P_H) = V_1(P_H) - k.$$

Similarly,

$$V_1(P_L) = V_0(P_L) - \ell.$$

Assume the so-called smooth-pasting conditions:

$$V_0'(P_H) = V_1'(P_H) \quad \text{and} \quad V_0'(P_L) = V_1'(P_L).$$

Write down the value-matching conditions and the smooth pasting conditions using the results in part (5). These four equations govern the variables A, B, P_H, and P_L.

(7) Show that

$$P_H > w + \rho k \quad \text{and} \quad P_L < w - \rho \ell.$$

Note. Part (7) is nontrivial. Our hint is to examine $G(P) = V_1(P) - V_0(P)$. For a discussion of this uncertainty effect and its proof, the reader is referred to Dixit (1989).

9. INVESTMENT LAGS

In the previous exercise, once the entry decision is made, the project is supposed to begin immediately. Bar-Ilan and Strange (1996) pointed out that most investment takes time. An obvious example is the time lag between a construction permit and the completion of a building. How does this *time to build* affect the entry and exit decision is the focus of their paper. Their model is an extension of Dixit (1989) in that, besides the idle firm and the active firm, there is another state, in which the project has started at time t and will begin generating revenues and incurring cost k at time $t + h$. This means that the entry cost at time t is $ke^{-\rho h}$. The time h is the time to build.

Let τ be the remaining time to build, $\tau \in (0, h]$. Let $V(P, \tau)$ be the value of the firm which is in the process of construction and will pay

k to enter the market at time $t + h$ (or $\tau = 0$), if optimal policies are followed.

(1) Show that the expected capital gain in period $[t, t + dt)$, satisfies

$$E\left[V\left(P + dP, \tau - dt\right) - V_0\left(P, \tau\right)\right] = \rho V\left(P, \tau\right) dt.$$

(2) Derive the differential equation governing $V\left(P, \tau\right)$:

$$(\sigma^2/2)\, P^2 V_{PP}\left(P, \tau\right) + \mu P V_P\left(P, \tau\right) - \rho V\left(P, \tau\right) - V_\tau\left(P, \tau\right) = 0.$$

(3) An alternative way of deriving the differential equation for $V\left(P, \tau\right)$ is to show that $V\left(P, \tau\right)$ satisfies

$$V\left(P, \tau\right) = E[e^{-\rho dt} V(P + dP, \tau - dt)].$$

Compare this equation with equation (11) of Bar-Ilan and Strange (1996).

(4) Solve the differential equation in (2).

Note. The differential equation in (2) is a variant of the heat equation discussed in Chapter 3. For the effect of introducing the time to build on P_H and P_L, the interested reader should consult Bar-Ilan and Strange (1996).

10. BOND PRICE DYNAMICS

Consider a zero coupon (no default) bond with a finite maturity date. Denote by $P\left(t, T\right)$ the price at time t of a bond maturing at T. Let the instantaneous *forward rate* at time t be

$$f\left(t, T\right) = -\frac{d \log P\left(t, T\right)}{dT}.$$

The *spot rate* at time t, $r\left(t\right)$, is the instantaneous forward rate at time t maturing at t, i.e., $r\left(t\right) = f\left(t, t\right)$. Let $\{W_1\left(t\right), \ldots, W_n\left(t\right)\}$ be a family of independent Wiener processes. Heath, Jarrow, and Morton (1992) postulated that the forward rate follows the stochastic process

$$df\left(t, T\right) = \alpha\left(t, T\right) dt + \sum_{i=1}^{n} \sigma_i\left(t, T\right) dW_i.$$

In integral form,

$$f(t, T) = f(0, T) + \int_0^t \alpha(v, T) dv + \sum_{i=1}^n \int_0^t \sigma_i(v, T) dW_i(v).$$

As pointed out in Heath, Jarrow, and Morton (1992), the only substantive economic restrictions are that the forward rate processes have continuous sample paths and that they are subject to a finite number of shocks across the entire forward rate curve.

(1) Normalize $P(T, T) = 1$. Show that

$$P(t, T) = \exp\left\{-\int_t^T f(t, s) ds\right\}.$$

(2) Show that the dynamics of the spot rate is

$$r(t) = f(0, t) + \int_0^t \alpha(v, t) dv + \sum_{i=1}^n \int_0^t \sigma_i(v, t) dW_i(v).$$

(3) Define

$$a_i(t, T, \omega) = -\int_t^T \sigma_i(t, v, \omega) dv,$$

$$b(t, T, \omega) = -\int_t^T \alpha(t, v, \omega) dv + \frac{1}{2} \sum_{i=1}^n a_i(t, T, \omega)^2.$$

Show that

$$\log P(t, T) = \log P(0, T) + \int_0^t [r(v) + b(v, T)] dv$$

$$- \frac{1}{2} \sum_{i=1}^n \int_0^t a_i(v, T)^2 dv + \sum_{i=1}^n \int_0^t a_i(v, T) dW_i(v)$$

(4) Show that the bond price $P(t, T)$ satisfies the following stochastic differential equation:

$$dP(t, T) = [r(t) + b(t, T)] P(t, T) dt + \sum_{i=1}^n a_i(t, T) P(t, T) dW_i(t).$$

The nicety about this bond price dynamics is that it is in general non-Markov, since the drift and the instantaneous variance can depend on past history.

Note. Part (3) is nontrivial. Our hint is this: From part (1), we have

$$\log P(t, T) = -\int_t^T \left[f(0, s) + \int_0^t \alpha(v, s)\, dv \right.$$
$$\left. + \sum_{i=1}^n \int_0^t \sigma_i(t, s)\, dW_i(v) \right] ds.$$

Then use Fubini's theorem. The details are in Heath, Jarrow, and Morton (1992). In fact, they used the method of martingale representation discussed in Chapter 5 to find a probability measure to price any interest-sensitive contingent claims.

11. ROTATION PROBLEMS AND GEOMETRIC GROWTH

Now suppose the tree growth follows

$$dX_t = \mu X_t\, dt + \sigma X_t\, dz_t,$$

instead of

$$dX_t = \mu\, dt + \sigma\, dz.$$

This geometric Brownian motion of tree growth has the advantage (in economics) that $X_t > 0$ w.p.1. Recall that c is the seedling cost, x is the seedling size, and the first passage time τ_b is defined by

$$\tau_b = \min\{t : X(t) = b\},$$

Then the rotation problem is

$$\max_b \left\{ \frac{(b - c)\, E\, [e^{-r\tau_b}]}{1 - E\, [e^{-r\tau_b}]} \right\}.$$

(1) Find $E\, [e^{-r\tau_b}]$.
(2) Find equation that governs the optimal cutting size.

(3) Find the upper and lower bounds for the optimal cutting size. The bounds should be in terms of the given parameters of tree growth, interest rate, and cutting cost.

(4) Find the upper and lower bounds for the optimal value of the rotation. Again, the bounds should be in terms of the given parameters of tree growth, interest rate, and cutting cost.

Note. Compare your results with Willassen (1998) and Chang (2003).

12. ENDOGENOUS SEEDLING COST

The stochastic rotation problem discussed in the text and the previous exercise all assume that the seedling cost is exogenous. In practice, the seedling cost should be endogenous. For example, the seedling size x is positively related to the seedling cost c, i.e., $x = x(c)$ with $x'(c) > 0$. This is what Sødal (2002) called the "seed production" function. Then the seedling cost (and the seedling size) can be chosen optimally. What, then, is the optimal investment rule?

To motivate the problem, we return to the simplest case that tree growth follows

$$dX_t = \mu \, dt + \sigma \, dz.$$

Then as shown in the text

$$E_x[e^{-r\tau_b}] = e^{-a_2(b-x)}.$$

If $x = x(c)$, then clearly

$$E_x[e^{-r\tau_b}] = e^{-a_2(b-x(c))}$$

is a function of b and c.

Sødal (2002) assumes that in general $E[e^{-r\tau_b}]$ is a function of b and c and can be written as

$$E[e^{-r\tau_b}] = f(b, c).$$

with $f_b(b, c) < 0$ and $f_c(b, c) > 0$. Then the stochastic rotation problem with endogenous seedling cost is

$$\max_{b,c} \left\{ \frac{(b-c) f(b, c)}{1 - f(b, c)} \right\}.$$

(1) Find the first-order conditions.

(2) Denote by $\eta(f, \theta)$ the elasticity of f with respect parameter θ, i.e.,

$$\eta(f, \theta) = \frac{\theta}{f} \frac{\partial f}{\partial \theta}.$$

Show that the optimal investment rule satisfies

$$f_b(b, c) + f_c(b, c) = 0,$$

which has a nice economic interpretation,

$$\frac{b}{c} = -\frac{\eta(f, b)}{\eta(f, c)}.$$

(3) Show that, if the tree growth is geometric, the expected discounted factor $f(b, c)$ is given by

$$f(b, c) = \left[\frac{x(c)}{b} \right]^{\gamma},$$

where

$$\gamma = \frac{-(\mu - \sigma^2/2) + \sqrt{(\mu - \sigma^2/2)^2 + 2r\sigma^2}}{\sigma^2} > 0.$$

(4) Show that, if the tree growth is geometric, the optimal investment rule satisfies

$$\frac{c}{b} = \eta(x, c) = \frac{c}{x} \frac{\partial x}{\partial c}.$$

Bibliography

Abel, Andrew (1983), "Optimal Investment under Uncertainty," *American Economic Review*, 73, 228–233.

Arnold, Ludwig (1974), *Stochastic Differential Equations: Theory and Applications*, John Wiley & Sons, New York.

Arrow, Kenneth (1965), "The Theory of Risk Aversion," lecture 2 of *Aspects of the Theory of Risk-Bearing*, Yrjö Jahnssonin säätiö, Helsinki.

Arrow, Kenneth (1984), *Individual Choice under Certainty and Uncertainty*, Belknap Press of Harvard University Press, Cambridge, MA.

Bar-Ilan, Avner and William C. Strange (1996), "Investment Lags," *American Economic Review*, 86(3), 610–622.

Barro, Robert (1976), "Integral Constraints and Aggregation in an Inventory Model of Money Demand," *Journal of Finance*, 31(1), 77–88.

Barro, Robert and James Friedman (1977), "On Uncertain Lifetimes," *Journal of Political Economy*, 85, 843–849.

Baumol, William (1952), "The Transactions Demand for Cash: An Inventory Theoretic Approach," *Quarterly Journal of Economics*, 66, 545–556.

Becker, Robert (1980), "On the Long-Run Steady State in a Simple Dynamic Model of Equilibrium with Heterogeneous Households," *Quarterly Journal of Economics*, 95, 375–382.

Becker, Robert and John Boyd (1997), *Capital Theory, Equilibrium Analysis and Recursive Utility*, Blackwell Publishers Ltd., Malden, MA.

Benveniste, Larry and Jose Scheinkman (1982), "Duality Theory for Dynamic Optimization Models: The Continuous Time Case," *Journal of Economic Theory*, 27, 1–19.

Bhattacharya, Rabi and Edward Waymire (1990), *Stochastic Processes with Applications*, John Wiley & Sons, New York.

Billingsley, Patrick (1995), *Probability and Measure*, 3rd edition, John Wiley & Sons, New York.

Birkhoff, Garrett and Gian-Carlo Rota (1978), *Ordinary Differential Equations*, 2nd edition, John Wiley & Sons, New York.

Black, Fischer and Myron Scholes (1973), "The Pricing of Options and Corpo-
    rate Liabilities," *Journal of Political Economy*, 81(3), 637–654.
Borch, Karl (1990), *Economics of Insurance*, North-Holland, Amsterdam.
Boyd, John, H., III (1990), "Symmetries, Dynamic Equilibria, and the Value
    Function," in *Conservation Laws and Symmetry: Applications to Economics
    and Finance*, R. Sato and R. V. Ramachandran (eds.), Kluwer Academic
    Publishers, Boston.
Brekke, Kjell and Bernt Øksendal (1994), "Optimal Switching in an Economic
    Activity under Uncertainty," *SIAM Journal on Control and Optimization*,
    32(4), 1021–1036.
Brennan, Michael J. and Eduardo S. Schwartz (1985), "Evaluating Natural Re-
    source Investment," *Journal of Business*, 58(2), 135–157.
Brock, William A. (1974), "Money and Growth: The Case of Long Run Perfect
    Foresight," *International Economic Review*, 15(3), 750–777.
Brock, William A. (1975), "Some Results on Dynamic Integrability," Report
    7551, Center for Mathematical Studies in Business and Economics, University
    of Chicago.
Brock, William A. and Mukul Majumdar (1978), "Global Asymptotic Stability
    Results for Multisector Models of Optimal Growth under Uncertainty When
    Future Utilities are Discounted," *Journal of Economic Theory*, 18, 225–243.
Brock, William, Michael Rothschild, and Joseph Stiglitz (1989), "Stochastic
    Capital Theory," in *Joan Robinson and Modern Economic Theory*, George
    Feiwel (ed.), New York University Press, New York.
Chang, Fwu-Ranq (1982), "A Note on Value Loss Assumption," *Journal of
    Economic Theory*, 26, 164–170.
Chang, Fwu-Ranq (1988), "The Inverse Optimal Problem: A Dynamic Program-
    ming Approach," *Econometrica*, 56(1), 147–172.
Chang, Fwu-Ranq (1991), "Uncertain Lifetimes, Retirement and Economic Wel-
    fare," *Economica*, 58, 215–232.
Chang, Fwu-Ranq (1993), "Adjustment Costs, Optimal Investment and Uncer-
    tainty," Indiana University Working Papers in Economics, 93-006.
Chang, Fwu-Ranq (1994), "Optimal Growth and Recursive Utility," *Journal of
    Optimization Theory and Applications*, 80(3), 425–439.
Chang, Fwu-Ranq (1999), "Homogeneity and the Transactions Demand for
    Money," *Journal of Money, Credit and Banking*, 31(4), 720–730.
Chang, Fwu-Ranq (2003), "On the Elasticities of Harvesting Rules," Working
    Paper, Indiana University, Bloomington.
Chang, Fwu-Ranq and A. G. Malliaris (1987), "Asymptotic Growth under
    Uncertainty: Existence and Uniqueness," *Review of Economic Studies*, 54,
    169–174.
Chung, Kai Lai (1974), *A Course in Probability Theory*, 2nd edition, Academic
    Press, New York.
Chung, Kai Lai (1982), *Lectures from Markov Processes to Brownian Motion*,
    Springer-Verlag, New York.

Cinlar, Erhan (1975), *Introduction to Stochastic Processes*, Prentice-Hall, Inc., Englewood Cliffs, NJ.

Clark, Colin (1990), *Mathematical Bioeconomics: The Optimal Management of Renewable Resources*, Wiley-Interscience, New York.

Clarke, Harry and William Reed (1989), "The Tree-Cutting Problem in a Stochastic Environment: The Case of Age-Dependent Growth," *Journal of Economic Dynamics and Control* 13, 569–595.

Constantinides, George (1990), "Habit Formation: A Resolution of the Equity Premium Puzzle,"*Journal of Political Economy,* 98(3), 519–543.

Constantinides, George and Scott Richard (1978), "Existence of Optimal Simple Policies for Discounted-Cost Inventory and Cash Management in Continuous Time," *Operations Research,* 26(4), 620–636.

Cox D. R. and H. D. Miller (1965), *The Theory of Stochastic Processes*, John Wiley & Sons, New York.

Cox, John and Chi-Fu Huang (1989), "Optimum Consumption and Portfolio Policies When Asset Prices Follow a Diffusion Process," *Journal of Economic Theory*, 49, 33–83.

Cox, John and Chi-Fu Huang (1991), "A Variational Problem Arising in Financial Economics," *Journal of Mathematical Economics*, 20, 465–487.

Crandall, Michael, Hitoshi Ishii, and Pierre-Louis Lions (1992), "User's Guide to Viscosity Solutions of Second Order Partial Differential Equations," *Bulletin of the American Mathematical Society*, 27, 1–67.

Crandall, Michael and Pierre-Louis Lions (1983), "Viscosity Solutions of Hamilton–Jacobi Equations," *Transactions of the American Mathematical Society*, 277(1), 1–42.

Dasgupta, Partha and Geoffrey Heal (1974), "The Optimal Depletion of Exhaustible Resources," *Review of Economic Studies*, Symposium, 3–28.

Dixit, Avinash (1989), "Entry and Exit Decisions under Uncertainty,"*Journal of Political Economy,* 97(3), 620–638.

Dixit, Avinash and Robert Pindyck (1994), *Investment under Uncertainty*, Princeton University Press, Princeton.

Doob, J. L. (1953), *Stochastic Processes*, John Wiley & Sons, New York.

Duffie, Darrell (2001), *Dynamic Asset Pricing Theory*, 3rd edition, Princeton University Press, Princeton, NJ.

Duffie, Darrell and Larry Epstein (1992), "Stochastic Differential Utility," *Econometrica*, 60, 353–394.

Duffie, Darrell, Wendell Fleming, H. Mete Soner, and Thaleia Zariphopoulou (1997), "Hedging in Incomplete Markets with HARA Utility," *Journal of Economic Dynamics and Control*, 21(4–5), 753–782.

Duffie, Darrell and Peter Glynn (1996), "Estimation of Continuous-Time Markov Processes Sampled at Random Time Intervals," Working Paper, Graduate School of Business, Stanford University.

Elandt-Johnson, Regina and Norman Johnson (1980), *Survival Models and Data Analysis*, John Wiley & Sons, New York.

Elliot, Robert (1982), *Stochastic Calculus and Applications*, Springer-Verlag, New York.

Epstein, Larry (1983), "Stationary Cardinal Utility and Optimal Growth under Uncertainty," *Journal of Economic Theory*, 31, 133–152.

Epstein, Larry and J. A. Hynes (1983), "The Rate of Time Preference and Dynamic Economic Analysis," *Journal of Political Economy*, 91, 611–635.

Epstein, Larry and Stanley Zin (1989), "Substitution, Risk Aversion, and the Temporal Behavior of Consumption and Asset Returns: A Theoretical Framework," *Econometrica*, 57(4), 937–969.

Fama, Eugene (1970), "Efficient Capital Markets: A Review of Theory and Empirical Work," *Journal of Finance*, 25(2), 383–417.

Fischer, Stanley (1973), "A Life Cycle Model of Life Insurance Purchases," *International Economic Review*, 14, 132–152.

Fischer, Stanley (1975), "Demand for Index Bonds," *Journal of Political Economy*, 83(3), 509–534.

Fleming, Wendell H. and Raymond W. Rishel (1975), *Deterministic and Stochastic Optimal Control*, Springer-Verlag, New York.

Fleming, Wendell and H. Mete Soner (1993), *Controlled Markov Processes and Viscosity Solutions*, Springer-Verlag, New York.

Fleming, Wendell and Thaleia Zariphopoulou (1991), "An Optimal Investment–Consumption Model with Borrowing," *Mathematics of Operations Research*, 16, 802–822.

Frenkel, Jacob and Boyan Jovanovic (1980), "On Transactions and Precautionary Demand for Money," *Quarterly Journal of Economics*, 95, 25–43.

Friedman, Avner (1975), *Stochastic Differential Equations and Applications*, Vol. 1, Academic Press, New York.

Friedman, Milton (1963), "Windfalls, the 'Horizon,' and Related Concepts in the Permanent-Income Hypothesis," in *Measurement in Economics*, C. F. Christ (ed.), Stanford University Press, Stanford.

Gikhman, I. and A.V. Skorokhod (1969), *Introduction to the Theory of Random Processes*, Saunders, Philadelphia.

Gould, John P. (1968), "Adjustment Costs in the Theory of Investment of the Firm," *Review of Economic Studies*, 35(1), 47–55.

Grinols, Earl and Stephen Turnvosky (1998), "Consequences of Debt Policy in a Stochastically Growing Monetary Economy," *International Economic Review*, 39(2), 495–521.

Hahn, Frank (1968), "On Warranted Growth Paths," *Review of Economic Studies*, 35, 175–184.

Hall, Robert (1978), "Stochastic Implications of the Life Cycle–Permanent Income Hypothesis: Theory and Evidence," *Journal of Political Economy,* 86(6), 971–987.

Hansen, Lars and Jose Scheinkman (1995), "Back to the Future: Generating Moment Implications for Continuous-Time Markov Processes," *Econometrica*, 63(4), 767–804.

Harrison, J. Michael (1985), *Brownian Motion and Stochastic Flow Systems*, John Wiley & Sons, New York.

Hartman, Philip (2002), *Ordinary Differential Equations (Classics in Applied Mathematics, 38)*, 2nd edition, Society for Industrial & Applied Mathematics.

Hausdorff, Felix (1962), *Set Theory*, 2nd edition, Chelsea Publishing Co., New York. (Translated from the German by John R. Aumann et al.)

Hayashi, Fumio (1982), "Tobin's Marginal q and Average q: A Neoclassical Interpretation," *Econometrica*, 50(1), 213–224.

He, Hua and Chi-Fu Huang (1994), "Consumption–Portfolio Policies: An Inverse Optimal Problem," *Journal of Economic Theory*, 62, 257–293.

Heath, David, Robert Jarrow, and Andrew Morton (1992), "Bond Pricing and the Term Structure of Interest Rate: A New Methodology for Contingent Claims Valuations," *Econometrica*, 60(1), 77–105.

Hertzler, Greg (1991), "Dynamic Decisions under Risk: Application of Ito Stochastic Control in Agriculture," *American Journal of Agricultural Economics*, 73(4), 1126–1137.

Hicks, John (1965), *Capital and Growth*, Oxford University Press, Oxford.

Hotelling, Harold (1931), "The Economics of Exhaustible Resources," *Journal of Political Economy*, 39(2), 137–175.

Howe, Roger (1982), "Most Convex Functions Are Smooth," *Journal of Mathematical Economics*, 9, 37–39.

Hubbard, John and Barbara Burke Hubbard (1999), *Vector Calculus, Linear Algebra, and Differential Forms: A Unified Approach*, Prentice-Hall, Upper Saddle River, NJ.

Intriligator, Michael (1971), *Mathematical Optimization and Economic Theory*, Prentice-Hall, Englewood Cliffs, NJ.

Jehle, Geoffrey and Philip Reny (2001), *Advanced Microeconomic Theory*, 2nd edition, Addison-Wesley, Boston.

Jensen, Bjarne and Chunyan Wang (1999), "Basic Stochastic Dynamic Systems of Growth and Trade," *Review of International Economics*, 7(3), 378–402.

Joshi, Sumit (1997a), "Turnpike Theorems in Nonconvex Nonstationary Environments," *International Economic Review*, 38, 225–248.

Joshi, Sumit (1997b), "Recursive Utility, Martingales, and the Asymptotic Behavior of Optimal Processes," *Journal of Economic Dynamics and Control*, 21, 505–523.

Joshi, Sumit (2003), "The Stochastic Turnpike Property without Uniformity in Convex Aggregate Growth Models," *Journal of Economic Dynamics and Control*, 27, 1289–1315.

Kamihigashi, Takashi (2001), "Necessity of Transversality Conditions for Infinite Horizon Problems," *Econometrica*, 69(4), 995–1012.

Karatzas, Ioannis, John Lehoczky, Suresh Sethi, and Steven Shreve (1986), "Explicit Solution of a General Consumption/Investment Problem," *Mathematics of Operations Research*, 11(2), 261–294.

Karatzas, Ioannis and Steven Shreve (1991), *Brownian Motion and Stochastic Calculus*, 2nd edition, Springer-Verlag, New York.

Knight, Frank B. (1981), *Essentials of Brownian Motion and Diffusion*, American Mathematical Society, Providence, RI.

Krylov, N. V. (1980), *Controlled Diffusion Processes*, Springer-Verlag, New York.

Kurz, Modecai (1968), "The General Instability of a Class of Competitive Growth Processes," *Review of Economic Studies*, 35, 155–174.

Kurz, Modecai (1969), "On the Inverse Optimal Problem," in *Mathematical System Theory and Economics I*, by H. W. Kuhn and G. P. Szegö (eds.), Springer-Verlag, Berlin.

Kushner, Harold (1971), *Introduction to Stochastic Control*, Holt, Rinehart and Winston, Inc., New York.

Leung, Siu Fai (1991), "Transversality Condition and Optimality in a Class of Infinite Horizon Continuous Time Economic Models," *Journal of Economic Theory,* 54, 224–233.

Lions, Pierre-Louis (1983), "Optimal Control of Diffusion Processes and Hamilton–Jacobi–Bellman Equations," *Communications in Partial Differential Equations*, 8(11), 1229–1276.

Lucas, Robert E., Jr. (1967), "Adjustment Costs and the Theory of Supply," *Journal of Political Economy*, 75(4), Part 1, 321–334.

Lucas, Robert E. (1978), "Asset Prices in an Exchange Economy," *Econometrica*, 46(6), 1429–1445.

Lucas, Robert E., Jr. and Nancy Stokey (1984), "Optimal Growth with Many Consumers," *Journal of Economic Theory,* 32, 454–475.

Malliaris A. G. and William A. Brock (1982), *Stochastic Methods in Economics and Finance*, North-Holland, New York.

Marsden, Jerrold and Anthony Tromba (1976), *Vector Calculus*, W. H. Freeman & Co., San Francisco.

McDonald, Robert and Daniel Siegel (1986), "The Value of Waiting to Invest," *Quarterly Journal of Economics*, 101(4), 707–727.

McKean, H. P., Jr. (1969), *Stochastic Integrals*, Academic Press, New York.

Merton, Robert (1971), "Optimal Consumption and Portfolio Rules in a Continuous Time Model," *Journal of Economic Theory*, 3, 373–413.

Merton, Robert (1973), "Erratum," *Journal of Economic Theory*, 6, 213–214.

Merton, Robert (1975), "An Asymptotic Theory of Growth under Uncertainty," *Review of Economic Studies*, 42, 375–393.

Merton, Robert (1990), *Continuous-Time Finance*, Blackwell, Cambridge, MA.

Michel, Philippe (1982), "On the Transversality Condition in Infinite Horizon Optimal Problems," *Econometrica*, 50(4), 975–985.

Michel, Philippe (1990), "Some Clarifications on the Transversality Condition," *Econometrica*, 58(3), 705–723.

Milbourne, Ross (1988), "A Theorem Regarding Elasticities of the Transactions Demand for Money," *Economics Letters*, 27, 151–154.

Miller, Merton and Daniel Orr (1966), "A Model of Demand for Money by Firms," *Quarterly Journal of Economics*, 80, 413–435.

Miller, Robert and Karl Voltaire (1980), "A Sequential Stochastic Tree Problem," *Economics Letters*, 5, 135–140.

Miller, Robert and Karl Voltaire (1983), "A Stochastic Analysis of the Tree Paradigm," *Journal of Economic Dynamics and Control*, 6, 371–386.

Mirman, L. and Itzhak Zilcha (1975), "On Optimal Growth under Uncertainty," *Journal of Economic Theory*, 11, 329–339.

Mussa, Michael (1977), "External and Internal Adjustment Costs and the Theory of Aggregate and Firm Investment," *Economica*, 44, 163–178.

Nickell, S. J. (1978), *The Investment Decisions of Firms*, Cambridge University Press, Cambridge.

Pindyck, Robert (1980), "Uncertainty and Exhaustible Resource Markets," *Journal of Political Economy*, 88(6), 1203–1225.

Pindyck, Robert (1982), "Adjustment Costs, Uncertainty and the Behavior of the Firm," *American Economic Review*, 72, 415–427.

Protter, Philip (1990), *Stochastic Integration and Differential Equations: A New Approach*, Springer-Verlag, New York.

Rebelo, Sergio and Danyang Xie (1999), "On the Optimality of Interest Rate Smoothing," *Journal of Monetary Economics,* 43, 263–282.

Reed, Michael and Barry Simon (1972), *Methods of Modern Mathematical Physics I: Functional Analysis*, Academic Press. Revised and enlarged edition, 1997, under the title of *Functional Analysis*.

Reed, William and Harry Clarke (1990), "Harvest Decisions and Asset Valuation for Biological Resources Exhibiting Size-Dependent Stochastic Growth," *International Economics Review*, 31(1), 147–169.

Richard, Scott (1975), "Optimal Consumption, Portfolio and Life Insurance Rules for an Uncertain Lived Individual in a Continuous Time Model," *Journal of Financial Economics*, 2, 187–203.

Rosen, Joe (1983), *A Symmetry Primer for Scientists*, John Wiley & Sons, New York.

Scarf, Herbert (1960), "The Optimality of (*S, s*) policies in the Dynamic Inventory Problem," in *Mathematical Methods in the Social Sciences*, K. Arrow, S. Karlin, and P. Suppos (eds.), Stanford University Press, Stanford.

Sethi, Suresh and John Lehoczky (1981), "A Comparison of the Ito and Stratonovich Formulations of Problems in Finance," *Journal of Economic Dynamics and Control*, 3, 343–356.

Sødal, Sigbjørn (2002), "The Stochastic Rotation Problem: A Comment," *Journal of Economic Dynamics and Control*, 26, 509–515.

Solow, Robert (1956), "A Contribution to the Theory of Economic Growth," *Quarterly Journal of Economics*, 70, 65–94.

Sundaresan, Suresh (1989), "Intertemporally Dependent Preferences and the Volatility of Consumption," *Review of Financial Studies*, 2(1), 73–89.

Tobin, James (1956), "The Interest Elasticity of the Transactions Demand for Cash," *Review of Economics and Statistics*, 38, 241–247.

Treadway, Arthur (1969), "On Rational Entrepreneurial Behavior and the Demand for Investment," *Review of Economic Studies*, 36(2), 227–239.

Treadway, Arthur (1970), "Adjustment Costs and Variable Inputs in the Theory of the Competitive Firm," *Journal of Economic Theory*, 2, 329–347.

Uzawa, H. (1968), "Time Preference, the Consumption Function, and Optimum Asset Holdings," in *Value, Capital, and Growth: Papers in Honor of Sir John Hicks*, N. J. Wolfe (ed.), Edinburgh University Press, Edinburgh.

Varian, Hal (1992), *Microeconomic Analysis*, 3rd edition, Norton & Company, Inc., New York.

Vila, Jean-Luc and Thaleia Zariphopoulou (1997), "Optimal Consumption and Portfolio Choice with Borrowing Constraints," *Journal of Economic Theory*, 77, 402–431.

Wan, Henry, Jr. (1970), *Economic Growth*, Harcourt Brace Jovanovich, New York.

Wang, Susheng (1993), "The Integrability Problem of Asset Prices," *Journal of Economic Theory*, 59, 199–213.

Whalen, Edward (1966), "A Rationalization of the Precautionary Demand for Cash," *Quarterly Journal of Economics*, 80, 314–324.

Willassen, Yngve (1998), "The Stochastic Rotation Problem: A Generalization of Faustmann's Formula to Stochastic Forest Growth," *Journal of Economic Dynamics and Control*, 22, 573–596.

Zariphopoulou, Thaleia (1994), "Consumption–Investment Models with Constraints," *SIAM Journal on Control and Optimization*, 32(1), 59–85.

Index

317